To Cynthia,
on behalf of all of us in
HQUSACE! Washington, DC
will not be the same without you!
Steve K

D1712466

CAPITAL ENGINEERS

THE U.S. ARMY CORPS OF ENGINEERS
IN THE DEVELOPMENT OF WASHINGTON, D.C.
1790–2004

Cynthia –
It has been a
real pleasure working
with you and you
did a great job for
us! Lee

Cynthia – I'm still in denial!
You can't leave us!
It's been great to work with the times
you again. Seems like the
Hopefully you will be back.
EVIe

PAMELA SCOTT

Cynthia,
It has been
great working with
you! I hope that
Jacksonville treats
you well and we see
you soon!!!
Jeremy

Cynthia –
Thank you so much
for coming up to the PJT
and helping us out. I hope
you learned a lot about HQ
and the people that work here...
I know I learned a lot...
I especially enjoyed the
Spanish lessons
Stacey

Cynthia –
It was nice going to
the baseball games
with you. Go YANKEES!
John Misik

Office of History
Headquarters, U.S. Army Corps of Engineers
Alexandria, Virginia

2008

EP 870-1-67

Cynthia,
Thank you for all
your great assistance.
I will miss you! I
hope your return
to Jacksonville is
smooth!

Cynthia –
You've made
a wonderful addition
to the HQ USACE team
Hope to have you
back soon!

Scott, Pamela, 1944–

Capital engineers : the U.S. Army Corps of Engineers in the development of Washington, D.C. 1790–2004 / Pamela Scott.

p. cm.

"EP 870-1-67."

Includes bibliographical references and index.

1. Military engineering—Washington (D.C.)—History. 2. United States. Army. Corps of Engineers. Washington District—History. 3. Washington (D.C.)—Buildings, structures, etc. I. Title.

UG24.D58S36 2008

307.1'41609753—dc22

2005025779

First printing 2005

Second edition 2008

For sale by the Superintendent of Documents, U.S. Government Printing Office
Internet: bookstore.gpo.gov   Phone: toll free (866) 512-1800;   DC area (202) 512-1800
Fax: (202) 512-2104 Mail: Stop IDCC, Washington, DC 20402-0001

ISBN 978-0-16-079557-2

CONTENTS

FOREWORD

The U.S. Army Corps of Engineers is best known for its water resources and environmental work and its construction of facilities on military bases; however, in its long history the Corps has performed many missions, some of which continue to the present and others that reflected the needs of a particular period of our nation's history.

Although not forgotten, but perhaps imperfectly remembered, the Corps' critical role in the development of Washington, D.C., is a fascinating and important chapter in U.S. Army Engineer history. The Corps' role began when the federal government called on the expertise of the few formally educated engineers in the early republic to provide urban services such as a reliable water supply or to contribute to the expansion of the Capitol.

As the small and rudimentary city expanded during and after the Civil War, the requirement for greatly increased engineering services became evident, both for the city's governmental center and for its neighborhoods where residents lived and businesses operated. For almost seventy years, Army Engineer officers supervised the monumental, federal core of the city as the Mall grew, evolved, and became the primary focus for the tributes the nation erected for its heroes. The Office of Public Building and Grounds was at the heart of the transformation of the city's federal center.

At almost the same time, Army Engineers were given a critical role in governing the city where Washingtonians lived and worked. As one of three commissioners who ran the city, the Engineer Commissioners were powerful figures directing public works and providing the expanding public urban infrastructure that a modern city needed as it grew in size and complexity after the Civil War.

And finally, Army Engineers performed their traditional missions in the Washington area by maintaining navigation on the city's rivers and building facilities on its many military installations. But those missions were magnified as the Washington Engineer District literally created new land that became the site of a national airport, monuments, and parks on the banks of the Potomac River.

By the fourth decade of the twentieth century, the Army Engineers' role in the capital began to decline as new federal agencies, such as the National Park Service, created to maintain the country's natural and man-made monuments, assumed duties formerly performed by the Corps. Three decades later, Washingtonians received more self-rule as elected officials replaced the federally-appointed city government. Only the water resources and military construction roles remain for the Corps, now performed by its Baltimore District.

Army Engineers fulfilled the needs of the time but eventually the needs evolved in new directions. In the process the Corps relinquished its central role in Washington, D.C., proud of its accomplishments and ready to fulfill its remaining duties. This book chronicles their contributions to the city and to the nation.

R. L. Van Antwerp

Lieutenant General, US Army

Chief of Engineers

Preface

Capital Engineers began as a revision and update of Albert E. Cowdrey's *A City for the Nation: The Army Engineers and the Building of Washington, 1790–1967*, published in 1979 by the Office of History, Headquarters, U.S. Army Corps of Engineers, under its old title, the Historical Division. Cowdrey's book was a quarter of a century old, long out of print, and did not, of course, reflect the tremendous growth of interest and research in the history of Washington, D.C., since its publication. In addition the book did not reflect the growing interest in and capability of providing sophisticated and valuable graphic material. While *A City for the Nation* included many images, it did not begin to tap the rich visual resources available on the history of Army Engineer work in the city. So the desire for an improved, more current, and better illustrated history of the role of Army Engineers in the development of the nation's capital led to this book.

The new publication began when Dr. Martin Gordon, a historian in the office and specialist in the history of the District of Columbia, engaged Ms. Pamela Scott, a well-known and well-respected architectural historian and historian of Washington, to revise the Cowdrey text. When Dr. Gordon left the office for a new position, I inherited the project. When I saw the excellent revised text that Ms. Scott was producing and looked at the now dated look and concept of the old history, it seemed to me that both the subject matter and the resources available argued for a much more ambitious publication.

The office had already engaged Mr. Douglas J. Wilson and Ms. Emelie M. George of R&D Associates, a historical research and writing company, to undertake an intensive inventory of the visual resources available on the history of the Corps of Engineers, including its work in Washington, in local archives and libraries. Mr. Wilson's research was unearthing a wealth of images beyond the already substantial collection in the office's own Research Collections.

The new technology of digital photography and scanning made access to this visual material easier and more effective. For example, the *Annual Reports of the Chiefs of Engineers* are filled with maps, charts, and photographs that have scarcely been exploited due partially to the difficulties of reproducing the material. Now very large maps and charts can be scanned and enhanced if they are in poor condition and used very effectively as illustrations. Ms. Jean Diaz, editor, Office of History, and Ms. Jessa Poppenhager, a student formerly employed in the office, were adept at scanning difficult images, especially large ones that had to be reassembled digitally, and cleaning and enhancing these historic maps and images without losing their authenticity and charm.

An excellent text and access to a plethora of visual materials led me to envision a publication that relied on both text and images. After all, the Army Engineers' work involved to a large extent construction of edifices, and it makes little sense to write about the built environment and not show it. Text and images with captions can be intertwined to both complement and supplement each other producing a more nuanced and sophisticated historical product than either could produce alone. So the new conception of this publication involved a heavy investment of time in both textual and image writing and research.

The group responsible for producing this history readily agreed to the new conception and worked long hours to make it a reality. Ms. Scott gave (and I use that word partially in its literal sense) generously of her time and effort. The newly-conceived book was much more than she had originally anticipated and would not have been possible without her enthusiastic support. She also kindly shared material from her own rich collection of documents and images on the history of Washington.

Douglas J. Wilson combined a talent for image research with a talent for image management. In some ways the revolution in printing that allows books to go to print on CDs has complicated the job of the book's producers. The entire team played a role in selecting the images for the book from the wealth of choices Mr. Wilson provided. He deftly managed paper copies, photographic copies, and digital scans of images and combined them with captions, credits, and other information along with the status and even size of the image into a complex but essential Excel chart that became the Bible of the group. Mr. Wilson and I wrote the captions and Ms. Scott reviewed, corrected, and embellished them. In addition the entire group reviewed the text and the page proofs.

No publication can succeed without the services of a good editor. Ms. Jean Diaz was a key member of the group. She carefully and conscientiously edited the text and captions and reviewed all the page proofs. We relied on her not only to correct our grammar and punctuation but also to clarify our meaning. She watched our schedule closely urging us on to greater efforts as deadlines grew near. Her patience and good humor helped everyone through those days and weeks that were the most trying. Even in this digital age, mistakes are made, and an editor is on the front lines and in the most exposed position in the battle to find and correct them. Jean's careful eye on the text, images, and design of the book were critical to the production of this publication.

My colleagues in the Office of History assisted in the preparation of this book in a variety of ways. Dr. John Lonnquest and Dr. Michael Brodhead read early chapters of the text and provided invaluable comments. Mr. James Garber assisted with image research and scanning. Ms. Anna Punchak, administrative officer, provided administrative support. Other colleagues were interested and encouraging and helped by relieving me of some of my other duties. Dr. Paul K. Walker, chief of the office, supported the project enthusiastically but critically from the beginning. All departures from standard practice and every commitment of resources received his careful scrutiny helping us to focus on what was important and clarify our decisions to embark in new directions. But he never hindered our creativity nor dampened our enthusiasm.

Mr. Mark Baker, historian in the Baltimore Engineer District, provided valuable comments on the final chapter, and he and Dr. Charles Walker, a historian and former executive assistant in the district, helped define the areas in which the Baltimore District played a role in the recent history of Washington. In addition Mr. Baker provided very useful photographic material. Mr. Thomas Jacobus, chief of the aqueduct; Mr. David MacGregor; and Mr. Billy Wright of the Washington Aqueduct Division of the district gave us access to the collection of images stored in the head-quarters building at Dalecarlia, and Mr. Wright was both patient and very helpful as we delved into the rich resources of the collection.

We were fortunate to obtain the services of EEI Communications for the production of the book. About a decade ago, EEI worked for a multi-service group, including the Office of History, to produce Robert P. Grathwol and Donita M. Moorhus's *American Forces in Berlin: Cold War Outpost, 1945–1994* (Washington, DC: Department of Defense Legacy Resource Management Program Cold War Project, 1994), a visually striking publication. Fortunately the project manager for the earlier book, Jayne Sutton, was also EEI's project manager for this publication. A book that relies so heavily on visual material requires the early participation of the production team. We explained our concept of the book to Jayne and her colleagues, especially Roy Quini who was responsible for design of the cover and special features of the book, and Sharon Martin, and worked closely with them to define what was possible and worked interactively to obtain a visu-ally attractive and effective design. Everyone worked on a tight schedule and sought to accommo-date our vision of the book and the realities of time and funding. EEI's handsome and intelligent design helped us approach the goal of maximizing the effectiveness of both text and images.

Authors get their names on a book's cover and spine, but good authors know that many other names should accompany theirs. This book in particular because of its conception and its history was truly a collaborative effort. Every member of the group was critical to its completion, and every member of the group is willing and able to say that they share in its failings and accomplishments.

William C. Baldwin

September 2005

ACKNOWLEDGMENTS

Capital Engineers began life as a revised and expanded version of Albert E. Cowdrey's *A City for the Nation: The Army Engineers and the Building of Washington, 1790–1967* (1979). The only one of Cowdrey's six chapters to be completely rewritten was the first devoted to L'Enfant's design for the federal city. Occasional paragraphs and frequent sentences from his other five chapters were incorporated in the text of *Capital Engineers,* as was some text taken from manuscripts for new final chapters by Roberta Weiner on file in the Office of History.

    Capital Engineers benefited from a wide range of contemporary scholarship on Washington's built environment including unpublished Ph.D. dissertations and reports by government agencies as well as recent and older books, articles, and newspaper accounts. The result remains an overview of the Corps' extensive contributions towards making Washington one of the world's great cities. Readers might expect bridges and management of the Potomac and Anacostia rivers, possibly even the engineering expertise to raise the Washington Monument to its lofty height, but most will be surprised by the Engineer Commissioners' nearly century-long service as the city's leading municipal authorities. Every part of public and private Washington has been informed by decisions made by a Corps engineer.

    My first thanks go to Dr. Martin K. Gordon, formerly of the Corps' Office of History, Alexandria, Virginia, who commissioned the new edition of *A City for the Nation.* Corps historians Mr. Mark Baker, Dr. Michael J. Brodhead, and Dr. John Lonnquest corrected errors and questioned assumptions. Mr. Douglas J. Wilson collected a broad range of wonderful photographs and drafted many of their captions. Mr. Michael R. Harrison copied relevant parts of the Corps' annual reports and digested their technical aspects. Colleagues who quickly responded to queries were Mr. William C. Allen, Dr. William B. Bushong, Dr. Kay Fanning, Dr. Kenneth Hafertepe, Dr. Christopher A. Thomas, and Dr. Barbara Wolanin. Ms. Jean R. Diaz, editor, Office of History, was an excellent and congenial editor. At EEI Communications, Jayne O. Sutton's enthusiasm and Roy Quini's beautiful book design made the last stages of the project a pleasure. I am very grateful for all their contributions.

My greatest debt of gratitude is owed Dr. William C. Baldwin, Office of History, who patiently, thoughtfully, and with great humanity shepherded *Capital Engineers* through its completion. Dr. Baldwin checked every fact, identified and provided me copies of many little-known contemporary sources, researched and selected images and drafted their captions, and wrote several paragraphs for the last two chapters that strengthened them immeasurably. I have never had a better colleague.

Pamela Scott

August 2005

GEORGE TOWN

PART OF VIRGINIA

ROCK CREEK

POTOMACK

WITHIN THE TERRITORY

Presidents House

PLAN
of the CITY of
Washington,
in the Territory of Columbia
ceded by the States of
VIRGINIA AND MARYLAND
to the

1 | *The Grand Design*
1790–1800

THE GRAND DESIGN

"To found a city in the center of the United States, for the purpose of making it the depository of the acts of the Union, and the sanctuary of the laws which must one day rule all North America, is a grand and comprehensive idea," were the opening words of the "Essay on the City of Washington," published in the *Washington Gazette* on November 19, 1796. The anonymous essay described Washington in extravagant allegorical terms, some of them very suggestive of ideas discernable in Major Peter Charles L'Enfant's visionary 1791–92 plan, but most did not correspond to what was being implemented. The first description of the federal city, written by "Spectator" and appearing in the September 26, 1791, issue of the *Maryland Journal*, was a reliable description of the strikingly picturesque land adjacent to Georgetown, Maryland. Moreover, it was a laudatory précis of the city's revolutionary design—"everything grand and beautiful that can possibly be introduced into a city." In 1794 President George Washington's secretary, Tobias Lear, published *Observations on the River Potomack*, a factual account that focused on what businessmen and developers would need to know about local conditions and services.[1]

Silhouette of Peter Charles L'Enfant. This is the only known authentic image of L'Enfant.
Diplomatic Reception Rooms,
U.S. Department of State

Thus, before the federal government moved to the permanent capital in 1800, the public already had been apprised of its unique character because the entire range of L'Enfant's intentions had been discussed in the public press. To design a beautiful city that addressed the political realities of its location within the country, its pragmatic problems due to its site, and its symbolism as an expression of the Revolution's achievements were the French engineer-architect's goals. L'Enfant (1755–1825), the son of a painter at the French court of Louis XVI, came to America in 1777. Although no record has been found in France of L'Enfant's military training, and only cursory notice of his artistic education as his father's student, from the age of twenty-two, L'Enfant served first in the French and then in the Continental Army as a military engineer. During the winter of 1778, he served with the Continental Army at Valley Forge where he was one of the illustrators for acting inspector general Friedrich Wilhelm von Steuben's manual of military maneuvers, and served as one of Washington's trusted couriers. L'Enfant was appointed captain of engineers in April 1779, after which he was assigned to work with General Johann de Kalb. Fighting in the southern theater, L'Enfant was wounded at the battle of Savannah in October 1779, taken prisoner at Charleston in May 1780, and exchanged in November.[2]

L'ENFANT PROPOSES CORPS OF ENGINEERS

On January 1, 1784, when L'Enfant was honorably discharged from the Continental Army, he decided to remain in the United States because he expected that he would lead the Corps of Engineers in his adopted country's reorganized peacetime Army. On December 15, 1784, he wrote the president of Congress:

> *Having been led to expect that such an establishment would take place I should now be doubly disappointed if it should not as by remaining here I have lost the opportunity of getting employment in my own Country from which I have been the more encouraged to absent myself as Brigadier General Kosciuszko at leaving this Continent gave me the flattering expectation of being at the head of a department in which if successful I shall endeavour to render my services agreeable to the United States.*[3]

The accompanying "memorial" L'Enfant submitted to Congress proposed a peacetime Corps, with an emphasis on a broad technical and cultural education for engineers. He proposed that they be proficient in mathematics, mechanics, architecture, hydraulics,

Detail from L'Enfant's
panorama of West Point, 1780
U.S. Military Academy Library

drawing, and "natural philosophy," the latter "necessary to judge of the nature of the Several materials which are used in building" because L'Enfant foresaw the Corps as playing a key role in the development of the country's public as well as its military infrastructure.

> *The duty of the said Corps shall be to attend to and have the direction of all*
> *the fortified places that of all military and civil building, the maintenance of*
> *the Roads bridges and Every Kind of work at the public charge. [S]urveys of*
> *the several places Shall be by them made and properly drawn with a view to*
> *make out an atlas of the whole Continent from which the Supreme power may*
> *be able to obtain a more just idea of its situation and forme a distinct opin-*
> *ion upon its advantages and defects. [T]o these plans Shall be added proper*
> *Notes and Remarks with Schemes for taking advantage of good positions or*
> *of preventing the defects of some unavoidable inconveniency.*[4]

The visionary rather than practical nature of L'Enfant's proposed Corps of Engineers, coupled with his self-serving and convoluted means of expression, probably led the congressional committee that reviewed it to conclude, "the situation of the military posts in the U. States does not require the establishment of a Corps of Engineers on the plan of the memorialist." Yet the elite, educated Corps that L'Enfant envisaged became a reality within a quarter century.[5]

L'Enfant's model for the American Corps of Engineers was a synthesis of the French government's system for commissioning public and military works: public architecture was centralized under the king, the "architecte du roi" holding a ministerial post equivalent to the secretary of war who oversaw all military installations. In contrast, the traditional English system for overseeing large civic building projects was to appoint commissioners (typically three, one of whom often was the architect), leading citizens who posted a bond to guarantee their honesty as they had control of the project's finances; jointly they made all decisions regarding design and construction.

THE FEDERAL CITY PROPOSED

During the late 1780s L'Enfant kept in close contact with his former military comrades, including Washington, while he pursued a civilian career as an architect and engineer. L'Enfant later claimed, "when it was contemplated by the old Congress to establish a federal city on the bank of the river delawar in the year 1787 I had made considerable progress in the survey of ground, and in the preparation of the plan of a city first intended there, but the project of that national establishment having been given up, I was encouraged to expect due compensation at some future day." L'Enfant may have been mistaken about the date; on February 2, 1785, Samuel Hardy nominated L'Enfant as one of two commissioners "for erecting the federal buildings." Ten months later L'Enfant wrote the Marquis de Lafayette about his disappointment concerning failed projected plans for a federal city.[6]

In 1789 Congress debated "laying the foundation of a city which is to become the Capital of this vast Empire" on the Susquehanna River. L'Enfant wrote Washington in September seeking the appointment as its projector and renewed a suggestion he made in his 1784 proposal, the need to fortify America's seacoast.

> [H]aving had the honor to belong to the Corps of Engineer acting under your orders during the late war, and being the only officer of that Corps remaining on the Continent I must confess I have long flattered myself with the hope of a reappointment....I view the appointment of Engineer to the United States as the one which could possibly be most gratifying to my wishes and the necessety of such an office to superintend & direct the fortifications necessary in the United States is sufficently apparent[.] [T]he advantage to be derived from the appointment will appear more striking when it is considered that the sciences of Military and Civil architecture are so connected as to render an Engineer equally serviceable in time of Peace as in war, by the employment of his abilities in the internal improvement of the Country.[7]

THE IMPACT OF L'ENFANT'S 1780S DESIGNS

L'Enfant's most significant non-military national contributions in the 1780s were in the realm of spectacles, emblematic designs, and public architecture. The form and general content of these projects contributed to his appointment as the federal city's designer early in 1791. In 1782 L'Enfant designed a forty-foot by sixty-foot dancing pavilion at the Philadelphia residence of French Minister Chevalier de la Luzerne for a party to celebrate the birth of the French Dauphin. Newspapers and journals described L'Enfant's design and decorations as the intermingling of French and American symbols, principally a rising sun representing America and a sun at its zenith representing France. On June 10, 1783, L'Enfant sent to von Steuben, President of the Society of The Cincinnati of which L'Enfant was a founding member, drawings and a description of the society's eagle badge; L'Enfant subsequently traveled to France to arrange for its diploma to be engraved and its eagle badges to be made by a French jeweler. America's official emblem, the Great Seal of the United States, evolved between 1776 and 1782: an American eagle with a shield of thirteen stripes on its breast and an aureole of thirteen stars over its head, an olive branch with thirteen leaves symbolizing peace grasped in one claw, and in the other, thirteen arrows symbolizing war. Its first non-governmental use was on the emblems L'Enfant designed for the Society of The Cincinnati.[8]

L'Enfant's watercolor of the Eagle Badge of the Society of The Cincinnati
Courtesy of the Society of The Cincinnati

Of all the constructions made by American cities in 1788 to celebrate ratification of the U.S. Constitution (generally floats in parades), the largest and most symbolically inclusive was L'Enfant's banqueting tables erected in New York at the destination of its July 23rd parade. Ten 440-foot-long tables represented the states that voted for the Constitution, each terminating in a pavilion decorated with state flags and insignia for state officials. They radiated from a central podium where members of the federal government and foreign ministers dined under a dome surmounted by a figure of fame. Six thousand people were served dinner at L'Enfant's banqueting tables, which were erected in less than five days.[9]

The success of New York's Federal Procession was L'Enfant's success and, in September 1788, led to the acceptance of his proposal to renovate New York's old City Hall into Federal Hall. L'Enfant added a neoclassical façade and a Senate chamber to the existing building where the First Federal Congress met for two sessions and where George Washington was inaugurated president on April 30, 1789. His emblematic decorations for the façade—the eagle of the Great Seal of the United States in the pediment above the balcony, thirteen stars representing the original states in the entablature below the pediment, and relief sculpted panels with olive branches and arrows above the second story

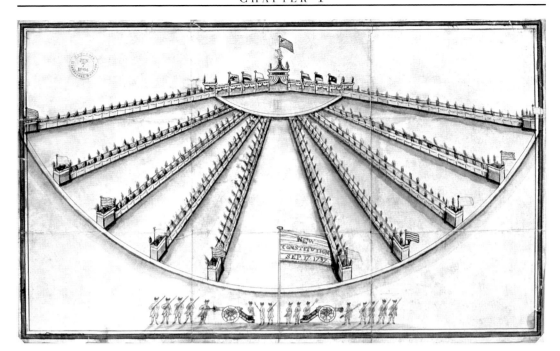

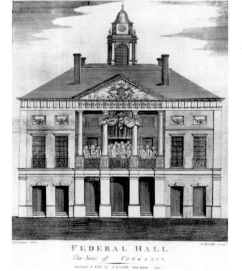

windows—identified Federal Hall's function. L'Enfant designed elaborate nationalistic decorations for the House of Representatives (a room he totally renovated), and Senate chambers so large and architecturally complex that they were not completed before they were dismantled. Federal Hall's rich and imposing appearance was a great success among Federalists, but suspect among many Democratic-Republicans who found it too grand to represent a republican government. Yet, the success of all these projects convinced many that L'Enfant had a genius for innovative design and worked well with craftsmen who built his elegant structures quickly, albeit not economically.[10]

WASHINGTON HIRES L'ENFANT

On July 16, 1790, Congress passed the Residence Act that established the permanent seat of government on the Potomac River. The city's boundaries were to be defined by three commissioners appointed by the president, its design "according to such plans as the President shall approve, the said commissioners, or any two of them, shall, prior to the first Monday in December 1800, provide suitable buildings for the accommodation of Congress, and the President, and for the public offices of the government of the U.S." On January 22, 1791, Washington appointed Daniel Carroll and Thomas Johnson of Maryland, and Virginian David Stuart, all personal friends and political allies, as the commissioners for the District of Columbia. A week later Secretary of State Thomas Jefferson wrote Johnson that Washington had written L'Enfant (letter not found) because he considered him "peculiarly qualified to make such a draught of the ground as will enable himself to fix on the spot for the public buildings." Jefferson and Washington both wrote Georgetowners Francis Deakins and Benjamin Stoddert on March 2, to alert them of L'Enfant's arrival.[11]

The same day, Jefferson ordered L'Enfant to Georgetown where he would find Major Andrew Ellicott already engaged on

> *a survey and map of the federal territory. The special object of asking your aid is to have drawings of the particular grounds most likely to be approved for the site of the federal town and buildings. You will therefore be pleased to begin on the Eastern branch, and proceed from then upwards, laying down the hills, vallies, morasses, and waters between that, the Patowmac, the Tyber, and the road leading from George town to the Eastern branch, and connecting the whole with certain fixed points on the map Mr. Ellicot is preparing. Some idea of the height of the hills above the base on which they stand would be desireable.*[12]

No further written instructions, nor offer of payment, to L'Enfant have been located. Major Ellicott (1754–1820), whose Revolutionary War commission was with the Maryland militia rather than the Corps of Engineers, began working as a surveyor in 1784 on the Pennsylvania boundaries. Early in 1791 Washington appointed him to survey the District of Columbia's ten-mile-square, assisted by the African-American amateur astronomer Benjamin Banneker, and later, his brother, Benjamin Ellicott. In 1799 Ellicott published his account of the survey in the *Transactions of the American Philosophical Society*, thirteen years after election to that body's membership. He continued to receive federal and state government commissions to survey state boundaries in Florida, Pennsylvania, Georgia, and South Carolina until his appointment in 1813 as professor of mathematics at West Point, a position that L'Enfant refused.[13]

Jefferson continued to send L'Enfant his orders, but L'Enfant addressed most of his reports to Washington. By the autumn of 1791, L'Enfant was in open revolt against the authority of the commissioners; when he turned to Washington for support he was told that the commissioners represented the law and that he was answerable to them. Washington cited L'Enfant's letter of appointment from the commissioners, which has not been found. Understandably, L'Enfant was confused about the chain of command, receiving orders from Washington, the commissioners, and Jefferson—if, in fact, he received all three letters. We only know that Jefferson asked L'Enfant initially to make a topographical survey of the land between Georgetown and the Eastern Branch, later called the Anacostia River. L'Enfant believed that Washington commissioned him to design the federal city and all of its public buildings, to be in effect the "engineer-architect to the President" on the French model he proposed to Congress in 1784 and again to Washington in 1789. He either ignored or did not understand the import of the traditional English system of building commissioners who met regularly, made decisions, and paid the bills, the common practice in America during the eighteenth century.

SITING THE FEDERAL CITY WITHIN THE FEDERAL DISTRICT

In his first report written on March 11, 1791, L'Enfant gave Jefferson his impressions of the varied and extensive ground between Georgetown and the Anacostia River as he sought the best location for a "small town," although he ventured that "the intended city on that grand Scale on which it ought to be planed" was more appropriate to express the United States. Jefferson's reply was to order L'Enfant to make topographical drawings of the land between Georgetown and Tiber Creek, the area where Jefferson himself located his own federal city design, which he presented to Washington sometime between August 1790 and March 1791. In a postscript to his letter, Jefferson cautioned L'Enfant not to divulge the results of his surveys.

> There are certainly considerable advantages on the Eastern branch: but there
> are very strong reasons also in favor of the position between Rock creek and
> Tyber independent of the face of the ground. It is the desire that the public
> mind should be in equilibrio between these two places till the President
> arrives, and we shall be obliged to you to endeavor to poise their expectations.

L'Enfant's surveys over the entire ground excited great speculation in Georgetown because one of two local groups—those landowners whose holdings were contiguous to Georgetown or those whose property lay near the town of Carrollsburg near the Eastern Branch— would benefit materially by his decision as to where to locate the federal city within the ten-mile-square federal district.

Three weeks later, when Washington came to Georgetown in late March, L'Enfant handed him an eight-page report that described the beauty of the Eastern Branch site, evaluated it in practical terms, and enumerated its potential as the capital of an "Extensive Empire." The engineer immediately saw the need for two bridges, one across the Eastern

Branch above Evans Point (where East Capitol Street now crosses the Anacostia River), and the other across the Potomac River where Key Bridge now crosses the Potomac. Both bridges were depicted on the surviving manuscript map and some of the early published maps, which also show the location of the ferry that crossed the Anacostia near the Navy Yard. They were crucial to L'Enfant's initial scheme of centering the federal city on Jenkins Hill: "begining the Setlement of the Grand City on the bank of the eastern branch and promoting the first improvement all along of the Height flat as far as w[h]ere it end on Jenkins Hill."

To connect the federal city to Georgetown, L'Enfant planned a

> *large avenue [now Pennsylvania Avenue] from the bridge on the potowmac to that on the Eastern branch....with a midle way paved for heavy carriage and walks on each side planted with double Rows of trees to the end that by making it a communication as agreeable as it will be convenient....*

L'Enfant speculated that such an avenue traversing the entire city would encourage owners to build on contiguous properties and thus visually diminish its length, as well as reflect the "Greatness which a city the Capitale of a powerful Empire ought to manifest."[14]

L'Enfant's intention from the outset was to benefit all the local inhabitants, a principle that he incorporated into his final design. No topographical surveys of the two locales Jefferson requested are known to survive and L'Enfant seemingly ignored the Secretary of State's order to turn his attention to the area adjacent to Georgetown. Moreover, he far exceeded both Jefferson's and Washington's expectations by recommending the Eastern Branch site. L'Enfant's independence in this regard was a precursor of his future behavior.

On March 28, 1791, Washington met with the "contending interests of Georgetown and Carrollsburg" to settle on the federal city's site. He laconically noted in his diary that after meeting with them he examined the works of L'Enfant, who had been (reiterating for the record) "engaged to examine, & make a draught of the grds in the vicinity of George town and Carrollsburg." Washington's response to L'Enfant's report and his meeting with him is recorded in the agreement he made with the proprietors of land, information he immediately conveyed to Jefferson on March 31, 1791.[15]

> *The terms agreed on between me, on the part of the United States, with the Land holders of Georgetown and Carrollsburg are. That all the land from Rock creek along the river to the Eastern-branch and so upwards to or above*

the Ferry including a breadth of about a mile and a half, the whole contain-

ing from three to five thousand acres is ceded to the public, on condition That,

when the whole shall be surveyed and laid off as a city, (which Major

L'Enfant is now directed to do) the present Proprietors shall retain every other

lot; and, for such part of the land as may be taken for public use, for squares,

walks, &ca., they shall be allowed at the rate of Twenty five pounds per acre.[16]

On April 4 Washington wrote L'Enfant, "it will be of great importance to the public inter-est to comprehend as much ground (to be ceded by individuals) as there is any tolerable prospect of obtaining." Washington then outlined the land he wanted included in the federal city.

Washington, who began his career as a surveyor, also suggested that L'Enfant include land as far north as the Bladensburg Road—presently K Streets, NW and NE—and across Rock Creek above Georgetown. Thus, stimulated by L'Enfant's visionary idea of a great city as an analogue of an "extensive empire," and influenced by the political need to reconcile all of the local inhabitants in order to ensure the success of the entire under-taking, Washington decided on a city that he estimated would be three to five thousand acres in extent. L'Enfant's final plan encompassed 6,111 acres and the public reserva-tions and streets comprised 54.6 percent of the total land area to the decided advantage of the government. Writing to Alexander Hamilton on April 8, L'Enfant took credit for suggesting the city's immense scale: "I gave imagination its full Scope in invading all the property....and carrying on my scheme further in extending my ideas so to lead the way to future and progressive improvement[.] I ventured some remarks thereon the which I submitted to the President on his arrival at this place and was fortunate enough to see meet with his approbation."[17]

L'ENFANT'S DESIGN PROCESS

On the same day Washington wrote L'Enfant, the engineer wrote Jefferson asking him for the "number and nature of the publick building with the necessary appending" and for maps of eight specific European cities "together with particular maps of any such sea ports or dock yards, and arsenals as you may know to be the most compleat in their Improvement." Six days later Jefferson sent L'Enfant maps of twelve cities he collected during his five-year tenure as America's minister to France between 1784–89; only Paris and Amsterdam corre-sponded with those on L'Enfant's list. Jefferson reiterated Washington's suggestion about

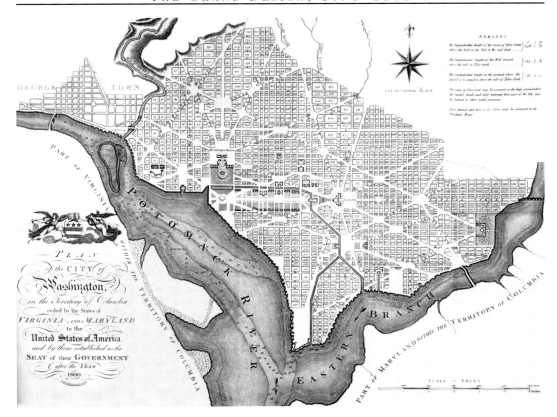

L'Enfant's "Plan of the City of Washington," 1792
Library of Congress, Geography and Map Division

generous apportionment for public grounds. "Considering that the grounds to be reserved for the public are to be paid for by the acre, I think very liberal reservations should be made for them."[18]

When he wrote his April 10, 1791, letter, Jefferson must have seen the pencil sketches L'Enfant had given Washington, read the engineer's March 26 report, or the president had explained L'Enfant's general concepts, because Jefferson further noted "those connected with the government will prefer fixing themselves near the public grounds in the center, which will also be convenient to be resorted to as walks from the lower & upper town." Washington enclosed Jefferson's own federal city plan in the letter he sent L'Enfant on April 4; one of its outstanding features was extensive "public walks" along the shores of the Tiber Creek that connected the "Capitol" and "President." In his April 10th letter, Jefferson wanted to ensure that L'Enfant knew the federal city's genesis was a collaborative effort on the part of many individuals. "[H]aving communicated to the President, before he went away, such general ideas on the subject of the town, as occurred to me, I make no doubt that, in explaining himself to you on the subject, he has interwoven with his own ideas, such of mine as he approved."[19]

In this same letter, Jefferson looked forward to the design of the public buildings. "[W]henever it is proposed to prepare plans for the Capitol, I should prefere the adoption of some one of the models of antiquity which have had the approbation of thousands of years; and for the President's house, I should prefer the celebrated fronts of Modern [Renaissance and post-Renaissance] buildings which have already received the approbation of all good judges. [S]uch are the Galerie du Louvre, the Gardes meubles, and two fronts of the Hotel de Salm."[20]

L'Enfant's second report to Washington made on June 22, 1791, was accompanied by a now lost map of the city. The grandeur of his conception is evident throughout this report, but apparently he only designed the city's central core at that point. The "Congressional building" would be located on the west side of Jenkins Hill "which stand as a pedestal waiting for a monument" and the "presidential palace" would combine the "sumptuousness of a palace the conveniance of a house and the agreableness of a country seat situated on that ridge which attracted your [Washington's] attention at the first inspection of the ground." While L'Enfant the visionary was the predominant voice in this report, L'Enfant the engineer (albeit a visionary one) did surface. Speaking of the Capitol's site, he noted that other locations might require less labor to "be rendered agreable" than Jenkins Hill, "but after all assistance of arts none Ever would be made so grand."[21]

...the "presidential palace" would combine the "sumptuousness of a palace the conveniance of a house and the agreableness of a country seat situated on that ridge which attracted your [Washington's] attention at the first inspection of the ground."

The Mall, canal, executive department offices (adjoining the president's house), "grand Equestrian figure" (presumably of Washington), and forty-foot-tall cascade "issuing from under the base of the congress building," had been conceptualized by mid-June. Although they were told some details would change, L'Enfant's unique fusion of the orthogonal grid of streets irregularly transversed by wider diagonal avenues to be the city's plan was shown to the proprietors of land on June 28 after they signed the deeds. Prior to its public display, Washington himself chose the exact location of the public buildings, moving the president's house "more westerly for the advantage of higher ground." The proprietors also were promised a "Town house, or exchange" located between the two principle government complexes.[22]

L'ENFANT'S INDEPENDENCE

During July 1791 L'Enfant began making inquiries about engraving the map. This seemingly simple task became a major complication, partly because he wanted the map to be on a large scale and no copper plate of sufficient size could be found in Philadelphia. In addition, L'Enfant did not want sales of lots to go forward until the city's true complexity shown on the plan also was apparent on the ground; he feared that only lots near the Capitol and president's house would be sold. Once again, he made an important political decision based on his own perspective without Washington's, Jefferson's, or the commissioners' prior knowledge or approval. In August Washington ordered him to Philadelphia, and on the 19th he delivered two maps, one, a "map of doted lines" that indicated the progress of the survey, the second, the city's virtually completed design with its many public buildings delineated. L'Enfant concluded his accompanying report with a discussion of how the city's development should be managed, suggesting that a loan be sought rather than a public sale of lots: "it is in this manner and in this manner only I conceive the business may be Conducted." Washington, Jefferson, and James Madison met with L'Enfant on August 27; the following day Jefferson wrote the commissioners proposing a meeting on the 7th or 8th of September so that "certain measures may be decided on and put into a course of preparation" to ensure that a sale of lots could take place on October 17th.[23]

Beginning in September the commissioners took a more decisive role in the affairs of the city. On the 24th they ordered L'Enfant to employ 150 laborers "to throw up clay at the presidents house and the house of Congress" to begin the process of laying their foundations. On October 10th they resolved that the surveyor Andrew Ellicott "proceed to lay off directly a number of Lots immediately around and fronting the Squares on which the president's house and Capitol are to be built." These orders were given before L'Enfant had produced plans for either building. After the engineer had been dismissed, Jefferson wrote Commissioner Thomas Johnson on March 8, 1792, that "Majr. L'Enfant had no plans prepared for the Capitol or government house. [H]e said he had them in his head. I do not believe he will produce them for concurrence." The dimensions of L'Enfant's president's house have been calculated to be about 696 feet east to west and 206 feet north to south based on the convergence of sightlines of the neighboring streets. (James Hoban's building is 170 feet long by 86 feet deep.)[24]

Jefferson and Johnson were cognizant of the discrepancy between the scale of the public spaces and the probable buildings that would be located there. "I fear your other apprehension is better founded," Jefferson wrote Johnson, "to wit, that the avenues are made to converge to the ends of a building of supposed extent, that the building may very probably be of less extent, and consequently not reach the points of view created for its use." The larger issue was the credibility of the entire federal city: if the published maps showed plans of buildings that did not correspond with those being built, sales of lots would suffer and those who wished to keep the government in Philadelphia would prevail. On April 11, 1792, the commissioners wrote Jefferson concerning the problem with L'Enfant's location of the Capitol. Notley Young's new house stood within the grounds designated for the Capitol and he would have to be compensated as much as fifteen thousand pounds unless the Capitol were moved about nine hundred feet. Their concern was the public's negative perception of changes to the plan (the map had not yet been published but its characteristics were widely known).

> *We cannot but be uneasy of the situation Chosen for the Capitol....Ellicott says...it will not take above 3, or 4 weeks to correct what will be necessary. This may be shortened, we have no doubt by introducing a few accurate measures, and the difference of expence much in favour of it....[Ellicott] says and the Fact is that the Deviation from the Plate will be imperceptable but on measuring, and that the Plate will convey an Idea of the work sufficiently exact to any man living.*[25]

Descriptions of the problems of placing L'Enfant's plan on the varied topography abound. For example, Benjamin Ogle Tayloe came to Washington in 1801, and later recalled that the "distinguished John Cotton Smith told me that when he was a Senator from Connecticut he attended President Adams's levee in Washington, in 1801, and that members of Congress living, like himself, on Capitol Hill, found it necessary to send to Baltimore for hackney coaches to convey them to the President's House; and to avoid the swamps of Pennsylvania Avenue, they had to travel along F Street and the high grounds adjoining." Although the same difficulties would be faced implementing any geometric plan, the combination of the federal city's immense scale; the difference in widths between its grid streets (meant for neighborhoods) and its avenues (meant to be processional); the unequal size of the blocks (necessary for the diagonals and grid to interlock); very hilly terrain; multiple streams and two rivers; and, tidal marshes complicated the matter considerably.[26]

The time between L'Enfant's arrival in March 1791 and when he was expected to produce the finished map and drawings of the public buildings was unrealistic. However, he created this situation himself when he convinced Washington to include more than six thousand acres in the city; the heavily wooded land could not be adequately surveyed before the October sale of lots. Washington recognized these difficulties. "The work of Majr. L'Enfant (wch. is greatly admired) will shew that he had many objects to attend to and to combine; not on paper merely, but to make them corrispond with the *actual*

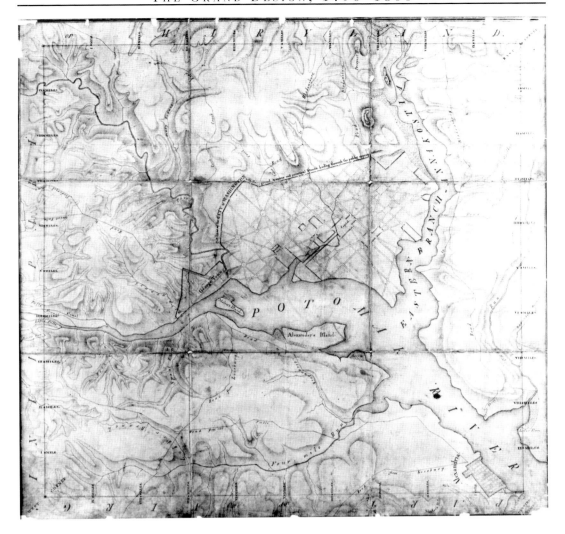

Andrew Ellicott's "Map of the District of Columbia," 1793. Andrew Ellicott, assisted by Benjamin Ellicott and Benjamin Baneker, surveyed the boundaries of the ten-mile-square District of Columbia while L'Enfant was designing the federal city.
Library of Congress, Geography and Map Division. 1069.1

circumstances of the ground." L'Enfant's projected public buildings could not be drawn on the scale and with the elaborateness that he conceived within a few months without a large number of draftsmen. Again, L'Enfant was responsible for this situation; he may well have made sketches of the dozen buildings whose convincing plans were on his manuscript map and, later, engravings. However, to translate such sketches into presentation and then working drawings for construction was the labor of months.[27]

L'Enfant's known assistants were Isaac Roberdeau, Stephen S. Hallet, and Charles de Krafft. Roberdeau was his most trusted ally, eventually arrested in January 1792 for following L'Enfant's orders rather than those of the commissioners. In 1816 Roberdeau, now a major in the Topographical Engineers, returned to Washington and had an important career carrying forward one of L'Enfant's 1784 dictates for the Corps—mapping the continent. Hallet, a French-trained architect who emigrated at the outbreak of the French Revolution, worked as L'Enfant's draftsman during the autumn of 1791, making a reduced version of the plan for the engravers. His design in the 1792–93 Capitol competition placed second and, in a compromise intended to take advantage of his superior architectural education, he was put in charge of constructing the Capitol—the exteriors following the winning design by William Thornton, the interiors designed by Hallet. In 1794 Thornton, now one of the commissioners, fired Hallet for deviating from this compromise plan. Little is known of Hallet's later career, although he remained in Washington for a short time, hired by real estate developer Theophile Cazanove to design houses.[28]

The *Georgetown Weekly Ledger* of July 2, 1791, reported that "a large number of gentlemen attending, a plan of the city, which had for several weeks occupied the time and talents of Colonel L'Enfant, assisted by the Baron de Graff, and which, with some small alterations [Washington] had determined to adopt" was shown to the public. Scholars have long speculated who "Baron de Graff" was. In 1800 "Charles de Krafft, Surveyor and Draftsman" advertised in a local newspaper that he "was employed by [the] government in the year 1791 (at Georgetown) to assist Major L'Enfant to plan and lay down the first draft, for the city of Washington."[29]

L'ENFANT'S URBAN INTENTIONS

Variations on traditional urban planning concepts make L'Enfant's plan for Washington a unique physical and symbolic solution to city design. The beauty of L'Enfant's city was achieved by his sympathetic exploitation of the picturesque landscape. In his "Observations explanatory of the plan," printed on the manuscript map placed before Congress on December 13, 1791, and first published in Philadelphia newspapers on December 26, L'Enfant outlined his methodology. He began by choosing prominent topographical features "commanding the most extensive prospects" for numerous public squares. He then connected them through a system of broad, diagonal avenues for both "prospect and convenience." Lastly, L'Enfant inserted a grid of city streets oriented in the cardinal directions to create neighborhoods around the squares. Fifteen of the squares were dedicated to the states, L'Enfant intending to encourage prominent citizens to buy property contiguous to their states' square. Thus, fifteen far-flung neighborhoods would gradually coalesce with those that would naturally grow up around the public buildings. This ambitious scheme supposed a large population within a few years. However, the multiple squares solved an immediate political problem: treating the proprietors with some equality, although everyone understood that those owning land near the president's house and Capitol had a distinct advantage.[30]

View of Georgetown and the site of the federal city
Library of Congress, Prints and Photographs Division. LC-USZ62-4702

To this simultaneity of functions—a beautiful city that also served pragmatic and political ends—must be added the city's symbolic meaning. On September 9, 1791, Jefferson, Madison, and the commissioners met, choosing "Washington" as the city's name to be located within the "Territory of Columbia." They also determined that the streets on the grid be denominated by letters and numbers. Three days later, Ellicott wrote L'Enfant, "the diagonal Streets are to receive names." The names for the diagonals first appeared on Samuel Hill's engraved map published in the May 1792 issue of the *Massachusetts Magazine*. No known surviving document tells who chose to name the avenues after the states.[31]

Washington's symbolic meaning is embedded in the names of the avenues and their relation to the public squares. There are at least three patterns discernable in the arrangement of the state-named boulevards. Those named for the New England states were located in the northern part of the city, the central states were in the city's center, and the southern states were located on Capitol Hill, the southernmost part of the city. The three largest states (also the only commonwealths)—Massachusetts, Pennsylvania, and Virginia—gave their names to avenues that traversed the entire city. They fell geographically within the city as the states do in the country, Massachusetts to the north, Pennsylvania in the center, and Virginia in the south.

The avenues also seem to have been grouped to reflect America's founding political history. With the exception of Delaware, those radiating from the Capitol were states where the Continental and Confederation Congresses met—Maryland, Pennsylvania, and New Jersey. Delaware may have merited this special location because it was the first state to offer a federal district and the first to ratify the Constitution. The White House and its grounds probably bisect New York Avenue because Washington was inaugurated at Federal Hall in New York. Because L'Enfant determined the placement of the avenues before they were named, and the complex system has such internal logic, it would seem that he originated their names as part of the city's symbolic meaning. Grand scale, the idea that power radiates from centers, and building the names of the states into the national capital's plan all were elements of urban design that L'Enfant would have known from his French heritage.[32]

> *"Grand scale, the idea that power radiates from centers, and building the names of the states into the national capital's plan all were elements of urban design that L'Enfant would have known from his French heritage."*

L'ENFANT'S DOWNFALL

L'Enfant's inability to adapt to the fluid situation the federal government was undergoing during this initial evolutionary period was his downfall. Washington lost faith both in his honesty and judgment, but showed remarkable understanding of his character. In November 1791 L'Enfant ordered his workmen (without consulting the commissioners) to tear down the house Daniel Carroll of Duddington (a nephew of Commissioner Daniel Carroll) was erecting in the middle of one of the new streets. After the episode was settled, Washington wrote the commissioners in mid-December. "His aim is obvious. It is to have as much scope as possible for the display of his talents, perhaps for his ambition....I submit to your consideration whether it might not be politic to give him pretty general, and ample powers for *defined* objects; until you shall discover in him a disposition to abuse them." On February 22, 1792, Jefferson wrote L'Enfant outlining the conditions of his continued employment in subordination to the commissioners. L'Enfant's response on the 26th was a diatribe against the commissioners and the following day Jefferson replied

> *It is understood that you absolutely decline acting under the authority of the present commissioners. If this understanding of your meaning be right, I am instructed by the President to inform you that notwithstanding the desire he has entertained to preserve your agency in the business, the condition upon which it is to be done is inadmissible, and your services must be at an end.*[33]

By the first of August 1792 Alexander Hamilton invited L'Enfant to design an industrial town—both a radiating town plan and a scheme for harnessing the falls of the Passaic River to power adjacent mills—for the Society for the Encouragement of Useful Manufactures at Paterson, New Jersey. L'Enfant remained in the society's employ for less than a year. In 1794 he was in Philadelphia working on Fort Mifflin on an island in the Delaware River. Private employment followed, but he quit all of his projects before they were completed. Most of the rest of L'Enfant's life was spent airing his grievances. Beginning in 1800 (he waited until after Washington's death), L'Enfant submitted ten memorials to Congress asking to be compensated for what he had lost monetarily and in reputation. "Major L'Enfant was of ordinary appearance, except that he had an abstracted manner and carriage in public," wrote painter and art historian William Dunlap in 1834. "It appears that he had the irritability belonging to ambition, but which is falsely made appropriate to genius; and that he thought himself wronged."[34]

> *"It is understood that you absolutely decline acting under the authority of the present commissioners. If this understanding of your meaning be right, I am instructed by the President to inform you...your services must be at an end."*

2 | *The Antebellum City 1800–65*

THE FEDERAL GOVERNMENT MOVES TO WASHINGTON, 1800

In 1800 the three branches of the federal government moved in stages from Philadelphia to Washington. The 1790 Residence Act required Congress to convene in the Federal City on the third Monday in November 1800, but in May, President John Adams ordered the executive departments to be open for business by June 15, 1800. Secretary of War Samuel Dexter had four clerks and a messenger, while the accountant for the War Department had ten clerks and a messenger out of the government's 130 full-time employees. Because the War Department's designated building was not yet finished, it leased Joseph Hodgson's brick building on the south side of Pennsylvania Avenue between 21st and 22nd Streets. On November 8, 1800, most of the department's records were lost when the building was destroyed by fire.[1]

In 1798 the English-born and -trained architect George Hadfield designed a standardized office building for the Treasury Department on the east of the president's house and the War Department on the west side. The Treasury Department's building was

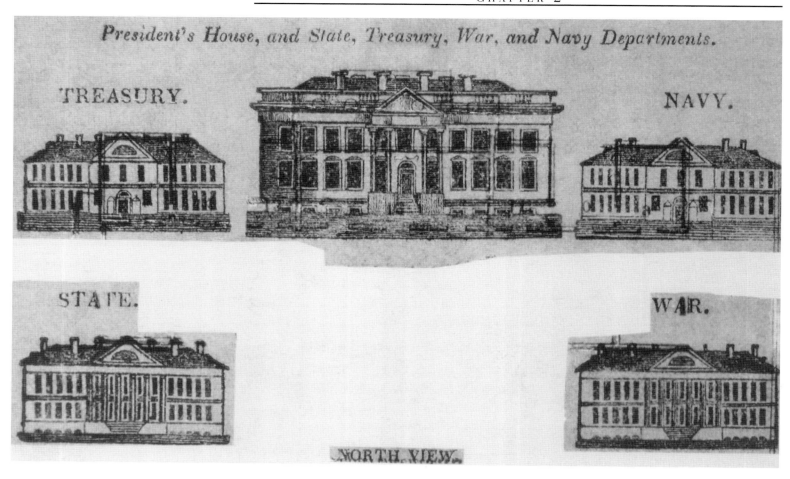

President's House, and State, Treasury, War, and Navy Departments.

TREASURY.

NAVY.

STATE.

WAR.

NORTH VIEW.

The four executive department buildings in the 1820s. The Corps of Engineers' headquarters was located in the War Department Building west of the president's house.
Washingtoniana Division, D.C. Public Library

completed first because it was the largest executive department with sixty-nine employees. On August 6, 1799, Maryland builder Leonard Harbaugh contracted to erect the War Department building at the corner of 17th Street and Pennsylvania Avenue for $39,511. It was finished in late 1800 or early 1801 and its twenty-four rooms were occupied by both the War and Navy Departments until 1819 (except for the two years when it was being rebuilt after being burned by the British on August 24, 1814). The Navy Department moved into the former War Department, which occupied a new, larger building at the corner of 17th Street and Pennsylvania Avenue in 1819.[2]

The legislation that appropriated monies for the government's move to Washington authorized $10,000 to be spent by the four cabinet secretaries to pave streets in the embryonic city, establishing the precedent for the cabinet officers sharing responsibility in carrying out congressional mandates concerning the city's physical development. House and Senate Committees on Public Buildings and Grounds, the Library, and the District of Columbia decided what measures needed to be taken in developing Washington's public spaces and securing designs for the public buildings. Initially, as was the case with James Hoban and the president's house, architects also superintended construction. With complex buildings, such as the U.S. Capitol, and the emergence of architecture and engineering as separate intellectual professions—exemplified by the arrival on the scene of the British-born and pan-European-educated architect-engineer B. H. Latrobe (1764–1820)—the need to divide design and construction superintendence to ensure building craftsmanship became evident. Latrobe educated apprentice architects in the first decade of the nineteenth century to carry on his conviction that the intellectual aspects of architecture were separate from the work of America's eighteenth century builder-architects, such as William Buckland, whose work in the Chesapeake Bay region was, and is, admired.[3]

THE MILITARY ACADEMY AT WEST POINT AND THE CORPS

Although the Corps of Engineers eventually played the leading role in managing the building of Washington, this responsibility evolved slowly during the first half of the nineteenth century. When the Continental Congress established the Continental Army on June 16, 1775, a Chief Engineer was among its ranking officers. As early as September 20, 1776, the Continental Congress appointed a committee who resolved that "the Board of War be directed to prepare a Continental Laboratory, and a Military Academy, and provide the same with proper Officers."[4] In 1783 at the end of the Revolution, most of the U.S. Army, including the Corps of Engineers, was disbanded, with only a small contingent left headquartered at West Point, New York.

In 1802 newly-elected President Thomas Jefferson persuaded Congress to re-establish the Corps of Engineers and create a national military academy at West Point staffed by the engineers, thus forging a strong link between the Corps and the academy. Jefferson wished, as did George Washington, to establish a National University in the city of Washington, but decided that a military school would better serve the country's needs by educating civil and military engineers. In Jefferson's view, the Corps, running the nation's first school of engineering, might have more than military duties, and he considered having its headquarters located in Washington. Poor in science but rich in resources, the United States might in the future look to its Army Engineers for internal improvements as well as defense. By 1816 approximately twenty-seven civilian civil engineers were active in the United States, and West Point's small early graduating classes gradually produced military engineers whose civic works paralleled those of civil engineers working for states or for private canal companies. For example, Joseph G. Totten, who became Chief Engineer, was the academy's tenth graduate, one of three in the class of 1805.

However, by 1837 Secretary of War John C. Calhoun noted that West Point had 940 graduates in total, most of them becoming artillery officers.[5]

The Congressional Act of March 16, 1802, that established the military's role during peacetime, stipulated: "The 27th section provided that the said Corps, when organized, shall be stationed at West Point…and shall constitute a Military Academy….and that the Engineers, assistant Engineers, and cadets, shall be subject to do duty at such places, and on such service, as the President of the United States may direct."[6] Traditionally West Point's top students were commissioned into the Corps of Engineers and their tours of duty allowed them to confront problems in many parts of the country involving surveying, building fortifications, or laying out roads and canals.

Jefferson's choice of the first peacetime Chief of Engineers emphasized the unusual, even elite, nature of the Corps despite his determination to establish a meritocracy in the federal government's civil, judicial, and military branches. As American minister to France, Jefferson in 1785 met Jonathan Williams (1750–1815), grandnephew to Benjamin Franklin, whom Jefferson replaced in the Paris diplomatic post. Upon his return to America, Williams completed his education at Harvard College in 1787, and the following year became a member of the American Philosophical Society, eventually serving as its vice president. Williams's scientific talents were variously expressed in practical articles on thermometric navigation and the study of mathematics, botany, and medicine. In 1801 President John Adams commissioned Williams as a major in the Second Regiment of Artillerists and Engineers, and in the spring of 1802 he was appointed the first superintendent of the Military Academy. There Williams "occasionally read lectures on fortifications, gave practical lessons in the field, and taught the use of instruments generally," while colleagues taught mathematics.[7] During his superintendence, Williams hired professors of drawing and French (most contemporary engineering treatises were written in French), skills that in conjunction with their engineering prowess gave the academy's students a combination of abilities that undoubtedly was unique in American education at this time.

Thus, from the outset, members of the Corps of Engineers were drawn from the best students at West Point who had been educated primarily in practical aspects of the arts and sciences. To provide his faculty and students with wider intellectual horizons, in 1803 Williams founded the U.S. Military Philosophical Society at West Point, whose motto was *Scientia in Bello Pax*, "Science in war guarantees [leads to; promotes] peace." Although the academy's early years were halting, increasingly larger numbers of students

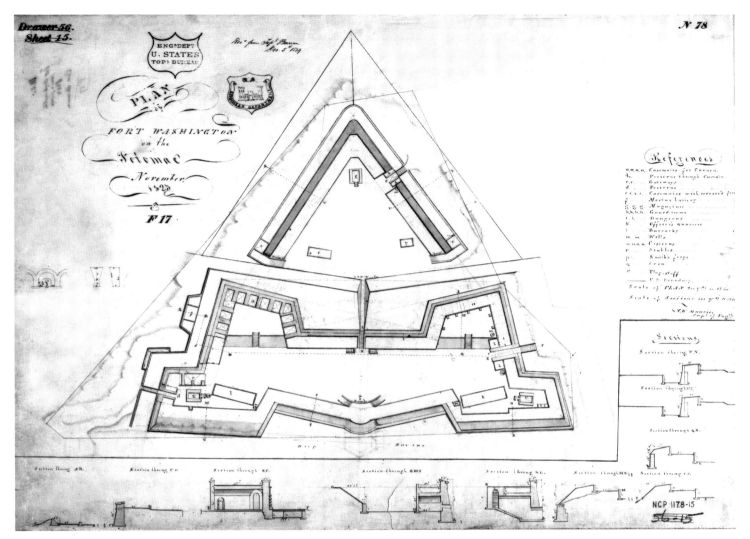

Plan of Fort Washington, 1823. American troops blew up Fort Warburton, a weak and ill-positioned battery, in 1814 upon the approach of the British fleet. Afterwards L'Enfant was placed in charge of demolishing the old fort and beginning a new one. He was relieved by the War Department scarcely a year later.
National Archives no. 79-117.8-15

were among the country's few men formally educated in the practical sciences and they soon proved their worth. No post designed by a West Point graduate was captured by the British during the War of 1812. By the 1820s and 30s, "internal improvements" nationally either relied on surveying and mapping undertaken by the Topographical Engineers, or these public works were directed by members (and sometimes former members) of the various branches of the Corps. In 1812 L'Enfant was offered a professorship at West Point in the "Art of Engineering in all its Branches," but he declined.

CORPS-DESIGNED FORTS PROTECT WASHINGTON

Both the Corps' military and civil expertise were used in and near the District of Columbia from an early date. On March 20, 1794, Congress authorized a series of forts to protect the harbors of American cities, the country's first permanent defensive system to be built. George Washington, concerned for his new capital, chose a bluff, Digges's Point, on the Maryland side of the Potomac, for the location of a future fortification. But it was not until 1807, when an incident in the Napoleonic Wars—a British attack on an

Drawing of Fort Washington (n.d.). Lieutenant Colonel Walker K. Armistead and Captain Theodore W. Maurice designed and built the new fort that was completed in 1824.
Office of History, Corps of Engineers

American frigate in coastal waters—prodded the government into action, and the government's second system of fortifications was begun. On October 31, 1807, the Secretary of War ordered Chief Engineer Jonathan Williams to Washington to draw plans for defending American ports and harbors. Williams also was to examine the site at Digges's Point, six miles downriver from Washington and within sight of Mount Vernon. Arriving in 1808, the Chief Engineer noted that Digges's Point commanded the river but was overlooked by higher ridges. However, the government purchased land for the fort and ordered Captain George Bomford (c. 1780–1848), an 1805 graduate of the Military Academy who had been commissioned a lieutenant of engineers on graduation, to lay out a fortification at the site.[8]

By mid-summer, 1808, Bomford reported that Fort Warburton was "in a condition of forwardness," and by the first of December 1809, it was "completed, to placing the merlons of sod on the parapet."[9] A water battery and little more, the work had semi-elliptical face and circular flanks, mounted thirteen guns, and enclosed quarters for two ordnance companies. "The parapet of this squat and sprawling fort was a solid ten feet, four inches thick and soared forty-one feet above the river."[10] Atop the bluff was an octagonal brick citadel—an ineffective defense against attack from the land, in the opinion of the Army's senior general, James Wilkinson, who declared, "being calculated against musketry only, [it] could have been knocked flat by a twelve pounder."[11]

Colonel Decius Wadsworth, Army Chief of Ordnance, however, was of a different opinion when advising about strengthening the country's defenses after the War of 1812 was declared. On May 28, 1813, he wrote Secretary of War John Armstrong that Fort Warburton's "situation is so elevated, the result of a cannonade by ships from the river should not be dreaded," and he discounted an attack by land.[12] Wadsworth concluded his report advising against additional heavy guns at Fort Warburton or constructing a neighboring fort.

On August 24, 1814, a British force defeated the Americans at Bladensburg, Maryland, and pushed on to capture Washington and burn the public buildings. Meanwhile, a squadron of the British fleet worked slowly up the Potomac River, maneuvering through a maze of shoals and unknown currents against contrary winds. On the evening of August 27, the invaders bombarded Fort Warburton for two hours. Shortly after arriving to take command of the fort on August 6, and convinced that he would have to lead a rear-guard action, Captain Samuel T. Dyson told Lieutenant James Edwards, who had formerly been in command of the fort's small garrison, to "plan the trail of gunpowder in case they had to demolish the fort themselves." Seeing the smoke rising from Washington where the Capitol had been fired on the evening of August 24, and the other public buildings the following day; receiving reports from civilian visitors to the fort on the 25th and 26th about the enemy's advance; and sighting the British fleet sailing up the Potomac River on the 27th, Dyson ordered the fort's cannons spiked and its evacuation that evening. (During the day President James Madison returned to Washington where he appointed James Monroe the new Secretary of War.) Dyson led his retreating forces only fifty paces before the first shell fired from the English warships landed near them; they had walked about three miles before the powder magazine containing 3,346 pounds of powder blew up from their own charges while mortars and rockets launched by the British were landing on and near the fort. At his court martial, which began on November 1, Dyson asked, "Was I not justified in concluding that the overwhelming force of the enemy had driven back all opposition and that my miserable post and little band was all that survived the general wreck?" The following day, Sunday, August 28, the British occupied the fort and the now defenseless city of Alexandria surrendered; Dyson was court martialed and barred from future military service.

Major Peter Charles L'Enfant was called as a witness in Dyson's defense at his court martial, but it is not certain he testified. He had played some part in defending the city. From March until July 1815, L'Enfant oversaw the reconstruction of the wharf at Fort Warburton

and the building of a ravelin at the water's edge. Early in 1816 the Topographical Engineers, Colonel Walker K. Armistead and Captain Theodore Maurice, began a new fort, now renamed Fort Washington, on the higher bluff above the earlier work.[13]

CORPS ENGINEERS CONSULT ON CAPITOL CONSTRUCTION

On March 17, 1817, President James Monroe consulted with Army Engineers about rebuilding the Capitol that had been gutted by explosions and fire on August 24, 1814. After architect Benjamin Henry Latrobe made proposals for its reconstruction, Monroe sought the expertise of Brevet Brigadier General Joseph G. Swift (1783–1865), one of the first two graduates of West Point in 1802, and a decade later Chief Engineer, and Colonel George Bomford, since 1815 the chief of the Ordnance Department. Latrobe proposed vaulting with brick the rebuilt House and Senate chambers (which originally had been vaulted). Monroe was concerned about the weight of the vaults compromising the safety of the Capitol (its foundations had been damaged in the fire), but also stressed that "this building should be finished with the greatest possible expedition." Although Swift and Bomford agreed that Latrobe's structural engineering of the vaults was sound, they reluctantly agreed to wood vaults, citing time, reduced cost, and public fears about masonry vaulted rooms. Latrobe responded to the engineers on March 31, arguing that wood domes above a stone colonnade and entablature were inadvisable because they would be susceptible to dry rot, "expand and contract with the weather," be subject to fire, and "would require more time to erect, plaster, and paint than to turn a brick dome." Monroe and the engineers prevailed and wood domes were built over both chambers, however, in 1901 they were replaced with cast plaster supported by steel trusses.[14]

Swift and Bomford, who had known Latrobe through their joint membership in the U.S. Military Philosophical Society, were asked by Monroe to mediate a quarrel between Latrobe and George Blagden, the superintendent of the Capitol's stonecutters. Latrobe wished to use a small deposit of a variegated breccia stone found in a Virginia quarry near the Potomac River for the colonnades in the legislative chambers, but Blagden believed the stone to be inferior in quality. Monroe accompanied Swift, Bomford, and Latrobe to inspect the quarry and decided that the government should take over the quarry's operation. This collaboration of Swift, Bomford, and Latrobe affected the range of American materials that Latrobe then used in rebuilding the Capitol as he could now call upon experienced construction engineers to help him select the best limestone and marble. In 1817 Swift traveled to New York to oversee preparation of the marble entablatures for the Senate chamber, taking Latrobe's drawings with him.[15]

ISAAC ROBERDEAU AND THE CORPS' TOPOGRAPHICAL BUREAU

In October 1817 President James Madison appointed South Carolinian John C. Calhoun as Secretary of War. A gifted administrator with his eyes on the White House, Calhoun was determined to create a better Army. Among other reforms, he ordered Chief Engineer Swift to Washington, declaring, "he should be stationed at the seat of Government, to superintend, under its immediate control, the great and important duties assigned to the corps." November found Swift packing for the move from Brooklyn, and on April 1, 1818, he was in his new "office in Washington City." Swift, however, did not remain in Washington long; he resigned from the Army in October when Calhoun appointed the French-born engineer Simon Bernard his equal in rank (but his subordinate within the Corps).[16]

Major Isaac Roberdeau
*Courtesy of Historical Society
of Pennsylvania*

Born in Philadelphia in 1763, Isaac Roberdeau studied engineering in London and returned to the United States in 1787 to write about, survey, and study astronomy. In 1816 he was commissioned a major, his time divided between West Point and Washington until 1818 when the Topographical Engineers' headquarters were permanently located in Washington and Roberdeau became its chief. During the early 1820s, Roberdeau accompanied Calhoun on intermittent inspection tours, but most of his time was spent caring for the Topographical Corps' maps, plans, and mathematical instruments. Before his death in 1829, Roberdeau collected public and private surveys of all parts of the country, his composite maps redrawn from them used by many government offices as well as private individuals during the decade the American frontier began to expand dramatically. This was only one part of the War Department's "collections in geology, paleontology and ethnology, including the remarkable series of paintings of Indians and Indian scenes." Roberdeau's two decades spent surveying and superintending the construction of canals (1792 until 1813), combined with his military experience, gave him the expertise to author the unpublished "Mathematics and Treatise on Canals," written about 1828, a decade before the first published work by an American on canals. John Quincy Adams, a fellow savant, spent "many hours discussing astronomy and other sciences" with him. Roberdeau's duties as the curator of the War Department's collection of maps, surveys, and instruments were seemingly not strenuous for someone of his education and capabilities. When Congress questioned his light responsibilities, Roberdeau was defended by both the Chief of Engineers and the Secretary of War, rather than transferred, which suggests that his unofficial duties may have included moving in diplomatic circles, perhaps even gathering information gleaned during his notably active social life.[17]

"Among the residents of our town," the Metropolitan and Georgetown Commercial Gazette reported on October 19, 1824, "we noticed at the Mayor's [reception for the Marquis de Lafayette] the Secretary of War, the Post Master General, the gallant Generals McComb [sic] and Jessup, and Col. Roberdeau of the Corps of Engineers." After visiting Georgetown College, Lafayette "repaired to the Secretary of War's residence. He was handed down from his carriage by Colonels Cox [Georgetown's mayor] and Roberdeau." Between October 12, 1824, when the Marquis de Lafayette first arrived in Washington, and September 9, 1825, when the frigate Brandywine passed Cape Henry light returning him home to France, Roberdeau was a frequent guest at several of the official functions honoring the Revolutionary War general during his farewell trip to America. President John Quincy Adams led the dignitaries at Roberdeau's funeral on January 17, 1829; he and Adams had been fast friends as well as fellow amateur astronomers, with Roberdeau's daughters frequent guests at the White House where they often assisted at banquets.[18]

In 1813 Congress created the Topographical Engineers to carry out surveys of seacoasts, rivers, and the country's interior to support the work of the Corps, which was engaged in building fortifications. The Topographical Engineers were abolished on June 15, 1815, but revived the following year. In 1816 Isaac Roberdeau was commissioned a Major, his time divided between West Point and Washington until 1818 when the Topographical Engineers' headquarters were permanently located in Washington and Roberdeau became chief of the newly established Topographical Bureau. During the early 1820s, Roberdeau accompanied Calhoun on intermittent inspection tours, but most of his time was spent caring for the Topographical Bureau's maps, plans, and mathematical instruments. Before his death in 1829, Roberdeau had collected public and private surveys of all parts of the country, his composite maps redrawn from them used by many government offices as well as private individuals during the decade the American frontier began to expand dramatically. This was only one part of the War Department's "collections in geology, paleontology and ethnology, including the remarkable series of paintings of Indians and Indian scenes."

THE CORPS' INCREASING RESPONSIBILITIES

The Corps of Engineers and its Topographical Bureau played an intermittent role in government construction and public works in the District of Columbia before 1853. As Congress gradually took a bolder line in local spending, engineer officers contributed to individual projects as their expertise was required. In 1822, for example, when Congress appropriated funds for the installation of cast-iron pipes to carry water from the government-owned spring in Franklin Park to the executive buildings in the President's Park, Roberdeau supervised the work. In 1830 a civil engineer employed by the Topographical Bureau made a pioneer study of Washington springs, and two years later Congress voted $45,700 to improve water service for the government by purchasing Smith Spring north of the city and piping its water to the Capitol.[19]

In 1831 a freshet swept away part of the wooden superstructure of the Long Bridge, which crossed the Potomac from the foot of 14th Street in Washington to Arlington, Virginia. Authorized in 1808, and built by a chartered company, for decades this toll bridge connected Washington to Virginia. Although temporary repairs were made, Congress purchased the bridge in 1832 to improve the connection to the south and provide public access without a toll. The president selected topographical engineer Lieutenant Colonel James Kearney to survey the condition of the existing bridge and propose a plan for its

*Long Bridge across the
Potomac River, 1860, taken
from its landfall at 14th Street
and Maryland Avenue, SW*
Office of History, Corps of Engineers

reconstruction.[20] When Congress authorized funding for the actual rebuilding, however,
it delegated the work to the Secretary of the Treasury, who chose the West Point-educated
civil engineer George W. Hughes to superintend the work.[21]

Congress also took an interest in the Aqueduct Bridge in Georgetown, which
provided another link to the Virginia shore. Congress had invested $1 million in the
Chesapeake and Ohio Canal when, in 1831, the Alexandria Canal Company began to
construct a branch south of the Potomac. Congressional appropriations backed this
new venture, and when an aqueduct—essentially a wooden trough and causeway on
massive stone piers—was needed to carry the canal across the river, "the company
considered it advisable...to have its expenditure placed under the direction of an
officer of the corps of topographical engineers." This would provide direct federal
oversight of federal monies, and, "in so difficult and rather unprecedented an undertaking, allow the company to avail themselves of the presumed science of [the
Topographical] officers."[22]

Topographical Captain William Turnbull (1800–1857) was assigned the aqueduct
work. He initially worked in close collaboration with the engineer of the Canal Company,
surveying the riverbed, designing the structure, and devising the means of its construction. After building cofferdams to hold out the river, Turnbull laid the foundations of the

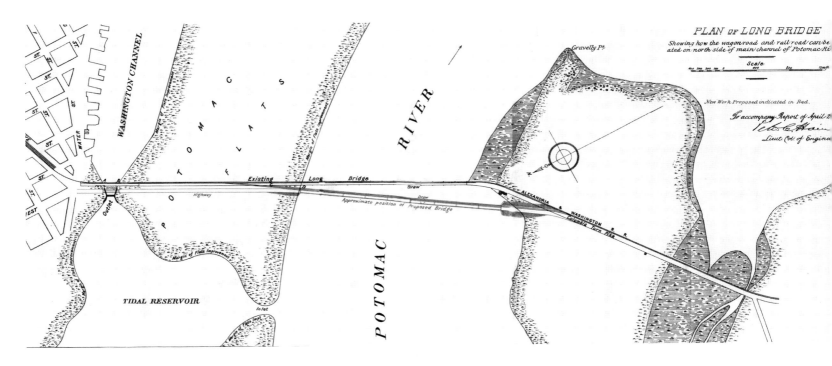

Scale

New Work Proposed indicated in Red.

To accompany Report of April —

Lieut. Col. of Enginee—

WASHINGTON CHANNEL

P O T O M A C   F L A T S

P O T O M A C   R I V E R

Gravelly Pt.

Existing   Long   Bridge   Draw

Highway

Approximate position of Proposed Bridge

Draw

ALEXANDRIA & WASHINGTON R R

Columbia Turn Pike

TIDAL RESERVOIR

Inlet

P O T O M A C

piers nearly forty feet deep to reach bedrock covered by twenty feet of mud, noting that the sight "of men busily at work so far below the surface of the river, seemed to interest the public exceedingly; but to the engineer, whatever might be his confidence in the ability of the dam to resist the immense weight which he knew to be constantly pressing upon it in the most insidious form, the sight was one which filled him with anxiety, and

Plan of Long Bridge, showing the existing span and a modification proposed in 1890
Office of History, Corps of Engineers,
ARCE 1890

POTOMAC AQUEDUCT.
Perspective view of the interior of the Cofferdam for Pier Nº 5.
SEPTº 1838.

Perspective view of the interior of the cofferdam for the construction of pier 5 of the Aqueduct Bridge, 1838
Office of History, Corps of Engineers

Aqueduct Bridge from the east bank of the Potomac River above Georgetown, 1860s, with the Georgetown Canal on the left
National Archives no. 77-HCS-1B26

urged him to the most unceasing watchfulness." Turnbull was assisted by Lieutenant M. C. Ewing, an artillery officer, and briefly by another officer from the infantry. At the end of 1835, as one of the project's many dams went up, Turnbull lamented, "it could not have been altogether completed and tested this season; but a force of mechanics sufficient for the purpose could not be obtained. Another extensive work in the vicinity being in progress at the same time, the demand for labor was very great." Begun in 1833 and completed in 1843, the bridge remained in private hands when completed, with the United States as a shareholder in the company.[23]

As Federal construction work grew, Army Engineers increasingly supplied the skills that made its accomplishment possible. A young lieutenant, Andrew A. Humphreys,

Barge using the Aqueduct Bridge across the Potomac River (n.d.)
Office of History, Corps of Engineers

superintended construction of a bridge over Rock Creek, and spent the summer of 1843 determining the grades of Washington streets. By 1838 citizens were complaining about the dust on the rapidly wearing Pennsylvania Avenue, and, at Senate request, head of the now independent Topographical Bureau, Colonel John James Abert (1788–1863), suggested repairs in his report on the paving of Pennsylvania Avenue west of the White House. George W. Hughes and Topographical Bureau Captain Campbell Graham repaired Pennsylvania Avenue, directed the paving of 15th and 17th Streets, and constructed the 15th Street sewer. The two worked with architect Robert Mills on unrealized designs for the new War Department building during the early 1840s.[24]

Colonel John James Abert
Courtesy of Historical Society of Pennsylvania

During the 1820s Mills had been the architect for the South Carolina Board of Public Works, which undertook civic projects on the state level similar to the Corps' national projects. Throughout this period, Mills sought employment with the Corps of Engineers. He first wrote Secretary of War (and fellow South Carolinian) John C. Calhoun on October 4, 1824, sending him his map and treatise on cutting a canal between the Susquehanna and Potomac Rivers. Nearly two years later, on September 12, 1826, Mills again wrote Calhoun asking to be appointed to the Board of Engineers for Internal Improvements and reapplied in May 1827. On November 8, 1827, Mills wrote Brigadier General Macomb concerning how the Corps of Engineers might use his *A Manuel on Railroads*. Brigadier General Charles Gratiot responded to Mills's August 15, 1829, letter of application sent directly to President Andrew Jackson; Gratiot again informed Mills that there were no openings for civilian engineers. Mills continued to correspond with Gratiot during the 1830s concerning water supply systems and brick manufacturing.[25]

In 1838 Mills's persistence resulted in Secretary of War (and fellow South Carolinian) Joel R. Poinsett appointing him to design the new barracks at the Military Academy at West Point and its Library and Philosophical Apparatus (scientific laboratories), which was slightly altered when constructed by Army Engineer Richard Delafield. This contributed to the growing competition between the Corps of Engineers and private architects who worked for the government, an antagonism present until the end of the nineteenth century and often inflammatory and counterproductive.

In 1831 the Topographical Bureau was separated from the Corps of Engineers, and throughout the next two decades the activities of the parent branch were largely confined to military construction. Although the Corps was not actively involved in building the city, its headquarters was staffed by some of the country's best-educated men drawn principally

Bvt. Maj. Gen. Joseph G. Totten
by Robert W. Weir
West Point Museum Art Collection, United
States Military Academy, #7511

from prominent families who easily fit into the federal city's intellectual and political circles. A key figure in the Corps' growing prestige and in its later role in public buildings was Colonel Joseph G. Totten (1788–1864), appointed Chief of Engineers in December 1838.[26]

CORPS ENGINEERS AND THE SMITHSONIAN INSTITUTION

Genial and courteous, a skilled soldier, and a scientist whose interests ranged from sea shells to ballistics, Totten found full scope for his talents in the nation's capital. A friend of powerful men, in 1840 he joined John Quincy Adams, Secretary of War Poinsett, and Chief Topographical Engineer Lieutenant Colonel John J. Abert to found the National Institute for the Promotion of Science. The group, which included many Army and Navy officers stationed in Washington, held monthly meetings where members occasionally delivered papers of general scientific interest. More frequently, they viewed and discussed books, drawings, and objects (historical as well as scientific) sent by sister organizations or collected by their own members. One of the chief reasons for founding the National Institute was to be the intellectual society in place able to accept the bequest of English scientist James Smithson "to found at Washington…an establishment for the increase and diffusion of knowledge among men." The 1846 law establishing the Smithsonian Institution stipulated that two members of its board of regents be members of the National Institute. Totten, and scientist and former Army Engineer Alexander Dallas Bache, superintendent of the U.S. Coast Survey, both were chosen and served with six members of Congress, the vice president, chief justice, secretary of state, the mayor of Washington, and a few private citizens who were known educators, a total of fifteen eminent professionals who each contributed their expertise.[27]

At the first meeting of the regents in September 1846, Representative Robert Dale Owen of Indiana, Totten, and Washington Mayor William W. Seaton (also the publisher of the *National Intelligencer*) were named to the executive committee. They, along with the Smithsonian's chancellor, Vice President George M. Dallas, and temporary Secretary of the Smithsonian, Representative William Jervis Hough, constituted the new institution's building committee. "The committee was to determine the best methods of warming, lighting, and ventilation, the best material for the exterior of the building, and the best site." Beginning on September 14, 1846, some building committee members interviewed architects in Philadelphia, New York, and Boston, visiting some of their buildings. Totten was unable to join the team until they arrived in Boston where they

Smithsonian Institution, ca. 1852,
with some of the evergreens and
deciduous trees planted under the
direction of A. J. Downing
Smithsonian Institution Archives, Record
Unit 95, Box 30, Folder 7, image #36881

consulted with architects Isaiah Rogers and Ammi B. Young, both mature builder-architects who successfully completed federal works.[28]

Although Totten initially supported Francis Markoe (a clerk in the State Department and a founding member of the National Institute) to be the Smithsonian's permanent secretary, he became one of Joseph Henry's most influential allies after the Princeton scientist was chosen to lead the institution in December 1846. About Totten, Henry confided to his wife: "Bache told me that when we became acquainted with each other we would draw together. Now that he is on the ground many things will go on well with reference to the building." In December 1847 Totten asked to be excused from the building committee because consulting on contracts and checking the quality of workmanship on the building was becoming too time consuming. Eighteen months later, the Smithsonian's youthful architect, James Renwick, was required to submit to Totten several alternative plans for the arrangement of rooms in the east wing (which contained laboratories and the chemical lecture hall) when the original configuration was found to be unworkable. It fell to Totten to choose the best scheme and he continued to support Henry when the secretary proposed other internal changes.[29]

Smithsonian interior
Smithsonian Institution Archives, Record
Unit 95, Box 41, Folder 7, image #16847

In the spring of 1850 Totten was one of six regents appointed to a special committee "to determine the extent of any contractual violations and to estimate the cost of repairing the damage" after part of the floor in the Smithsonian's main hall collapsed. This

THE SMITHSONIAN INSTITUTION.

THE LECTURE ROOM.

Smithsonian Institution lecture hall, designed by Captain Barton S. Alexander, who, between 1853 and 1855, redesigned many interiors to be fireproof

Smithsonian Institution Archives, Record Unit 95, Box 31, Folder 40, image #43804K

committee called in three impartial experts: Colonel William Turnbull of the Corps of Topographical Engineers and two architects who were currently constructing government buildings elsewhere, South Carolinian Edward B. White and Baltimorean John R. Niernsee. In August Totten played a key role that allowed Renwick (who had several important Washington connections) to submit final bills indicating the Smithsonian was completed.

Immediately, Captain Barton S. Alexander (1819–1878) of the Corps of Engineers prepared drawings for fireproofing the unfinished central block. Two years later Alexander was detailed to design the first building for the Soldiers' Home and supervise its construction.[30]

Between 1853 and 1855 Alexander worked closely with Henry to redesign and construct rooms in the Smithsonian's main block and to rebuild some parts of the east wing, adding a second story to serve as the secretary's residence. Alexander's function at the Smithsonian differed from Totten's; he was the superintendent of construction, consulting with Henry and the building committee and suggesting changes to Renwick's design. His most important contribution was the spartan, two-story lecture room that dominated the top two floors of the central section of the main block. Henry considered Alexander as "rather too extravagant, having been used to the purse of the government." Alexander considered his room to have dignity and simplicity: "There is not much ornament, but still enough, I think, to enable the building to do its duty with grace and dignity."[31]

Fireproof, masonry-encased iron beams installed by Alexander in 1853–54 did their job on January 24, 1865, when a fire broke out on the roof above the lecture room.

The roof collapsed and the second floor was gutted, but Alexander's beams prevented the total destruction of the building. Henry immediately applied to Secretary of War Edwin M. Stanton asking for the Army's help in raising a temporary roof. Alexander surveyed the damage, discovered the cause of the fire, and estimated that thirty to forty carpenters could erect a temporary roof in two days, work that was completed under the Army's supervision by January 31. German émigré architect Adolf Cluss was given the job of rebuilding and once again the Smithsonian's interiors were changed to adapt to the institution's changing nature with the lecture hall eliminated. The role of the Corps reverted once again to a supervisory one; General Richard Delafield served as the chairman of the Smithsonian's building committee during Cluss's rebuilding campaign.[32]

SUPPLYING WASHINGTON WITH WATER

The Corps' more traditional role as hydraulic engineers occupied a number of men who designed and built Washington's water system during the 1850s. President Millard Fillmore declared in his first annual message to Congress in 1851 that "nothing could contribute more to the health, comfort and safety of the city and the security of the public buildings and records than an abundant supply of pure water." A few months before, in

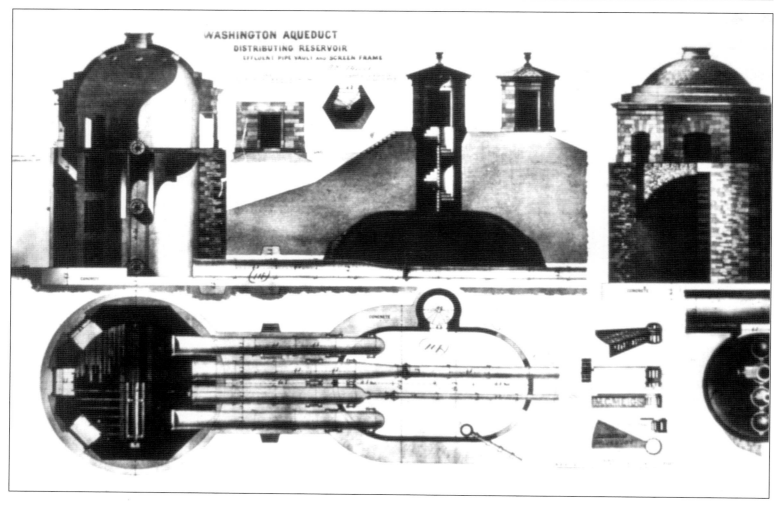

WASHINGTON AQUEDUCT
DISTRIBUTING RESERVOIR
EFFLUENT PIPE VAULT and SCREEN FRAME

*Drawing of Aqueduct
equipment, 1857*
*Office of History, Corps
of Engineers*

the fall of 1850, Congress confronted the long-standing problem of the city's water supply by voting $500 for a War Department survey to locate the best sources. The survey was undertaken by Captain George W. Hughes of the Topographical Corps, who, due to the limited amount appropriated, confined his report to the use of Rock Creek as a supply.[33]

In December 1851 a fire broke out in the Capitol, destroying the Library of Congress and threatening the wooden dome. The following summer Congress voted $5,000 for "surveys and estimates of the best means for affording the cities of Washington and Georgetown an unfailing and abundant supply of good and wholesome water." This bill was prepared by Fillmore's Secretary of the Interior, assisted by local banker William W. Corcoran and by Chief of Engineers Colonel Totten. Fillmore assigned the survey to the Corps. Totten turned the job over to Captain Frederick A. Smith, his long-time deputy, but Smith died one month later. Casting about for a successor, in October 1852, Totten picked a young lieutenant, Montgomery C. Meigs.[34]

"Thus quietly and unostentatiously was commenced the great work. Which is destined I trust for the next thousand years to pour healthful water into the Capital of our union. May I live to complete it & connect my name imperishably with a work greater in its beneficial results than all the military glory of the Mexican War."

Captain Montgomery C. Meigs with Aqueduct equipment, 1859
Office of History, Corps of Engineers

For three months, Meigs, assisted by civil engineer William H. Bryan, surveyed the countryside northwest of Washington and worked on his report. After careful study, he proposed that the city draw its water supply either from Rock Creek or from the Potomac River at either Little Falls or Great Falls. Using Great Falls would entail the greatest engineering effort and cost the most money, but it would produce the largest and most reliable supply. Meigs preferred an aqueduct capable of serving a growing city for centuries to come. "Let our aqueduct be worthy of the Nation," he wrote. "Let us show that the rulers chosen by the people are not less careful of the safety, health, and beauty of their Capital than emperors [of Rome]."[35]

When Congress asked the president to choose among the three alternatives Meigs suggested, newly inaugurated Franklin Pierce chose the Great Falls plan. On March 29, 1853, Jefferson Davis, secretary of war and strongman of the new cabinet, selected Meigs— scion of a prominent Democratic family—to head the project. A demonstration of his individualistic style followed. Meigs refused to give bond, telling Davis, "The security of

1858

CONSTRUCTION OF CABIN JOHN BRIDGE

The Corps built the bridge using the Roman arch construction technique of a central keystone holding wedge-shaped stones (voussoirs) in position.

May 1858

December 1858

June 1859

August 1861

Civil War Era

an Engineer officer's commission and character [is] better than the bond of a civil agent." A new force had arrived on the Washington scene.[36]

Over the decade that followed, Meigs directed the building of a dependable water supply system marked by touches of striking originality. The main conduit was a circular masonry tunnel nine feet in diameter and ten miles long. It ran from the Potomac to a fifty-acre receiving reservoir near the district line, created by damming the Little Falls Branch, which provided sedimentation and storage. Two miles further along, a thirty-six-acre distributing reservoir on the Potomac Palisades served for additional storage, before two cast-iron mains, one thirty inches and the other twelve inches in diameter, carried the water into the city. A third storage reservoir was a domed rotunda building fifty feet high on the heights of Georgetown at the corner of Wisconsin Avenue and R Street. Additional pipes carried the Aqueduct's water to the Capitol and then as far as the Navy Yard, the total length of the system being 18.6 miles.[37]

Underground work was craftsman-like and durable; that aboveground was graceful and bold. Meigs built classical temples to hide the machinery and serve as gatehouses. At Cabin

John Run, he adopted a design prepared by his gifted assistant, Alfred L. Rives, and spanned the deep ravine with the longest ashlar masonry arch in the world. He carried the Aqueduct across Rock Creek by an ingenious bridge in which two forty-eight-inch cast-iron tubes served both as supporting arches and water mains. The structure carried both the city's water supply and the traffic of Pennsylvania Avenue. Throughout its length, the Aqueduct bore the marks of an original engineering mind.[38]

It also bore Meigs's name, for vanity was no small foible of his. He recorded in his diary for October 31, 1853, the turning of the first spade of soil at Great Falls. "Thus quietly and unostentatiously was commenced the great work. Which is destined I trust for the next thousand years to pour healthful water into the Capital of our union. May I live to complete it & connect my name imperishably with a work greater in its beneficial results than all the military glory of the Mexican War." Although the workforce of seven hundred free and slave laborers received no memorial, Meigs did order the names of his assistants—Alfred Rives, W. H. Bryant, C. Crozel, C. G. Talcott, and W. R. Hutton—engraved on stone tablets, though Rives's name, like that of Secretary Davis, was later erased when he joined the Confederacy.

Pennsylvania Avenue Bridge over Rock Creek supported by forty-eight-inch cast-iron water mains with Georgetown in the background. In 1876 the Engineer Officer in Charge of Public Buildings and Grounds decided that the bridge was no longer capable of carrying heavy loads, provoking outrage from Montgomery Meigs. The Chief of Engineers appointed a board of engineer officers to examine the bridge, which was declared sound and remained in service until 1916.
Office of History, Corps of Engineers

But Meigs saw the Aqueduct largely as a memorial to himself. Throughout the Aqueduct's length, he had his name engraved on and cast into bridges, gatehouses, pipes, staircases in pipe vaults, even on the derricks and hoisting gear. No one then or later would forget that the project was his.[39]

In 1852 Captain Alexander H. Bowman (1803–1865), an 1825 graduate of West Point, was chosen to head up the new Bureau of Construction in the Treasury Department and promoted to major. His previous experience constructing defenses on the Gulf of Mexico and Charleston (he built Fort Sumter), while at the same time working on rivers and harbors, prepared him to manage several large-scale projects simultaneously. In his 1853 annual report to Congress on the state of finances, Secretary of the Treasury James Guthrie appended a list of thirty-eight "Regulations for the construction of custom-houses and other buildings." The regulations were probably written largely by Bowman to summarize his experience with divided administration and working with local contractors in areas distant from Washington but answerable to the War Department. The regulations laid out in some detail the responsibilities of everyone along the chain of command on what procedures to follow if an officer in charge suspected poor quality construction in a fail-safe bureaucratic system of checks and balances in order to avert fraud both in the field and in Washington.[40]

This emphasis on accountability led to Bowman being detailed to the Treasury Department. Until 1860 he worked with architect Ammi B. Young erecting approximately seventy federal buildings throughout the country during the government's second great building campaign. In 1855 President Franklin Pierce chose Bowman and Young to undertake their largest project, to carry out Thomas U. Walter's design for the Treasury Extension. Walter and Meigs hoped to secure the job in addition to their other work, principally superintendence of the Capitol Extension. Three years earlier Walter and Meigs had replaced Robert Mills as the architect and engineer of the Patent Office Extension and a few weeks before Pierce's decision on the Treasury Building, Walter's design for the General Post Office Extension was chosen with Meigs put in charge of its construction.[41]

The Aqueduct was the Corps' major project in Washington before the Civil War, but not its only one. In 1857 the mayor of Georgetown, concerned about the navigability of the Potomac, asked the secretary of war to assign an Army Engineer to superintend a survey of the river's Georgetown Channel. Secretary John Floyd delegated Captain Isaac C. Woodruff, an assistant in the Corps of Topographical Engineers, to the task.

Woodruff's January 1858 report was the first thorough description of the river's conditions in the district since 1792. It noted both the Potomac's central role in supporting local commerce and in moving materials for the Aqueduct and the Treasury Building extension. Woodruff quoted a letter from Bowman, citing "great delays and inconveniences [that] have arisen from the detention of vessels loaded with granite, by grounding on the bars, with serious loss to the contractor, in detention and lighterage on granite intended for [the Treasury] building." The city undertook dredging the channel and private entrepreneurs built a new dock in Foggy Bottom to unload materials for the Aqueduct and the Treasury Extension.[42]

U.S. General Post Office Extension under construction, August 1858. Captain Meigs was in charge of constructing the extension to the General Post Office, 1855–60, at the same time Captain Bowman was in charge of building the Treasury Building's south wing extension.
Library of Congress, Prints and Photographs Division, LC-USZ62-88920

U.S. CAPITOL EXTENSION

Two American titans in their respective professions clashed over control of Washington's major mid-nineteenth century building projects, the extension of the U.S. Capitol and the design and construction of its new cast-iron dome. For nine years Captain Montgomery C. Meigs of the Corps of Engineers and Philadelphia architect Thomas U. Walter divided the responsibilities for these monumental tasks, initially working in concert, but eventually in competition with one another professionally and personally.

The Capitol's extension began before the formal competition of 1850–51 that resulted in Walter being named architect of the Capitol Extension. On March 3, 1843, Congress requested the Secretary of War to direct the Corps to prepare a design "for the better accommodation of the sittings of the House of Representatives," a room with serious acoustical faults that defied the efforts of three architects, Charles Bulfinch, William Strickland, and Robert Mills, and the Corps engineers who worked with them during the 1820s and 30s.[43]

THE WASHINGTON MONUMENT GROUNDS WERE NOT ALWAYS MONUMENTAL. THE GROUNDS WERE FENCED IN DURING THE CIVIL WAR AND CATTLE WERE RAISED THERE TO FEED UNION TROOPS STATIONED IN WASHINGTON. THE SOUTH WING OF THE TREASURY BUILDING, ON THE RIGHT, WAS COMPLETED UNDER THE DIRECTION OF CAPTAIN BOWMAN SHORTLY BEFORE THIS PHOTOGRAPH OF 14TH STREET WAS TAKEN IN THE 1860S. THE BOARD OF PUBLIC WORKS IN THE 1870S FILLED IN THE CANAL NORTH OF THE CATTLE. TODAY, THE FILLED CANAL IS CONSTITUTION AVENUE.

National Archives no. 111-B-5147

Corps of Topographical Engineers' 1845 drawing of the extension of the Capitol, with porticoed lateral wings attached directly to the original building
Architect of the Capitol. 63447

During the spring and summer of 1843 Topographical Corps engineer A. A. Humphreys (1810–83), working under Colonel Abert, determined that lateral additions to the existing Capitol would solve the need for increased space for congressional business, offer the opportunity to construct new legislative chambers upon better acoustical principles, and improve what the Corps and others considered the aesthetic fault of the disproportionate height of Charles Bulfinch's dome, completed in 1824. Humphreys and Abert reported that a new House wing, 103 feet by 152 feet placed symmetrically at right angles directly against the Capitol's south wall, could be constructed without disrupting the normal work of Congress. The engineers consulted the writings of acoustical experts and concluded that the new House of Commons in London would be the appropriate model. Corps engineers designed a rectangular room 75 feet by 105 feet within the wing to have a flat ceiling and level floor overlooked by public galleries on two sides. The Corps made detailed estimates that also included modern methods of heating and ventilating such a large room.

After determining the form, position, and scale of the wing additions (the new Senate Wing would be built following that for the House), Abert asked Strickland to suggest an alternate interior arrangement for the House wing, and to calculate its cost to compare to the government's estimates for the Topographical Corps' design. Strickland designed a rectilinear, galleried House, its flat, cast-iron ceiling admitting light through four cupolas with its lateral galleries able to accommodate six hundred spectators. Estimates for both the Humphreys-Abert and Strickland schemes were just under $300,000 per wing, a sum apparently too great at this time because Abert wrote the architect on April 5, 1844, that the entire idea had been abandoned. However, the early formula

Capitol with its low dome, 1851. South, or House wing, extension, in relationship to Charles Bulfinch's dome built in 1823

Library of Congress, Prints and Photographs Division, LC-USZ62-62168

for how to extend the Capitol and design new legislative chambers on better acoustical principles, first suggested by the Corps, was further developed during the 1850s by Walter and Meigs.

Six years later Congress decided to go ahead with the project to extend the Capitol. On July 4, 1851, the cornerstone for the extension was set, and Walter, hired by the Department of the Interior, contracted for a year's work on foundations. Immediately he encountered difficulties prompted primarily by aesthetic issues—republican simplicity versus the Victorian splendor and opulence of his winning design. The government's financial situation also changed dramatically when the mineral rights gleaned from the Gold Rush began filling the federal treasury.[44]

Walter's first skirmish was over the Massachusetts marble chosen for the wings. The Secretary of the Interior appointed General Totten, Smithsonian secretary Joseph Henry, the commissioner of the Patent Office, and Walter to a commission to test various marbles. The result of their December 22, 1851, report was the decision to use marble from Massachusetts, Maryland, and New York. The second difficulty Walter encountered concerned the foundations of the wings; on April 2, 1852, engineers Frederick A. Smith and J. L. Mason reported that the gneiss and hydraulic cement

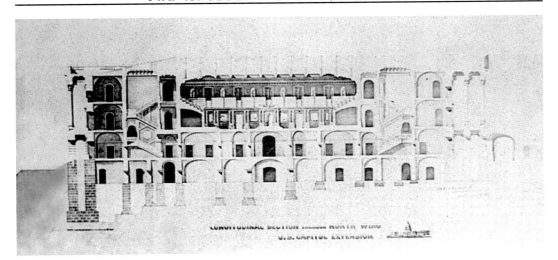

being used were excellent, the Corps having been called in as consultants by the
Senate's Committee on Public Buildings.

On December 24, 1851, fire destroyed Bulfinch's Library of Congress, which
spanned the west wing's top two stories. Between March 1852 and July 1853, Walter
replaced it by inserting a three-story cast-iron cage of shelves and balconies manufactured by the Janes, Beebe & Company of New York. Although the new Library of
Congress officially had America's first cast-iron ceiling suspended from an iron truss
roof, all of the rooms' other iron elements were the logical conclusion of Walter's earlier
Philadelphia works using iron construction. Walter's innovative use of cast-iron in the
library soon became the basis for Walter's and Meigs's design and construction of the
Capitol's wings as well as additions they made to the Patent Office (1853–67) and
General Post Office (1855–69).[45]

When the administration changed in 1853, Democrat Franklin Pierce quickly
transferred oversight (on March 23) of the Capitol's construction from the Interior
Department to the War Department at the request of Secretary of War Jefferson Davis.
Allegations against Walter concerning his contracts for materials were investigated and
explained but the government was leery of any appearances of malfeasance. On April 4,
1853, Davis chose Captain Meigs to carry out Pierce's executive order calling for the
Corps' general supervision and control of the whole work. In April 1854 the propriety of
having military engineers supervise civil works in general, and public buildings in particular, was debated by two Washington newspapers. The *Daily Union*, reporting on Kentucky
Congressman Richard H. Stanton's charge that about seventy Army officers were currently
unlawfully involved in civil projects, noted that the engineers were carrying out their legitimate duties "in compliance with the laws of Congress and the orders of their government."

The *Washington Sentinel* disagreed on the grounds that it was foolhardy to assign engineers to civil works projects when there was a critical shortage of engineers to carry out military projects. The *Sentinel* particularly argued that Meigs's supervision of the Capitol Extension was contrary to the original legislation and cited an 1824 law that allowed the Army to hire civilian engineers when its workload required extra expert labor.[46]

In spite of the controversy over military control of civilian projects, Meigs took over the writing and managing of all contracts for materials and labor from Walter, while the architect retained his responsibilities as the Capitol's designer. With Meigs as the "engineer in charge," a working relationship was established that became the model for the design and construction of the government's post-Civil War buildings in Washington. Meigs's

Montgomery C. Meigs
Office of History, Corps of Engineers

Meigs combined exceptional mental gifts, physical stamina, and an indomitable will—characteristics that made him the Corps' most colorful personality on the Washington scene for more than three decades. He was "high-tempered, unyielding, tyrannical towards his brothers, and very persevering in pursuit of anything he wishes" at the age of six, according to his mother. Oversight of the Capitol's extension might have been full-time work, but during the 1850s Meigs also was in charge of the Washington Aqueduct, extensions to two other major government buildings, and a score of lesser projects. Descended from a Revolutionary War General, Meigs was born in Augusta, Georgia, on May 3, 1816, the son of a Yale-trained physician, and the grandson of a Yale professor. Meigs was raised in Philadelphia and at the age of fifteen entered the University of Pennsylvania while awaiting an appointment to West Point. He graduated fifth in his 1836 class of forty-nine cadets, was commissioned an officer in the Corps of Engineers, and began the typical round of two- to four-year assignments by surveying the Mississippi River followed by building forts on the Great Lakes. By 1839 Meigs was in Washington serving on the Board of Engineers for Atlantic Coast Defenses where he married Louisa Rodgers, daughter of Commodore John Rodgers of the U.S. Navy. They lived in the Rodgers house on H Street, a short walk to the War Department and St. John's Episcopal Church, of which they were members. After other tours of duty, in 1852, Totten called Meigs back to Washington to survey the best route for Washington's aqueduct. Except for a few months in 1859 and 1860, Meigs spent the remainder of his career in Washington.[47]

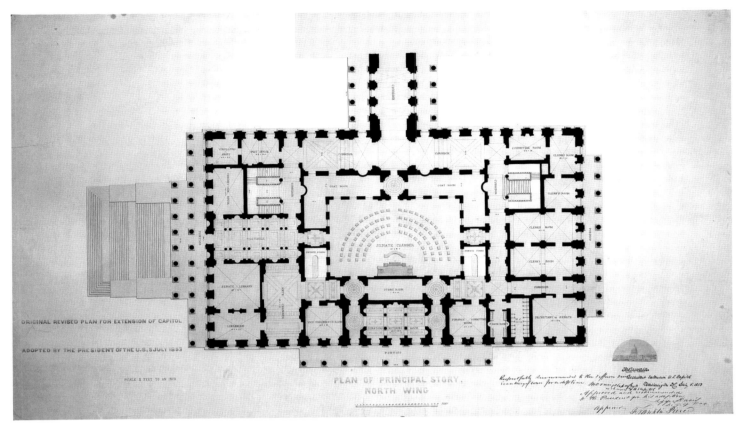

instructions gave him wide latitude. "As upon you will rest the responsibility for the proper and economical construction of these buildings, you will consider yourself fully empowered to make such changes in the present administration as you may deem necessary, and to regulate the organization thereafter as your experience may dictate." Meigs might have taken this opportunity to fire or replace Walter, but he did not do so. Meigs's first assignment under orders was to reexamine the foundations, the source of charges brought against Walter. At the same time he and Walter collaborated on a major change in the wings. Walter had placed the chambers on the west sides of the wings for views over the Mall and city; Meigs suggested moving them to the center of each wing. This improved circulation between them and congressional committee rooms, and allowed the chambers to be sunken wells with public galleries on all sides to ensure acoustical quality. Meigs's arrangement meant illuminating the rooms with skylights, the entire design already suggested in the Abert-Strickland scheme of 1843. Meigs claimed

> we obtain a pleasanter light, ample for all useful purposes, as proved by its
> adoption in all the best constructed picture galleries. We also exclude the
> sounds of the exterior, which, saturating the air, as it were, distract the atten-
> tion, and even overpower the voice we wish to hear....Open windows for
> hearing will be worse than closed ones; they not only let irregular, disturbing
> currents of air in, but they let the voices out.[48]

53

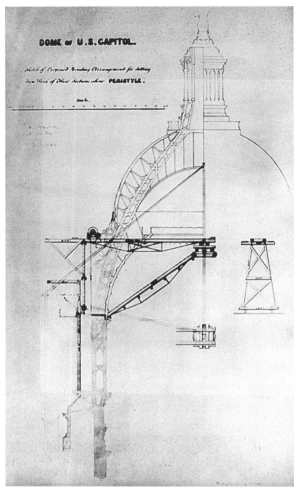

DOME of U.S. CAPITOL.

PERISTYLE.

*Sketch of Meigs's arrangement for
hoisting the cast-iron pieces of
the new dome*

Library of Congress, Prints and Photographs
Division, LC-USZ62-88572

*"I do not see why a
republic richer than the
Athenian should not rival
the Parthenon in the front
of its first public edifice."*

Meigs's revised 1853 plan included two monumental imperial marble staircases per wing, "the most stately in the country and when embellished with our beautiful native marbles," Meigs claimed, "will, I trust, compare favorably with any abroad." These staircases were primarily to take visitors to the public galleries, and their Victorian splendor reflected the contemporary taste of a newly rich country. Meigs's reports describe the new plans "in terms of richness, luxury, and elegance, reflecting the administration's determination that the Capitol extension" be comparable to contemporary European public buildings increasingly being visited by congressmen, cabinet officers, and high government officials.

Walter continued to control the design of the Capitol's exteriors with one exception. Meigs suggested including pediments above the east porticoes of the wings to match the central pediment above the portico that led to the rotunda. These pediments were to be filled with sculpture, and Meigs chose the artists, suggested appropriate themes to them, critiqued their work, and ensured they were paid.[49]

In July 1853 Meigs wrote Edward Everett (a former president of Harvard as well as former congressman and governor of Massachusetts) asking for recommendations for sculptors; Everett recommended Hiram Powers and Thomas Crawford. In August 1853 Meigs wrote Crawford, who like some other contemporary American sculptors, lived and worked in Rome. "The pediments and doorways should be part of the original construction of the building, and I do not see why a republic richer than the Athenian should not rival the Parthenon in the front of its first public edifice." Meigs cautioned Crawford that complex allegories were not acceptable to the American public and Crawford responded with a design for the Senate wing's pediment titled the *Progress of Civilization.* Crawford's central statue allegorized America while twelve flanking figures represented the Euro-Americans in appropriate dress bringing European civilization to the new world and a Native American family in great sorrow. Once the Capitol's dome was underway, Meigs turned again to Crawford for a figure of *Freedom.*[50]

Meigs's attention to construction details was legendary. When he noticed that windowsills on the eastern side of the south wing were a little more than an inch higher than those on the west, he had it corrected. His professional logs and personal journals record such daily minutiae as the cost of laying one thousand

*Roof over the House of
Representatives' chamber, with
Meigs's glass roof suspended by
a truss system he designed*
Library of Congress, Prints and
Photographs Division, LC-USZ62-62170

bricks ($4.07), the number of government employees and contractors' workmen per day, and the progress of minor construction details. Obtaining good quality materials, especially bricks in sufficient quantities, was an ongoing problem and the Capitol's letter books attest to Meigs's visits to quarries and brickyards along the eastern seaboard and his rejection of shoddy products.[51]

Meigs was particularly anxious to use America's richly veined native marble and pursued sources at the same time Army (and Navy) Engineers were testing their strength and durability for general use. It was not solely the Capitol's stability and construction technology, however, that Meigs wanted to his credit, but its place among the world's great buildings. He argued early in 1854 that the 100 new exterior columns should be monoliths cut from single pieces of stone, a subtle but effective aid to the appearance of stability, but, more importantly, a rare architectural achievement in Europe. Steam engines to cut monoliths from quarries, steam engines to convey them to the site, and steam engines to hoist them in place made a once vastly expensive architectural luxury perfectly possible; Meigs convinced Congress to bear their extra cost, double that of shafts composed of individual drums.[52]

In 1854, the enemies of the "military rule" at the Capitol questioned Meigs's competency as the Capitol's design partner, but not his abilities as an engineer, at a time when radical changes in national taste were occurring. Representative Richard H. Stanton of Kentucky, in particular, was very outspoken about preferring Walter's "refined" taste to the opulence, even garishness, that Meigs was introducing in highly colored marble, tiles, and fresco

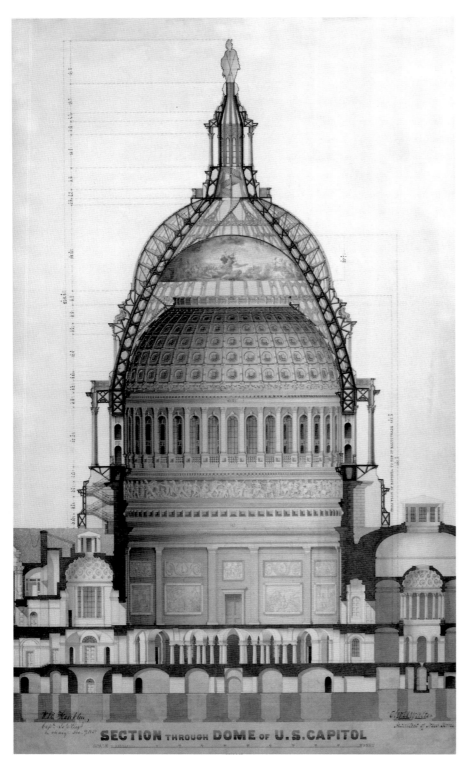

Thomas U. Walter and Capt. W. B. Franklin, "Section through Dome of U.S. Capitol," Dec. 9, 1859. Both the trusses and the dome's exterior and interior decorative parts are made of cast-iron.
Architect of the Capitol, 74001

paintings. Such enmity also was motivated by congressional power struggles and partisan politics, a constant factor throughout the Capitol's history of construction beginning in 1793. Walter himself was initially delighted with the division of responsibilities between architect and engineer and admired Meigs. He wrote his father-in-law on June 20, 1854:

*The Captain is as noble a man as the country can produce, and he is better fitted for his post than any one they could find whether **soldier** or **civilian**, and I most sincerely desire that he may not be removed; such a thing would be a disaster for the country in general and me in particular—you have no idea what a luxury it has been to me during the past year to be able to devote myself to the legitimate professional duties, and be freed from the annoyances of contractors, appointments, disbursements, and the like, all of which take time, unhinge the mind, and create an army of enemies.[53]*

From his youth, Meigs was part of the government and he understood the ways of politicians and the bureaucracy and how to manipulate the one and navigate the other, while Walter was often at the mercy of both. Both men had their friends and enemies in Congress and often that was the arena where differences of taste and credit were fought.

In May 1854 Walter began working on a new dome, from the outset planned to be built of cast-iron. He excited Congressmen with spectacular drawings—one seven feet long—and Meigs regretted that he did not have a larger part in its design. On December 26, 1854, he recorded in his diary: "I think the sketch I have made is a better outline than the one Mr. Walter and myself settled upon before, and I wish to have had something to do with this design myself. I can make a little greater height and more graceful outline and a very noble and beautiful interior arrangement."[54]

Meigs's journal entry for December 29, 1854, indicates the kind of suppressed hostilities between architect and engineer that later broke out into open warfare.

I showed Walter today my sketch for the dome....He was very decided in his opinion that his is better but offered to have both worked up so that they could be [compared]. It was evident that he is disgusted that I should attempt such a thing as design a dome. The arrangement of the rooms is mine. The form of the ceiling is mine. The style of decoration is that which I directed....He has not a dome in the building. I have introduced many. So that, in fact, the design is quite as much, if not more, mine than his....[55]

Meigs acted speedily in February 1855 to ensure that both houses of Congress voted to place the dome's construction under the Corps of Engineers, it not having been

> *"The Captain is as noble a man as the country can produce, and he is better fitted for his post than any one they could find whether soldier or civilian...."*

January 1856

1857

March 4, 1861

ENLARGEMENT OF THE CAPITOL DOME

Partially completed for President Abraham Lincoln's first inauguration on March 4, 1861, construction continued during the Civil War. By January 1856 the old dome had been removed in preparation for construction of the new, larger dome. The 1857 photograph shows new iron work projecting from the support wall of the old dome. This new iron work would support the peristyle of the new dome.

ca. 1861–62

November 1862

***Tholus and Statue of Freedom
of the New Dome of the Capitol***
*Library of Congress, Prints and
Photographs Division, LC-USZ62-88881*

part of the original legislation for the Capitol Extension. In order to get the greatest exterior width at the dome's base, Meigs suggested embedding iron brackets in the existing octagonal brick drum to support a cantilevered iron ring from which thirty-six columns would rise. Meigs designed a special scaffold with a triangular base to avoid a weak spot in the center of the rotunda's floor, later raising a mast and boom powered by a steam engine that Meigs fueled with wood from Bulfinch's dismantled outer dome. This structure made it possible to raise the large iron pieces efficiently and economically, a great savings in time. Meigs kept up to date with European and American advances in technology and was quick to apply what he learned to projects under his direction. Because of concern about the weight of the much larger new dome, the old dome was weighed as it was dismantled, the cast-iron dome found to weigh only twenty-percent more than Bulfinch's dome. When the original congressional appropriation of $100,000 was deemed inadequate, Meigs claimed that he repeatedly refused to estimate the new dome's cost based solely on Walter's elevation drawing; the dome eventually cost $1,047,271.[56]

Within two months of Congress authorizing the new dome, Meigs asked sculptor Thomas Crawford to sketch a figure for its summit, an element present on Walter's drawings but its subject undefined. On May 11, 1855, Meigs wrote the sculptor: "We have too many Washingtons; we have America in the pediment, Victories and Liberties are rather pagan emblems, but a Liberty I fear is the best we can get." Crawford's design was received on July 12, its subject "Freedom Triumphant in Peace and War," its emblems consisting of a sword, olive branch, and shield of the United States, all elements readily comprehensible to the American people. Meigs returned the design asking for a base to be added that would fit the tholos on which it was to stand; Crawford's photograph of his revised sketch maquette arrived in January 1856, with the figure wearing a liberty cap, a Roman emblem of freed slaves that had been revived first during the American Revolution and then the French Revolution. Secretary of War Jefferson Davis objected to this addition to the statue, arguing, "history renders it inappropriate to a people who were born free and would not be enslaved." In January 1856 Meigs noted in his diary that despite Davis's objection to the liberty cap, "he leaves the matter to the judgement of Mr. Crawford," who was sent Davis's letter and decided to give "Freedom" an eagle headdress.[57]

Marble in a great variety of colors and patterns from many American quarries were the Capitol extension's most expensive elements and Meigs had complete control over their choice and contracting for them. Although marble floors originally had been specified, Meigs substituted English Minton encaustic tiles—highly patterned and very colorful, as well as being very durable. He substituted iron door and window frames for marble because they could be made more rapidly. During the nine years that Meigs oversaw the Capitol's construction, he was always conscious of applying new technologies to save time and money without sacrificing the quality of construction. He used steam power whenever possible to replace man-hours. However, cost savings in these areas was more than balanced by Meigs's expenditures on beautifying the Capitol according to his (and currently popular) taste, all duly authorized by Congress.[58]

Meigs began seeking artists to decorate the Capitol's interiors in 1854, and in January 1855, when the Roman expatriate fresco painter Constantino Brumidi came to the Capitol seeking work, Meigs invited him to paint a lunette in his office, the subject being the *Calling of Cincinnatus from the Plow*. Meigs considered this an appropriate theme because it fused the Revolution's military and civic history in an allegory cast in the timelessness of classicism. The Society of the Cincinnati had been founded in 1784, with George Washington its first president, to honor American military officers who served their country during the Revolution. Contrary to Crawford's realistic sculpture for the Capitol, Brumidi carried out under Meigs's direction great cycles of paintings in which American historical events were cast in the visual language of traditional European allegories. The architectural and decorative frameworks in which they were placed were derived from Italian Renaissance buildings, considered to be the acme of human civilization by Meigs's generation. Some of Brumidi's paintings were portraits of actual people engaged in real events, but the majority, including the grisaille frieze and the *Apotheosis of Washington* in the rotunda, used the traditional allegorical language drawn from ancient mythology as more appropriate to the European origins of the Capitol's architecture.[59]

Meigs also received a great deal of credit during the nineteenth century for his engineering work on the Capitol Extension. Because of frequent night sessions in the House of Representatives and because of its large size, the chamber was lit by an impressive array of 1,260 gas burners on the ceiling containing forty-five thousand individual jets. The jets reportedly ignited in twenty seconds when the system was first used on December 2, 1857. Meigs also was responsible for the Capitol's unique steam heating system, "thought to be superior to anything of the kind ever invented." Air was heated as it passed over "seven or eight miles" of steam pipes and dispersed to the Senate chamber and committee rooms.[60]

When James Buchanan was sworn in as president in 1857, he appointed Virginia Governor John B. Floyd as secretary of war. Meigs's championing by the War Department gradually came to an end because Floyd saw the Capitol's large workforce as an opportunity to exercise political patronage. Meigs repeatedly refused at first hints and then direct orders to replace his trusted and experienced workmen with those suggested by Floyd. At the same time, competition between Walter and Meigs for credit of the Capitol's design erupted over the issue of the new Hall of Representatives. Walter complained that Meigs had undertaken all of its decorations without consulting him and that "it is the most vulgar room I was ever in." Meigs wrote the *National Intelligencer* on December 7, 1857, promoting his design.[61]

> *The style is new in this country where our public buildings generally, through the poverty of the public purse or perhaps the greater poverty of the architect's taste, starve in simple white-wash. This, new in this country, rich and magnificent decoration, naturally, when first seen excites surprise. The colors are so rich, so various, so intricate, so different from anything seen before, that the impression is that it must be, what? Gaudy? But what is gaudy? Are the colors of the autumnal forest gaudy?...Let not the noisy babble of ignorance forestall public opinion on its merits.[62]*

On November 1, 1859, Floyd relieved Meigs of his duties at the Capitol. Meigs recounted in his journal a particularly acrimonious meeting with Floyd on September 15, 1858.

> *He said that he thought the skill and taste of Mr. Walter could not be spared, that he supposed I would not be ready to assume a sufficient skill as an architect to complete the building without him or someone in his place.*

> *I told him that he was mistaken. I assumed to be able to complete it as well as Mr. Walter or any man living, that it was now mine, the exterior alone being Walter's, and that not entirely his; that the interior was my design, Mr. Walter having been the draftsman only, to execute such drawings as I directed; that the design and construction of the halls for legislation were entirely mine and to me alone was due the success of the building its great object. That the reputation which I had thus won, Mr. Walter endeavored to*

"...it is the most vulgar room I was ever in."

"The colors are so rich, so various, so intricate, so different from anything seen before, that the impression is that it must be, what? Gaudy? But what is gaudy? Are the colors of the autumnal forest gaudy?"

rob me of, etc. That I was entirely unfitted to take the position he proposed,
of a mere executive agent, a disbursing officer, to carry out the designs of
Mr. Walter or any other architect. That I had made a reputation which
neither Walter nor any other man could take from me.[63]

Meigs was more extreme in his attitude towards architects than other Corps engineers who worked as superintendents of construction on post-Civil War buildings in Washington. His exceptionally strong ego combined with his rightful intellectual ownership of many design decisions at the Capitol led him to believe that his artistic contributions were not being properly recognized. Meigs, as many West Point engineers of his generation, was trained to solve architectural problems including issues of design; recognition of his own considerable abilities as a designer and acutely conscious of contemporary aesthetics so different from those of Walter's more sedate generation, drove him to adopt this position. Seemingly, Meigs was unable to recognize the differences between his education in design, which focused on literal reinterpretations of prototypes (but innovative solutions of technical problems), and the architects' education, which emphasized the transformation of traditional historical archetypes in the creative process. Walter, one of the founding members of the American Institute of Architects, began a campaign to assert the supremacy of architectural design over the mechanics of coordinating the construction of such a complex building. He was unwilling to recognize Meigs's actual architectural and design contributions; personal jealousies between the two men became institutionalized during the following decades when Congress dictated that architects design public buildings and Army Engineers build them.

Throughout his private journal kept during the 1850s, Meigs lamented that his captain's salary was barely enough to support his family, certainly not enough to entertain as he felt his position required and merited. Despite his grumbling that he could earn a much higher salary as a civilian engineer, Meigs remained a military man to the end of his life. Two factors offset his desire for a larger salary: the opportunity to have so much control over such momentous projects as the Capitol Extension and the Washington Aqueduct, and the entrée into Washington society that his position and family connections afforded him. It was not until well after the Civil War that General Meigs was given the opportunity at the Pension Building to fully exploit his talents as both engineer and architect in a highly individual work of architecture.[64]

"I had made a reputation which neither Walter nor any other man could take from me."

The Winder Building, at the corner of 17th and F Streets west of the White House, was built in 1847–48 by William H. Winder, who leased most of the space to the U.S. government. The Corps of Engineers made it their headquarters from then until 1889. The building, seen here in the Civil War era, has been subject to very few alterations and still stands today.

THE CORPS IN CIVIL WAR WASHINGTON

The Corps of Engineers contributed extensively to the physical makeup of the district during the Civil War.[65] At the end of May 1861, Union troops occupied defensive positions on the Virginia side of the Potomac, and there established the first defensive works to protect the capital from southern military threats. After the July 1861 Union defeat at Manassas, greater emphasis was placed on the thorough planning of a protective system for the city. The next month Major General George B. McClellan assigned engineer Major John G. Barnard to be chief engineer of the city's defenses, in charge of construction of a planned ring of batteries, redoubts, lunettes, and forts. Barnard began by protecting major roadways, first on the Arlington Heights, then on the roads connecting the city to towns in Maryland to the north. By the end of 1861, forty-eight defensive works protected Washington—twenty-three in Virginia, seventeen on the northern sweep from the Potomac to the Anacostia, and eleven to the southeast and south of the Anacostia. Much of the labor was supplied by soldiers, supervised by the dozen or so engineer officers assigned to the work. As the war progressed, the Army Engineers came

Fort Stevens in the Northwest section of the district. Engineers built the fort to defend Washington from attack along the 7th Street Pike (now Georgia Avenue). On July 11, 1864, confederate Lieutenant General Jubal Early's forces attacked that section of the city's defenses but were driven off.
National Archives no. 66-DC-18-4

to rely upon numerous civil engineers and civilian overseers. A pair of civil engineers, previously employed on the Aqueduct, directed substantial work done in 1863: "They exhibited great zeal and intelligence, and soon mastered all those branches of military engineering which concerned their duties of construction. They were required to execute the plans prepared in the office of the chief engineer, to exercise a close supervision over their respective divisions, and generally to act as administrative officers in the details of the work."[66] As subsequent military campaigns moved soldiers to the field, Barnard also relied increasingly on hired labor. As he wrote after the war, "Details of troops were used whenever (and to the fullest extent) practicable; but this force was variable and uncertain, generally furnished with reluctance by the commanding officers, and comparatively inefficient when furnished....During the year 1863 large details were drawn from the convalescent, stragglers, and deserters' camps south of the Potomac, and made up in numbers what they lacked in individual efficiency."[67]

The initial detached line of forts was only later filled in and strengthened with supporting fortifications. Congressional appropriations in 1862 could not be used to start new works, although reevaluation of the defenses of the capital city came after the Battle of Antietam in October. A commission created by Secretary of War Edwin Stanton reported that twenty-five thousand infantry, nine thousand artillerymen, and three thousand cavalry were needed to defend the city adequately—plus another twenty-five thousand additional men to act as a mobile force outside the ring of defenses. The commission also called for changes to the existing works, the creation of half a dozen new forts, and additional shore defenses. Stanton's commission was well positioned to help the secretary of war gain congressional approval for expanded defenses: it included Chief of Engineers Totten and Quartermaster General Meigs, in addition to W. F. Barry, Chief of Artillery; G. W. Cullum, chief of staff to the General-in-Chief; and J. G. Barnard.

Despite labor and funding difficulties, by the end of 1863 Washington possessed 60 forts, 93 batteries, and 837 field guns. Rifle pits wide enough for two ranks of soldiers tied the ring of defenses together. The campaigns of 1864 removed both troops and guns from Washington. Lieutenant Colonel Barton S. Alexander replaced Barnard, reassigned to General Grant's staff as his chief engineer. When Confederate Lieutenant General Jubal Early moved on Washington in July—the only substantial fighting the city actually saw—only nine thousand soldiers manned the defenses. The engineers worked to improve and perfect the city's defensive works through the end of the war, although no major threat followed Early's unsuccessful campaign. By April 1865 the Corps had overseen the use of $1.4 million to construct twenty miles of rifle pits and thirty miles of military roads serving more than fourteen hundred gun emplacements in sixty-eight forts and ninety-three batteries. Among the roads was a five-and-a-half-mile stretch connecting Fort Sumner along the Potomac to Fort Stevens to the east of Rock Creek, "a very excellent road, thoroughly drained by side ditches and with substantial bridges and culverts…to

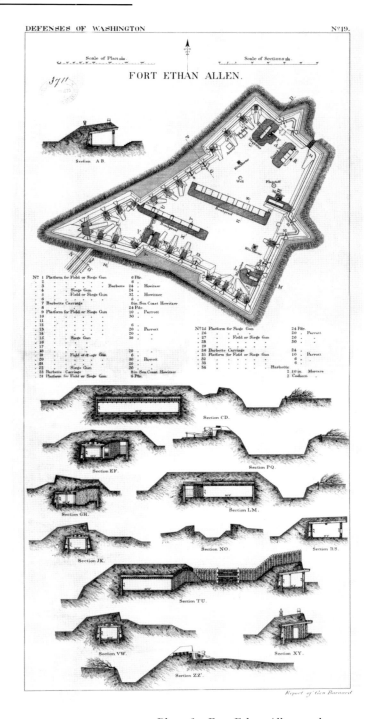

Plans for Fort Ethan Allen on the western side of the Potomac River, one of the many earthen and wood fortifications built to defend Washington during the Civil War
Office of History, Corps of Engineers

BUILDING THE BRIDGE.

A PONTON.

ROPE BRIDGE.

INFLATING THE PONTON.

WAGON WITH TIMBER PONTON.

CAMP ALEXANDER. WASHINGTON D.C.

No. 498.—PONTOONING IN THE ARMY—EXPERIMENTING WITH ROPE SUSPENSION BRIDGES AND INDIA RUBBER PONTOONS AT CAMP ALEXANDER, WASHINGTON, D. C., BY THE 15TH REGIMENT NEW YORK VOLUNTEER ENGINEERS, COLONEL McLEOD MURPHY BRIDGING THE ANACOSTIA.

Lithograph of the 15th New York Volunteer Engineers experimenting with rope suspension bridges and India rubber pontons and ponton bridges at Camp Alexander on the Anacostia River during the Civil War

which was given a width of forty-five feet and a full, rounded surface." Within a few years after the return of peace, the defensive works—which had briefly made Washington one of the most heavily fortified cities in the world—had been abandoned, although some of the roads and parks on the grounds of former forts became lasting contributions to the city.[68]

OPPOSITE PAGE: ENGINEER MAP OF THE DEFENSIVE POSITIONS SURROUNDING WASHINGTON DURING THE CIVIL WAR

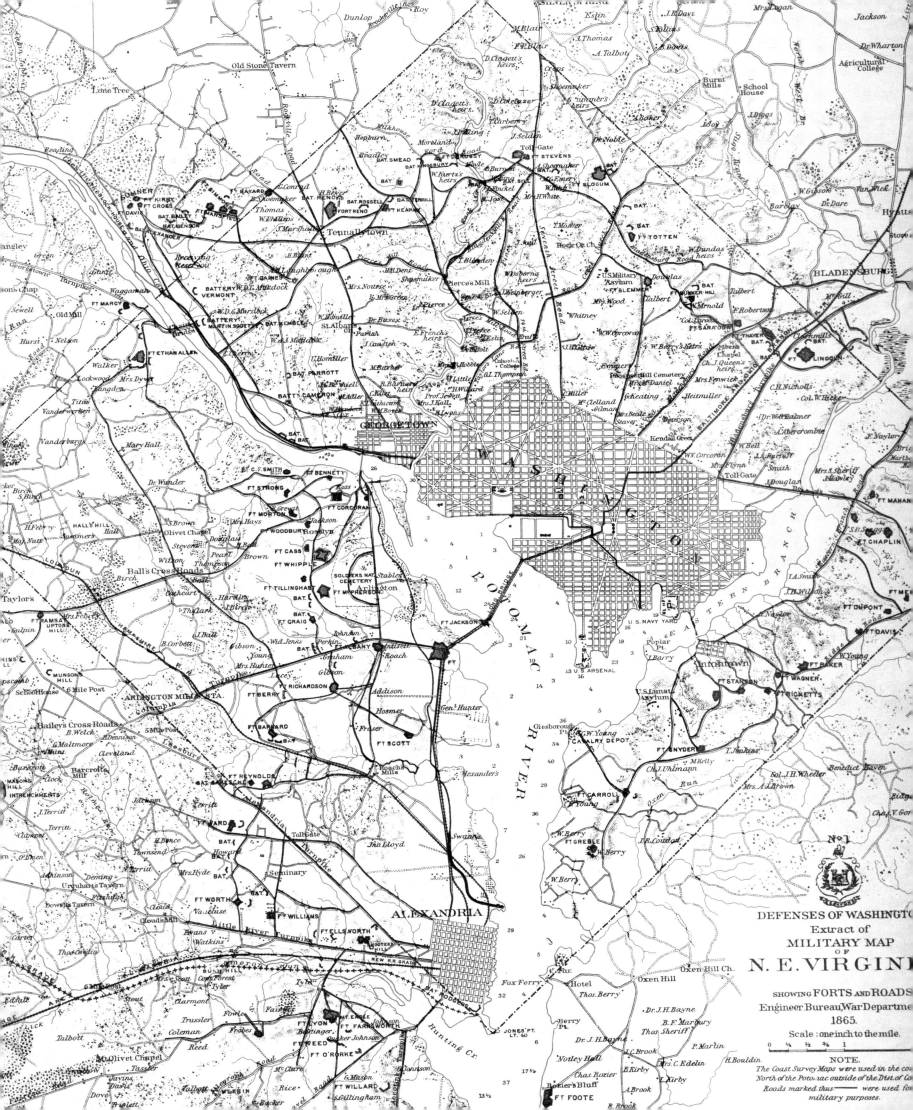

DEFENSES OF WASHINGTON
Extract of
MILITARY MAP
OF
N. E. VIRGINIA

SHOWING FORTS AND ROADS

Engineer Bureau War Department
1865.

Scale : one inch to the mile.

NOTE.
The Coast Survey Maps were used in the co
North of the Potomac outside of the Dist. of C
Roads marked thus ———— were used for
military purposes.

OCT. 16. 1894.

3 | *The Victorian City*
1865–90

INTRODUCTION

Within a decade of the Union Army's three-day victory march down Pennsylvania Avenue celebrating the end of the Civil War, late May 1865, three major administrative changes involved U.S. Army Engineers in the unanticipated tasks of overseeing the construction of Washington's most important late nineteenth century buildings, rebuilding and expanding the city's municipal infrastructure, and reclaiming the Potomac flats. In 1863 the Army Engineers had been reunited when the Topographical Engineers merged with the Corps. Four years later, on March 2, 1867, largely as a result of Congress's approval of Meigs's supervision of the Capitol Extension and the Aqueduct, the Office of Public Buildings and Grounds was transferred from the Interior Department to the War Department. (Another factor was the civilian building commissioner B. B. French's support of Andrew Johnson during congressional impeachment proceedings.) This act meant that the Chief of Engineers became responsible for overseeing construction of some individual government civilian buildings in Washington, in addition to military ones. In 1874 Washington's short-lived territorial government failed, and a temporary board of three civilian commissioners,

OPPOSITE PAGE: PLASTER CASTS OF STOCK SCULPTURES USED TO DECORATE THE LIBRARY OF CONGRESS, OCTOBER 1894

Library of Congress, Prints and Photographs Division. LC-USZ62-120936

assisted by an Army Engineer in charge of public works, took over running Washington's municipal affairs. The commissioner form of government was made permanent in 1878 and lasted until 1967 with an Army Engineer now one and perhaps the most powerful of the three commissioners. Finally, in 1875, the Washington Engineer District was formed, its initial responsibilities being the management of the Potomac River. The tidal flats adjacent to the west end of the Mall were filled and the Tidal Basin created, the long-term result being Potomac Park, which more than doubled the public grounds of the Mall.[1]

OFFICE OF PUBLIC BUILDINGS AND GROUNDS

The Corps of Engineers returned to peacetime civil projects in 1866 when the Senate ordered a report recommending sites for a major public park and a new Executive Mansion. Major Nathaniel N. Michler (1827–1881) quickly assembled the requested information. The next year, a youthful Major John A. Tardy took charge of Fort Washington and the surveying of the Potomac.[2] Of greater significance, lawmakers that year decided to remove the care of public buildings from a civilian commissioner. They transferred it, along with "the superintendence of the Washington Aqueduct and all the public works and improvements of the government of the United States in the District of Columbia" to the Corps of Engineers. The Office of Public Buildings and Grounds was the result. Chief of Engineers General A. A. Humphreys appointed Michler as the logical man to fill the new post, and for the first time the Corps took a regular and routine hand in running the nation's capital.[3]

The transfer of responsibility for the federal lands and property in the District of Columbia made Michler the chief maintenance man for the federal buildings and the landscape architect of the federal reservations. "Not since L'Enfant had anyone examined the physical city as broadly and with as much care as Michler,"[4] as evidenced by his 1867 report. He carefully made a copy of Andrew Jackson Downing's 1851 picturesque plan for the Mall for the use of his office. The seriousness of his commitment to his job and to Washington's development set a high standard for the Corps' engineers and was rarely dishonored. Like subsequent members of the Corps of Engineers to hold such an important position in Washington, Michler had broad practical experience in many parts of the country before being given administrative responsibilities in Washington.

Moreover, Michler continued the precedent set by L'Enfant, Roberdeau, Totten, and others of the gentleman-engineer tradition, descended from families long in public service

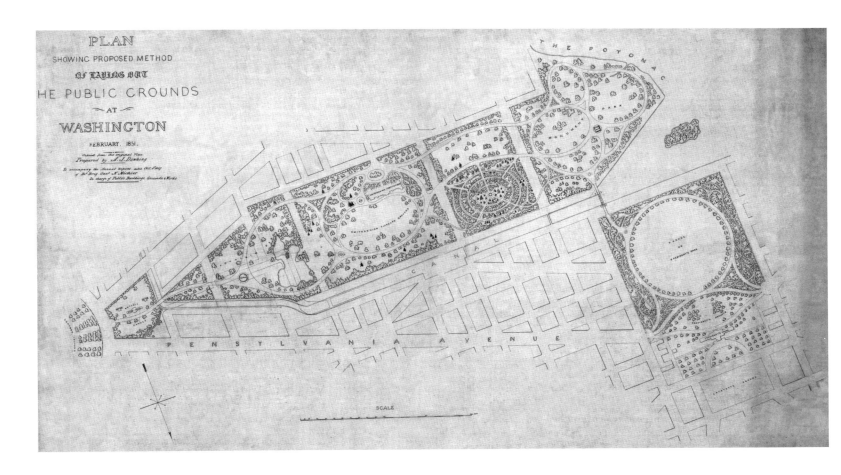

and educated in far more than the arts of war. A Pennsylvania Moravian and the son of a state legislator, Michler excelled at surveys and map-making. He rebuilt the White House conservatories in 1867, doubling their size and even selecting some of the new plants, outlined plans for the development of the Mall, began to beautify parks and squares, and started grading some of the streets and avenues. He lobbied for money to cover "that pestiferous ditch of water styled the 'Washington City canal,'"[5] and managed a workforce of watchmen, doorkeepers, clerks, and gardeners. In 1869 when Congress allowed the Mount Vernon Ladies' Association a $7,000 indemnity for the loss of revenue when the Potomac River was blockaded during the Civil War, Regent Ann Pamela Cunningham specifically asked that Michler be placed in charge of its disbursement for Mount Vernon's restoration. Finally, Michler was responsible for disbursing "one of the most charitable and disinterested appropriations…[,] that for the care of such transient paupers as are in need of medical advice and treatment."[6]

On June 12, 1866, R. D. Mussey, formerly a military secretary to the president, wrote Thaddeus Stevens, chairman of the House Committee on Appropriations, upon learning that Stevens's committee was looking for a new executive mansion with the intention of turning the White House over to the State Department. Mussey, "painfully conscious of the imperfections and deficiencies of the present building,"[7] because of its low-lying situation

Andrew Jackson Downing's Plan for the Mall, 1851, was copied by Lieutenant Colonel Nathaniel Michler to aid the Office of Public Buildings and Grounds in implementing its five sections, including the Ellipse south of the president's house intended as a military parade ground.
National Archives, Cartographic Branch, RG77, Civil Works File F116-1.

near the malarial Potomac River, suggested Meridian Hill as the best locale in the city for a new executive residence. The historic White House might then become entirely offices. On July 18 the Senate directed the Secretary of War to select a "park and site for a Presidential Mansion that shall combine convenience of access and healthfulness, good water and capability of adornment."[8]

Michler's January 29, 1867, report addressed the "park and site" separately, beginning with a lyrical and emotive description of the picturesque beauties of the Rock Creek valley and an impassioned plea that the government purchase large tracts in anticipation of future growth. "There should be a variety of scenery, a happy combination of the beautiful and picturesque—the smooth plateau and the gently undulating glade vying with the ruggedness of the rocky ravine and the fertile valley, the thickly mantled primeval forest contrasting with the green lawn, grand old trees with flowering shrubs."[9] These were the effusions of a mid-nineteenth-century romantic soul and not the stuff of the usual engineer's report to Congress. (Michler's obituary in the *New York Times* noted that his father, Peter Michler, was the "owner of one of the finest estates in that portion [Easton] of Pennsylvania.")[10] Michler's intensity of commitment to secure the best possible location for the executive is complemented by his foresight in thinking about the city's future needs. He compared the extent of European (London's 6,000 acres) and American (Central Park's 840 acres) public parks to land available along Rock Creek ranging from tracts of 1,800 to 2,540 acres. Michler appended to his report "Remarks on the Vegetation of the District of Columbia," by Dr. Arthur Schott, which characterized the habitats and characteristics of trees and shrubs in Washington.

A pragmatic concern for the safety of a future presidential residence is also evident in Michler's discussion of Rock Creek, as is the flexibility he was allowed to fulfill his special duty: to find suitable sites for both a public park and a presidential mansion. He identified four possible sites and their probable cost for the mansion that would "combine convenience of access and healthfulness, good water and capability of adornment,"[11] as he was directed to do. All were on high ground within four miles of the White House and he rejected two of them because Meridian Hill was "too near the city to afford any retirement and repose for the Chief Magistrate," and Eckington because it was "not sufficiently high to afford any extensive views." W. W. Corcoran's already beautifully landscaped estate, Harewood, "would be a most eligible site for a presidential mansion" near the Soldier's Home off North Capitol Street.[12]

However, Michler favored Moncure Robinson's estate, also adjacent to the Soldier's Home, because it fulfilled all of his criteria as to a beautiful and healthful locale, was three

"There should be a variety of scenery, a happy combination of the beautiful and picturesque—the smooth plateau and the gently undulating glade vying with the ruggedness of the rocky ravine and the fertile valley, the thickly mantled primeval forest contrasting with the green lawn, grand old trees with flowering shrubs."

miles from the Capitol, and would be the least expensive to purchase. It is possible that Michler designed a new presidential mansion for this site, but no drawings have been found. Michler's aspirations set a precedent for future Army Engineers who invested a great deal of time and effort in planning for better quarters for the presidents' private, ceremonial, and official lives.

Alongside these civic duties, Michler received additional engineer assignments, including being made chief of the Aqueduct. In 1868 he prepared a report on the Potomac River for the House of Representatives. Comparing his data with surveys from 1792, 1858, 1862, and 1867 (the 1858 report being topographical engineer Woodruff's report, while the studies from the 1860s were made by the U.S. Coast and Geodetic Survey), Michler reported the dramatic increase over time of the tidal flats between the river's Virginia and Washington channels. Michler recommended extensive dredging to preserve navigation in the channels. With the rock causeway of Long Bridge obstructing half the width of the river and exacerbating the accumulation of silt, he stressed the need to modify or remove the bridge.[13]

Colonel Orville E. Babcock turned the Mall into a Victorian pleasure garden, planting trees, shrubs, and flowers during his tenure as the superintendent of Public Buildings and Grounds from 1871 to 1877.
Library of Congress, Prints and Photographs Division, LC-BH83-3715 (detail)

The Office of Public Buildings and Grounds was responsible for the improvement and maintenance of Washington's federal reservations, which included both large public parks and hundreds of small triangular and trapezoidal parcels, by-products of L'Enfant's combining grid and radial systems of streets. Many of these lots had never been improved, and Michler and his successor, Colonel Orville E. Babcock (1835–1884), who was appointed in 1871, set about systematically identifying and improving them citywide. Toward the end of making these "places of sand and mud" into sites that were "green and beautiful,"[14] the office published in 1872 its first location and condition survey of the entire park system. This survey was updated periodically; the 1894 version, which became the official reservation map by act of Congress in 1898, showed 301 reservations covering about 405 acres.[15]

As the street plan of Washington was formally extended beyond L'Enfant's original boundaries at the end of the nineteenth century, even more reservations were added to Office of Public Buildings and Grounds' responsibilities. An 1898 act placed the District of Columbia park system under the "exclusive charge" of the engineers, and specified that they were to take care, as well, of any land the District Commissioners set aside from the street system to be parks.[16] Consequently, as the district improved and modified its road system, additional small reservations were transferred to the Office of Public Buildings and Grounds. By the same token, engineer-controlled reservations also were periodically returned to the District Commissioners when needed "for street purposes."[17]

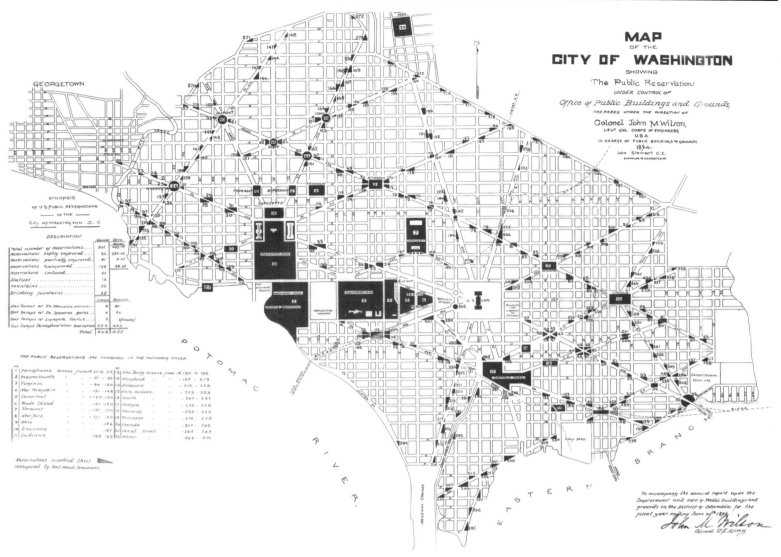

Map of Federal Reservations, 1894. The Office of Public Buildings and Grounds was responsible for these 301 parcels of land, large and small, scattered throughout the city.
Office of History, Corps of Engineers, ARCE 1894

Work on these lands included grading; planting trees, shrubs and flowers; irrigating; and building walks and roads. In Babcock's first year in office, workers in his employ laid forty-six thousand feet of sod, constructed one thousand feet of curbing, ten thousand yards of pavement and walks, and put in four miles of drains.[18] As Theodore Bingham put it when he was in charge in 1899, "the parks in and around Washington should form a systematic and well-considered whole….an emerald setting for the beautiful city within."[19] Consequently, the engineers built watchmen's stations and fountains in some larger parks and purchased benches, lamps, and ornamental vases. In 1874 Mary Clemmer Ames exclaimed: "Seats—thanks to General Babcock—everywhere invite to sit down and rest beneath trees which every summer cast a deeper and more protecting shadow." The office even requested sixteen statues and six vases from the St. Louis Louisiana Purchase Exposition for public decoration during the inaugural of 1905, and these were subsequently installed in Potomac Park and President's Park.[20]

Babcock introduced worm- and insect-eating European sparrows to the parks,[21] and accepted donations of eagles, prairie dogs, deer, and owls.[22] When public funds fell short for feeding the animals, he dipped into his own pocket.[23] The Territorial Government's Board of Public Works praised Babcock for his "cordial co-operation with local authorities, his wise counsel, energy, and ability."[24] The Office of Public Buildings and Grounds encountered periodic difficulties keeping the parcels free from illegal private occupation—dumps, gardens, buildings, and railroad tracks appeared on them—and undertook to mark unimproved reservations with six-inch granite markers and to surround improved lots with post-and-chain fences and, later, concrete copings.[25]

The standing bronze figure of Civil War Naval hero Admiral Samuel F. Dupont was erected under the auspices of Colonel Almon F. Rockwell in 1884 when Pacific Circle was renamed Dupont Circle. The present fountain replaced it in 1921.
Washingtoniana Division, D.C. Public Library

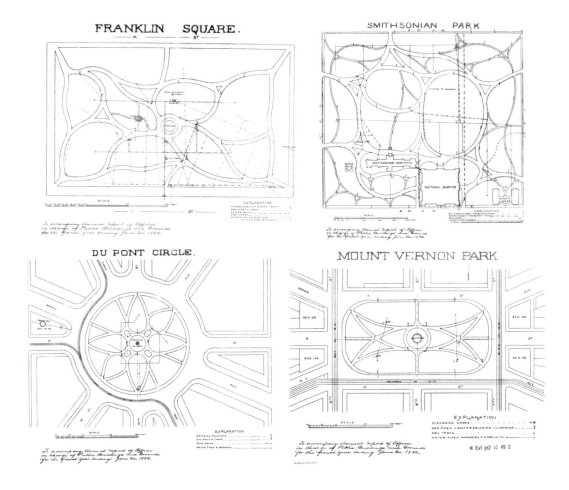

FRANKLIN SQUARE.

SMITHSONIAN PARK

DU PONT CIRCLE.

MOUNT VERNON PARK

Four designs for parks and squares done by the Office of Public Buildings and Grounds in 1886 to serve Washington's rapidly expanding residential neighborhoods
Office of History, Corps of Engineers, ARCE 1886 (photo illustration)

A joint congressional resolution of March 2, 1867, authorized a statue of Lieutenant General Winfield Scott, the first of many of the Union Army's Civil War generals to be so honored. The July 15, 1870, act appropriating funds for the statue directed the Secretary of War to choose a location, contract with the sculptor and architect of the base (both of whom had been chosen by a commission), and oversee all aspects of construction, including disbursing the funds. These duties, which were carried out by the Corps Officer in Charge of Public Buildings and Grounds (Babcock for the Scott statue), became routine for all of the statues destined for Washington's public parks. By 1872, when the Major General John A. Rawlins's statue was approved by Congress, the Officer in Charge of Public Buildings and Grounds (again, Babcock) served on the design jury, along with the Architect of the Capitol and the Librarian of Congress. Thereafter it became the accepted practice for the Secretary of War to be appointed to the commission that chose designs for Washington's public

Logan Park undergoing improvements, 1913. The District Commissioners transferred the public reservation (260 feet long and 40 feet wide) in the middle of what was then called Pierce Street in Anacostia, to the Office of Public Buildings and Grounds in 1907. At the request of the Anacostia Citizens' Association in 1908, the office named the area Logan Park in honor of Major General John A. Logan.
National Archives no. 42-SPB-12

art if some private organization had not already initiated the project and chosen the artists. Some secretaries chose to be directly involved; when they delegated this privilege, the public buildings engineer officers were their logical surrogates because they would manage all the affairs of dealing with both artists and contractors while they oversaw construction. Babcock himself may have designed the base for the Major General James B. McPherson statue for which $25,000 was appropriated in 1875. Most of these sculptures were minor duties for the engineer officers, but their daily lives were generally consumed with overseeing a number of small and medium-sized projects.[26]

In 1872 Babcock began a cleanup of the Washington Monument grounds and within a year had transformed them from the cattle pen they had been during the Civil War into a beautiful park. Natural depressions were replaced by ornamental ponds and a fish hatchery called Babcock Lake. Drained, graded, its depressions filled, planted with trees, and surrounded by a broad carriage drive, the area became a respectable setting that invited completion of the monument itself. Babcock added a fountain jet in the middle of the lake on axis with the monument and noted in his report that "during cold weather the lake formed safe and good skating for children, and was much enjoyed by them."[27] Soon after Babcock's work was finished, local columnist George Alfred Townsend was effusive in his praise:

"...every day last fall equestrians and carriages enlivened this old haunted corner by the river side, and a sense of gratitude toward the Engineer was felt by every thoughtful visitor."

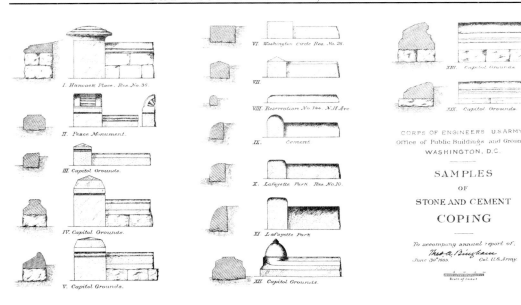

Samples of stone and cement coping used by the Office of Public Buildings and Grounds, 1899, as low walls setting off the public reservations under its control
Office of History, Corps of Engineers, ARCE 1899

The old grounds around the Washington Monument, which the very goats disdained to frequent and truant school-boys passed through with awe; where the stench of the canal and the river's miasma blended their odors, and half-dismantled houses, sheds, and hulks of boats dozed on the unsightly margin, were now brought into civilization...so that every day last fall equestrians and carriages enlivened this old haunted corner by the river side, and a sense of gratitude toward the Engineer was felt by every thoughtful visitor.[28]

The Office of Public Buildings and Grounds continually oversaw the labor-intensive maintenance of the federal reservations for almost sixty years. "The employees of this office...are mostly laboring men," Babcock reported in 1872. "The work necessary to improve the public grounds is of such a character that it cannot be done by contract."[29] In addition to designing new improvements, the office's yearly tasks included painting, raking, planting, cutting, gutter cleaning, snow removal, road

repair, and record keeping. The engineer officers in charge oversaw the park watchmen and sought to increase their numbers and pay. They even arranged in the summer of 1904 for military band concerts in the public parks, including some performances by "the Engineer Band from Washington Barracks."[30]

One of the most pleasant duties inherited from the civilian Commissioner of Public Buildings was the care and maintenance of the president's house. Although

Residents facing Lafayette Square demanded a public hearing to review the placement and design of the new "gardener's lodge" in 1914. Vine-covered trellises were to obscure the building's main purpose— public restrooms.
National Archives no. 42-SPB-9

Dedication of statue of Major General George B. McClellan at the intersection of Connecticut Avenue and Columbia Road, NW, 1907. The Office of Public Buildings and Grounds frequently orchestrated large public dedication ceremonies.
National Archives no. 77-H-8859-6

seemingly mundane, these tasks gave the military public buildings' officers in charge control over alterations and redecorations of the house, cabinet room, and presidential offices. Babcock orchestrated the Victorianization of the East Room during the Grant administration. Because the Officers in Charge of Public Buildings and Grounds were de facto the military attaché to the president, they enjoyed broad exposure at a variety of diplomatic and social events. They arranged presidential levees with the power to contribute to the guest list and were frequently themselves dinner guests at the president's house. Other functions they planned included unveiling ceremonies for statues, welcoming official guests, and national parades. All of these duties required coordinating the efforts of several groups of people, the same skills used in supervising a building project.

Babcock, who had been President Grant's secretary until his 1871 appointment to the Office of Public Buildings and Grounds, was one of territorial governor Alexander R. Shepherd's best friends. Shepherd appointed three of the Corps' engineers who were already engaged in the city's public works for the government—Babcock, Meigs, and Humphreys—as well as Boston landscape architect Frederick Law Olmsted, to a panel to advise the city's Board of Public Works.[31] Babcock defended Shepherd and his Board of Public Works before Congress more than once, and when the Territorial Government fell, he was discredited and suspected of defrauding the public in some way because he, like Shepherd, had accomplished a

great deal in a very short time. Evidence for such suspicions included Babcock hiring Shepherd (a building contractor by profession), in 1872, to install a copper roof on the White House for nearly $35,000.[32] In 1876 Babcock was accused of planting documents stolen from a safe on one of Shepherd's critics—but was acquitted.[33] Ben Perley Poore mentions Babcock in his *Reminiscences of Sixty Years in the National Metropolis* (1886), recounting the two-week federal trial implicating Babcock in the 1875 Whiskey Ring, a conspiracy to defraud the government of liquor taxes.[34] Babcock was again acquitted, but the Army Engineer who had graduated third in his 1861 class at West Point now had the same kind of shady reputation as some architects and engineers involved in public works in other American cities. Babcock damaged one of the Corps' great boasts, its disinterestedness and probity in handling large government contracts. One of Grant's biographers noted "Babcock seems to have had intimate contacts with most of the corrupt men of a corrupt decade. He fished for gold in every stinking cesspool, and served more than any other man to blacken the record of Grant's Administration."[35]

WASHINGTON MONUMENT

One of the greatest achievements of the Office of Public Buildings and Grounds was completion of the Washington Monument. The Washington National Monument Society was founded in 1833 by local Washingtonians—many of them military officers—who were dismayed that the previous year Congress commissioned a statue of Washington to commemorate the centenary of his birth rather than an important monument. Although no design was chosen from among the entries submitted in their 1836 competition, the

Sketch Washington Monument & grnds
24 Sept 1850 M C Meigs   Wash Monument

*Montgomery Meigs's 1850 sketch
of the unfinished Washington
Monument with Jefferson's 1803
meridian stone shown in its
original location near the banks
of the Washington City Canal*
National Museum of American History,
Smithsonian Institution, negative #38876-B

society mounted a nation-wide campaign to raise $1 million to erect the largest monu-
ment in the world in recognition of Washington's greatness.

   In 1845 the society selected a design proposed by one of its members, architect
Robert Mills, for a 600-foot obelisk surrounded by a colonnaded pantheon base 250 feet
in diameter and 100 feet high. Soon after the monument's cornerstone was laid on July 4,
1848, many members of the society doubted their ability to raise the money for such a
complex design. Their alternate choice was the obelisk supported by a stepped pyramidal
base composed of thirteen levels to commemorate the original states. Construction
progressed smoothly until 1854 when a controversy arose over including a piece of the
Temple of Concordia from the Roman Forum, sent by the Vatican as one of several
emblematic stones to be included in its stairwell. The anti-Catholic Know Nothing, or
Native American party, strongest in the Baltimore-Washington region, objected to including what they dubbed the "Pope's Stone." Their real objection was to the large number
of recent Irish immigrant laborers who, working cheaply, were building the monument.
During the night of March 5, 1854, members of the Know Nothings broke into the

Washington Monument grounds, stole the Pope's Stone, and reputedly dumped it in the Potomac River. The following year they attended the monument society's annual meeting and voted in their own officers. After the original society was deposed and members of the Know Nothing Party took over, public support for the monument's completion waned.[36]

The Corps' involvement in the post-Civil War history of the Washington Monument changed character as the monument passed from private to public ownership. During the decade following the war, the two goals of the Washington National Monument Society were raising money for the obelisk's completion, and convincing Congress to accept the structure they believed should have been undertaken by the government in 1832. Several structural reports by Corps engineers were commissioned, some agreeing with the 1859 assessment by Lieutenant Colonel J. C. Ives of the Corps of Topographical Engineers that the original foundations were adequate, and others disagreeing. Ives was unequivocal in his report:

> To those who are aware of the care which was taken in laying the foundation of the Monument, both in the selection and preparation of the bed, and in the execution of the masonry work, it will be scarcely necessary to enter into any statements in regard to its present condition. The test, to which it has been already subjected, may however be mentioned. If raised to the height of six hundred feet, the weight of the entire shaft, together with the foundation, will be a little more than seventy thousand tons. The weight of the portion now built is more than forty thousand tons. For five years, therefore, while the work has been suspended, the foundation has been bearing about four sevenths of the pressure that it will ultimately be required to sustain, and, in the recent examination, I was unable to detect any appearance of settling or indication of insecurity.[37]

Lieutenant William L. Marshall (1846–1920), however, wrote two contradictory reports that suggested continued questioning of the monument's stability was putting pressure on the engineers to find fault with the original construction. On February 19, 1873, he noted, "all questions as to the stability of the shaft itself have been answered by Lieutenant Ives, in whose conclusion I concur."[38] However, a year later, on April 20, 1874, Marshall reported, "it seems inadvisable to complete the Washington Monument to the full height of 600 feet. The area covered by its foundations is too small for a structure of the proposed dimensions and weight, causing an excessive pressure upon a soil

"I was unable to detect any appearance of settling or indication of insecurity."

"The area covered by its foundations is too small for a structure of the proposed dimensions and weight...."

Although Robert Mills's 1845 design for the Washington Monument, lithographed by his son-in-law Charles Fenderich, called for a pantheon base 100 feet high and 250 feet in diameter, he designed the obelisk's foundations to carry the monument's weight without buttressing.
Library of Congress, Prints and Photographs Division, LC-USZ62-58544

not wholly incompressible."[39] Yet in the same report, Marshall noted "there are no sufficient grounds for doubting the security of the foundation under the present load."[40] He calculated that the monument shaft was already exerting a weight of 4 8/10 tons per square foot.

As a compromise, Marshall recommended the monument be raised to only 400 feet; in 1875 the society agreed to reduce the monument's height to 437 feet. Marshall recommended reducing the thickness of future masonry walls by four feet, using brick on inside walls of the future shaft, and roofing the finished obelisk with cast-iron rather than stone vaulting, all to reduce additional weight. Marshall also proposed that a broad terrace be built up to the height of the doors, its stone abutments and fill providing additional support at the monument's base. A commission of three senior engineers stationed in New York, headed by J. G. Barnard, reported to Chief Engineer A. A. Humphreys on August 7, 1874, on Marshall's second report, and concluded "there is a lack of accepted data on this important subject of the weight bearing capacity of soils." They compiled data on the weights of several recent American buildings and concluded, "5 tons is an excessive pressure for soils composed of clay and sand. We could not, therefore, with the information before us, recommend that any additional pressure should be thrown on the site of the Washington Monument."[41]

A joint resolution of July 5, 1876, required Congress to "assume and direct the completion" of the monument, and on August 2nd, Congress appropriated $200,000. This act established a Joint Commission whose members were the president, Supervising Architect of the Treasury, Architect of the Capitol, Chief of Engineers, and the first vice-president of the Washington National Monument Society. The society intended to continue raising funds for the monument's erection but transferred all their property rights to the government. The Joint Commission named Lieutenant Colonel Thomas Lincoln Casey, the new head of the Office of Public Buildings and Grounds, succeeding Babcock in 1877, as construction manager for the project.

The Joint Commission's first goal was to definitively settle the question of the existing foundation's capacity to support an obelisk between 500 and 600 feet tall. In 1877 a board of three engineer officers, Lieutenant Colonel J. D. Kurtz, Lieutenant Colonel Q. A. Gilmore, and Lieutenant Colonel J. C. Duane, submitted a lengthy and detailed report, the results of further investigation by Second Lieutenant Dan C. Kingman. Robert Mills's reports on the original excavations and all previous engineers' reports, both pro and con, were examined in detail. They concluded that the earth around the monument was not sufficiently resistant to compression and had already been compressed, weight added to the 156-foot-tall shaft would probably cause splitting of the marble at the base, and that Mills's foundations had not been spread sufficiently to buttress the full weight of the finished obelisk. Kingman's report was received critically on technical grounds but also aroused particular concern that it might lead to the existing shaft's demolition.

Shortly after this report was published, Washington architect Henry R. Searle published a pamphlet illustrating and describing his design for completing the monument. He specifically cited the Kurtz report as determining his scheme of erecting three massive terraces ranging from twenty-four to forty feet in width to buttress the shaft. Other designs for the completion of the Washington Monument featuring substantial buttressing were published in art and architectural journals during the 1860s–70s and also may have been influenced by reports made by the Corps' various engineers on the obelisk's stability.[42]

The great disparity among the findings of several of the Corps' engineers suggests there were internal and external political forces at work. Competition between the Army's engineers and Robert Mills had been fierce, was ongoing, and involved other architects who were supervising construction of public buildings in Washington that they had designed. Another possibility was the desire to discredit Ives's report; in 1861 he declined a captaincy in the Union Army and joined the Confederacy where he became a colonel of engineers and one of Jefferson Davis's aides-de-camp.[43] Whether reinforcing the Washington Monument's foundations was necessary, or not, is now of academic interest only. In the 1870s the issue was public confidence in any major undertaking by Congress. The Corps' decision to provide for all foreseeable structural problems the finished monument might encounter protected the government's interests and assured the longevity of the monument itself.

On June 14, 1878, Congress authorized $36,000 to strengthen the monument's foundations, and on July 1st, the Joint Commission ordered Colonel Casey to proceed. Casey chose Captain George B. Davis as his assistant to manage daily operations and administer contracts. Bernard Green (1843–1914), a Harvard-educated civil engineer and civilian employee of the Corps of Engineers, was Casey's partner in devising the system of underpinning the monument and constructing its pyramidion. Casey examined two proposals on how to secure the foundations but found both inadequate. Within a month he "decided to

Architect Henry R. Searle's 1877 design to complete the Washington Monument conformed to recommendations made by three Corps engineers regarding buttressing the obelisk's base.
Library of Congress, Prints and Photographs Division, LC-USZ62-4055

COMPLETION OF THE WASHINGTON MONUMENT

The view of the monument before construction began shows the Department of Agriculture Building (left) on the Mall and the Potomac River and Tiber Creek close behind the incomplete structure. Before the engineers began work on the monument, they struggled with the question of whether the old foundation could support an obelisk that should be 550 feet tall according to ancient Egyptian proportions. Casey ordered the foundation strengthened and completed the monument in 1885 at 555 feet with a tall pyramidion topped by a cast aluminum capstone that served as a lighting rod.

ca. 1879

October 1879

January 1880

May 1880

September 1882

1885

February 1884

underpin and extend the surface of the base of the foundation." A pyramid of Portland concrete covered the original stepped tiers of stone and a concrete bed twelve feet deep that extended eighteen feet under the existing foundation was inserted along with a "leg of concrete under the middle of the foundation."[44] Casey's estimate for this work was $99,102 in comparison to the $36,000 Congress had appropriated, and the increase was authorized on June 27, 1879.[45]

The height of the obelisk and its termination were additional aspects of the Washington Monument's design addressed by Casey during construction. The width of its base was fifty-five feet and Casey's correspondence with George Perkins Marsh, ambassador to Italy, led the engineer to taper the shaft to terminate at 550 feet. This accorded with Marsh's study of the numerous Egyptian obelisks in Rome, which he determined had been designed to be ten times as tall as their width at the base. Moreover, Marsh noted that the angled sides of the Egyptian pyramidions were the same height as the width of the obelisk's base, and eventually Casey's pyramidion was fifty-five feet tall. In 1878, however, he proposed to top the Washington Monument with a twenty-five-foot-tall, iron and glass pyramidion to light the interior of the shaft whose walls were to be decorated with more than 200 memorial stones. It was Green who designed the final pyramidion, its exterior cladding in marble, but iron was used for its interior structure, deck, stairs, and elevator shaft.[46]

In 1880 Casey estimated it would take an additional $677,000 to complete the monument in four years. He was so determined to meet his schedule that the 100-ounce aluminum capstone was set during a raging storm on the day appointed, December 6, 1884. The aluminum capstone was part of the Washington Monument's system of lightning rods but also recalled the gold-topped pyramidions of the Egyptians. Obelisks were sacred to the sun god and caught the first rays of the morning sun. Copper, bronze, or brass, each platinum-plated, were Casey's first choices of material for the capstone, but Philadelphia founder William Frishmuth convinced Casey to use aluminum even though its first successful casting occurred only five years earlier. Frishmuth, the only American supplier of aluminum at the time, argued that the material's "conductivity, color, and non-staining qualities" merited experimenting with casting a pyramidion of the size needed. When completed in 1884, the Washington Monument was the tallest structure in the world, surpassed five years later when the Eiffel Tower was erected in Paris. An 1885 thunderstorm caused a small crack in the aluminum, and copper rods connected to the aluminum were inserted. Subsequent lightning strikes further damaged the aluminum but repairs were possible allowing the original capstone to remain in place.[47]

State, War and Navy Building

Immediately after the close of the Civil War, Montgomery Meigs, now Quartermaster General, was the key figure in promoting a new War Department Building. On April 12, 1866, he sent Secretary of War Edwin Stanton alternate designs for extending the Winder Building, across 17th Street from the War Department, for its short-term use. He noted, "at some future time Congress will doubtless make provision for the erection of a building on 17th Street and Pennsylvania Avenue in style and construction to correspond in some degree with the Treasury Building." Three months later Congress passed the necessary legislation and Meigs was one of six generals charged with obtaining a design. The design competition was announced in the autumn of 1866, Meigs bringing to the October 26 board meeting plans of the Treasury Building and White House grounds, as well as "wood cuts from the London Times of the British Foreign and India Offices and Museum at South Kensington," massive French Second Empire style buildings.[48]

The information circular sent to 144 respondents addressed the new building's architectural character in general terms. "The Board desires to have the designs of rich architectural effect, but as the building is for use for office purposes, would exclude designs with large porticos, long colonnades and heavy and expensive columns." In February 1867 John Crump of Philadelphia won the competition for his imposing Second Empire style design, a U-shaped building facing Pennsylvania Avenue that allowed for future expansion into a rectangular building enframing a courtyard. Although Crump was not notified that he had won, his design became the basis for the State, War and Navy Building begun in 1871.[49]

Several political factors led to housing the three departments in a single building located on the west side of the president's grounds. The State Department Building was razed in 1866 when the north wing of the Treasury Building on the east side of the White House was begun. In April 1869 Architect of the Capitol Edward Clark, Supervising Architect of the Treasury A. B. Mullett, Officer in Charge of Public Buildings and Grounds Lieutenant Colonel Nathaniel Michler, and the secretaries of State, War, and Navy, were appointed to a special Senate committee to select a site for the State Department and possibly the War Department.[50]

Which department was to occupy the choice location on the president's grounds was one issue; the second was which of the government's architectural and engineering offices was to take the lead. Mullett was immediately given the job of designing the State Department Building by Secretary of State Hamilton Fish. It was a modified version of Crump's 1867 design for the War Department. In April 1870 Fish announced that the

"[A]t some future time Congress will doubtless make provision for the erection of a building on 17th Street and Pennsylvania Avenue in style and construction to correspond in some degree with the Treasury Building."

multi-departmental building, a rectangular version of Mullett's State Department, was to be built. While proposals to move the federal capital to a mid-western location were under consideration by Congress, no appropriations for Washington buildings were considered. Soon after Congress placed the city's administration under federal control in February 1871, the first government building to be funded was the State, War and Navy Building. Mullett was placed in charge of its construction from June 21, 1871, until he resigned as Supervising Architect effective January 1, 1875. The south wing housing the State Department was completed in November 1875 under his successor William A. Potter, Mullett having declined to supervise the entire building's completion as a private architect. On January 26, 1875, Fish requested that he "be relieved from further scrutiny and control in the construction of the remaining part of the building."[51]

Mullett's very large, relatively ornate, and extremely expensive building was a major project of the Ulysses S. Grant administration, intended as a symbol of the federal government's stability and resurgence after the Civil War. By 1877, when Grant's presidency

Brigadier General Thomas Lincoln Casey as Chief of Engineers
Office of History, Corps of Engineers, U.S. Army Signal Corps Photo

Born into a military family (the son of Major General Silas Casey), Lieutenant Colonel Thomas Lincoln Casey (1831–1896) graduated first in his class at West Point in 1852, was a professor there for five years, and had ten years experience as head of the Fortification Division of the Corps of Engineers just prior to his appointment to complete the government's major office building. He finished his distinguished career as Chief of Engineers from 1888 to 1895.

His professional credentials as a creative engineer were excellent and his personal character impeccable; during the ten years when Casey supervised construction of the State, War and Navy Building, he acted as his own disbursing officer. Casey's contemporaries measured his successful completion of the building in financial terms. Upon his retirement in 1895, the Washington Star published a lengthy article recounting the highlights of Casey's entire career. At the State, War and Navy Building, "Gen. Casey put on the roof of the east wing and built the north, west and center wings entire. The total cost of the building was $10,038,482. The south and east wing and approaches cost $6,016,226 [sic], and the north and west wings and approaches and the center wing $3,992,236 [sic]. In other words, Gen. Casey did three-fourths of the work for about $2,000,000 less than the other fourth had cost." In his final report, Casey noted that $10,124,500 had been appropriated between 1871 and 1886, and that he was returning to the Treasury $86,017.58.[52]

ended amidst charges of widespread corruption, the State, War and Navy Building (along with Mullett's similar Second Empire-style government courthouses, post offices, and customs houses erected throughout the country) became highly visible evidence of political patronage and graft in awarding contracts to loyal Republicans. In addition, Mullett's role on the Territorial Government's Board of Public Works in expending $4 million on public improvements, particularly street grading and paving on 17th Street to benefit his building and the contractor, Territorial Governor Alexander Shepherd, was investigated by Congress. Multiple other allegations of patronage contracts and suspicions of even greater corruption forced Mullett to resign in October 1874.

After Fish's January 1875 removal from duties associated with the State, War and Navy Building, Grant specifically appointed (rather than leaving the choice to the Chief of Engineers) Orville Babcock, his former secretary and now Officer in Charge of Public Buildings and Grounds, to superintend the completion of the east, or Navy Wing, whose foundations had been laid in 1872. "If Mullett's resignation had been conceived as a gesture to placate reformers, Babcock's appointment counted as a reassertion of authority by Grant's inner circle." Babcock held his position as Officer in Charge of Public Buildings until the end of Grant's presidency, but was forced to resign the partly ceremonial White House post enjoyed by the commissioners of public buildings shortly after his acquittal in February 1876 for participation in a Whiskey Ring. None of the drawings produced by the office during Babcock's superintendence have his authorizing signature, making it difficult to assess his contributions to the development of the State, War and Navy Building. When he was relieved in March 1877, the "masonry of the [east] wing had been carried to the level of the fourth-story window sills in front and to the top of the courtyard walls in the rear."[53]

Lieutenant Colonel Thomas Lincoln Casey, appointed to replace Babcock on March 3, 1877, was the antithesis of his predecessor. Casey's efficiency, well established before he took over superintendence of State, War and Navy, was integral to his ability to devise "new methods for novel challenges which he encountered in building fortifications, especially on tidal sites." He was able to cut costs dramatically on three quarters of the State, War and Navy Building by changing the way the government conducted its construction business. By hiring its own employees and contracting only for materials and specialty services such as heating systems, plumbing, and elevators, Casey was able to implement different ways for work teams to function most effectively. One example was the elaborate doors at State, War and Navy. "The Government bought mahogany, white pine, maple for

"Babcock's appointment counted as a reassertion of authority by Grant's inner circle."

CONSTRUCTION OF THE STATE, WAR AND NAVY BUILDING

After the Supervising Architect of the Treasury Department completed the south wing of the State, War and Navy Building, Colonel Orville Babcock, Officer in Charge of Public Buildings and Grounds, continued the east wing until he was relieved in 1877. His successor, Lieutenant Colonel Thomas Lincoln Casey, completed the rest of the building, including the middle wing, in 1888. Shown is the construction of the west, or War Department, wing.

1884

October 1884

October 1884

June 1885

February 1886

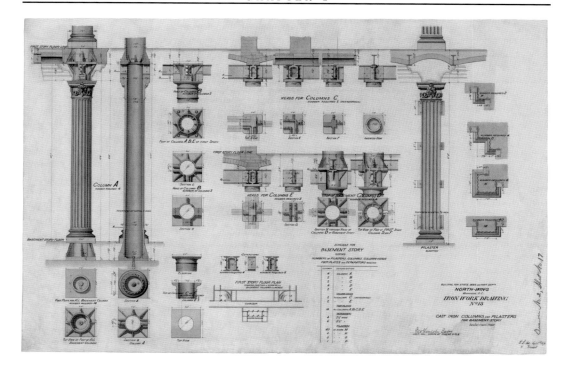

Cast-iron columns and pilasters for the basement story of the north wing of the State, War and Navy Building, 1879. Thomas Lincoln Casey signed the drawings.
National Archives, Cartographic Branch, RG121, Folder 47, Drawing 13.

"[T]he version chosen by Casey contained no figures, but instead drew on the Roman cuirass, Phyrigian helmet and battle standards of the official seal of the United States Army, and surmounted the group with an American eagle."

dowels, zinc sheets, and hardware, and craftsmen made the doors on the site. The veneering, paneling, and doweling demanded skills of high order. The same workmen also cut and joined the mahogany handrails for the staircases, fabricated the window sashes, and built the screen doors."[54]

Casey's close associate on this project, as well as on the completion of the Washington Monument and the Library of Congress, was the civil engineer Bernard Green. Both respected the integrity of Mullett's design by removing two courses of granite and the coping at the top of the walls on the east front (done under Babcock's direction) in order to match the height of Mullett's south wing. Casey wished the entire building to appear as a seamless construct, rather than one done piece-meal, as it indeed was. Also at stake was Casey's own professional pride. Both Casey and Green worked closely with the Venetian-born and Austrian-trained engineer and designer Richard von Ezdorf (1848–1926), who had been hired as a draftsman by the Office of the Supervising Architect of the Treasury on July 14, 1873. Ezdorf worked with Mullett on interior designs and structure, especially relating to cast-iron, for the south wing. In 1876 Ezdorf was transferred to the War Department specifically to work with Babcock to maintain continuity of design in the east wing's interiors and details.[55]

Ezdorf's greatest achievements were his three cast-iron libraries, designed as multi-tiered balconies overlooking central, sky-lit wells with shallow book stacks located behind the balconies. This horizontal layering of open spaces connected to quasi-open spaces was based on Thomas U. Walter's cast-iron Library of Congress built behind the Capitol's west front balcony between 1851 and 1853, the first room to be built with a cast-iron ceiling. Walter used cast-iron because it was fireproof, inexpensive, and rapidly assembled; because he designed its decorative parts to imitate carved stone or wood classical details, the mass of iron was physically and visually heavy. Ezdorf embraced in part the modern French Neo-Grec (New Greek to distinguish from the Greek Revival of the early nineteenth century) attitude toward the use of iron that emerged in the 1860s. This French theory, in part, held that decorative cast-iron should reflect visually its structural facts as well as the mass production methods by which it was made, rather than imitate naturalistic ornament hithertofore carved in wood or stone. Often, the resulting ornaments looked mechanistic and even included elements like gears and ball bearings. Thus Ezdorf's cast-iron libraries used iron more sparingly than Walter's massive, hollow shells that appeared to be solid. His State Department library's balconies, designed under Mullett and finished under Babcock, give the appearance of a filigree cage composed of multiple linear elements set in front of cast-iron walls. Ezdorf's War Department library, designed for the west wing's central pavilion in 1884 under Casey, was a filigree cage, its fragmented walls and pierced balconies calculated to use a minimum of materials.

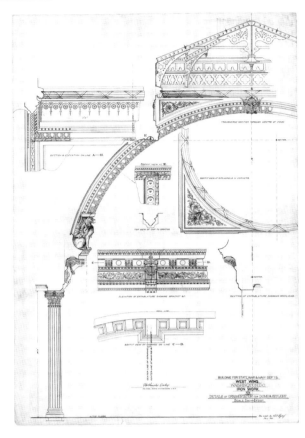

Details of the iron work ornamentation on the dome and skylight of the west wing of the State, War and Navy Building designed by Richard von Ezdorf under Casey's supervision
National Archives, Cartographic Branch, RG121, Folder 63, Drawing 88

In many cases alternate designs by Ezdorf survive and Casey's choice between them reflects his own contributions to the State, War and Navy Building's aesthetic development. One of Ezdorf's two designs for the cast-iron ornament in the north wing's pediment "featured undraped allegorical figures of War (male) and Peace (female) flanking a laurel wreath, emblematic of victory." However, "the version chosen by Casey contained no figures, but instead drew on the Roman cuirass, Phyrigian helmet and battle standards of the official seal of the United States Army, and surmounted the group with an American eagle."[56] Modest allegorical sculpture in each wing's pediments identified its occupants and Casey chose the least expensive alternatives as well as those that were more comprehensible to most Americans. Casey also independently hired other architects or designers to undertake special projects. On January 15, 1887, Casey wrote Secretary of War William Endicott: "I have the honor to request authority to employ the personal services of Stephen D. Hatch as architect; for the purposes of making under my directions, designs for the finish of certain rooms in the west wing of this building." Hatch, a New York architect, designed very elaborate decorations for the Secretary of War's suite, the most ornate of any of the offices in the building.[57]

U.S. NATIONAL MUSEUM

Montgomery Meigs, the Army's most distinguished prewar builder, completed a number of significant projects in Washington after the Civil War. Two trips to Europe in 1867–68 and 1876, during which he studied ancient, Renaissance, and contemporary architecture and engineering projects of all kinds, particularly in Italy, influenced his postwar work. The first was for the Smithsonian Institution. The United States National Museum (now the Arts and Industries Building, Smithsonian Institution) had emerged in the 1850s when government-owned collections were transferred to the Smithsonian and federal money was appropriated for their care. These collections crowded the institution's Mall building, and, when a flood of donations of objects arrived in the wake of the 1876 Centennial Exposition, Smithsonian Regents petitioned Congress to fund a separate museum building. A February 5, 1877, memorial to Congress stated, "Careful inquiries have been instituted to ascertain the smallest sum which would be adequate to [erect a building], and the plan of a convenient structure has been made by General Meigs...."[58]

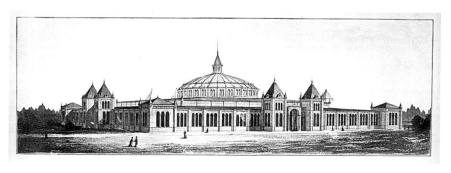

Preliminary drawing by Adolf Cluss and General Montgomery C. Meigs of the proposed United States National Museum, February 1877

Smithsonian Institution Archives, Record Unit 95, Box 32, Folder 2, image #1307

The House Committee on Public Buildings and Grounds noted the constraints on the museum project. "To erect an edifice of the necessary magnitude, in the style of architecture heretofore adopted by the Government for its use in Washington, would involve expenditure of many millions of dollars, and it could not be completed and available for occupation in a shorter period than from five to eight years. Nevertheless on a simple plan originally suggested by General Meigs, a building somewhat similar in character to those erected for the National Exposition...perfectly fireproof, amply lighted, and properly adapted for all its objects, can be constructed for about $250,000, and can be ready for occupation within ten months, or at most a year." Meigs's experience with iron used in constructing the Capitol, General Post Office, and Patent Office Extensions in the 1850s led him to study alternative uses of iron in fireproof construction.[59]

Congress appropriated exactly that amount and approved the building site in 1879. The Regents established a National Museum Building Commission, chaired by regent General W. T. Sherman. "The committee at the outset invited Gen. M.C. Meigs...to act in the capacity of consulting engineer to the commission, and also selected Messrs. Cluss & Schulze, whose plans for the new building were those approved by Congress, as superintending architects."[60] Ground was broken in April 1879, on the single-floor brick and iron structure, to be set without a basement on concrete foundations. The U.S. National Museum was substantially finished by the end of 1880, and its final cost, including additional appropriations to cover buildings systems and marble flooring, came to $315,400, the least expensive, permanent government building constructed in Washington up to that time, according to the final report.[61]

A major factor in the museum's low construction cost was Meigs's suggestion of a "tent" roof, an exposed iron truss that had been used in industrial and manufacturing buildings since it was introduced in 1835. Meigs had concealed iron roof trusses above the drop ceilings that spanned the House and Senate chambers in the Capitol Extension in 1855. Just four years earlier, at London's Crystal Palace, Joseph Paxton used exposed iron trusses for the exhibition hall's entire structure. It established a precedent for using iron to roof temporary exhibition buildings, a technology soon used for permanent exhibition halls that required large interconnected spaces. At the National Museum, many different roof heights and shapes, as well as numerous monitors, had to be accommodated; the underside of the roof and the upper walls, and perhaps the trusses themselves, were painted a light sky blue to appear nearly invisible and heighten the effect of open, airy spaces. The trusses themselves were not decorated in any way to mask their industrial character and their simple bolted joints were left exposed.

Adolf Cluss's 1885 design for the Army Medical Museum, located on the Mall's south side at 7th Street, SW, was built by Colonel Thomas Lincoln Casey using inexpensive brick, terra cotta, and iron materials. The building, on the site now occupied by the Hirshhorn Museum, was razed in 1969. (Photographed ca. 1940s)
Library of Congress, Prints and Photographs Division, LC-A7-4130-Lot 11661-9 (G)

ARMY MEDICAL MUSEUM, RAZED 1969

The museum, library, and historical records of the Surgeon General's Office were housed in Ford's Theater from 1866 until the Army Medical Museum was built on the south side of the Mall at the corner of B (now Independence Avenue) and 7th Streets, SW, between 1885 and 1887. Secretary of War Robert T. Lincoln, son of President Abraham Lincoln who had been assassinated at Ford's Theater in 1865, sent a special message to Congress on January 19, 1882, urging construction of a building. These records and objects (that included the bullet that killed Lincoln) were in "imminent danger of destruction" if they remained in the decaying theater. Two recent museum fires in Washington—at the Smithsonian Institution in 1865 and the museum in the Patent Office in 1877—were given as reasons to erect a building to house the Surgeon General's collection. Although Congress appropriated $200,000 on February 28, 1883, for a "plain, fire-proof [building] with a large amount of floor space," opponents felt that the library could be merged with the Library of Congress and the museum artifacts displayed either at the Pension Building or the State, War and Navy Building, both then under construction.[62]

President Chester Arthur signed the legislation on March 2, 1885, to place the metal and brick museum on the site selected by a commission composed of the Secretary of War, the Architect of the Capitol, and the Secretary of the Smithsonian, with the War Department overseeing construction. On April 14, 1885, Colonel Casey was put in charge of its construction. Adolf Cluss had earlier designed the Medical Museum to complement his nearby National Museum Building and was able to comply with the government's mandate for an inexpensive and fireproof building by using mass produced bricks and decorative molded terra-cotta panels for exterior walls and easily maintained glazed bricks for interior walls. The Army Medical Museum employed metal roofs with monitor lights supported with iron trusses that covered the two forty-seven-foot-tall exhibition wings—an inexpensive and fireproof system similar to what Cluss and Meigs had employed in the National Museum and Meigs was to use at the Pension Building. On November 9, 1887, Colonel John Wilson, now in charge of the Office of Public Buildings and Grounds, transferred the museum to the Surgeon General's Office after only a three-month delay in its completion.[63]

PENSION BUILDING

Based on his role in making the National Museum building a success by keeping construction costs low, in 1881 the Senate Appropriations Committee appointed Meigs to design and construct a building to centralize the operations of the post-Civil War Pension Bureau's 1,500 clerks. The building's second mandate, possibly suggested by Meigs himself, was a large hall for Washington's great social and state occasions, partic-ularly inaugural balls. The Pension Bureau was under the Interior Department, but from the outset it was determined that Meigs would be both the architect and the superin-tendent of construction. Thus the legislation was co-sponsored with the War Department, and construction supervision was specifically placed under the Quartermaster General's Office, rather than the Chief of Engineers. Meigs retired from active service in 1882, the year the Pension Building was begun, and he devoted all of his formidable energy for the next five years to produce "a building the like of which is not to be seen anywhere else in the country."[64]

The Pension Building often is judged as Meigs's masterpiece; it was the only monumental architectural work over which he had total control and he put into it his

Montgomery C. Meigs began his Washington career in the 1840s as a lieutenant and ended it in the 1880s as a major general. His most prominent post-Civil War project was the Pension Building, designed to be fireproof, inexpensive, and provide a humane, naturally air conditioned environment for its office workers—mainly Union Army veterans.
Library of Congress, Prints and Photographs Division, LC-BH83-137 (detail)

"...a building the like of which is not to be seen anywhere else in the country."

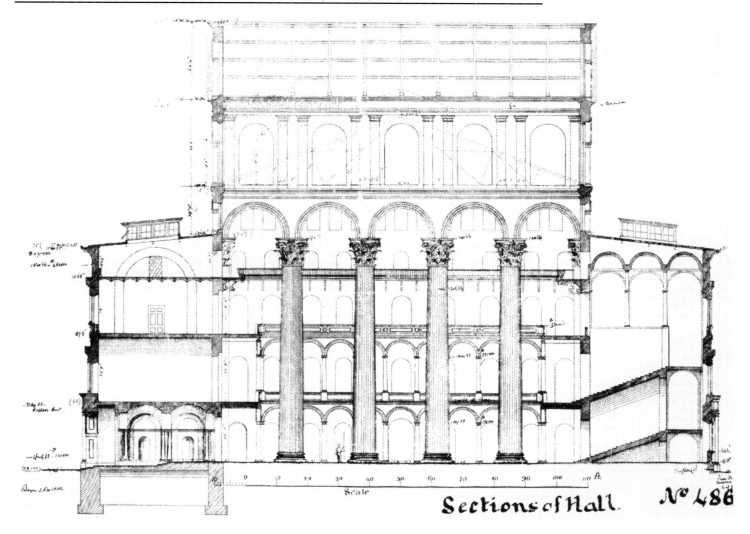

Sections of Hall.   Nº 486

considerable accumulated knowledge of architecture and engineering. The Pension Building is unique among Victorian buildings but partakes of many late Victorian architectural characteristics: synthesizing several historical models to create something new; combining traditional building methods with new ones born of modern technology; and, symbolizing by its form and its symbolic decoration nineteenth-century positivism that promoted the idea of progress driven by technological and scientific advances. The engineering aspects of the Pension Building are inventive, ingenious, and imaginative, as Meigs considered all the pragmatic issues involving its construction, especially its ventilation, because one major goal was a humane physical environment for the bureau's employees.

While in Rome on February 16, 1868, Meigs sketched an idea for the War Department Building, a solid three-and-a-half-story Roman palazzo. Fifteen years later he executed a very similar design for the Pension Building. Rome's brown brick Palazzo Farnese (ca. 1515–46), the largest of the Renaissance urban palaces, provided Meigs

Montgomery Meigs, "Section of Hall," April 16, 1886. This drawing created mid-way through the Pension Building's construction shows its fourth floor and skylights added during construction as well as the final configuration of the roofs. The fluted finish for the massive columns in the courtyard was not carried out.
National Archives, RG 15

Pension Building under construction showing holes for shallow domes on the third floor, November 1883
Library of Congress, Prints and Photographs Division, LC-USZ62-59413

Pension Building under construction showing the massive brick central columns and the rows of columns on the first and second floors, November 1885
Library of Congress, Prints and Photographs Division, LC-USZ62-51277

with the Pension Building's form of a hollow rectangle with offices ranged around its exterior, and internal circulation around arcaded loggias that lined the inside of the rectangle. Some of the Farnese's details, including staircases constructed with shallow risers and deep treads to allow the bureau's clerks, who were disabled war veterans, to easily traverse, demonstrate how Meigs, the Victorian, selectively chose from history any element that served his purpose.[65]

Two additional Roman buildings provided Meigs with historical design models, the courtyard loggia of the Cancelleria palace, and the massive ancient Roman columns incorporated into the Renaissance church Santa Maria degli Angeli—appropriate sizes to serve as the prototype for the seventy-five-foot-tall columns needed to support the Pension Building's roof. Meigs doubled the size of the Farnese palace and used 15.5 million bricks to build the Pension Building, the largest brick building in the world, he claimed, when it was finished. Brick and terra cotta—the Pension Building's decorative details were in terra cotta—were the only truly fireproof materials in Meigs's opinion. Ancient and much of Renaissance Rome had been built of brick and Meigs consciously designed and built the Pension Building to stand for a millennium and then be as impressive as a fallen ruin dominating its entire Washington block.

As the architect of the Pension Building, Meigs was committed to giving it an important artistic character within the confines of his limited budget. Brick allowed him to erect a massive building cheaply, but to make it appear monolithic, he colored the mortar the same color as the brick. He hired the Bohemian-born sculptor Caspar Buberl to model in clay a 1,200-foot-frieze based on subjects he chose, a continuous parade depicting the infantry, cavalry, artillery, naval, quartermaster, and medical corps that comprised the men in whose service the building was erected. No such frieze existed on the Palazzo Farnese; rather Meigs and Buberl turned to ancient and modern monuments for their inspiration. The Parthenon in Athens is often cited as their model because Meigs and Buberl corresponded on the "pedestrian figures

Exterior of Pension Building under construction, November 1885. The city block occupied by the Pension Building was not one designated for public buildings on the L'Enfant plan.
Library of Congress, Prints and Photographs Division, LC-USZ62-56363

followed by the youths of Athens on horseback" that were familiar from the Parthenon's Panathenaic Procession. But this procession depicted a recurring religious event; Meigs's and Buberl's buff-colored terra cotta frieze depicted a victorious marching army in the uniforms of their time—not unlike the frieze on Paris's Arc de Triomphe, completed in 1836 to celebrate the feats of Napoleon's armies. Soldiers stand like sentinels at attention on the corners of each nineteenth-century structure as the entire panoply of their respective modern armies pass in review. Again, Meigs and Buberl were participating in the eclecticism of their age by fusing together ancient (Athen's Parthenon) and modern (Paris's Arc de Triomphe) in the frieze's sculptures.[66]

As the Pension Building's engineer, Meigs was equally creative in the way he used brick, incorporated heating and ventilating, and roofed the 116-foot by 316-foot courtyard. The solid bearing walls—four feet wide at their foundation—were tied into the cross walls that supported the vaults of each twenty-five-foot by thirty-seven-foot office. Meigs chose brick domes on pendentives for office ceilings and structural supports for the floors above them. This elegant design, rare in the United States, required the use of "more expensive experienced bricklayers and careful supervision."[67]

Meigs's system of heating and ventilating the Pension Building was integral to his entire design because it required the exterior walls, offices, courtyard, and roof to function in concert. Airshafts under each window (observable as the three stretcher bricks missing under each window) passed through an L-shaped conduit that opened at the base of each of the two windows per office. Steam radiators under each window warmed this air during cold weather. During warm weather, air was drawn through the offices, which had tall arched openings rather than doors, by suction artificially created in the courtyard via windows in its three-part roof. Meigs redesigned the roof three times in order to perfect this system (and to add a fourth floor for document storage). The building's maintenance engineers could open different sized windows, including monitors in the higher, central section, either with pulleys reached from the top balcony or from the exterior. Meigs spent months determining the number of degrees the temperature would drop in offices on each side of the building depending on the time of day and the direction of the prevailing wind. He calculated that the courtyard's air could be completely exchanged once every two minutes under optimum conditions. After one year in the new building, the Pension Bureau reported that employee absenteeism was down 8,622 days. Yet there were problems with the system because after two years, employees petitioned that it be shut down as their offices were wind tunnels filled with flying papers. They also found that their offices were too cold during the winter months and so the arches were filled and doors installed.[68]

The immense size of the enclosed courtyard and the powerful effect of its eight plaster-coated Corinthian columns that divide it into thirds was made possible by the iron and steel trusses that support the hollow clay tile roofs. These columns were later painted to resemble veined marble. The columns in the first-floor arcade are terra cotta covered with cement while those on the second floor are hollow cast-iron. The only wood used in the building (other than for window frames and sashes) was behind the cornice because Meigs could find no other economical way of attaching terra cotta heads of lions to the cornice. The wood soon rotted and the lions' heads were removed. Meigs wanted to install trees and shrubs in the courtyard for oxygen/carbon dioxide exchange, but settled for hanging plants from urns on the top balcony for reasons of economy.[69]

In 1881 Congress appropriated $250,000 for the Pension Building's site, an entire city block. The Pension Building was first occupied in 1885 and completed in 1887 at a cost of $866,614.04, which, according to Meigs, was $4.69½ per square foot and 10¾ cents

"The sum for which it is to be built, amounting only to five dollars for every square foot of ground covered, is very small for a fire-proof building, but the lesson to be learned from it will be none the less useful, as showing the dignity which can be given to simple materials in the hands of one who knows how to use them."

per cubic foot of space. The final cost of the State, War and Navy Building—seventeen years in construction—was about $10 million. In the previous generation, the Smithsonian Institution's medieval revival architecture (and its Seneca Creek brownstone) cost 17¼ cents per cubic foot compared to the Treasury Building's neoclassical style (and Aquia Creek sandstone) at 42½ cents per cubic foot. The 1882 *American Architect and Building News* article that briefly described Meigs's design and its projected cost, concluded: "The sum for which it is to be built, amounting only to five dollars for every square foot of ground covered, is very small for a fire-proof building, but the lesson to be learned from it will be none the less useful, as showing the dignity which can be given to simple materials in the hands of one who knows how to use them."[70]

LIBRARY OF CONGRESS

Revisions in 1870 to the copyright law centralized its functions in the Library of Congress and further required that multiple copies of materials to be copyrighted be deposited and registered. Its passage made T. U. Walter's 1853 cast-iron Library of Congress, located in the Capitol, too small to accommodate anticipated amounts of new books and other materials. The 1873 competition to design a new library building was the beginning of a protracted history that resulted in the adoption in 1886 of one of several designs submitted by the Washington-based German-American architects, John L. Smithmeyer and Paul Pelz; they were hired to oversee its construction under the jurisdiction of the Department of the Interior.[71]

A three-man building commission included Librarian of Congress Ainsworth Spofford, who in 1873 had conceptualized how the building was to be laid out with a central octagonal reading room and corner pavilions linked by curtains. Within a year, lawsuits brought by contractors caused construction delays and an investigation led to Smithmeyer's dismissal. Between May and September 1888, hearings held by the House Committee to Investigate Contracts for the Construction of the Library of Congress Building recommended transferring jurisdiction of the library's construction to the Treasury Department. The new Secretary of Interior, William F. Vilas, suggested that the Corps of Engineers take over its construction supervision; on October 8 General Casey, now Chief of Engineers, was put in charge. Thus Casey reported to the Secretary of the Treasury, not the three-man commission.

This decision led to contradictory claims of authorship for many of the Library's most notable features and culminated in a second lawsuit brought by the architects. Modern scholarship has not yet unraveled where all the credit is due during the complex quarter

"[T]hanks to the perfect discipline of Mr. Green, the 300 men engaged on the work move almost as one, without jar or friction, nobody getting into his neighbor's way."

Civilian engineer Bernard R. Green spent most of his career working with Corps engineers on Washington projects. For the Library of Congress, where he worked closely with Thomas Lincoln Casey, Green invented a pneumatic tube and conveyer belt system to order and transport books from the stacks to the reading rooms.
Library of Congress, Prints and Photographs Division, LC-USZ62-90221

century when dozens of architects, specialty contractors, engineers, muralists, and sculptors were directly involved or consulted. In reality, the design process, once responsibilities began to be shared, was so fluid and so interwoven with constructing the decorated parts of a very ornate building, that several people might have or did contribute many elements of the Library's facades, interiors, and art works.

Civil engineer Bernard Green, who had been hired in the spring of 1888 by the building commission, was promoted to "Engineer and Superintendent of Construction" in charge of day-to-day operations by Casey, while Pelz retained the title and functions of the Library's architect. The *Evening Star,* which generally reported favorably on supervision of architectural projects by the Army Engineers, on September 24, 1889, commented "thanks to the perfect discipline of Mr. Green, the 300 men engaged on the work move almost as one, without jar or friction, nobody getting into his neighbor's way." Green kept a daily diary from October 4, 1888, to August 19, 1902, the source of much detailed information about the Library's construction.[72]

Under Casey's direction Pelz made two sets of drawings for the Library, presented to Congress based on Smithmeyer and Pelz designs done in 1884–85. The more costly was for a larger building than originally planned by the architects in 1873. Designs for a smaller building were estimated at $4 million before members of the Joint Committee on the Library toured European national libraries during the summer of 1885. Working with a joint congressional committee, Casey secured appropriations for a $5.5 million building "capable of extension without marring its symmetry or involving costly demolitions." This appropriation was eventually increased to $6,245,000.[73]

Casey and Green worked closely with Spofford, who provided them with fifteen functional considerations relating to abundant light, ventilation, dimensions of rooms, and efficient movement between them, as well as innovative alcove and stack systems. Because of Spofford's insistence on the rapid movement of books and other materials from stacks to reading rooms, Green invented a "bookcarrying apparatus," the first pneumatic tube and conveyor belt system in an American library. Green's most famous invention was his 1890 patent for cast-iron book stacks, manufactured for the Library of Congress in Louisville, Kentucky, then subsequently available for general library use.[74]

In his first annual report, Casey predicted that construction of the Library of Congress would take eight years. The engineer's ability to efficiently manage the logistics of

October 1890

November 1892

January 1894

Library of Congress under construction
Library of Congress, Prints and Photographs Division, Lot 12042-1 no. 12 (OSE)
Library of Congress, Prints and Photographs Division, Lot 12042-2 no. 42 (OSE)
Library of Congress, Prints and Photographs Division, Lot 12042-2 no. 58 (OSE)

Private reading room, House of Representatives, under construction, designed by Edward P. Casey
Library of Congress, Prints and Photographs Division, LC-USZ62-102087

> *"If Gen[eral] Casey had stated to the Committee his program, it is quite likely it would have been approved....I suppose it did not occur to him that such statuary was anything more than architectural decoration."*

constructing a very large, complex, and highly decorated building in which traditional masonry walls, cast-iron-supported floors, roofs, and dome, modern utilities including nine pneumatic elevators, multiple lavatories, and electric lights was proven beyond doubt in the Library of Congress. Knowing when and where to employ each subcontractor's team in concert with the library's own workforce of about 400 men was coordinated with the delivery of materials and pre-fabricated elements, such as the patented book stacks. The Corps of Engineers, along with architects trained in the Treasury's Office of the Supervising Architect, brought to such large projects a coordination matched by few large private architectural or engineering firms during the era that typically overran budgets and schedules. Casey's estimate that the Library could be built in eight years was exceeded by only a few months; costs were $200,000 less than appropriated.

The efficiency of Casey's and Green's management of the Library of Congress construction, particularly in containing its costs, is most remarkable when one considers the considerable extra expense of ornamenting the building. Casey's most visible contribution to the building, always credited to the architects Smithmeyer and Pelz, was to enlarge upon and realize the library's iconographical and decorative schemes. Spofford was particularly adamant that the central reading room's walls be "decorated" with tier upon tier of books, rather than "crass architectural display."[75] Smithmeyer had from the beginning considered the Library of Congress to be "more of a museum of literature, science and art, than strictly taken as a collection of books," and thought that the building itself should provide visitors with an insight into the range of human knowledge.[76]

Casey started hiring muralists and sculptors as early as 1890 but they were not singled out in his reports. By subsuming the work of the sculptors under "marble work," and that of the artists under "painting," in his annual reports, Casey may have wanted to avoid lengthy congressional debates and public criticism by the many vocal opponents of elaborate government buildings. Green's report for 1896 (Casey having died on March 25) summarized which contractors had been responsible for supplying materials or building specific parts of the building, information not given by Casey in his reports that listed that year's accomplishments. Significantly, Green included two pages (out of ten) listing all of the artists and their works.[77]

Grand staircase in the Great Hall of the Library of Congress
National Archives no. 200(S)-MHW-8

Casey embarked on the library's decorative scheme without prior approval by Congress, or even the knowledge of the members of the Joint Committee on the Library. It is a mark of the general respect for, and confidence in, Casey that Senator Justin Morrill of Vermont, when he learned in 1893 that Casey had contracted with artists, asked first if the library's decoration could be done without additional appropriations. "Morrill admitted that it did 'look strange that the Gen[eral] sh[oul]d not have talked over with us so important [and] valuable [a] point in the progress of his great work,' but explained this away by adding, 'If Gen[eral] Casey had stated to the Committee his program, it is quite likely it would have been approved....I suppose it did not occur to him that such statuary was anything more than architectural decoration.'"[78] American government buildings, with the exception of the Capitol, had little allegorical painting and sculpture in comparison to their European counterparts and many American municipal and commercial buildings.[79]

Each of the key participants in the library's formation contributed some part either to the literary or artistic realization of its theme of collective world knowledge and culture. In 1894 Casey set up a "committee of selection" to choose artists and their themes consisting of himself, his Columbia University educated son, architect Edward Pearce Casey (whom he designated the Library's "decorative designer,") and Green as supervisor of construction.

Main reading room of the
Library of Congress, (n.d.)
Library of Congress, Prints and
Photographs Division, LC-USZ62-59277

"So Casey and I just went
ahead and hired artists
on our own."

They wrote to and met with the country's leading artists to ensure high quality work. Yet Green later recounted: "So Casey and I just went ahead and hired artists on our own." Casey did direct the muralists and sculptors, leaving them free to choose their subjects within the established schema, but subject to his approval. Both the architects and engineers sought credit for what they realized would be one of America's most important buildings.[80]

General Casey and his son invited three prominent sculptors to be members of a committee to advise on the building's sculptural decoration.[81] John Quincy Adams Ward, Olin Levi Warner, and Augustus Saint-Gaudens, all of whom had undertaken many public commissions, first met with the engineers on January 26, 1894, when they collectively laid out a sculpture program for forty-four free-standing figures or relief panels. Casey and Green carefully managed contracts so that the art works were accomplished within their regular construction budget.[82]

Spofford chose the subjects of the portrait busts set in the bull's-eye windows above the central entrance. He also chose the sixteen great men to be commemorated by bronze statues

Muralist Henry Oliver Walker's "Lyric Poetry" located in the south corridor of the Great Hall
Library of Congress, Prints and Photographs Division, LC-USZ62-104456

embodying ancient and modern practitioners of the eight branches of knowledge represented by each side of the reading room: art, science, religion, history, law, commerce, poetry, and philosophy. But Casey and Green had the authority to veto his choices and they rejected his selection for "modern law." The engineers also invited Harvard president Charles W. Eliot to choose the quotations for the main reading room, while Spofford selected those for literature within the Great Hall. Spofford set the height of the reading room's dome at seventy feet in his original instructions to competing architects in 1873. Casey and Green raised the dome to 195 feet, a height that appeared on Pelz's revised design accepted by Congress on March 2, 1889. This height interfered with vistas of the Capitol along Pennsylvania Avenue from the west and the east.[83]

On March 29, 1892, Casey terminated Pelz's services "as you have now entirely completed the designs of the [library's] architectural characteristics and features."[84] During these early years of construction, professional relations between Green and Pelz were antagonistic because each claimed credit for solutions to design problems and because Pelz had joined with Smithmeyer in a lawsuit against the government seeking full monetary compensation and intellectual ownership of the library's design. Edward Pearce Casey was officially named architect of the Library of Congress on March 12, 1896, two weeks before his father's sudden death. When he exhibited a section drawing of the Library of Congress in New York in 1895 claiming the

Plaster casts of stock sculptures used to decorate the Library of Congress, October 1894
Library of Congress, Prints and Photographs Division, LC-USZ62-120936

design as his own, the Washington chapter of the American Institute of Architects wrote a letter of censure and New York architectural critics questioned his rights to this claim.[85]

In his 1889 annual report on the library's construction, Casey quoted the Congressional act of March 2, 1889, that stated "said building shall be constructed in accordance with the

plans marked 'D,' submitted by the Chief of Engineers with his annual report to Congress" in 1888. In the same report, Casey noted that "the architect, Mr. Paul J. Pelz, has been engaged in preparing the drawings necessary for the work for the coming year as well as for the year past, in all their varied and complicated details, and the progress made on the building [masonry cellar walls] has been materially assisted by his work."[86]

At congressional hearings held on November 20, 1896, Green claimed that the plans from which the library was built "were made in the office under General Casey's and my own direction between October 2 and November 23, 1888," but in the same hearing acknowledged that the "small plan was a reduction and modification of the original Smithmeyer plan." Several hundred signed and dated drawings for the Library of Congress preserved in its Prints and Photographs Division indicate that all design aspects were determined by Smithmeyer and Pelz except for the patented system of metal stacks and the decoration of very extensive areas beyond the vestibule and main reading room. Certainly, Casey expanded the scope and extent of this program and chose the artists to execute the work.[87] General Casey provided additional intellectual stimulus for the library's symbolic ornamentation and the organizational abilities to build it. Upon the Library's completion in 1897, Green wrote an illustrated article, "The Building for the Library of Congress," concentrating on their joint functional, rather than artistic, achievements.[88]

ENGINEER COMMISSIONERS

Part country town, part capital city, Washington after the Civil War promised much to its residents but provided little in necessary urban services. "Upon the whole," Walt Whitman wrote during the war, "the city, the spaces, buildings, etc., make no unfit emblem of our country, so broadly planned, everything in plenty." Yet, he added, "the fruit of the plans, the knit, the combination is wanting...many a hiatus yet."[89] L'Enfant's public reservations remained empty, weed-grown fields or had been turned to other uses, a few even having had churches built on them illegally. The Washington Monument stood incomplete on the unkempt Mall, its grounds having been used to pen cattle during the war. Sloops and scows nosed along the Washington Canal beside North B Street. Tiber Creek, the canal, and other streams were open sewers. Slash Run marsh and tidal flats near Foggy Bottom were breeding grounds of malaria, and the Potomac Flats were a noisome marsh uncovered twice a day when the river fell. Cursed with slums adjacent to mansions, Washington in many ways remained a village where cattle, geese, and chickens roamed at will.[90]

The sheer discomfort of the capital, combined with memories of its Southern sympathies, convinced many that it was not a fit place for the government. At the end of the Civil War, Congress debated proposals from mid-western states to move the capital to America's heartland, the Ohio or Mississippi valleys. Worried by the agitation to move the government, Washingtonians embarked on a new effort to recreate their city as a worthy national capital. Alexander R. Shepherd, a native Washingtonian, an alderman, a wealthy contractor, as well as a friend of President Grant, led local boosters who advocated a more active district government and a building program to make the city handsome and to revitalize it with modern amenities becoming common in other American and European cities.[91]

Washington's population of 130,000 in 1870 had doubled since 1860, yet the city "was less advanced in the matter of civic conveniences than many a State capital of smaller size." The aqueduct's water did not serve all parts of the city and water in all of the city's quadrants continued to be pumped from wells or from springs; septic systems were rudimentary and individual to each structure; and the hilly landscape over which L'Enfant's streets had been laid was picturesque to look at but very difficult to

"[T]he city, the spaces, buildings, etc., make no unfit emblem of our country.... [T]he fruit of the plans, the knit, the combination is wanting..."

navigate for carts, carriages, and pedestrians. These rolling streets also impeded organized urban growth, especially the siting and building of row houses. Moreover, "Pennsylvania Avenue alone enjoyed the distinction of being lighted and that but poorly." Sewers, a healthy supply of water, street lighting, and street paving and grading were of the first importance.[92]

Urged on by these forces, on February 21, 1871, Congress fused L'Enfant's original city with the "county," the land ceded by Maryland that still comprised the District of Columbia (the Virginia portion had been retroceded in 1846), into a single national territory under a territorial form of government. A governor to serve four years was to be appointed by the president, as was an eleven-member council, each serving two years, representing eleven new districts, two in Georgetown and two in the old county. Washington's citizenry, however, elected the twenty-two members of the House of Delegates. The president also was to appoint four members of a board of public works to serve four-year terms, the fifth member to be the governor. The duties outlined for the Board of Public Works (the Board of Health being the only other municipal office under the territorial government) gave them: "entire control of and [the power to] make all regulations which they shall deem necessary for keeping in repair the streets, avenues, alleys, and sewers of the city, and all other works which shall be entrusted to their charge by the legislative assembly or Congress." Army Engineers later inherited this authority.[93]

President Grant chose as governor Henry D. Cooke, brother of banker Jay Cooke, whose name and connections would be useful in selling bonds. But it was Shepherd, appointed vice president of the Board of Public Works in May 1871, and governor, and thus its president, in 1873, who emerged as the dominant figure in transforming the district. In his three-year reign, "Boss" Shepherd worked with architects Alfred B. Mullett and Adolf Cluss to pave over a hundred miles of streets, build sidewalks, set up about three thousand streetlights, install a sewer system, and cover the Washington Canal as far as Third Street. Most noticeable to visitors was the landscaping that went hand-in-hand with paving and grading the streets, as public reservations were planted with trees and flowers and the "parking" (public land between the streets and building façades), was landscaped on the wide avenues; this amenity can still be appreciated on East Capitol Street where the public "parking" is maintained by private owners as their front gardens. Although Shepherd's Board of Public Works of 1871–74 (notably its architects Cluss and Mullett) are always given credit for conceptualizing as well as overseeing the "parking" and paving of Washington's streets, Army engineer Nathaniel

The city "was less advanced in the matter of civic conveniences than many a State capital of smaller size."

"…an officer of the Engineer Corps of the Army, because… under such an officer, whatever work is done will be well done, and by an officer responsible to the executive and to Congress."

Michler reported on the results of Meigs's 1867 study trip to Europe concerning the most advanced technology for roadbeds being employed in Berlin and Paris. The engineers also suggested "parking" on these European models as the way to humanize L'Enfant's inordinately wide avenues. Shepherd's pell-mell pace, ruthless treatment of property owners, and financial juggling brought the territorial government down in a major scandal. In the summer of 1873 the bankrupt district faced a major change in its political life.[94]

The board's maladministration led to a federal takeover of the city. In 1874 congressional investigators probed the board's work, discovering irregularities (but no positive evidence of fiscal corruption), that led them to recommend a new government of three civilian commissioners to be appointed by the president. To assume the duties of the abolished Board of Public Works, the committee recommended "an officer of the Engineer Corps of the Army, because…under such an officer, whatever work is done will be well done, and by an officer responsible to the executive and to Congress."[95] Cluss had been discredited by allegations of contract irregularities during the 1873 investigations, and Mullett (whose term ended in June 1873) was overworked and under criticism in his main position as the Supervising Architect of the Treasury.

Tours of duty for the engineer officers were frequently rotated, giving them valuable experience solving difficult engineering problems in difficult situations all over the country. Throughout their careers they were required to write (and illustrate) concise reports stating the problems they faced, their solutions, and their costs. Thus they were uniquely equipped to go beyond the administrative and oversight duties that Mullett and Cluss had performed from 1871 to 1874. President Grant chose another protégé as the municipal engineer in what was thought to be a temporary form of government, First Lieutenant Richard L. Hoxie (1844–1930), a West Point friend of his son Frederick Grant. In 1878 an act made the Board of Commissioners permanent and stipulated that one of the three commissioners be an engineer officer above the rank of a captain. In 1890 a joint resolution of the board required that its engineer officer must have served fifteen years in the Corps of Engineers as a requirement for appointment.[96]

The sensational is news and Washington's short period of territorial government was reported widely in local and national newspapers and journals because Shepherd became at first infamous for his reckless extravagance and later famous for his vision. "The work of reconstructing the city had been so thoroughly begun that there was no option but to complete it. This was cautiously and carefully done," reported the *Century Magazine* in 1884. Although Shepherd's name figured prominently in this article on "The New Washington," Hoxie's name was not linked with his accomplishments during the decade he worked first as the sole engineer during the temporary government beginning in 1874, and after 1878, as one of the assistants to Major William J. Twining, who served as engineer commissioner until his early death in 1882. In fact, the *Century Magazine* writer who found little to criticize in Shepherd's accomplishments—wood paving blocks that "went to pieces very quickly" being the exception—was in reality praising the results of much of Twining's, Hoxie's, and Captain F. V. Greene's (assistant from 1879 to 1885) work. "Year by year the wood has been replaced with asphalt, which now covers a length of fifty miles, and is a great luxury for all who use the streets, whether with cushioned carriage or heavy express wagon. By far the greater part of the streets used for residences are covered with these asphalt pavements, which are somewhat similar to those in Paris, but cover an extent three times as great."[97]

Beginning in 1878 one of the Engineer Commissioner's two assistants was assigned to sewers and the other to streets. Twining developed plans for increasing the water supply, extended the sewage system, paved many miles of streets, and urged upon Congress a plan for reclaiming the Potomac flats. In the course of work to drain and fill the old city canal, Greene employed 1,500 people, "laborers, carts, and water-boys…selected by the police from among the needy and deserving poor."[98] In 1879 Greene urged Congress to prevent further unplanned growth in the district by adopting a unified street plan, although nothing happened until 1888. Such essential, but mundane, jobs were the underlying infrastructure of the "new Washington," but did not lend themselves to the sensational when no scandal was involved.

Humane and competent administration won Twining great popularity, and his death from overwork in 1882 was regarded as a public misfortune and grave loss to the Corps. President Chester A. Arthur, members of the cabinet, and lawmakers from both houses of Congress attended his funeral.[99]

The three members of the temporary commission appointed in 1874 were Republican politicans, but when the commissioner form of government became permanent in 1878, President Rutherford Hayes initiated the practice of appointing a civilian commissioner from each major political party, a practice that became customary. Congress apparently believed that the third member should be a non-partisan expert. According to Congressman Joseph Blackburn of Kentucky, "No third man could be found who would come nearer meeting the requirements and demands made than an officer of the U.S. Army, who ought not to be burdened with politics; an officer detailed from the Engineer Corps than who

> *"By far the greater part of the streets used for residences are covered with these asphalt pavements, which are somewhat similar to those in Paris, but cover an extent three times as great."*

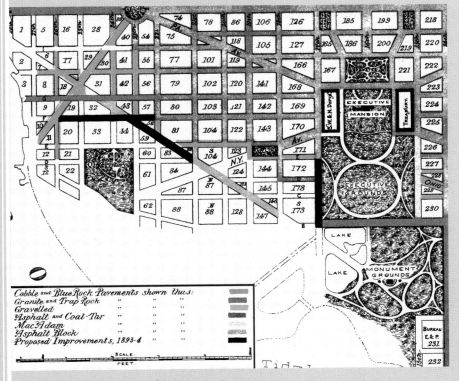

Cobble and Blue Rock Pavements shown thus:
Granite and Trap Rock   "   "   "
Gravelled   "   "   "
Asphalt and Coal-Tar   "   "   "
Mac Adam   "   "   "
Asphalt Block   "   "   "
Proposed Improvements, 1893-4   "   "

SCALE.
FEET.

THIS 1885 VIEW SHOWS THE SPARSE DEVELOPMENT OF MUCH OF THE AREA SOUTHWEST OF THE WHITE HOUSE, INCLUDING NEWLY RECLAIMED LAND. VIRGINIA AVENUE APPEARS GRADED THOUGH UNIMPROVED. THE ENGINEER COMMISSIONER MAP (DETAIL) REVEALS THAT BY 1893 THE COMMISSIONERS HAD PAVED PORTIONS OF THE AVENUE AND SURROUNDING STREETS. THE SECTION FROM THE WASHINGTON MONUMENT TO B STREET REMAINED UNIMPROVED AND WOULD EVENTUALLY BE ABANDONED. THE PORTIONS BETWEEN 18TH AND 21ST STREETS AND BETWEEN F AND G STREETS WERE COVERED WITH GRAVEL; THE SMALL SECTION BETWEEN 25TH AND 26TH STREETS PAVED WITH COBBLE AND BLUE ROCK; AND THE STRETCH FROM 21ST TO 23RD STREETS PROPOSED FOR IMPROVEMENT THE FOLLOWING YEAR.

I am free to say there is no set of men to be found in all the land who have maintained through war and peace an escutcheon more perfectly free from stain and blot."[100]

After many upheavals, Washingtonians largely acquiesced to the 1878 "Organic Act." Blacks saw Congress as their protector, while white property owners noted Congress's apparent promise to pay half the expenses of the district and to underwrite the local debt. Local finances failed at last under the strain of supporting Shepherd's building program, and the federal government had taken over the city. At the cost of the franchise, the district became the nation's city under the nation's care. As a direct result, the Army Engineers acquired an unprecedented role in the regular, peacetime government of an American city. The Organic Act remained in force until 1967 with a member of the Corps of Engineers one of three people who conducted the city's business for nearly nine decades.

In 1902 Rufus Rockwell Wilson noted the social and political results of Washington's governance by the Board of Commissioners:

> *Free from scandal of every sort, successive boards of commissioners of ability and character have administered the affairs of the District during the past twenty-seven year more efficiently and economically than the affairs of any other American municipality have been administered, and to such general satisfaction that there has been no lasting criticism. Indeed, to quote the words of an experienced and acute observer, "Washington is one of the best governed cities in the world. There is no political party to profit from the knavery of contractors or the finding of places for henchmen, no boss to whom universal tribute is paid. Its streets are clean and well lighted, its policemen polite and conscientious, its fire department prompt and reliable, its care for the public health of the sick and indigent admirable, and its rate of taxation one of the lowest in the country."*

Wilson went on to describe many beauties and amenities found in Washington at the turn of the century, noting, "all money for street improvements is virtually controlled by the engineers."[101]

The engineer commissioners and their assistants lived in the city they administered and participated in its social and cultural life. Hoxie's life and career were unusual for a career American military officer, in that he was educated in Italy in his youth and joined the Union Army in 1861 while a student at Iowa State University. His gallantry in combat led to his appointment to West Point in 1864. After working on engineering projects in New York

"No third man could be found who would come nearer meeting the requirements and demands made than an officer of the U.S. Army, who ought not to be burdened with politics; an officer detailed from the Engineer Corps than who I am free to say there is no set of men to be found in all the land who have maintained through war and peace an escutcheon more perfectly free from stain and blot."

and Boston, at the age of thirty, his exceptional talents led to his appointment as the temporary municipal engineer. In 1878, the year he became Twining's assistant, Hoxie married the sculptor Vinne Ream, to whom he had been introduced by Lieutenant General William T. Sherman. The Hoxie's house on Farragut Square, the setting for Ream's famous salon of artists and intellectuals, overlooked her statue of Admiral Farragut, one of her many notable monumental works of sculpture. Hoxie's social standing in Washington matched his professional achievements; his erudition in hydraulics and astronomy was particularly notable and he retired in 1908 a brigadier general.[102]

BUILDING CODES

The most pervasive influence the engineer commissioners had over the city's architectural appearance was adding to, administering, and enforcing its building regulations. Washington's 1790s building codes focused primarily on the city's urban appearance, addressing materials, building heights and their position on lots, party walls, temporary structures (such as gateways), and projections into the public spaces beyond individual lot lines. The 1871 act that established the Board of Public Works gave it the authority to "make all necessary regulations respecting the construction of private buildings in the District of Columbia." The commissioners inherited this authority. As published on August 19, 1872, the comprehensive Building Regulations addressed safety in terms of fire protection and structural stability. The regulations called for building permits for new buildings and substantial alterations, outlined several rules ranging from roofing contiguous buildings to fireplace flues for private buildings, and addressed safety in theaters and other public halls that included their seating capacity and ventilation.[103]

In 1875 the District of Columbia Commissioners appointed a committee to update the regulations to include more stringent safety measures and to address health issues such as requiring either a water closet or an outhouse for every structure in the city. In 1877 the engineer commissioner required non-combustible materials, such as iron for cornices and eaves, on buildings erected to a height of sixty feet or more, and by 1887 fire escapes were required for buildings fifty feet in height. Bay windows had been allowed by the Territorial Government in 1871; the 1877 regulations allowed towers and projecting shop windows as well as bays, but all required building permits issued by the commissioner. By 1887 "oriel" (a bay window above the first floor) windows were allowed. For nine decades the engineer commissioners helped formulate and regulate the appearance of

"Washington is one of the best governed cities in the world. There is no political party to profit from the knavery of contractors or the finding of places for henchmen, no boss to whom universal tribute is paid."

"All money for street improvements is virtually controlled by the engineers."

Washington's streetscapes and much of the character of its housing developments and individually designed homes erected in suburban neighborhoods.[104]

In 1870 neighborhood associations began forming to enable the collective voices of citizens to exert influence on the Board of Commissioners in the daily running of the city. The associations routinely wrote to the board to express their local concerns or banded together to influence decisions of citywide import. The House and Senate committees on the District of Columbia depended on reports and recommendations issued by the engineer commissioners and almost invariably acted as the engineer advised.[105]

PERMANENT SYSTEM OF HIGHWAYS

Piecemeal suburban development in the county of Washington beginning in the late 1860s threatened to ring L'Enfant's organized city with a patchwork of individual and mismatching street plans. In 1879 assistant engineer commissioner Greene urged the formulation of a master street plan for the entire district, based on "a thorough geodetic and topographical survey" that he proposed be created under a collaboration between the city's engineer department and the Coast and Geodetic Survey.[106] Congress began funding this ten-year mapping project the next year, but took no action on controlling suburban growth until 1888. In August the District Commissioners received authority for the first time to approve the plats of new subdivisions, which were required to conform to the city's "general plan."[107]

Lacking an overall master plan on paper made it problematical to interpret whether street patterns of real estate developments in the county accorded with the city's plan. The Highway Act of March 2, 1893, attempted to solve this problem. It directed the creation of a Highway Plan for the entire district be formulated and mapped in four sections beginning with the area outside Florida Avenue between North Capitol Street and Rock Creek Park that contained a majority of Washington's nonconforming subdivisions. Each section of the plan was to be approved, after public comment, by the Board of Commissioners and finally by a special Highway Commission comprised of the Secretaries of War and Interior and the Chief of Engineers.[108] Engineer Commissioner Captain Charles F. Powell named civil engineer William P. Richards the assistant engineer in charge of highway extensions, and he directed the extensive work of developing and implementing the Highway Plan until 1905.

The Highway Act called for extensive condemnations of rights-of-way through many of the district's oldest and most developed suburban subdivisions. Legal challenges,

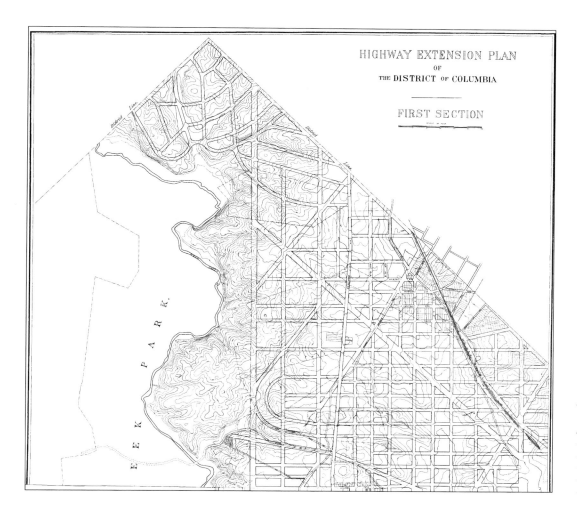

"Highway Extension Plan of the District of Columbia, First Section, 1898." Shown is the Engineer Commissioner's projection for extending a modified version of L'Enfant's plan to the northwestern section of the city.

Image Archives of the Historical Map & Chart Collection/Office of Coast Survey/National Ocean Service/NOAA, MSPHS1C

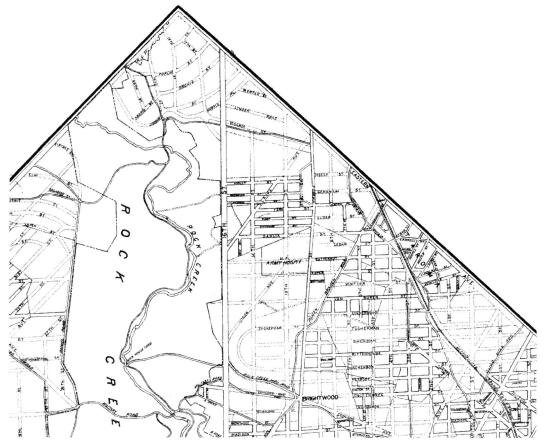

"Map of the Permanent Highway System of the District of Columbia. Prepared in the Office of the Engineer Commissioner, 1914." Sixteen years after the highway system became law, its implementation was still spotty east of Rock Creek Park.

Image Archives of the Historical Map & Chart Collection/Office of Coast Survey/National Ocean Service/NOAA, MSSH (detail)

Chain Bridge undergoing repairs, 1928. One end of the wrought-iron bridge built by Babcock in 1874 was lifted to repair one of its piers.
Library of Congress, Prints and Photographs Division, LC-USZ62-77637

condemnations, and a flawed system set up in the act for determining damages and benefits in condemnation cases held up implementation of the Highway Plan from mid-1895 until mid-1898. An act of June 28, 1898, however, broke the stalemate by amending the Highway Act to exempt most pre-August 1888 subdivisions from revision under the Highway Plan. The fourth and final section of the plan, which covered all the land south of the Anacostia River, was completed in 1900, assuring that L'Enfant's vision of a monumental city would be preserved, under the oversight of the Engineer commissioner, as the city grew into the twentieth century.[109]

POTOMAC AND ANACOSTIA RIVER BRIDGES

The relation of the Potomac and Anacostia Rivers to Washington is similar to that of the Thames to London with wide, deep, and swiftly flowing waters dividing rather than connecting disparate parts of each city. A succession of early nineteenth century wood bridges connected Washington to the Virginia shore and the Eleventh Street Bridge connected the Navy Yard to Anacostia. These bridges were rebuilt and additional ones erected across the Potomac River during the middle decades of the nineteenth century. Land east of the Anacostia was slow to develop and be incorporated into the city partially because of the paucity of bridges and partially because of the river's wide flood plain. Throughout the last quarter of the century, engineers detailed to the Office of Public Buildings and Grounds and the Washington Engineer District updated the city's river connections by overseeing the planning of six, and the installation of five, similar iron bridges over both rivers.

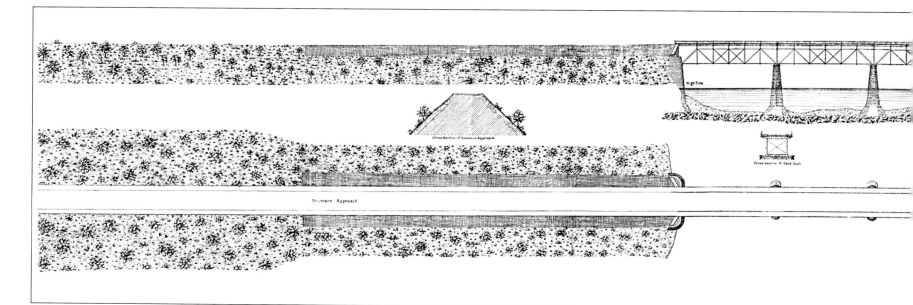

"A substantial wrought-iron bridge, 1,352 feet long, was built over the Potomac at the site of 'Chain Bridge,'" reported Babcock in an 1877 summary of his achievements as Officer in Charge of Public Buildings and Grounds.[110] Six bridges had successively occupied a site below Little Falls since 1797, including three of the chain-suspension type. Flooding in 1870 destroyed the heavy timber superstructure of an 1850s span, leaving its stone piers in place. In August 1872 Babcock contracted with S. R. Dickson of New Haven, Connecticut, for a new wrought-iron bridge on the standing piers. He annulled the contract fourteen months later, when no work had been done, and made a new one with Clark, Reeves and Co. of the Phoenixville Bridge Works in Pennsylvania. They completed the bridge four months later, in March 1874. This iron bridge stood until replaced in 1939.[111]

The Office of Public Buildings and Grounds next replaced the Anacostia River Bridge east of the Navy Yard. The existing wooden structure on the site had been almost entirely rebuilt by the Army during the Civil War to cope with the heavy use it received. In 1868 Michler proposed that a new, permanent iron bridge either replace the old bridge or supplement it up the river where direct communication would be made with Virginia or Pennsylvania Avenues. No action was taken and the bridge continued to accommodate "an immense travel" and require "almost constant repairing." In July 1873, "as a four-horse team belonging to the Government Insane Asylum was crossing the Navy Yard bridge, a span of the bridge broke, and let them through into the water. A patient from the hospital was seated with the driver, and narrowly escaped being drowned. Two of the horses were drowned."[112] More repairs followed, and the

Plan and elevation drawings of the Aqueduct Bridge, 1887, showing its low landfall in Arlington, Virginia (on the left) and Georgetown, which was higher in elevation
Office of History, Corps of Engineers, ARCE 1887

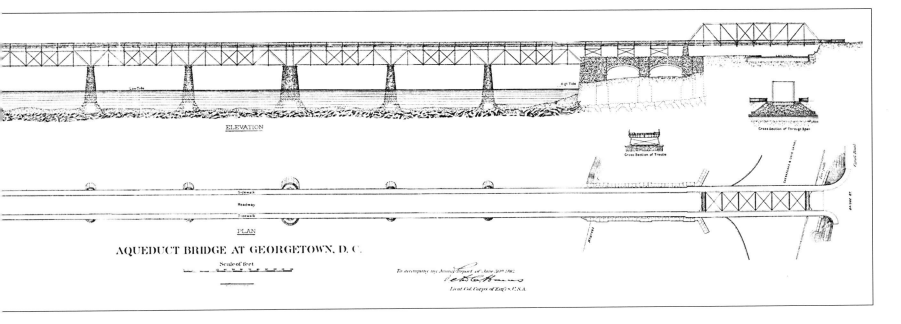

ELEVATION

PLAN

AQUEDUCT BRIDGE AT GEORGETOWN, D. C.

Scale of feet

next year Congress authorized a completely new wrought-iron truss bridge set on masonry piers. The Office of Public Buildings and Grounds under Babcock again contracted with Clark, Reeves and Co., which built the bridge to plans and specifications it had drawn up as part of the bid process. This structure lasted until 1908, when a heavy steel arch bridge designed by a civil engineer in the D.C. Bridge Division replaced it.[113]

During the Civil War, the Army converted the trough of the Aqueduct Bridge, which connected Georgetown to Virginia, into a wagon way. The bridge's private owners turned it into a toll bridge in 1868. Engineers inspected the bridge several times in the following decades but did not condemn it as unsafe until 1886, when the private owners agreed to sell the bridge. The federal government set up an engineer board under the auspices of the Washington Engineer District, composed of Lieutenant Colonel William E. Merrill, Lieutenant Colonel Peter C. Hains, and Major W. R. King. This board was charged with

Pennsylvania Avenue Bridge across the Anacostia River, built between 1887 and 1890, was replaced by the John Philip Sousa Bridge in 1940. (Photographed October 1926)
Office of History, Corps of Engineers

planning the reconstruction of the bridge. It proposed erecting a new iron-truss super-structure with wood floor joists and planking on the existing 1830s piers. Limitations in the federal appropriation for construction prevented the building of a drawbridge that the board had strongly recommended, but construction proceeded and the bridge opened on June 30, 1888. Hains supervised the construction.

In May 1886 the long process to erect a Memorial Bridge linking the District of Columbia at Observatory Hill to Arlington National Cemetery began with a congressional resolution; Hains proposed an iron-truss bridge composed of four 300-foot spans. The job fell to Captain Thomas W. Symons who collaborated with architect Paul Pelz to design a monumental stone bridge with two towers masking a central bascule draw, their model being Tower Bridge in London. This bridge, conceived as the Grant Memorial Bridge, was never built both because of its perceived insult to Virginia and the South and because of congressional opposition to the Corps' involvement with its design.[114]

While work on the Aqueduct Bridge progressed, District Engineer Hains took up another river-spanning project. Lobbying efforts by a local citizens' association led Congress to authorize a bridge extending Pennsylvania Avenue over the Anacostia River in 1887. No bridge had occupied this site since the privately owned Middle Bridge had burned in 1845. A board of Army Engineers planned the structure at Congress's request, and Hains contracted the work to the Groton Bridge and Manufacturing Co. A dispute over the placement of the west abutment arose with the Baltimore and Potomac Railroad, over whose tracks the bridge passed. Hains worked out an alteration to the plans that met the

Major General Peter C. Hains during World War I. Many long-retired engineer officers returned to service during the war as district engineers throughout the United States so that active duty officers could serve in France. Hains's most lasting contribution to Washington was dredging the flats of the Potomac and Anacostia Rivers to improve the healthfulness of the entire city.
Office of History, Corps of Engineers,
U.S. Army Signal Corps Photo (detail)

Construction of the inlet bridge for the Tidal Basin, 1909. The inlet and outlet bridges served as actual bridges at the same time their substructures were designed to flush out the Washington channel with each tide.

needs of the government, the railroad, and the contractors, and the bridge was completed in July 1890. This bridge was replaced by the John Philip Sousa Bridge in 1940.[115]

Benning's Bridge, crossing the Eastern Branch in line with H Street, NE, was another of the city's nineteenth-century wooden bridges, and it, like the others, was perpetually being repaired. It was strengthened by the Corps of Engineers to handle heavy guns during the Civil War, and it was later maintained by the Office of Public Buildings and Grounds, surviving until 1934.[116] A second bridge constructed of iron was built in 1892 under the authority of the Engineer Commissioner, whose highway department contracted its construction with the Keystone Bridge Co.[117]

District engineers made surveys and plans for two additional Anacostia bridges that were not built. Major Charles E. L. B. Davis considered placing one at the foot of First Street, SW, in 1895, and two years later Major Charles J. Allen planned one extending Massachusetts Avenue, SE, to connect the city's divided southeast sector. Both Anacostia River bridges would have employed steel-truss systems on masonry piers.[118]

WASHINGTON ENGINEER DISTRICT

Alongside the challenges of constructing the government's major public buildings and its bridges, as well as running the district government, the Corps of Engineers brought its expertise in river control and land reclamation to bear in Washington at the end of the nineteenth century. In 1875 the Washington Engineer District came into existence when the Chief of Engineers chose civilian Sylvanus T. Abert (son of Colonel J. J. Abert, who had been Chief of Topographical Engineers during the middle of the century) to undertake the improvement of the Potomac River.

The Potomac flowed through the District of Columbia in two channels. The easternmost of these, the Washington Channel, was prone to filling as the Potomac emptied into its broad estuary and dropped its burden of silt. As settlement and deforestation increased upstream, the flats around the channel gradually became larger, forming a marsh that threatened navigation. A dam built by Virginia from Analostan Island to the shore and the causeway of Long Bridge accelerated the marsh's growth. Submerged at high water, these shoals formed at low water a foul-smelling mud bank stretching from not far south of the White House to below the Long Bridge. Reeds and grasses covered the muck, and wastes from the Washington Canal—later to be the B Street sewer—decayed in the sun. The flats were widely believed to be a breeding ground for malaria. "The Presidential mansion," Hains once commented, "being distant only about half a mile, got the full benefit of the condition of affairs when the wind was from the south."[119] Repeated efforts at the end of the century to build a new White House elsewhere in the city were in part motivated by the existence of the flats.

Little was done about the situation until federal expenditures for rivers rose following the Civil War. Then engineers dredged channels and removed the rocks obstructing Georgetown harbor. They pointed to the condition of the canal and the flats and recommended that the causeway of Long Bridge be replaced with pilings. Dredging, suggested Michler in 1868, could provide spoil to reclaim the flats.[120]

In 1872 a board of survey that included Officer in Charge of Public Buildings and Grounds Babcock, vice president of the Board of Public Works Shepherd, and Chief of Engineers Humphreys, plus the governor of the District of Columbia and two officials from the Coast and Geodetic Survey, proposed a general plan for improving the river. Specially noting the "immense marshy flat," the board wrote, "the reclamation of this flat is an absolute necessity for the preservation of the health of the city, and must be included in any plan...for the improvement of the water-front of Washington." Their plan proposed building a new Southwest waterfront out in the river and filling the

"[T]he reclamation of this flat is an absolute necessity for the preservation of the health of the city, and must be included in any plan... for the improvement of the water-front of Washington."

Periodic flooding of the Mall and downtown Washington, as in 1889 when Pennsylvania Avenue was flooded, declined markedly after Hains built up the Potomac flats.

Office of History, Corps of Engineers

Major Peter Hains's initial plan for reclaiming the Potomac flats, "Potomac River in the Vicinity of Washington, D.C., Showing the Proposed Improvements in Front of the City." Hains's Potomac flats would be a picturesque park like Downing's Mall.

Office of History, Corps of Engineers, ARCE 1883

area between its new docks and the old river's edge with the dredged mud. The result would have added more than one thousand acres to the city and completely covered the Washington Channel and the flats.[121] Seven years later Engineer Commissioner Twining proposed a similar solution, filling up the flats in front of the waterfront, but leaving the Washington Channel mostly intact as a tidal arm of the river. At the new upper limit of the channel, north of Long Bridge, he conceived the idea of providing four flushing ponds, or tidal reservoirs, on the reclaimed land. These lakes, fitted with inlet and outlet gates, were to assure a twice-daily flow of fresh water through the channel, thereby preventing stagnation and silting.[122]

With many elements of a comprehensive plan already worked out, Congress acted after the severe flood of 1881 inundated the Mall and Pennsylvania Avenue. The lawmakers first ordered a new survey, which was submitted by Sylvanus T. Abert, "U.S. Civil Engineer in charge of Washington and Georgetown Harbor Improvements," in January 1882.[123] The next month a Corps of Engineers' board comprised of Lieutenant Colonels Q. A. Gillmore, William P. Craighill, and C. B. Comstock assembled a plan combining elements of Twining's and Abert's proposals.[124] This report laid the groundwork for an act of August 2, 1882, appropriating $400,000 to improve navigation and raise the flats.[125]

The greater part of the work that followed fell to Hains (1840–1921), head of the Washington Engineer District from 1882 until 1891. Dredging the channel, Hains first had the dredged material moved on scows to a receiving basin, from there to be piped into hopper cars and hauled by railroad to the dumping ground. There it was dumped and spread by methods similar to those of contemporary levee work. Hains found the

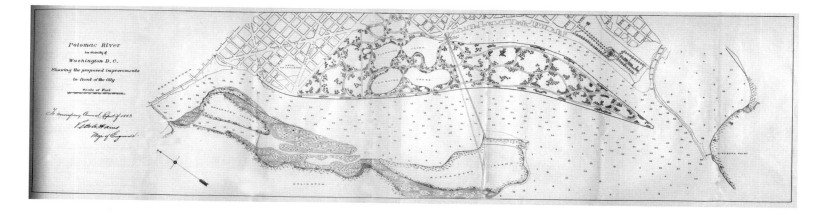

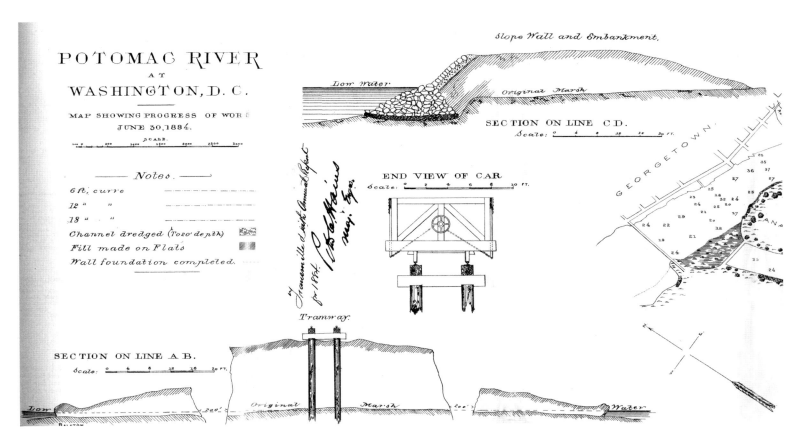

double dredging and repeated construction of railroad trestlework to be too expensive, and he subsequently switched the work to hydraulic dredges that could pump the spoil directly to its destination. For the twelve years prior to this monumental reclamation project, Hains had been on lighthouse duty as engineer for the 5th and 6th districts (the southern states on the Atlantic Ocean and Florida), where he gained invaluable experience in the varied conditions found in tidal rivers, marshes, and swamps. "In 1891, when he was called elsewhere, about three-quarters of the 12,000,000 cu. yd. estimated to be necessary had been placed on the flats. About 620 acres of malignant swamp had been transformed into healthful dry land."[126] Under Hains and his successors, Major Charles E. L. B. Davis and Lieutenant Colonel Charles J. Allen, the land that was to

Detail from map of the Potomac Flats Reclamation, June 30, 1884. A cross section of the early retaining walls and the hoppers that were initially used to move dredged material onto the flats to create landfill. The newly developed pipeline dredges allowed more efficient pumping of dredged material from the river bottom to areas to be filled.
Office of History, Corps of Engineers, ARCE 1884

Progress in reclaiming Potomac flats to June 1890
Office of History, Corps of Engineers, ARCE 1890

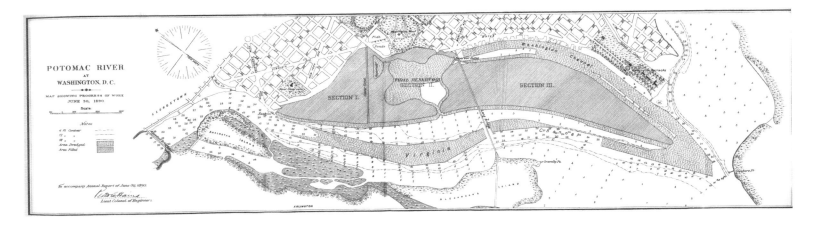

Aerial view of the Potomac reclamation project almost complete in 1892. The point at the downstream end of the park was named for Peter Hains, Washington District Engineer, who worked on the project for nine years.
Washingtoniana Division, D.C. Public Library/National Park Service

become Potomac Park rose from the waters of the estuary, while the river flowed through deeper and straighter channels.[127]

During the summer of 1889 Hains also oversaw the survey of three possible routes for a national road from the Virginia end of the Aqueduct Bridge to Mount Vernon. The "river route" followed the Chesapeake & Ohio Canal bed to Alexandria and then skirted swampland; the middle route went along Arlington Road and passed Alexandria north of Shuter's Hill; while the western route was along a ridge of hills, the Virginia highlands. Hains saw the national road as having the "character of a monumental structure" because its purpose was neither commercial nor military, but commemorative of Washington's virtues and to "satisfy the cravings of a patriotic sentiment that fills the heart of the American people" to visit Mount Vernon.[128] Hains hired B. F. Mackall to carry out the actual survey and the proposed costs ranged from about $1.3 million to $1.8 million. The river route was the most expensive, the highland the least costly, and Hains recommended the latter both for economic reasons and because the views were superb.

Between 1866 and the early 1890s, Washington's development as a city and as the national capital depended on the Corps' multiple activities as engineers, administrators,

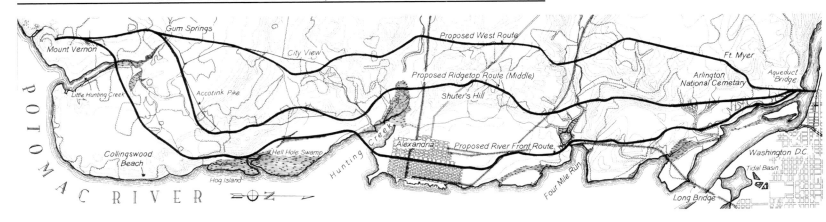

and designers. The magnitude of projects with which Congress entrusted them during peacetime was unprecedented in the country. From the Corps, Congress could draw upon an enormous pool of talent and expertise already on the government's payroll with an established administrative structure that was proving itself as efficient in peace as it had been in war. Casey was first in his class at West Point in 1852, Babcock third in his class in 1861, Michler fourth in his class in 1844, and Meigs fifth in his class in 1836. Successive chiefs of engineers chose for positions of authority from among their officers those whose training and experience best equipped them to succeed as construction engineers, hydraulic engineers, or whatever the current development needs of Washington required. Their responsibilities were often complementary and the engineers advised one another, consulted with national experts in the arts and sciences, and developed personal and institutional relationships with the country's political leadership. If one studied in detail what was being built in Washington during any single year between 1865 and 1890, dozens of members of the Corps would be quietly directing most of the work.[129]

In 1889 Hains oversaw the survey of three possible routes for a memorial parkway to take tourists from Washington to Mount Vernon.
Library of Congress, Historic American Engineering Record, National Park Service, Robert Dawson and Ed Lupyak, 1994

4 | *The Progressive City 1890–1915*

INTRODUCTION

On January 18, 1901, James McMillan of Michigan, chairman of the Senate Committee on the District of Columbia since 1892, opened the final stage of his campaign to devise a comprehensive plan for Washington's future aesthetic development. His report summarized the recent accomplishments and future projects that would make Washington a "beautiful capital city."

> *During the past decade Congress has provided the means for the artistic development of the District of Columbia in a manner befitting the capital city of the nation. The purchase of Rock Creek and the Zoological parks, the adoption of a permanent system of highways throughout the District, the improvement of the flats of the Potomac, and the creation of Potomac Park, and the extension of certain great thoroughfares of the city of Washington through the misfit subdivisions and thence to the District line all betoken the desire and intention of Congress to carry out the original idea of making Washington a beautiful capital city.*

Moreover, legislation well begun, but not yet completed, shows that this
purpose on the part of the National Legislature is continuous. The proposed
speedy completion of the sewer system according to a carefully matured plan;
the approaching completion of an increased water supply, and the installa-
tion of a filtration plant; the plans for elimination of all grade crossings on
steam railroads within the city of Washington, and for the building of
adequate railway terminals; the proposed reclamation of the Anacostia
Flats; the approaching transfer to the District authorities of the control of the
commercial water front of the city; these great projects that are even now in
process of being worked out serve to show how comprehensive and varied is
the movement now in progress for the development of Washington.[1]

McMillan was the catalyst who initiated many of these great public works and then
worked with various levels of the city and federal governments to bring them about
because he saw them as the necessary groundwork for the future beautification of
Washington. McMillan did not mention that each of these complex endeavors had been
or was being carried out under the direction of some member of the Corps of Engineers.
They were aided by the emergence of citizen involvement in several local organizations,
including the Board of Trade and numerous neighborhood associations. Members of
the Senate and House Committees in the District of Columbia sought the advice of the
Engineer Commissioners and they, in turn, worked with the citizens' groups who lobbied
them for city services.

THE SENATE PARK COMMISSION PLAN, 1902

On March 19, 1901, McMillan chaired a Senate subcommittee meeting that was the
formal beginning of the Senate Park Commission, also known as the McMillan
Commission, to coordinate the projects proposed or already underway with newly
proposed buildings to serve a variety of public functions—a municipal building, a public
library, a judiciary building (that included rooms for the Supreme Court), a government
printing office, an auditor's office, a geological survey, and even a national university.
McMillan wanted these buildings to be part of a coherent, comprehensive plan that would
take into account the city's growth for at least half a century. The Senate Park Commission
he established was composed of two nationally prominent architects, Daniel Burnham and
Charles Follen McKim; landscape architect Frederick Law Olmsted, Jr., whose father

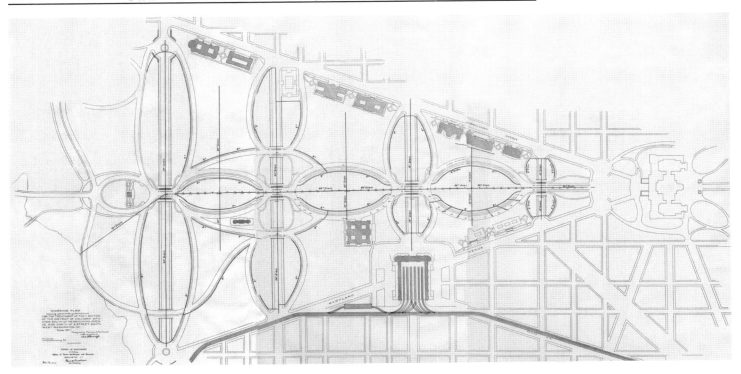

designed New York's Central Park; and America's most famous sculptor, Augustus Saint-Gaudens. McMillan's secretary, Charles Moore, acted as their guide through the Washington bureaucracy during their monthly meetings as they took seriously McMillan's injunction to be visionary in their outlook.

The commission's plan unveiled at the Corcoran Museum of Art on January 15, 1902, revealed that its members focused their talents on totally redesigning Washington's monumental core. Their Beaux-Arts scheme replaced the Mall's existing brick, brownstone, and terra-cotta-clad Victorian buildings with white marble neoclassical ones as an integral part of a new formal landscape placing the Washington Monument in the center of a vast, cruciform-shaped public garden incorporating the filled lands of East and West Potomac Parks. The plan not only called for dozens of new buildings, it required major alterations to the existing landscape, principally grading the Mall, which was considerably higher on its south side, building terraced overlooks around the Washington Monument, and re-positioning or creating major bodies of water in East and West Potomac Parks.

The Senate Park Commission plan was to have immense ramifications for the work of the Corps for the following quarter century. Its modern anti-Victorianism threatened to erase several post-Civil War buildings that Corps engineers had built on the Mall that would have to be rebuilt to modern designs; its vision transformed the Corps' reclaimed Potomac River flats not only into varied and extensive parklands but into spectacular sites for major new

At the behest of Col. Theodore Bingham, New York landscape architect Samuel Parsons, Jr., made a formal design for the Mall in 1900. Bingham himself proposed two designs for the Mall that would have left much of its picturesque gardens intact.
Office of Public Buildings and Grounds

memorials; and its scope promised work that would increasingly involve the Corps in the revolutionary transformation of Washington into the capital of an emerging world power. The Senate Park Commission was dissolved after its design was made public, but its members were so committed to the plan's implementation that they all continued to participate in the design and construction of Washington's buildings and landscapes, either in advisory positions as members of future commissions or in securing some of the new projects for their own firms.[2]

THE PRESIDENT'S HOUSE

In 1889 First Lady Caroline Harrison asked a young friend, architect and engineer Frederick Dale Owen, to design additions to the White House. Since 1800 presidential families shared the mansion's second floor with presidential offices (open to high government officials twenty-four hours a day) while its ground floor had served as the "official residence" often opened to the general public. Owen proposed adding enclosed circular colonnaded rooms (inspired by the open arcades at Mount Vernon) to function as pivots to connect two new wings to the 1792 building—on the west the "official" wing and on the east the "public" wing. They, in turn, were connected to a bank of low greenhouses on the south to form an enclosed rectangle; the new greenhouses were to replace a complex of glass houses that had gradually accumulated on the White House's west side.[3] The drama of the White House's fate was news and reported broadly in the popular and professional presses of the day:

> *Mrs. Harrison expressed her views to Col. John M. Wilson, U.S.A., engineer in charge of public buildings and grounds, whose daily routine is to visit the Executive Mansion and receiving the wishes of the presiding lady in reference to repairs or improvements, and suggested a proper recommendation on the subject of the present condition and requirements of the official residence of the President and family, in his annual report to the Secretary of the Interior for transmission to Congress.[4]*

Throughout the 1890s Corps officers repeatedly urged some solution to the problems of overcrowding at the White House. "Col. John M. Wilson, United States Army, who, by reappointment of President Cleveland, has now charge of the White House and adjacent grounds, has made a strong report on the necessity of some change in the arrangements for the domestic life of the Chief Executive." Wilson particularly urged that a presidential office be found either in the Treasury Building or the State, War and Navy Building or that a separate office be erected on the White House grounds. One of his successors, Colonel Theodore Bingham, expressed the same concerns; the White House's structure was adequate if it was used solely as a private residence but could not survive the wear and tear of heavy office usage and huge public receptions. At the New Year's reception held January 1, 1897, 251 guests entered through the south entrance, while 7,849 entered from Pennsylvania Avenue. Colonel Bingham, Officer in Charge of Public Buildings and Grounds, told President McKinley "if more than two thousand persons were invited to a single White House reception, he—the President—must assume responsibility for any accident that might occur. Owing to the fact that the offices in the second story are mainly over the large East Room, they have no adequate partition support, and cannot be strengthened by the putting in of underpinning." Indicative of the stress being placed on the building, a contemporary account noted seventeen men and their desks had recently been moved into one of the office rooms above the East Room.[5]

Perhaps Bingham considered his dual degrees from Yale and West Point sufficient education to undertake redesigning proposed additions to the White House. On December 12, 1900, Bingham displayed in the Blue Room a white plaster model of

Colonel Bingham...told President McKinley "if more than two thousand persons were invited to a single White House reception,... the President must assume responsibility for any accident that might occur."

White House east entrance and terrace under construction, September 1902

Office of History, Corps of Engineers, Restoration of the White House Report

his reduced interpretation of Owen's proposal for extending the president's house—enlarged versions of the two circular colonnaded rooms now serving as the mansion's sole additions. Bingham placed a new state dining room on the west side, its upper floor a series of hippodrome-shaped guest bedrooms. The new circular east wing was to contain two stories of executive offices. Bingham outlined his five guiding principles at the unveiling of his design:

1. *The present Executive Mansion to remain absolutely unchanged, and, if possible, not an outer door or window to be closed up.*

2. *The additions to be of such a character as not to dwarf nor obscure the present mansion; rather, if possible, to accentuate it.*

3. *Architectural harmony to be absolutely preserved.*

4. *The additions to be such as to relieve the pressure upon the present building, for, say, twenty-five or thirty years, and permit of still further extension in the future as may be found necessary, while at the same time presenting the appearance of a finished building.*

5. *Reasonable expenditure.*[6]

In 1900 Bingham also presented this plan at the annual meeting of the American Institute of Architects (AIA) being held in Washington, rousing the ire of the architectural profession. Architects found that the monumental scale of the two imposing domed rotundas detracted from the original building and considered the interior planning crude—Bingham simply ran straight corridors through the second floors, for example. Adverse opinions of

New White House east entrance and terrace, 1903

National Archives no. 77-WH-13

Bingham's additions appeared widely in newspapers and journals of the day. "Mustn't Spoil the White House," read the headline of one Philadelphia newspaper on December 31, 1900, prompted by opposition expressed by the members of the T-Square Club of that city. "Devoid of Dignity, Lacking in Unity" was the opinion of New York's Society of Beaux Arts Architects as reported in the *New York Herald* on January 23, 1901. Robert Gibson, a fellow of the AIA, was careful to clarify the institute's position.

> *The institute had in mind only what it was proposed to do and carefully refrained from any criticism of the department having the matter in charge. Yet a too hasty press almost nullifies this courtesy by many misstatements.*
>
> *The institute is not engaged in an effort to take this public building or the task of enlarging it out of the custody of the United States engineers, nor does it charge that the scheme proposed is lacking in reverential intent toward the historic monument in question.*
>
> *It simply seeks to show the custodians de facto the need of professional advice of a high order when the design of a house for the Chief Magistrate is in question, whether that house be or be not an addition to an existing one. The institute believes and declares that the thing to be done is important to the whole Nation and is worthy of the best skill procurable.*[7]

Under the leadership of Washingtonian Glenn Brown, secretary of the AIA, the architects succeeded in convincing President Theodore Roosevelt in 1902 to give the job of renovating the White House to the New York architectural firm of McKim, Mead & White. Brown used the same rhetoric that launched the 1902 Senate Park Commission plan—patriotic sentiment about George Washington's role in founding the city and originally commissioning the president's house.[8]

McKim's principles for his restoration were:

> *To put the house in the condition originally planned but never fully carried out.*
>
> *To make the changes in such manner that the house will never again have to be altered; that is to say, the work should represent the period to which the house belongs architecturally, and therefore be independent of changing fashion.*
>
> *To modernize the house in so far as the living rooms are concerned and provide all those conveniences which are now lacking.*[9]

(Top)
White House east room under construction, July 1902
Office of History, Corps of Engineers, Restoration of the White House Report

(Bottom)
New White House east room, 1903
National Archives no. 77-WH-21

"The institute had in mind only what it was proposed to do and carefully refrained from any criticism of the department having the matter in charge."

The *Architects and Builders Journal* in June 1902 reported, "it is President Roosevelt's idea to avoid gorgeousness in the decorations, which, wherever introduced or renewed, will be made rather simple, so as to harmonize with the rest of the mansion."[10]

Adherents of both aesthetic points of view believed they were accomplishing the goal of preserving the historic White House. In fact, Bingham's additions were respectable but naïve within the context of the waning Victorian period; he looked to Thomas U. Walter's 1850s additions to the Capitol, the exteriors of which both continued its regulating lines and details but multiplied its columns to achieve a richly three-dimensional screen effect. In his White House additions, Bingham did not employ a suitable hierarchy by diminishing the scale of the additions in relationship to the original, as well-trained Beaux Arts architects would have done. By 1900 Beaux Arts classicism—erudite, subdued, and elegant—had replaced the sumptuousness of Victorian classicism whose tenets Bingham was still following.

Of all his duties as Engineer Officer in Charge of Public Buildings and Grounds, Bingham was most comfortable with the ceremonial ones associated with his position as

Theodore Alfred Bingham (1858–1934), who made a determined effort to remedy the White House's problems, was born in Andover, Connecticut, and was intensely proud of his Revolutionary-era ancestry. Before entering the U.S. Military Academy in 1875 (and graduating four years later third in his class), Bingham attended Yale College for three years, later receiving a master's degree in 1896. Bingham's social background and skills led to his appointment as the military attaché in the U.S. legations at Berlin and Rome between 1890 and 1894. In 1897 Bingham was appointed Officer in Charge of Public Buildings and Grounds, a position that included serving as the president's military aide in charge of official functions. In 1903, after Roosevelt relieved him of this position, Bingham was transferred to Buffalo at his own request. On July 10, 1904, he was promoted to brigadier general and the following day retired for disability having lost his left leg when a derrick fell as he observed it hoisting a launch. Eighteen months

Colonel Theodore Alfred Bingham
*Office of History,
Corps of Engineers*

later Bingham was appointed New York's Commissioner of Police in charge of a force of nine thousand policemen, a position he held until 1909 when he became the city's chief engineer of highways and subsequently a consulting engineer with the city's department of bridges.[11]

Line outside the White House for a New Year's reception (n.d.). The Officer in Charge of Public Buildings and Grounds was responsible for organizing the variety of events held at the White House.
Library of Congress, Prints and Photographs Division, LC-USZ62-104065

Easter Monday egg rolling at the White House, 1900. Among the many duties large and small of the Engineer Officer in Charge of Public Buildings and Grounds was organizing this annual festivity for children.
National Archives no. 77-WH-9

the president's military aide. He collected newspaper and magazine accounts relating to all the White House's social functions that he organized, the invitations to ceremonies for the erection of monuments that he arranged, and the seating plans for the three annual state dinners over which he presided as major domo. His efforts on behalf of the White House dominated Bingham's annual reports; the defeat of his plan to enlarge the White House was probably made more bitter because it was his duty to supervise construction of the McKim, Mead & White design. He and McKim had an unpleasant encounter that McKim reported to Secretary of War Elihu Root: "I have just had it 'out' with Col. Bingham in his office and explained to him very frankly the reasons which compelled me to oppose him. Thanks to you and the President, the air is clearer than it has been from the beginning—and the Col. is now full of expressions of readiness & willingness to assist us. He comes tomorrow to our office in New York with copies of [the] Contract." In 1907 Charles Moore wrote McKim, "it seems not only desirable but absolutely necessary to secure the hearty, intelligent cooperation of the office of Public Buildings and Grounds, if real progress is to be made with the plans for the improvement of the District of Columbia. Almost all of the difficulties that have arisen in the past have come from misunderstandings with this office."[12]

GOVERNMENT PRINTING OFFICE

The diversity of types of government buildings erected during this period required of Corps' engineers not only an in-depth knowledge of the latest advances in building technology, but a better understanding of the design, planning, and engineering abilities of large American architectural firms. Second Lieutenant John S. Sewell, who graduated second in West Point's 1891 class, was one of the new generations of capable Corps engineers assigned to constructing these buildings. The Government Printing Office (GPO) began looking for a site for an additional building near its 1860s structure on North Capitol Street because it needed to be close to a rail line and the Capitol. Sewell was ordered to duty in Washington in July 1893, "in connection with the erection of public buildings," and between 1894 and 1896 designed and carried out a series of additions and repairs to the original building that had been described in 1891 as "unsafe and in every respect an objectionable structure."[13]

In 1899 the government acquired the block on North Capitol Street on the north side of H Street, NW; $2.4 million was appropriated for an additional building, and Sewell was assigned to design its interiors and erect the 408-foot by 175-foot structure. The original authorization specifically stated that the "selection and appointment of a competent architect to prepare the plans and specifications for the elevations of the building shall be made by the said Chief of Engineers and the Public Printer jointly." They chose Washington architect James G. Hill, who designed a seven-story red brick block on the Chicago formula for massive industrial buildings, its numerous, large, and regularly spaced windows providing abundant interior light for four thousand employees to work amidst machinery that often dwarfed them.[14]

From the outset, Sewell worked closely with the Public Printer, former congressman and Midwestern newspaperman Frank W. Palmer, who began lobbying for a new fireproof building soon after his appointment in 1889. Palmer wanted his mechanical staff, especially GPO's chief engineer and electrician, to be actively involved in both the design and construction of the building. Sewell noted:

> *I found that these gentlemen had made a careful study of the needs of the office, and had already arrived at perfectly definite conclusions in regard to many of the points brought up for discussion. Under these circumstances, it was deemed best for them, if possible, to design and supervise the installation of the mechanical, as they were more conversant with the needs of the office than any outside expert could possibly be.*[15]

Storage of paper in the basement required a dry environment, so Sewell ran conduits from each of the pits of the fifteen elevator shafts directly into the sewer line on North Capitol Street to lower the ground water by at least four feet. Because of the weight and vibration of the printing presses, the tremendous volume of paper printed daily and stored in the building, and the sandy construction site, Sewell devised concrete foundations "of truncated pyramids under interior columns and truncated wedges under the walls," their sides sloping sixty degrees to support loads up to twenty tons per square foot. Sewell devised this kind of foundation because he wished "to avoid putting steel grillages beneath the basement floor" where they would be exposed to moisture that might eventually weaken them. A dramatic rise in the cost of steel at the outset of the project forced Sewell to refine his calculations for the steel frame to keep within the budget yet still erect exterior steel and brick walls uniformly two feet, seven inches thick.

Sewell noted that the most perplexing part of the design was the structural system for the floors because electricity was the only source of power to be used in the building and each machine had its own motor. Moreover, Palmer's planned introduction of linotype and other hot metal printing technologies meant Sewell needed to plan for future holes in the floors and different configurations of machines. His solution was a sandwich of concrete

Colonel John S. Sewell. Sewell made his mark on Washington from 1899 to 1907 as head of two engineer offices for the construction of a new building for the Government Printing Office and the buildings for the Engineer School and the War College at Washington Barracks. In addition he supervised construction of the Department of Agriculture Building on the Mall.
National Archives no. 111-SC-159604

CONSTRUCTION OF THE NEW GOVERNMENT PRINTING OFFICE

Captain John S. Sewell worked closely with GPO to design and construct a fireproof building suitable for the site and for the technical work of the Public Printer. The truncated pyramids used to spread the weight of the steel frame are visible in August 1900. Sewell used both contractors and laborers hired directly by his office in constructing the building, which had the "health and comfort of employees" as one of its objectives. The rapidly increasing price of steel and other construction materials was a problem during the project.

August 7, 1900

October 30, 1900

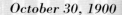

Office of History, Corps of Engineers, ARCE 1901
Office of History, Corps of Engineers, ARCE 1901

June 10, 1901

Post-1920

slab ceilings, a three-foot-tall crawl space to carry electrical cables and wires, and hollow clay tile floors, thus marrying structural solidity, access, and flexibility for each of the building's horizontal levels. Because GPO's engineers and electricians best understood how the complex electrical and mechanical systems needed to work, they directed the Corps' draftsmen in these aspects of the design. Sewell also allowed for more spacious vertical shafts than were common in large buildings of the era to run ventilating and heating pipes as well as electrical cables. When it was nearing completion, the *Washington Post* calculated that the GPO's eight acres of floor space could accommodate the entire populations of Washington and Baltimore. It was the largest printing office in the world and, when it was nearly complete, Sewell went on to design and build the Government Printing Office in Manila using the structural techniques he formulated for its prototype in Washington.[16]

ARMY WAR COLLEGE AND AGRICULTURE DEPARTMENT BUILDING

Sewell's expertise in designing advanced structural systems also was used at the Army War College and the Agriculture Department Building, both erected during the first decade of the twentieth century. Secretary of War Elihu Root created the new Army War College in 1901 for better integration of the Army's various branches. L'Enfant identified the military installation's location on Greenleaf's Point in 1791 and it has been in continuous use as one of Washington's principal military reservations since 1797. Since the 1840s the Washington Arsenal was at Greenleaf's Point, its buildings clustered at the south end of the peninsula and along its central roadway. Early in 1902 former Engineer Commissioner and Commandant of the Engineer School at Washington Barracks, Colonel William M. Black, carried a preliminary site plan for the War College to the Capitol where McKim, Root, and McMillan were lunching. McKim's legendary response was that Black had the "heel of the stocking where the toe ought to be," because the main buildings in the Army's plan were near the north end of the peninsula close to main transportation routes. Root immediately declared that McKim should design the complex in order to take advantage of the beautiful site and prevailing breezes. McKim and Sewell collaborated on the general plan that isolated the main War College building on the central axis at the south end of the point and ranged the officers' quarters along its western shore. On July 21, 1902, Sewell traveled to New York and spent the day working with McKim. "We really made progress, and Capt. Sewell left us with expressions of satisfaction which I feel sure it will please you to know," McKim reported to Root. "His readiness to meet us in every way was particularly gratifying and encouraging to us."[17]

"We really made progress, and Capt. Sewell left us with expressions of satisfaction which I feel sure it will please you to know."

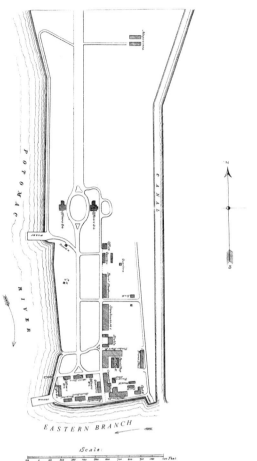

MAP OF
WASHINGTON ARSENAL, D.C.
AREA 69 ACRES.

BOARD ON ARSENALS,
Convened in pursuance of Act of Congress
approved March 3, 1875.

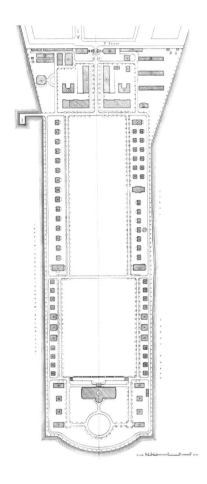

*Map of Washington Arsenal,
1875, and plan for the Army
War College and Washington
Barracks, 1908. In 1901 the
U.S. Army Engineer School
moved from Willets Point
near New York City to
Washington Barracks,
former site of the Washington
Arsenal. The newly-created
Army War College was also
located on the post, now
called Fort McNair. Not all
the buildings shown on the
1908 plan were built.*
Board of Arsenals; Monographs of
the Works of McKim, Mead, and
White, 1915-20 (photo illustration)

Sewell's great challenge in building the Army War College was the site conditions at the end of the peninsula. Preliminary plans had to be revised when trenching showed that the point had been filled with a mosaic of different fill materials and foundations of former buildings when the point had served as the arsenal. To support the buildings along "General's Row," Sewell turned to a new device—reinforced concrete pilings. Learning of the untried process, he negotiated a contract with the local licensee. Through weeks of trial and error, Sewell worked out the best method of using the pilings, then built the homes upon them. In 1906 Sewell received the American Society of Civil Engineers' Norman Medal for his paper on innovative reinforced concrete design.[18]

Sewell was placed in charge of constructing the new Agriculture Department Building on May 2, 1903. He oversaw the construction of the Agriculture Department's two laboratory wings (its connecting administration building was not erected until

Army War College under construction, July 1906. Designed by the architectural firm of McKim, Mead, and White, the Office of Public Buildings and Grounds built the war college building at the tip of Greenleaf's Point on the site of an old arsenal.
Courtesy National War College

Officers quarters at Fort McNair, June 1905. Quarters 2 and 3 are nearing completion and the remaining thirteen quarters on the west side of the post are complete. The Chiefs of Engineers have lived in Quarters 9 since the 1980s.
Office of History, Corps of Engineers

1927–30). Construction was delayed until the site was chosen and Sewell was involved in those negotiations. For more than two years congressional committees, the Secretary of Agriculture, and even President Roosevelt debated the relative merits of north and south Mall sites for the building. Sewell often acted as a go-between among the interested parties. Once the site on the Mall's higher south side was decided in February 1905 at a conference held in the Philadelphia office of the building's architects Rankin, Kellogg & Crane, the problem was how to situate it on its steeply graded block. McKim represented the Senate Park Commission's view and Bernard Green and Sewell represented the Corps because the siting and heights of the buildings under their charge would be materially affected. The decision was that the Agriculture Department Building should be built in a depression excavated ten feet below grade in order to conform to the Mall's overall grade proposed by the Senate Park Commission in its 1902 plan. At the February meeting it was decided that Sewell should convince the Department of Agriculture to accept the change. Sewell and McKim were allies in establishing the parameters for the Mall's present and future buildings.[19]

Sewell saw the laboratory wings of the Agriculture Department completed and was promoted to major on June 9, 1907. Six months later he resigned from the Army (on January 31, 1908) to become vice president (president in 1919) of the Alabama Marble Company. Sewell's resignation in mid-career was unusual among the elite Corps of Engineers. Like many other former engineers, Sewell was called back to active service

during World War I when he was named a Colonel of Engineers and after which he received the Distinguished Service Medal, and was named an officer in the French Legion of Honor and received the Belgium Order of Leopold. Sewell's last major professional contribution was as director of exhibits at the Century of Progress Exposition, held in Chicago in 1931.[20]

THE CORPS AND THE AMERICAN INSTITUTE OF ARCHITECTS

At the turn of the twentieth century, the Corps and members of the AIA (by no means the majority of Americans who worked as architects) increasingly collaborated on major projects in and near Washington. The AIA had established five percent of a project's total costs as the minimum fee its members should charge and was trying to enforce this rate for government projects. The government argued in turn that Corps engineers actually performed many of the services normally included in architects' fees. The Agriculture Department Building's architects, Lord & Hewlett, refused to sign the three and one-half percent contract proffered by the government and were replaced by Rankin, Kellogg & Crane of Philadelphia. While working together to ensure that the Mall's first two buildings would follow the Senate Park Commission's plan regarding building and grading lines,

Construction of the Department of Agriculture Laboratory B on the Mall, July 1905. After lengthy discussions, the department's laboratories were built on the higher south side of the Mall. In order to preserve the Senate Park Commission's plan for the siting and scale of buildings, the engineers built the building in a ten-foot depression that can be seen in this photograph.
National Archives no. 16-C-2-18

147

Sewell, Green (who was superintending the construction of the Natural History Museum), and McKim discussed in detail the issue of architects' fees.[21]

On April 18, 1904, McKim wrote Green, "our own agreement with the Government, in the work of the Army War College at Washington Barracks, has proved satisfactory both to the Government and to ourselves." He noted the three requirements of his firm's contract with the Army:

> *(1) 'To be charged with all questions of plan, location, disposition and general arrangement of buildings and grounds.*
>
> *(2) To prepare the preliminary studies, working drawings, details and specifications necessary for the construction of the building in accordance with the requirements of the War Department, and under the direction of the Chief of Engineers.*
>
> *(3) We should further expect to furnish such supervision and periodical inspection of the work, in process of erection, as we should find necessary to ascertain whether it was being executed in conformity with the design and specifications, approved by the Chief of Engineers, and the Secretary of War.'*[22]

McKim then compared "supervision" of a building's construction with its "superintendence," which he understood was to be done by the Corps. The superintendent was the purchasing agent in charge of engineering issues relating to drainage, heating, lighting, and plumbing, and inspected materials and workmanship, with some supervision allowed the architects.[23]

Surprising to everyone at the time, the twentieth century began with a sudden lessening of rancor between the architectural profession and the Corps of Engineers. Roosevelt's involvement in the Senate Park Commission's design and early implementation efforts included his Secretary of War, Elihu Root, also a cosmopolitan New Yorker and a member of the Century Club. There the country's leading artists mixed freely with its political and business leaders. Roosevelt and Root met McKim and other architects, who increasingly were seeking government work, at the Century Club. Roosevelt and Root themselves may have asked that the relative responsibilities of architects and Corps engineers working together on government projects be clarified, or McKim may have taken the initiative.

In 1902 the AIA invited Colonel John Biddle, the Engineer Commissioner, and Sewell to address its annual meeting. Biddle welcomed the architects to Washington and

National Museum (later the Smithsonian's Museum of Natural History) under construction, March 1909. The dome and columns are partially completed and the stone slabs for the stairs encased in their wood shipping crates seen in the foreground.

outlined the nature of his professional concerns in the age of skyscrapers, building codes, and private interests versus public convenience. Sewell's lengthy paper, on the contrary, addressed the issue that most concerned the AIA: "The Relation of the Architect and Engineer to the Design and Erection of Government Buildings." McKim, as the AIA's new president, introduced Sewell as "a master builder for the Government, a worthy successor of Casey and companion of Green, who aims to build for all time, as the Roman constructors impressed themselves on civilization." Sewell advocated a simple system applicable to all departments of government because "there is much complaint on the score of artistic merit, or structural excellence, or economical execution in many of the buildings erected under any of the existing [government] systems." His system was one that echoed the opinions of many in the architectural profession: "The engineer should be a Government official, with authority to disburse funds and make contracts; the architect should be in private practice."[24]

"The engineer should be a Government official, with authority to disburse funds and make contracts; the architect should be in private practice."

In 1903 McKim drafted a long memorandum titled, "An Architect's Service and Remuneration," in which he quoted several reports on the construction of government buildings. Sewell's November 3, 1903, report for the Government Printing Office calculated the Corps' office expenses at six and six-tenths percent of the building's total cost. "This is exclusive of the cost of experts in heating, ventilation, plumbing, electrical installation, and his own salary," McKim noted. Bernard Green had argued with McKim that "compensation of architects must be very moderate under Government employment" because the government paid all of its skilled and professional employees less than what they could make in the private world. He felt that there was an "acknowledged honor and prestige obtained from government employment in professional fields" and that a law should fix architects' fees at four percent for government work independent of the quality of the architect. McKim and other AIA members disagreed, partly because they used their own staffs for work that was then duplicated by members of the Corps. Green's solution was a new "Office of Construction of Public Buildings, District of Columbia," which would have the authority to select architects as well as have total supervision of all aspects of the construction of new buildings.[25]

GRANT MEMORIAL

The Grant Memorial Commission was established by Congress on February 23, 1901, and an unprecedented $2.5 million was appropriated for Grant's Memorial in comparison to the $2 million appropriated later for the Lincoln Memorial. General Grenville M. Dodge,

president of the Society of the Army of the Tennessee, chaired the commission, and its members were Rhode Island Senator George Peabody Wetmore and Secretary of War Elihu Root. From the outset, the commission planned "a statue or memorial," but prior to deciding on a memorial design it proposed locations either immediately south of the State, War and Navy Building, or on the northern part of the Ellipse. The sudden proliferation of commissions charged with Washington's development fostered conflicts. By June 3, 1901, three months after its initial meeting, the Senate Park Commission planned a huge triumphal arch dedicated to Grant to terminate the Mall's west axis at the Potomac River's edge. On June 7 Root convinced the Grant Memorial Commission to delay deciding on a site until all the design entries (anticipated to be sculptural in character) were received. The entries were not due for another ten months.[26]

About the same time, Root asked the Senate Park Commission to act as consultants to the Grant Memorial Commission, the two commissions having conflicting ideas about the location and character of the memorial to Grant. Daniel Burnham, chair of the Senate Park Commission, lobbied Root via a letter in late August, arguing that the Potomac

Park site for the Grant Memorial was one of the plan's "five great points." McKim followed up with a meeting with Root six days later on August 28, and reported that the secretary was personally in favor of the Mall site for the Grant Memorial but would not oppose Dodge, unwilling to "over-ride a man so near the end of his career, whose public services entitled him to such consideration." Moving the Grant Memorial to the Mall would have nullified the Grant Memorial Commission's competition and undoubtedly caused concern in Congress, which had appropriated a quarter of a million dollars for it. In late November 1901 McKim, the Mall's principal designer, decided to move the Grant Memorial to the foot of Capitol Hill just a month before the Senate Park Commission's plan was to be unveiled on January 1, 1902. This decision led to repositioning the Lincoln Memorial (also originally conceived as a triumphal arch), first located south of the White House on the far side of the Tidal Basin.[27]

On February 4, 1903, a design by the young team composed of sculptor Henry M. Shrady and architect Edward Pearce Casey was selected from among twenty-seven entrants in the Grant Memorial competition. In 1901 Root suggested that statues of General Philip Sheridan and General William T. Sherman be added as pendants to the figure of Grant. Shrady, however, chose to represent Sheridan and Sherman via multi-figure groups of artillery and cavalry, adding two relief panels depicting infantry on the pedestal base of the equestrian figure of Grant, and four recumbent lions, all modeled in clay, initially cast in plaster, and finally cast in bronze.[28]

The competition was contested, the choice of the former Botanic Garden as the site was assailed, and Shrady's relatively frail constitution led to repeated delays in meeting deadlines, all challenges that a succession of Corps officers successfully met, beginning with Theodore Bingham and ending with Clarence O. Sherrill. Bingham secured the Corcoran Gallery's exhibition space to display the entries, made arrangements for a second, limited competition, and reported to Root that Shrady's sense of personal and professional decorum was superior to that of Charles Henry Niehaus, the second-place contender. Shrady began working in February 1903, although the site had not yet been finalized. His 1903 contract had two financially burdensome stipulations—the posting of a $250,000 bond to ensure the project's completion, and incremental payments based on completion of plaster casts of each section. In 1910, with the help of Colonel Cosby, Shrady had the latter requirement

Designed by sculptor Henry M. Shrady, the central figure of the composition—the bronze equestrian statue of Grant—weighs 10,700 pounds and with its pedestal is forty feet high. The statue was hoisted atop its pedestal in 1919.
Library of Congress, Prints and Photographs Division, Lot 12654-5

Colonel William W. Harts (shown as Brig. Gen.). As Officer in Charge of Public Buildings and Grounds, Col. Harts played an important and delicate role in the design and construction of the Lincoln Memorial.

Office of History, Corps of Engineers

changed to the completion of the clay models. Casey's architectural setting was erected in 1908 and the four lions and eight candelabrum were installed shortly thereafter; the artillery group (the largest and most complex bronze cast to that date in the United States) was not put in place until 1911.[29]

By 1914 the Grant Memorial Commission was questioning Shrady about repeated delays. Shrady wrote to the executive officer of that commission, Colonel William W. Harts: "I am afraid Gen. Dodge [chairman of the commission] does not quite appreciate the great task before me." Colonel Harts, acting in his role as secretary of the Commission of Fine Arts, wrote its sculptor member, Daniel Chester French, asking him to visit Shrady's studio and report on his progress. French's reply to Harts echoed Shrady's assertion. Harts then wrote Dodge that the monument could not be unveiled before the spring of 1916. But Dodge remained impatient and Harts was forced to continue pressuring Shrady. Early in 1916 the Cavalry Group was placed on its pedestal and Shrady's family said Washington "officials" stopped "hounding" him. When the figure of Grant was raised on its tall pedestal in 1919, the central group was nearly forty feet high. "Shrady's daughter recalled that her father's government patrons had instructed him to make the Grant larger than the *Victor Emanuel*,…but that he had decided to make it two inches shorter for two reasons; in deference to the Italian workmen he employed to assist him in his studio as he enlarged the model to full size, and because he wanted his work to be distinguished by its merits, rather than by its size." The massive Victor Emmanuel II Monument on the north side of Rome's Capitoline Hill, dedicated to the first king of the united Italy, had been constructed between 1885 and 1911.

When the two relief panels depicting the infantry had not been added to the base of the Grant statue by June 1921, Colonel Clarence O. Sherrill, new Officer in Charge of Public Buildings and Grounds, wrote Shrady that if they were not finished by October, another sculptor would be hired to complete them. Sherrill reminded Charles Moore of the Commission of Fine Arts, who intervened on the sculptor's behalf, that Shrady's contract was extended ten times. Shrady hired a young sculptor, Edmund Amateis, to work on the relief panels, but he was unable to complete them. The monument was unveiled without them and the panels were not added until 1924. When the unfinished sculpture was unveiled on Grant's birthday, April 27, 1922, Shrady was already in the hospital with a fatal illness. The physical and psychological stress of creating one of America's greatest sculptural works, and the difficulties he encountered dealing with the Washington bureaucracy, are cited as the cause of his death at the age of forty-nine.[30]

LINCOLN MEMORIAL

In 1911 President William Howard Taft signed a bill establishing the Lincoln Memorial Commission, which he chaired. Its six other members were all congressmen, including Illinoisan Joseph Cannon, one of the bill's sponsors. This commission was a departure from others instituted to bring about Washington buildings and sculpture because the Secretary of War was not included. The Corps' particularly broad involvement in the Lincoln Memorial, however, was legislated in other ways. The major decision taken at the commission's first meeting on March 4, 1911, was to require the newly-formed Commission of Fine Arts (approved May 17, 1910) to advise on the "location, plan, and designs" of the Lincoln Memorial. The act establishing the Fine Arts Commission required that all federal commissions proposing buildings or sculpture in Washington consult the new commission.[31]

Three of the original seven congressionally appointed members of the Commission of Fine Arts had been instrumental in the formation and execution of the Senate Park Commission's plan of 1902: architect Daniel H. Burnham, landscape architect Frederick Law Olmsted, Jr., and layman Charles Moore, McMillan's trusted secretary. Its other members were respected American artists, and its secretary managed day-to-day operations, advised its members about pending and current legislation, and communicated recommendations to pertinent government officials. From June 17, 1910, the secretary of the Commission of Fine Arts was *ex officio* the Corps Officer in Charge of Public Buildings and Grounds. The first four secretaries of the Commission, who served during the creation of the Lincoln Memorial from 1910 to 1922, were all Army Engineers.[32]

At its second meeting on July 25, 1911, the Lincoln Memorial Commission chose a secretary and appointed the *ex officio* Engineer Officer in Charge of Public Buildings and Grounds as its disbursing officer. Colonel Spencer Cosby (1867–1962) held both positions until October 1, 1913; at the August 8, 1911, meeting of the Lincoln Memorial Commission, the engineer officer's responsibilities were increased to "executive and disbursing officer." Thus, duties at both levels of responsibility for achieving the Lincoln Memorial—that of influencing and communicating decisions about its design and that of managerial and construction oversight—were given to Cosby and his successors.

Choosing a design for the Lincoln Memorial was tied directly to the selection of its site, a rancorous process because Cannon opposed the Senate Park Commission's proposed site that was adopted by the Commission of Fine Arts. Cannon opposed the Park Commission from its founding because McMillan bypassed the House Appropriations Committee when Cannon was its chairman. Moreover, Cannon could not imagine that an

September 1, 1914

March 1, 1915

ca. May 1916

CONSTRUCTION OF THE LINCOLN MEMORIAL

Because the memorial was located on fill material dredged from the Potomac, its foundations had to be driven about 100 feet to bedrock. The tops of some of the 122 steel and concrete cylinders that supported the memorial are visible in September 1914. By May 1916 the memorial's columns were being assembled. As the war in Europe neared its end, the memorial was approaching completion.

July 1, 1916

July 1, 1918

area he first had known as a tidal marsh, and later as a desolate field of rubble after the Corps' reclamation operations of the 1880s, could ever be made appropriately beautiful to commemorate Lincoln.

A public competition for the Lincoln Memorial was expected and would have been normal for such an important structure, but in August 1911 the Commission of Fine Arts decided to select the young architect Henry Bacon (1866–1924), well respected among architects but without a national reputation. At the August 22, 1911, meeting of the Lincoln Memorial Commission, Cannon had enough votes to pass a resolution allowing the Executive and Disbursing Officer, with the chairman's approval, to contract with New York architect John Russell Pope to make designs for the Lincoln Memorial on two alternate sites. The resolution further authorized Pope to "make use of the office force of the Superintendent of the Capitol Building and Grounds."[33]

Thus Cosby oversaw a limited quasi-competition for removing the Lincoln Memorial from its Mall site, favored by one commission for which he was the executive officer and opposed by another for which he was the secretary and executive officer. The engineer favored Bacon's appointment as architect, and the Mall site, the position adopted by President Taft, one of the Senate Park Commission's staunchest supporters when he was Secretary of War and the creator of the Commission of Fine Arts in 1910. As chair of the Lincoln Memorial Commission, Taft was required to carry out any majority resolution and Cosby was required to implement its injunctions. For the next several months, Cosby attended the meetings of both commissions and was privy to their conflicting points of views and strategies, drew upon Army Engineers to gather data about the alternate sites, and communicated this information, as well as some of the changing political scene, to the architects and the various commission members.[34]

Public and professional opinion was divided over the designs but when the Lincoln Memorial Commission met on January 22, 1912, it was to debate the site and not the relative merits of the designs. Cannon was joined by Speaker of the House, James Beauchamp Clark of Missouri, in supporting first one and then the other of the alternate sites. The meeting ended with the resolution that the Commission of Fine Arts be consulted about erecting an obelisk dedicated to Lincoln similar to the Washington Monument "on a suitable site in the District of Columbia" when the members could not agree on any of the three sites under consideration. The Commission of Fine Arts rejected the idea of an obelisk and voted to retain the Mall site, inviting both Bacon and Pope to refine their designs to fit in West Potomac Park. Speaker Clark's response to his and Cannon's defeat on the site was to revive the popular idea of the Lincoln Memorial Highway between Washington and Gettysburg, Pennsylvania, one of the earliest ideas of how to memorialize Lincoln. The American Automobile Association was their ally in this protracted effort.[35]

In order to protect Bacon's building on the Mall, Glenn Brown of the AIA informed Congress that the highway would cost $34 million to construct and $3 million annually to maintain in comparison to the $2 million appropriated for the Lincoln Memorial. The memorial road association countered that the construction cost would be $1.5 million. The authoritative voice that decided the issue to the satisfaction of Congress was that of Major William V. Judson (1865–1923), Washington's Engineer Commissioner from 1909 to 1913. From his experience building roads in Puerto Rico and knowledge of Hains's survey for a memorial route to Mount Vernon, Judson informed Congress that the Gettysburg road would cost more than $20 million to build and "considerably over $1,000,000 for annual maintenance. The estimate of cost covers no ornamental features of any kind, not even trees."[36]

Bacon and Pope presented their revised designs to the Commission of Fine Arts on March 22 and 23 and to the Lincoln Memorial Commission on March 28. The Commission of Fine Arts preferred Bacon's design, but the Lincoln Memorial Commission could not agree then nor when they met again on April 10. Six days later, however, the vote was four-to-two in favor of Bacon's design. On December 4, 1912, with one dissenting vote, the Senate approved the resolution to build Bacon's Lincoln Memorial at the west end of the Mall and on January 29, 1913, the resolution passed both houses of Congress. Cosby's role then changed from intermediary and facilitator in this intensely political and cultural battle to supervisor of construction. Until he was relieved on September 10, Cosby reviewed foundation blueprints made by Bacon's engineer, L. J. Lincoln, and changed the concrete aggregate formula in the specifications to agree with Lincoln's calculations.[37]

On September 10, 1913, the day bids for the foundations were opened, Colonel William W. Harts replaced Cosby on the various commissions overseeing the Lincoln Memorial. He was immediately embroiled in a dispute about whether the Secretary of War or the president of the Lincoln Memorial Commission was authorized to award contracts. "It is understood that Mr. Taft is of the opinion that the commission has the power to award the contract, and that the Secretary's [of War] duties were merely perfunctory." The Attorney General ruled that the Secretary of War alone had the authority to award contracts while the Lincoln Memorial Commission had the power to select the design and oversee its construction. The *Washington Evening Star* viewed this as a business matter and urged that re-advertising for bids not cause delay in the memorial's construction. Bacon wrote Harts: "I feel as if I had been drawn through twenty knot holes, each one smaller than the previous one, and if the process had been kept up much longer, I should have been smaller mentally, morally and physically than the longest knitting needle in Christendom."[38]

During his four years as Officer in Charge of Public Buildings and Grounds, Harts presided over the Lincoln Memorial's construction from sub-foundations to carving the friezes. Lincoln Memorial scholar Christopher A. Thomas noted, "The Lincoln Memorial appears to be a peripheral temple standing on a hill, but this is a calculated deception, since the building is really more like the top story of a skyscraper that is buried for most of its height." The sub-foundations contain 122 circular concrete piers surrounded by steel cylinders that were driven down to bedrock 100 feet below the surface and anchored to it by reinforcing bars; this method was suggested by one of the contractors who submitted bids. This construction method had been used to erect piers of bridges, but not for dry-land construction. The upper foundations are concrete columns—some hollow and some reinforced—whose arched tops provide the platform on which the memorial's floor sits forty-five feet above the ground. The foundations were of great import because the memorial's thirty-six columns representing the states in the Union—ignoring Southern secession when Lincoln was president—were composed of 456 drums, each weighing tons. The total weight of the marble superstructure was calculated at 11,400 tons. Harts approved the Colorado Yule marble, more expensive than eastern marble, for the Lincoln Memorial's superstructure because it was the best material and the quarry was able to cut the large blocks Bacon wanted.[39]

The mutual respect of several urbane men—Moore, Harts, Bacon, and sculptor Daniel Chester French—made the Lincoln Memorial a masterpiece. Like Shrady, sculptor of the Grant Memorial, French personally spent more than he earned to produce the seated Lincoln because he made repeated sketch models in varying poses and increased the size until the figure fit perfectly into the space Bacon created for it. The original contract called for a ten-foot-tall bronze statue but French determined that a nineteen-foot-tall marble one was the only solution. When Harts did not reply immediately to his request to amend the contract, French wrote Moore that Harts "has a laudable ambition to build the entire Monument within the appropriation." Working with the Lincoln Memorial Commission, Harts wrote a supplemental contract for $43,000 to cover the additional cost of the marble carving company that turned French's model into the final

> *"I feel as if I had been drawn through twenty knot holes, each one smaller than the previous one, and if the process had been kept up much longer, I should have been smaller mentally, morally and physically than the longest knitting needle in Christendom."*

> *"The Lincoln Memorial appears to be a peripheral temple standing on a hill, but this is a calculated deception, since the building is really more like the top story of a skyscraper that is buried for most of its height."*

sculpture.[40] Although construction continued during World War I, the memorial would not be finished until near its end.

In his memoirs, Harts noted his role in the creation of the Reflecting Pool between the Lincoln Memorial and the Washington Monument.

> *In one of the early laws it had been prohibited to build any lake or lagoon in Potomac Park simply because Speaker Cannon [elected Speaker during the 58th Congress in 1903]...did not like them and thought it would be unwarranted as an expense. But when I excavated for the soil [to fill in around the memorial's raised foundations], water came in and made a lagoon anyway. One day, when Mr. Cannon was visiting the Memorial before it was quite finished as we stood on the steps looking toward the Washington Monument, I asked him why he objected to the lagoon which was an architectural feature already of much beauty....He chewed his cigar for a few moments and then said "The trouble with you fellows is that you start your kindergarten too late." This was quite an admission for him to make of his earlier mistakes. Now the Lincoln Memorial in its majestic beauty justifies all the struggle to select this memorial instead of a highway to Gettysburg.[41]*

Harts (1866–1961) was born in Springfield, Illinois, the son of a lawyer whose family had emigrated from Bavaria in 1709. He attended Princeton University from 1884 to 1885 but left to finish his education at West Point. When Harts was selected as military aide to the president in 1913, and automatically placed in charge of public buildings and grounds in Washington, he already had an eventful and varied career of postings from the Atlantic to the Pacific coasts.[42]

In his annual report for 1916, Harts outlined the twenty-six duties assigned to the Officer in Charge of Public Buildings and Grounds, the ongoing care of existing government buildings and parks, and the supervision of newly-launched projects—a variety of monuments, bridges, and buildings. His vivid account of the duties of the president's military aide, ranging from significant to menial, is an excellent record of how the city's military, political, diplomatic, and civilian populations interacted socially. His duties at the White House were "often trying and annoying...[b]ut my position likewise gave me a great prestige. I had to arrange the great receptions, introduce guests to the President on almost all occasions, lead the march to the State dinners, select military and naval aides for White

"'The trouble with you fellows is that you start your kindergarten too late.'...Now the Lincoln Memorial in its majestic beauty justifies all the struggle to select this memorial instead of a highway to Gettysburg."

House receptions, musicales and teas." Conversely, Harts "was responsible for the machinery of the parking of private carriages, at coming functions, the heating and lighting of the building[,] interior decorations and flowers, maintenance of furniture, the cloak-rooms, the green-houses, the guarding and care of the grounds, the upkeep of the building itself, payment of servants and many other items of the drudgery class." The simultaneous involvement of the Corps' officers in the multiple layers of official Washington that Harts described helped them speak with authority in all their positions.

ROCK CREEK PARK

The Senate Park Commission's proposed changes to Washington in 1902 were broad ranging in their extent because Senator McMillan intended the plan to coordinate the government's ongoing projects relating to infrastructure as well as to the city's future expansion. The Senate and House Committees on the District of Columbia, working with the Commissioners of the District of Columbia, were its de facto city government, a situation that McMillan balanced with his responsibilities as a member of Congress. Serious citizen involvement in Washington's municipal affairs had begun with securing amenities that other municipalities were providing for their residents. In early July 1866 a group of Washington residents, including Montgomery Meigs, sent a petition to Congress, asking that "some public park within a convenient distance of their residences, to which they could resort after the labor of the day, and to which they could send their wives and children during the heat of the day, for relief from the heated and impure air of the city" be undertaken.

A Senate resolution of July 18, 1866, instructed the Secretary of War to "make preliminary surveys and maps of certain tracts of land adjoining or near this city for the purposes of a public park and also a suitable site for a Presidential mansion." Major Nathaniel Michler was detailed by the Chief of Engineers to this task, and in his report he recommended separate sites to fit each of these purposes. He noted that the alternative of combining them would not be a problem, considering that "so many splendid situations present themselves from which to make a selection." For the public park he recommended part of the valley of Rock Creek and its tributaries, setting aside from 1,800 to 2,540 acres at a cost to Congress of between $360,000 and $580,000. "With its charming drives and walks, its hills and dales, its pleasant valleys and deep ravines, its primeval forests and cultivated fields, its running waters, its rocks clothed with rich ferns and mosses, its repose and tranquility, its light and shade, its ever-varying shrubbery, its beautiful and extensive views, the locality is already possessed with all the features necessary for the object in

"[M]y position likewise gave me a great prestige."

"With its charming drives and walks, its hills and dales, its pleasant valleys and deep ravines, its primeval forests and cultivated fields, its running waters,...the locality is already possessed with all the features necessary for the object in view."

view." He suggested starting the construction of the public park "as soon as practicable. It is a grand and beautiful undertaking and should be prosecuted with the greatest energy."[43]

Missouri senator Benjamin Brown, chairman of the Senate Committee on Public Buildings and Grounds, introduced a bill in the Senate in early 1867 that called for establishment of a park within the boundaries suggested by Michler. The bill provided for the establishment of a commission to acquire the necessary land, and it named Michler and then Brevet Major General Meigs to investigate further. The bill was tabled and, as Brown left the Senate at the end of that term, not taken up again. In 1880 assistant engineer commissioner Captain Richard L. Hoxie proposed another plan for Rock Creek valley. To ensure a clean and plentiful supply of fresh water for the growing city of Washington, Hoxie recommended damming Rock Creek to make a 1,300-acre lake above Georgetown, its shores to be used as a park. Banker W. W. Corcoran, Supreme Court Justice William Strong, and Josiah Dent, representing the city's businessmen, futilely urged creation of the park again in 1883. Additional legislative attempts to create the park failed in 1884, 1886, 1888, and 1889.[44]

On Thanksgiving Day 1888, the wealthy and well-connected Charles C. Glover, a partner in the banking firm of Riggs and Company, invited four influential friends on an outing into the area of the proposed park. After horseback riding through the country, these men agreed to work to get the park authorized. Glover's guests were his business partners James M. Johnson and Thomas Hyde, lawyer Calderon Carlisle, and Assistant Engineer Commissioner Captain Thomas W. Symonds. Not long after this excursion, Johnson and Carlisle drafted new legislation under the direction of Glover. Glover had a friend and ally in Crosby S. Noyes, editor of the *Evening Star*. In a December 1888 editorial Noyes wrote, "The project of converting the picturesque Rock Creek Valley into a public park has long been cherished by thoughtful citizens as the one thing needed to justify the claim of Washington to a rank among the most beautiful and attractive capital cities of the world." The following January 11, a citizen's meeting at the Atlantic Building elected an economically and politically well-connected executive committee to lobby Congress and organize public support for the park. The committee included Glover and Noyes.[45]

Extensive lobbying led to another attempt, in January 1889, to bring a park bill before the House. Its failure led to an effort to add the park to the then-pending National Zoological Park legislation. This had the effect of forcing the passage of the zoo bill, for park opponents agreed to authorize the zoo if park proponents agreed to kill the Rock Creek Park rider. The zoo was authorized on March 2, 1889, and with this partial victory

Park watchman in uniform at the beginning of the twentieth century. The Office of Public Buildings and Grounds argued in its 1904 report that the watchmen had the duties and responsibilities of policemen and should be formally called policemen. The watchmen patrolled the public parks, and each year the office provided statistics on the number of people arrested and their alleged crimes.
National Archives no. 42-SPB-93

Willow Tree Park, 1918

Garfield Park, 1910

THE OFFICE OF PUBLIC BUILDINGS AND GROUNDS' EFFORTS TO IMPROVE THE DISTRICT'S PUBLIC RESERVATIONS OFTEN FOCUSED ON LEISURE-TIME AMENITIES FOR WASHINGTON'S CITIZENS. THE 1910 CONCRETE WADING POOL BUILT IN CAPITOL HILL'S GARFIELD PARK AT SOUTH CAROLINA AVENUE AND 3RD AND E STREETS, SE, DOUBLED AS A FOUNTAIN. NEIGHBORHOOD ACTIVISTS SECURED GARFIELD PARK, ONCE SLATED TO CONTAIN A RAILROAD ROUNDHOUSE, AS A CHILD-FRIENDLY PLACE AS CORPS ENGINEERS GRADUALLY MOVED AN EXISTING PLAYGROUND TO A SHADIER CORNER, INSTALLED CEMENT AND GRAVEL WALKS, LAID OUT A TENNIS COURT, AND ERECTED TWELVE GAS LAMPS.

IN MARCH 1914 THE DISTRICT COMMISSIONERS CONDEMNED AN ALLEY BETWEEN 3RD AND 4½ AND B AND C STREETS, SW, AND TRANSFERRED IT TO THE OFFICE OF PUBLIC BUILDINGS AND GROUNDS WHO CREATED WILLOW TREE PARK. OVER THE NEXT SEVERAL YEARS, CORPS ENGINEERS PLANTED TREES, BUILT A WADING POOL, AND ERECTED A NEW LODGE AND "PUBLIC COMFORT STATION," AND DISTRICT COMMISSIONERS ENCLOSED IT WITHIN AN IRON FENCE. THE SITE OF THE PARK IS NOW OCCUPIED BY THE U.S. DEPARTMENT OF HEALTH AND HUMAN SERVICES BUILDING.

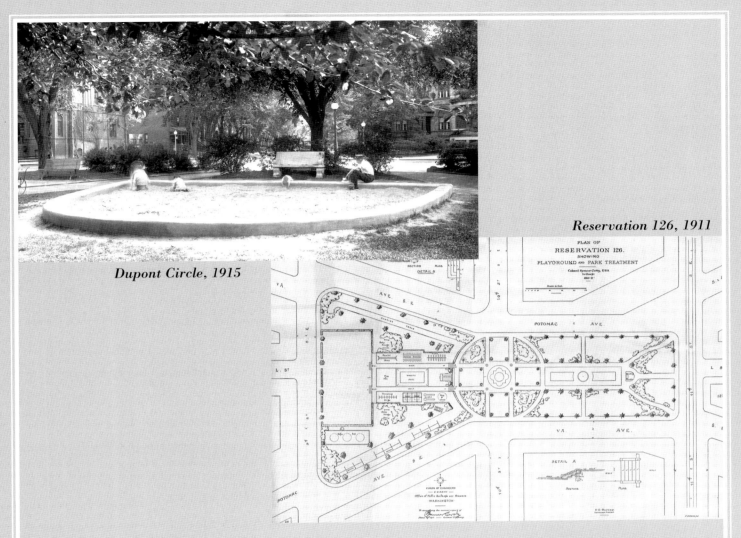

Dupont Circle, 1915

Reservation 126, 1911

CHILDREN LIVING NEAR DUPONT CIRCLE IN 1915 ENJOYED FOUR NEW SANDBOXES, TWO OF WHICH WERE REPLACED THE FOLLOWING YEAR BY ONES OF "MORE RECENT DESIGN." ALL THE NEIGHBORS BENEFITTED FROM THE CORPS' 1916 PLANTING OF NEARLY 2,000 TREES, SHRUBS, AND ROSE BUSHES.

IN 1911 THE OFFICE OF PUBLIC BUILDINGS AND GROUNDS IMPROVED THE PARK AT RESERVATION 126. LOCATED AT THE INTERSECTION OF VIRGINIA AND POTOMAC AVENUES, SE, THE WESTERN PART OF THE PARK RECEIVED A NEW PUBLIC PLAYGROUND. THE PUBLIC PLAYGROUNDS ASSOCIATION PROVIDED MANY OF THE FACILITIES INCLUDING A WADING POOL, SAND BOXES, AND A COMFORT STATION. THE OFFICE BUILT A RUNNING TRACK AND PLANTED NUMEROUS TREES AND OTHER PLANTS.

Timber footbridge over Rock Creek Park. This bowstring, or grapevine truss, bridge was located near Beach Drive and illustrates the rustic construction in the park.
Library of Congress, Prints and Photographs Division, LC-H823-B08-021

Glover was able to convince powerful Ohio Senator John Sherman to support the full park. Sherman introduced new legislation in 1890. While his bill passed the Senate at the end of January, it got stuck in the House as objections were raised (not for the first time) that the park was simply a device to aid local land speculators, including Senator Sherman, who owned extensive tracts in the northwest suburbs. The bill narrowly failed a vote in April, but was brought up again in May and passed. A conference committee reconciled the Senate and House versions, the final bill passed both houses, and Benjamin Harrison signed it into law September 27, 1890.[46]

The authorizing legislation set aside an area along both banks of Rock Creek from Klingle Ford Bridge to the district line "as a public park or pleasure ground for the benefit and enjoyment of the people of the United States, to be known by the name of Rock Creek Park."[47] The park was not to exceed two thousand acres nor was its land to cost more than $1.2 million. Half of the land acquisition cost and half of future maintenance and improvement costs for the park were to be paid by the District of Columbia. The legislation established a park commission consisting of the Chief of Engineers, the Engineer Commissioner and three citizens, in this case reporter and Civil War veteran officer Henry V. N. Boynton, Smithsonian Institution secretary Samuel P. Langley, and attorney R. Ross Perry. Major General Thomas L. Casey and Colonel Henry M. Robert (perhaps best known as author of *Robert's Rules of Order*) initially filled the first two roles. Captain William T. Rossell, assistant Engineer Commissioner, served as executive officer to the commission. Secretary Langley was a key figure in the creation of the zoo, and his knowledge of the Rock Creek valley recommended him to the commission charged with establishing the shape and size of the new park.[48]

The commission established a final map of the park by March 1891 and undertook the acquisition of land based on it. Most landowners did not accept the commission's offers for their property, and legal condemnation proceedings were required to obtain the land, which reduced the parcels' size to keep costs below the appropriation. All the land was purchased by mid-April 1892, the park containing just less than 1,606 acres. Rock Creek Park was placed under the joint jurisdiction of the District Commissioners and the Chief of Engineers. These men organized themselves into the Board of Control of Rock

Grant Road Bridge across Broad Branch Creek in Rock Creek Park. Built around 1898, this granite and brick arch bridge twenty-one feet wide and with a ten foot span was one of the earliest bridges that the engineers built in the park.
Library of Congress, Prints and Photographs Division, HAER, DC, WASH, 566-2

Creek Park and assumed control of the reservation on New Year's Day, 1895. Captain Gustav Fieburger was the board's first executive officer, and he had direct responsibility for administering and superintending the park.[49]

The established park was not improved quickly. Despite community petitions and resolutions to the District Commissioners and Congress, the first Congressional appropriation for park maintenance came only in 1899. Through 1912 less than $225,000 had been appropriated in total for park development. What resources were available went primarily to the construction or improvement of roads, bridges, and bridle and footpaths. Existing country roads and trails served as the basis for the Corps of Engineers' efforts to create public access to the park. Captain Lansing H. Beach was largely responsible for initiating the park's road building program in 1897, despite the dearth of funds, and he lessened park labor costs through the use of convict labor. The central role played by Beach and his successor engineers in the creation of Rock Creek's roads led to most of the roads being named after them. The Board of Control named the drive along Rock Creek, which Beach planned and superintended at the turn of the century, in his honor in 1901, while he was Engineer Commissioner.[50]

The *Washington Evening Star* reported on the progress of the park in 1901. "It may be interesting to know…that Rock Creek Park is twice as large as Central Park, upon which Greater New York plumes herself with so much pride, and that in natural beauties Rock Creek

Major General Lansing H. Beach.
Captain Beach served as assistant to
the Engineer Commissioner of the
District of Columbia from 1894 to
1898 and then as Engineer
Commissioner from 1898 to 1901.
He was a popular commissioner and
called the "guardian angel" of
Rock Creek Park, whose main
thoroughfare was named in his
honor. He completed his military
career as Chief of Engineers
from 1920 to 1924.
Office of History, Corps of Engineers

"The dominant
consideration, never to
be subordinated to any
other purpose in dealing
with Rock Creek Park, is
the permanent preservation
of its wonderful natural
beauty, and the making
of that beauty acessible to
people without spoiling the
scenery in the process."

Park is a hundred times much superior to the much vaunted parallelogram on Manhattan Island." The paper described Engineer Commissioner Captain Beach as "the guardian angel" of the park, "the moving spirit in the transformation now in progress, and his effective vicar in the good work has been and is Mr. W. B. Richards, of the District engineer office."[51]

The Senate Park Commission's 1901–02 proposals called for a comprehensive development plan for Rock Creek Park, to prevent piecemeal road and facility building from damaging the landscape. A proposal by the district surveyor in 1916 to create a "Municipal Play Grounds and Recreation Park" within the federal reservation led Chief of Engineers Major General William M. Black to request an assessment from Colonel William W. Harts. Harts, in charge of the Office of Public Buildings and Grounds, pointed out "the urgent need of having a carefully considered plan for the entire park prepared by a competent landscape architect."[52] Black therefore ordered Harts in early 1917 to prepare an overall planning study for the park. Just prior, however, Engineer Commissioner Colonel Charles W. Kutz, Black's colleague on the Board of Control, had contacted Frederick Law Olmsted, Jr. to engage his park-planning services. A contract with Olmsted, although eventually signed, was delayed until May 1917 as the Engineer Commissioner and the Chief of Engineers came to an agreement over whether a civilian firm or a military office was best to plan the park.[53]

The Olmsted brothers' December 1918 final plan began, "The dominant consideration, never to be subordinated to any other purpose in dealing with Rock Creek Park, is the permanent preservation of its wonderful natural beauty, and the making of that beauty acessible to people without spoiling the scenery in the process." Departing from patterns set by Frederick Law Olmsted, Sr.'s plans for Central Park in New York and Frederick Law Olmsted, Jr.'s for Washington's Mall, the firm recommended division of the valley into "use areas" and "growth areas." In the former, recreational features were discreetly introduced; in the latter, the natural forest was to be preserved except for necessary tending to prevent fire and disease. A corridor of natural forms, changing with the seasons, would curve through the densely settled district—principles the park's caretakers followed in developing Rock Creek Park. Before the Olmsted Brothers released their study, Congress acted to integrate the park into the District of Columbia's park system, assigning administration of the park to the Office of Public Buildings and Grounds on July 1, 1918. Army Engineers superintended the construction and maintenance of the structures, roads, and landscape in the park until it was transferred, along with the rest of the city's park system, to the National Park Service in 1933.[54]

The establishment of Rock Creek Park stimulated interest in protecting additional Rock Creek valley lands, particularly the stretch between the zoo and the Potomac River. For two decades beginning in 1889 there were two schools of thought about how to reclaim the lower valley. One, supported in large part by Georgetown business interests west of the creek, called for enclosing the stream and filling in the valley, using the new land for a wide ceremonial parkway. City of Washington interests proposed beautifying the existing valley and placing a scenic drive parallel to the streambed. In 1892 Engineer Commissioner Captain William T. Rossell undertook a congressionally mandated study of the closed valley plan; he proposed constructing a five-foot-high arch over the creek, with landfill over and around it to create useable real estate in the valley. While this land might add to the district's tax base, Rossell found the notion of enclosing the stream "wrong in principal and enormously expensive." In 1901 Beach cited crime in the lower valley as his primary reason for supporting the closed valley plan.[55]

Washington's powerful Board of Trade sponsored proposals in 1889 and 1899 for a scenic parkway in the lower valley. In 1900 Congress again looked into the matter, appropriating funds to hire a professional landscape architect to address the problem of linking West Potomac Park and the zoo. Colonel Theodore Bingham, head of the Office of Public Buildings and Grounds, hired New Yorker Samuel Parsons, Jr., (who had worked on Central Park and was a founder of the American Society of Landscape Architects) to investigate the parkway question, as well as propose plans for a park that would integrate newly reclaimed land south and west of the Washington Monument with the rest of the Mall. Parsons's ambitious plan for connecting the zoo with the Mall, while endorsed by the Chief of Engineers and the Secretary of War, was practically and politically unrealistic because it cut broad swaths through densely populated Washington neighborhoods.[56]

Parsons's parkway and Mall plans were designed to provide wide carriageways, either straight boulevards or along broad curves, because carriage drives were a major form of outdoor entertainment for Washington's elite during the 1890s. In 1900 Bingham proposed two plans for the Mall, both designs opening a central, tree-lined roadway beginning at the foot of Capitol Hill and progressing to a *rond point* encircling the

"Preliminary Design for the Treatment of Rock Creek and Potomac Parkway," 1916, *drawn by James G. Langdon, Office of Public Buildings and Grounds, who had been hired as the Senate Park Commission's draftsman in 1901*
Commission of Fine Arts

THE RESPONSIBILITIES OF THE OFFICE OF PUBLIC BUILDINGS AND GROUNDS EXTENDED TO WASHINGTON'S PUBLIC "RESERVATIONS," INCLUDING ITS MANY TRAFFIC CIRCLES. REPORTS WRITTEN BY CORPS ENGINEERS IN THE NINETEENTH AND TWENTIETH CENTURIES DETAIL GRASS SEED SOWN, SIDEWALKS POURED, WATER MAINS LAID, AND LIGHTING INSTALLED.

IN 1911 THE OFFICE RELANDSCAPED THOMAS CIRCLE AT THE CROSSING OF MASSACHUSETTS AND VERMONT AVENUES AND 14TH STREET, NW.

CORPS ENGINEERS RAISED THE GRADE OF THE CIRCLE, MOVED FOUR CANDELABRA LIGHT POSTS TO IMPROVE THE MAIN VIEWS OF THE CENTRAL STATUE, AND RECONFIGURED FLOWER BEDS. HOPING TO ALLEVIATE TRAFFIC CONGESTION, IN THE 1950S THE DISTRICT'S HIGHWAY DEPARTMENT TUNNELED MASSACHUSETTS AVENUE BENEATH THOMAS CIRCLE AND CUT 14TH STREET THROUGH IT. IN JANUARY 2005 DISTRICT AND FEDERAL AUTHORITIES BEGAN RESTORING THE CIRCLE TO ITS ORIGINAL APPEARANCE AND PROVIDING PEDESTRIAN ACCESS TO IT.

During 1916 the Corps' Office of Public Buildings and Grounds focused on Truxton Circle, which had been located near the intersection of Florida Avenue and North Capitol Street in 1891 as part of the extension of L'Enfant's plan into Washington county. In 1900 Col. Bingham moved a large fountain from Pennsylvania Avenue and 26th Street to Truxton Circle. In 1916 the Corps regraded, relandscaped, and installed seats at the circle's edge. Three decades later, the D.C. Highway Department argued that "the obstacles which it presents to the orderly and rapid flow of twentieth century traffic has made it one of the most inconvenient and hazardous intersections in the metropolitan area" and Truxton Circle was razed in 1947. In 2004, with the support of the Bloomingdale Neighborhood Association, the city's Department of Transportation began studying the feasibility of restoring the circle as part of the revitalization of the North Capitol Street corridor.

Office of History, Corps of Engineers, ARCE 1916

Washington Monument that connected to drives leading to Rock Creek. Bingham's plans also included pleasure drives around the perimeter of Potomac Park, including Hains Point, a feature of both areas today. Early in 1900 Bingham also hired Chicago architect Henry Ives Cobb to execute a design for "suggestions for locating future Government Building in the District of Columbia" that centered on a diagonal avenue through the Mall from the foot of Capitol Hill to the foot of New York Avenue, the terminus of the proposed Memorial Bridge. In all three of these cases, the intimate nature of the Mall's extensive picturesque garden would be preserved while providing drives through it; Bingham opposed the Senate Park Commission's open treatment of the Mall because it destroyed its bucolic character. A pragmatist, either by nature or training, Bingham (like most Washingtonians at the time) thought of the Mall as a pedestrian precinct, a shaded refuge rather than a monumental setting for public buildings.[57] None of these plans, however, would be executed until after World War I.

WASHINGTON AQUEDUCT

Population expansion in the federal city during and after the Civil War led, in the 1870s, to numerous calls for increased capacity in the city's water supply, the infrastructure need that the Corps had initially built and now needed to expand. Montgomery Meigs himself advocated the construction of a second distributing reservoir, reviving an unrealized component of his original 1853 plan. On July 15, 1882, Congress approved two solutions to the water problem. Following a recommendation first put forward by Lieutenant Colonel Thomas L. Casey in 1881, it permitted extension of the Great Falls Dam to the Virginia riverbank, and it authorized a second distributing reservoir and second tunnel from Great Falls. The dam spanned the Potomac by 1886, allowing the level of water above the intake to be controlled for the first time.[58]

Major Garrett J. Lydecker, engineer commissioner from May 1882 until May 1886, was given charge of the aqueduct in August 1882—one month after Congress authorized the new reservoir.[59] To improve water flow to the eastern parts of the city he chose the site of Smith Spring near Howard University for the new storage facility, on high ground east of Rock Creek. Rather than build a covered conduit from the Potomac, as Meigs had done, Lydecker planned to bring water through a deep, twenty-one-thousand-foot-long tunnel under the Rock Creek valley. Expecting favorable conditions that would not require a lined tunnel, Lydecker wrote, "There is no reasonable doubt that this tunnel can be carried through solid rock in a direct line between the terminal points."[60]

"[S]ubstantially the whole and every part of the lining of the tunnel is absolutely and enormously defective."

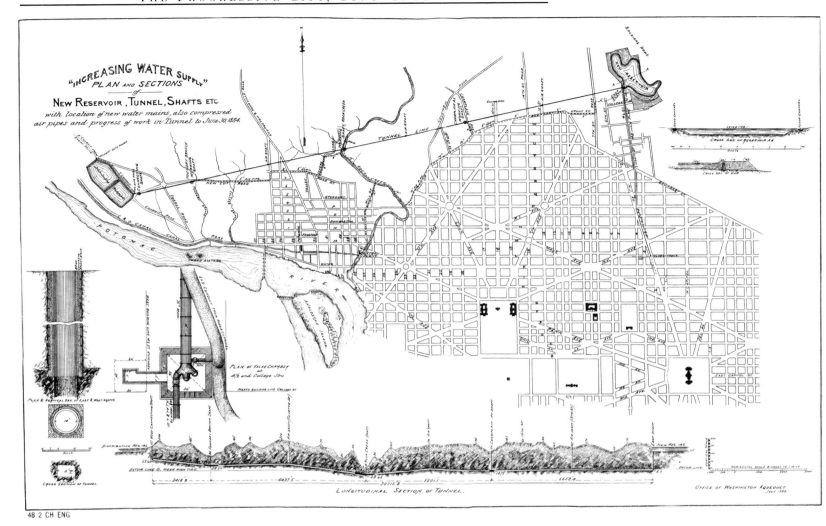

48 2 CH ENG

Numerous difficulties plagued construction of the Washington City Tunnel. Incomplete testing of the rock conditions along the route failed to reveal the poor quality of the rock, and the engineers realized after work began that much of the tunnel would have to be lined, adding significantly to the cost. When a new civilian assistant engineer resurveyed the route in 1885, he discovered misalignments that could have kept the various sections of the tunnel construction from meeting. Shoddy workmanship in the lining of the tunnel and escalating costs led to a congressional investigation of the project beginning in October 1888. At this point, the reservoir was almost done and the mains connecting it to downtown already laid.[61]

A select congressional committee, advised by a "board of three highly qualified civil engineers" that included Joseph M. Wilson of Philadelphia, criticized the contracting practices, management, and construction quality of the project. "It appears beyond all question," the committee's report declared, "that substantially the whole and every part of the lining of the tunnel is absolutely and enormously defective." With evidence of the contractors bribing government inspectors, the committee found Lydecker and his assistants negligent in the

Plan of the New Washington City Tunnel from the Distributing Reservoir (later renamed the Georgetown Reservoir) to the New Reservoir (later named the McMillan Reservoir in honor of Senator James McMillan who during the 1890s worked tirelessly to ensure a clean water supply for Washington), located east of Howard University, 1884
Office of History, Corps of Engineers, ARCE 1883

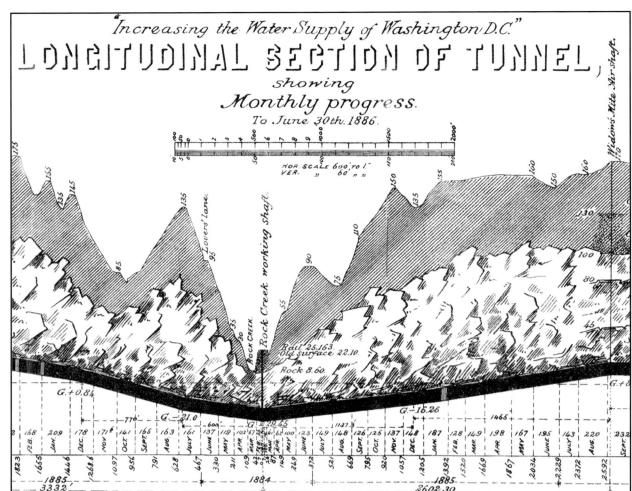

"Longitudinal Section of Tunnel Showing Monthly Progress to June 30th, 1886." This detailed drawing shows the ambitious plan to build a four-mile-long tunnel through the upland sections of the District of Columbia. Poor information on soil conditions and contractor problems led Congress to halt construction of the tunnel in 1888. The Corps resumed work in 1898 and completed the tunnel in 1901.

Office of History, Corps of Engineers, ARCE 1886

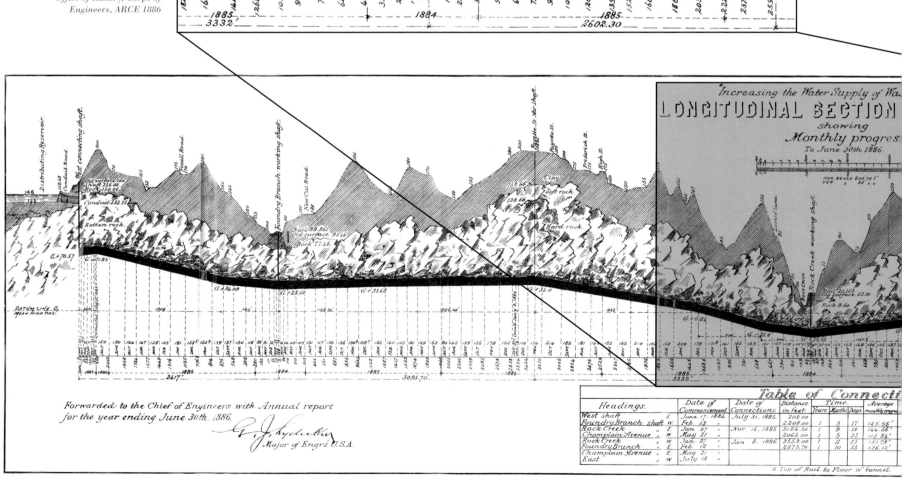

Forwarded to the Chief of Engineers with Annual report for the year ending June 30th, 1886.

Major of Engrs U.S.A.

project's oversight and the tunnel was abandoned. Acknowledging the continued need for better water service to the eastern parts of the city, the board of engineers recommended the speedy installation of additional mains out of the original distributing reservoir. With money approved March 2, 1889, the new officer in charge of the Aqueduct, Lieutenant Colonel George H. Elliot, brought the new pipes into use just over a year later.[62]

The city water was frequently turbid, however, a condition long noted by the officers in charge of the Aqueduct. Although it remained healthier to use than water from the city's numerous wells, its aesthetic qualities drove many citizens back to their wells. Public Health officials felt this preference left the city vulnerable to outbreaks of contagious disease, particularly typhoid fever. The Senate ordered a study of water filtering at the beginning of 1886. Completed by engineer Captain Thomas W. Symons, the study recommended filtration; however Colonel Elliot, in charge of the Aqueduct, did not feel filtration was necessary. Elliot moved, nevertheless, to add sedimentation capacity to the system by bringing the idle receiving reservoir near the Little Falls Branch back into service in 1893–95.[63]

The *Washington Star* commented, "Our nectar of the Alleghenies will, it is asserted, be as bright and clean as liquid diamond. Every time a Washingtonian holds a glass of redeemed Potomac water to his lips, he will say, 'Here's to Colonel Elliott.'" But this

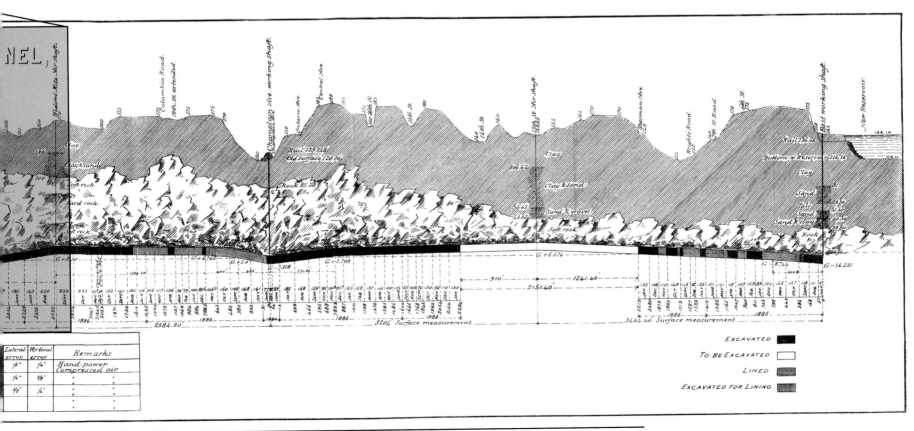

Foundry Branch shaft leading to the tunnel connecting the distributing reservoir and the new reservoir, 1884. The engineers built three shafts at Foundry Branch, Rock Creek, and Champlain Avenue.
Washington Aqueduct Division, Baltimore Engineer District

Section of the Washington City Tunnel under construction in July 1899. The section of the tunnel under Rock Creek was lined with cast-iron when tunnel construction recommenced in 1898.
Washington Aqueduct Division, Baltimore Engineer District

effort had limited effect, and the *Washington Star* printed further comments a year later: "A person of cleanly habits, who knows he is not as dirty as the contents of his tub, hesitates long before he takes his dip....But when it comes to using the stuff as a beverage, the matter takes on even a worse aspect. It is as dark in color as a glass of bock beer, and not nearly as translucent, or anything like as tempting."[64]

Thinking more sedimentation would help, on March 2, 1895, Congress ordered a detailed report on the feasibility of completing the second reservoir and its flawed tunnel. A board of four army and two civil engineers found in favor of the project, and in 1896 the Chief of Engineers asked Congress for money to resume work. Within two years money was appropriated and work resumed at the end of 1898. The tunnel was finished in 1901, and the reservoir was brought into full operation at the beginning of 1902.[65]

The Senate again requested information on filtering the Potomac water in January 1898, and the entire Congress ordered another filtering study in June. Lieutenant

Built to conceal the sluice gates that directed water under Conduit Road (now MacArthur Boulevard) to the tunnel, the gatehouse completed in 1902 was designed to resemble the Corps of Engineers' castle insignia on all four of its facades.
Washington Aqueduct Division, Baltimore Engineer District

Workers at the McMillan plant shoveling sand into a movable ejector during the construction of the slow sand filter plant, 1904. When the plant was in operation, workers shoveled about two inches of dirty sand into movable ejectors, like the one shown here, for transfer to the sand washers. In the background are the round towers used to store clean sand. Now vine-covered, the towers became local landmarks west of North Capitol Street.
Washington Aqueduct Division,
Baltimore Engineer District

Slow sand filter at the McMillan Slow Sand Filter Plant, ca. 1910. Twenty-nine slow sand filters, each one acre in size, filtered water through more than two feet of sand. The piles of clean sand shown here were dumped into the filters through manholes in the roof and distributed evenly over the sand already in place.
Washington Aqueduct Division,
Baltimore Engineer District

McMillan Reservoir with fountain in the foreground. In 1913 the citizens of Michigan paid for a fountain designed by Herbert Adams to honor their former senator. The federal government paid for the base and landscaping designed by Charles Adams Platt who also designed the Freer Gallery on the Mall.
Washington Aqueduct Division,
Baltimore Engineer District

Colonel Alexander M. Miller reported on March 28, 1900, recommending construction of mechanical (or rapid-sand) filters at the new Howard University Reservoir. Local professional and citizen's organizations objected to the chemicals used in this filtration process, and the Senate Committee on the District of Columbia chaired by James McMillan (who had been very involved in public works in Detroit before being elected to Congress in 1889) held hearings on the issue. A subsequent Senate-appointed committee of civilian experts recommended chemical-free slow-sand filtration, and Congress approved construction of such filters on March 1, 1901. This effective filtering system, substantially designed by Miller, was built between the spring of 1903 and the end of 1905. The following year, Secretary of War William Howard Taft ordered the reservoir and new filters named after the late Senator McMillan, who died in 1902.[66]

POTOMAC RIVER FLATS RECLAMATION

In 1897 Washington banker Charles C. Glover, a longtime advocate for the reclamation of the Potomac flats, persuaded Congress to order the 628 acres of land reclaimed by the engineers since the 1880s "forever held and used as a park for the recreation and pleasure of the people."[67] Though land building continued until 1913, the Washington District gradually transferred the reclaimed area to the Office of Public Buildings and Grounds,

Potomac Park looking northeast to Washington Monument with drive along the Tidal Basin, 1906
National Archives no. 77-H-3334F-27

Potomac Park, the Tidal Basin, the Outlet Gate, and Washington Channel from the Washington Monument, 1899. The propagating gardens are in the foreground and the reclaimed land along the Tidal Basin and in East Potomac Park is largely unlandscaped.
National Archives no. 77-H-3048-11

Potomac Park, the Tidal Basin, the Outlet Gate, and Washington Channel from the Washington Monument, 1910. By 1910 the propagating gardens had expanded and new buildings began to appear on the borders of West Potomac Park. Landscaping along the Tidal Basin improved significantly but East Potomac Park remained less improved. The new railroad (1904) and highway (1906) bridges appear in the upper right with the future site of National Airport in the distance.
National Archives no. 66-DC-19

beginning in 1901 with the land between the east side of the Tidal Basin and the monument grounds. Although some improvements had already been done on this land—the District Commissioners built a bathing beach after 1890—construction of a major park in place of the foul marsh had become possible.[68]

Theodore Bingham, Officer in Charge of Public Buildings and Grounds from 1897 to 1903, was an enthusiast convinced that parks improved the health and happiness of the "toiling masses crowded together in cities," and he planned drives, Japanese gardens, nurseries, polo grounds, athletic and military parade fields, and an electric fountain for the Tidal Basin in his grand scheme for the area. In the comparatively small first parcel transferred to his care, Bingham in 1902–03 raised the revetment wall along the Tidal Basin and completed it where the district bathing beach had been. He cleared and graded the area and built a 50-foot-wide macadam drive along the east side of the Basin. (This road opened in October 1903. The Annual Report for 1904 mentioned, "Saturday afternoons between 4 and 6 o'clock, have, by authority of the Chief of Engineers, been set aside for speeding purposes.") Through his efforts, the old two-story house that canal lock keepers had used as a gatehouse was deeded by the company's trustees to the Chief of Engineers for use by the public. Repaired and refurbished, the building became a watchman's lodge. Around it, workmen swept away sheds and mounds of rubbish, built a drive, planted trees, and seeded lawns.[69]

Under Bingham's successors, the Potomac Park area grew in size as district Engineers finished dredge-and-fill operations and transferred newly-made land to the office of buildings and grounds. In November 1903 the engineers added the land between the Tidal Basin and railroad causeway at the end of Long Bridge to the park, and by 1908, when Congress authorized the extension of B Street to the Potomac and the creation of a riverside drive, the rest of

(Above left) Colonel Spencer Cosby (center) with President Woodrow Wilson on the White House north portico prior to Wilson's inauguration, March 4, 1913. Officers in Charge of Public Buildings and Grounds had many duties including leading roles at inaugurations.
Office of History, Corps of Engineers, Cosby Personal Papers

(Above right) Reviewing stand for the inaugural parade, March 4, 1913. From left to right, Col. Spencer Cosby, Mrs. Wilson, Maj. Gen. Leonard Wood (Chief of Staff of the Army), and President Wilson. Cosby had a long association with Washington, serving as Washington District Engineer from 1905 to 1908, briefly in 1908–09 as Engineer Commissioner, and then as Officer in Charge of Public Buildings and Grounds and Military Aide to the President from 1909 to 1913. His thirty-seven year career in the Army ended with his retirement in 1928, and he died in Washington in 1962 at the age of ninety-four.
Office of History, Corps of Engineers, Cosby Personal Papers

Potomac Drive lined with statues from the St. Louis World's Fair, August 1905. As the Washington Engineer District created land in Potomac Park, it turned the new land over to the Office of Public Buildings and Grounds, which built roads and provided landscaping and other attractions.

National Archives no. 77-H-3334F-23

West Potomac Park was under Engineer care. "Construction of driveways, bridle paths, walks, grading and sowing lawn areas, laying water and drain pipe and planting trees and shrubs" continued throughout this time and into the 1910s. The end result was an orderly and scenic park with ample roads and paths, bathing facilities, a boathouse and dock, a nursery, extended propagating gardens, and an athletic field. In 1914, the year Congress officially made Potomac Park part of the D.C. park system and reaffirmed the Chief of Engineers' jurisdiction over it, the engineers improved earlier equestrian facilities and laid out a small golf course. Such recreational amenities have survived into the twenty-first century. Less extensive improvements to East Potomac Park, southeast of Long Bridge, began in 1912, although a comprehensive plan sent to Congress in 1916 proposed substantial facilities for making the park a "public recreation ground." Most of these were never built.[70]

In March 1912 final work began on one of the best-known Potomac Park improvements, as three thousand flowering cherry trees, a gift from the municipality of Tokyo, arrived to replace an earlier shipment that had proven to be diseased. First Lady Helen Herron Taft planted the first one on March 27, and by the end of April the engineers had overseen planting of the remainder around the Tidal Basin, where eleven years of care had created a perfect setting. In 1909 Colonel Spencer Cosby, Engineer Officer in Charge of Public Buildings and Grounds, had suggested that the cherry trees be planted around the Tidal Basin. After the second shipment of healthy trees was thriving, Cosby wrote Tokyo's mayor, predicting they would become a great American tourist attraction.[71]

ANACOSTIA RIVER FLATS RECLAMATION

Annual freshets, runoff from upriver agricultural land clearing, and extensive sewage dumping had narrowed the Anacostia River and created extensive tidal flats along both its banks. In 1891 Hains, in his last months with the Washington Engineer District, reported to the Chief of Engineers on the survey he had been assigned of that portion of the Anacostia in the District of Columbia. Hains proposed dredging a channel from the river's mouth to the Navy Yard. Just as he had done in the Potomac during the 1880s, the spoils from the Anacostia dredging would be used to reclaim the river's marshes. This effort would solve the problems of the approach to the Navy Yard being "narrow and crooked" and prevent the growth of unhealthy tidal flats. The Washington Engineer District oversaw limited dredging and reclamation below the Navy Yard in 1892.[72]

As the outline of the riverbank began to change, the District Commissioners asked the Secretary of War to fix harbor lines for the river. He created a board of engineer officers in 1892 that drew bulkhead and wharf lines for the section of the Anacostia River below the Pennsylvania Avenue Bridge. These development plans were a necessary guide for future reclamation work. In 1898 Congress again ordered an Anacostia survey and Lieutenant Colonel Charles J. Allen recommended further work to complete Hains's initial proposals. Dredging and land reclamation would provide for improved "access to the navy-yard," "increased facilities for commerce and navigation," and "removal of unsanitary conditions." No money was made available. In 1902 Allen was required to survey the land owned by the government within the Anacostia River flats, so as to assure proper title, and four years later Congress asked the District Commissioners to "report upon the improvement of the so-called flats…with recommendation and estimates of cost." The Commissioners repeated Allen's 1898 estimates.[73]

Increased development along the river's tributaries in the late nineteenth and early twentieth centuries increased the amount and rate of runoff and floods became more frequent and severe. Finally in 1911 money was appropriated for completing the reclamation of the Anacostia flats and an engineer board, comprised of the Officer in Charge of Public Buildings and Grounds, the Engineer Commissioner, and a District Engineer developed plans. Anacostia Park was developed during the 1920s and in 1927 Congress designated an area above the park as a "tree farm," the beginnings of the National Arboretum and Botanic Garden. Influenced by the 1902 McMillan commission recommendations, the engineer board recommended the construction of a dam and lock across the Anacostia River aligned with Massachusetts Avenue, SE, to protect the upper Anacostia River from Potomac River freshets and to create an aquatic park near their confluence for recreation. The Anacostia's dam would have functioned similarly to the Potomac Tidal Basin, with "influent gates at the upper end and effluent gates at the lower end." By 1915 additional engineer studies showed this dam would have detrimental effects, and the engineer board eliminated it in favor of a modified "aquatic park separated from the [Anacostia] river channel by a continuous bank." Kenilworth Gardens, a private water garden begun in the 1880s, in 1938 became part of the Anacostia's extensive waterfront park. As with the development of East and West Potomac Parks, Olmsted "was appointed [in 1915] by the Commission of Fine Arts a committee of one to consult with the board on the proposed modifications" that led to abandoning the bridge in favor of extensive parklands.[74]

CORPS ENGINEERS HAVE TRADITIONALLY SUPPORTED AESTHETIC ELEMENTS ASSOCIATED WITH WASHINGTON'S PUBLIC BUILDINGS AND SPACES, PARTICULARLY OVERSEEING THE DESIGN AND INSTALLATION OF THE CITY'S SCULPTURAL WORKS SUCH AS THOSE ON BRIDGES.

ROLAND HINTON PERRY'S PAIR OF 1908 CAST-CONCRETE LIONS GREET TRAVELERS APPROACHING THE TAFT MEMORIAL BRIDGE THAT CARRIES CONNECTICUT AVENUE ACROSS ROCK CREEK VALLEY. ERNEST C. BAIRSTOW DESIGNED THE BRIDGE'S ORNAMENTAL CAST-IRON LAMP POSTS, EACH FEATURING AN EAGLE ATOP A STANDARD WHOSE BASE IS DECORATED WITH CLASSICAL GARLANDS, ACANTHUS LEAVES, AND SCROLLS.

THE 16TH STREET BRIDGE CROSSING PINEY BRANCH VALLEY, ERECTED BETWEEN 1907 AND 1910, IS THE FIRST PARABOLIC ARCH BUILT IN THE U.S. ALEXANDER PHIMISTER PROCTOR'S FOUR BRONZE TIGERS FLANK THE BRIDGE.

PROCTOR ALSO DESIGNED THE SEVEN-FOOT-TALL BRONZE AMERICAN BISON ON THE CURVED Q STREET BRIDGE, POPULARLY KNOWN AS THE "BUFFALO BRIDGE," THAT CONNECTS GEORGETOWN TO THE SHERIDAN CIRCLE AREA.

THREE OF LEON HERMAN'S 1935 ART DECO RELIEF SCULPTURES DECORATING THE ABUT-MENTS OF THE CALVERT STREET BRIDGE DEPICT TRANSPORTATION BY WATER, AIR, AND HIGHWAY. THE BRIDGE'S ARCHITECT, PAUL CRET, DESCRIBED THE FOURTH FIGURE, REPRESENTING RAIL TRANSPORT, AS "A MALE FIGURE, TYPICAL OF THE POWERFUL MODERN STEAM ENGINE, FLYING OVER THE NETWORK OF TRACKS COVERING THE COUNTRY."

Railroad and highway bridges constructed across the Potomac in the early years of the twentieth century. This 1930 photograph shows the two bridges and the popular Arlington beach and amusement park along the Potomac where the highway curves north along the riverfront. Washington's earliest airports and the Pentagon were built in the large fields at the bottom of the photograph.

Office of History, Corps of Engineers

POTOMAC RIVER BRIDGES

The Washington District Engineers saw one major bridge to completion during the Progressive Era, repaired another, and planned a third. At the time of the Civil War, the mile-long Long Bridge that ran from the foot of 14th Street to Arlington, Virginia, was two-thirds rock causeway with pile sections and a draw at either end. Its wooden superstructure and draws were rebuilt by the Quartermaster's Department during the fall of 1861. In 1864 a parallel bridge set on piles was constructed as a railroad connection. After a few years of maintenance by the Corps, the bridge was transferred to the Baltimore and Potomac Railroad in 1870. Shortly thereafter, the whole length of the structure, including roadway, crib-work, piling, railing, and causeway, was damaged and required reconstruction.[75]

By the 1890s it was becoming increasingly impractical to repair and rebuild the bridge continually. By this time the railroad bridge was underlaid with a substantial amount of rock shoring dumped under its spans over the years to improve stability, and the structure blocked the free flow of the Potomac, contributing to flooding on the Mall during icy conditions. A flood in 1889 prompted the Senate to order a report on the reconstruction of the bridge, but

Colonel Hains's resulting plans were not acted upon. The general provisions of the railway act of 1901—the same one that eliminated grade crossings and threatened the Mall with a viaduct—directed the Baltimore and Potomac Railroad (a division of the Pennsylvania Railroad) to construct a new railroad bridge. This legislation also charged the Secretary of War (i.e., the Corps of Engineers) with creating a new highway bridge just up the river.[76]

The steel plate-truss railroad bridge opened in August 1904. Just up river, the Pennsylvania Bridge Company constructed the matching highway bridge beginning in October 1903. A board comprising Lieutenant Colonel Charles J. Allen, the Washington District Engineer, and three other officers chose its design—eleven steel-plate-truss spans with a central swing span. The 2,234-foot bridge, costing $1,189,702, opened to traffic in December 1906. Together the bridges reduced hazards to Alexandria traffic while ending floods caused by the old Long Bridge.[77]

The Washington District also helped write a new chapter in the continuing Memorial Bridge story. In response to congressional requests, the engineers carried out surveys in 1886 and 1890 for a potential bridge connecting the Naval Observatory grounds to the Arlington estate property. In 1899 Lieutenant Colonel Charles J. Allen joined Stanford White, Major T. W. Symons, Captain David D. Gaillard, and local architect James G. Hill on a jury that secured plans from prominent American bridge designers. Those invited to submit plans were William H. Burr, William R. Hutton, L.L. Buck, and George S. Morison. The jury chose Burr's $3.7 million masonry arch design, which included a steel draw span. The Secretary of War submitted the results of the competition to Congress in April 1900, but no appropriations were made to undertake construction.[78]

Along with construction of the highway bridge and the potential Memorial Bridge, the engineers undertook additional river-crossing work at the turn of the century. Between 1897 and 1907 they rebuilt three piers of the Aqueduct Bridge, and recommended a new bridge to connect Georgetown with Rosslyn. Congressional action on this matter did not follow for a decade. In 1897 Captain Gaillard submitted both steel and stone-arch bridge designs to carry Massachusetts Avenue across Rock Creek. Congress did not fund this engineer project either, leading the city to erect a simple culvert for the avenue in 1901.[79]

MISCELLANEOUS DISTRICT PROJECTS

The Corps participated in several significant mapping projects around the time of World War I. In 1914 the Office of Public Buildings and Grounds compiled a map of all District of Columbia public lands held under federal jurisdiction. Largely the work of

District surveyor Melvin C. Hazen and civil engineer Frederick D. Owen of the Office of Public Buildings and Grounds, it was prepared under Harts's supervision to assist the work of the Commission to Investigate the Title of the United States to Lands in the District of Columbia.[80]

> *"On the whole, my four years in Washington gave me more scope in originating new things to add to the beauty of the city than I had ever dreamed of and I look back with much pleasure and satisfaction at the success which has followed the lead then begun."*

In response to a need to relieve overcrowding in government offices, Congress authorized a commission in 1916 to "ascertain what public buildings are needed to provide permanent quarters for all the government activities in the District of Columbia." Its members were drawn from Congress, plus the Superintendent of the Capitol Building and Grounds, the acting Supervising Architect of the Treasury, and the Officer in Charge of Public Buildings and Grounds. Harts, followed by Colonel C. S. Ridley, served on the Commission, which reported its findings in 1917. It found, for example, that the War Department's 2,220 employees occupied 834,643 square feet of owned and rented building space, 330,442 of which was office space. It cost the government $757,448 each year to hold and operate this space.[81]

The Corps' engineers also exerted considerable influence on the design of some of Washington's civic buildings by serving on juries to select their architects. One appropriate example was the Municipal Building, now more commonly called the District Building. In August 1902, for example, the congressional commission to supervise the erection of the Municipal Building chose a jury composed of the three active members of the Senate Park Commission and, *ex officio*, the Supervising Architect of the Treasury and the District of Columbia Engineer Commissioner, then Colonel John Biddle. The offices of the Engineer Commissioners moved to the District Building when it was completed in 1908.

The remarkable coordination among presidents, cabinet officers, congressmen, artists, businessmen, contractors, and artisans in order to complete these interconnected projects required much more than the military organizational skills of the Corps officers involved. Astuteness, intelligence, tact, and diplomacy were required on a daily basis. Harts recalled: "When I reported to President Wilson he was very gracious, complimented me on my Princeton degree [an honorary A.M. degree conferred in 1913] and said we should be all the better able to get along on account of that." (Wilson was a former president of Princeton University.) In 1918–19, during Wilson's European visit, Harts often accompanied the president on official visits as one of his aides-de-camp, a position for which his tenure in Washington as the president's military aide had adequately prepared him. Harts noted that the Commission of Fine Arts meetings were always held in his office "and were a liberal education to me in artistic matters." He characterized his job in the Office of

Public Buildings and Grounds overseeing the Lincoln Memorial, the Amphitheater at Arlington Cemetery, and the Red Cross Building: "I was the engineer, the contractor for the U.S., the head inspector and paid all bills. I may have been too harsh at times in accepting work but no breath of suspicion of any missing of funds was ever raised. These buildings were all built by contract and under the eyes of the architects as well." Harts summed up his Washington years in a way that probably rang true to many of the Corps' officers who served in his position.

On the whole, my four years in Washington gave me more scope in originating new things to add to the beauty of the city than I had ever dreamed of and I look back with much pleasure and satisfaction at the success which has followed the lead then begun.[82]

District Building completed in 1908. The Engineer Commissioner served on the jury that chose the building's design and the District Commissioners' offices occupied the building.
National Archives no. 66-DC-16

5 | *The Expanding City*
1915–50

ENGINEER COMMISSIONERS

On January 26, 1915, Louis Brownlow—newsman, Woodrow Wilson's protégé, and future leader in American city management—walked with Engineer Commissioner Major Charles W. Kutz to the boardroom of the District Building. There Brownlow was sworn in as a commissioner. Already a friend of Kutz's—the two were members of a group of reporters and public servants dubbed the "Doughnut Cabinet" who met daily for lunch at the Willard Hotel's grillroom—Brownlow began to learn the art of government in the months that followed.

> *At the same time I was learning a great deal about administration from a master of the art, Majr. Kutz. He didn't lecture me. He didn't tell me directly that I had put my decisions and recommendations on too narrow a base. He didn't reprove me for my impetuosity…. He didn't tell me directly that there were some things I ought to look into more carefully and think about longer before I reached my final conclusions. He didn't tell me any of these things, but in every board meeting he gave me a lesson by example. For every recommendation he brought in, he was careful to explain the reasons for his determination….When I was too hasty, and I frequently was, Kutz*

OPPOSITE PAGE: ARLINGTON MEMORIAL BRIDGE CONSTRUCTION

Photo credit: Library of Congress, Prints and Photographs Division, LC-H824-T-321

sometimes would ask a question, always phrased in tentative form and always asked quietly.

As the months went on, it became more and more my habit, when issues were complex, to walk into the engineer commissioner's office and ask Kutz what he thought we should do.

Thus it happened that during the first months and the first two years of my actual experience as a public administrator, I found a teacher and a mentor, wise, kindly, and sympathetic, in the person of a then major of the Corps of Engineers of the United States Army, a graduate of West Point, a military man with a military mind, who still never permitted for an instant the rigidity of his training to overcome the flexibility of his mind and heart.[1]

Major Kutz became Engineer Commissioner in 1914, but was sent to wartime service when the United States entered World War I. Brigadier General John G. D. Knight came out of retirement to take his place. The commissioners faced a chaotic scene in Washington during the war. The city's population soared 50 percent. General Knight was competing with the war for men and materials to keep the city running. Normal construction was halted, a shutdown of sewerage and garbage service had been narrowly averted, and

Colonel Charles Willauer Kutz
Office of History, Corps of Engineers
U.S. Army Signal Corps photo

Charles Willauer Kutz (1870–1951) graduated from West Point in 1893, his first assignments working on fortification and river and harbor work in Baltimore, Maryland, and Portland, Maine, which became his particular area of expertise. Between 1903 and 1906 Kutz served as an assistant to the Chief of Engineers in Washington before spending two years as an instructor at West Point. In 1906 he was assigned to fortification and river and harbor work in Seattle subsequent to being named chief engineer officer of the Department of the Philippines in 1911. Beginning in 1914 Kutz served almost ten years in three separate terms as Washington's Engineer Commissioner, longer than any other incumbent, the first term broken by overseas service during World War I.

Potomac River pollution was on the increase. Thousands of new mouths drank city water, and Knight refused to estimate per capita consumption, since nobody knew any longer how many people were in Washington.[2]

Embroiled in a struggle to force rate schedules upon district utilities, Brownlow persuaded Secretary of War Newton D. Baker to secure Kutz's appointment to a second term as a District Commissioner when the war was over. "I shall never forget," said Brownlow, recalling a day in 1918, "the concerned, puzzled, and frustrated look on the face of one of the presidents of the utilities when he came into my office later that afternoon and I told him that Kutz would be back." Together Brownlow and Kutz forced exceptionally low rates on the utilities. Brownlow (a Democrat), whose father-in-law Representative Thetus W. Sims had been a member of the House Committee on the District of Columbia, was himself intensely interested in politics. Kutz, he recalled, "had not shared the partisan political approach to affairs toward which so many of us…were inclined. I was astonished when he disclosed to me that he had some misgivings about my attitude, that he was somewhat alarmed that I would violate the integrity of the District service by going too far in my partisan activities."[3]

The most significant achievement during Kutz's second term as Engineer Commissioner was a comprehensive zoning plan for Washington that passed Congress in 1920. Washington was the second American city to institute such an integrated plan. Working with St. Louis planner Harland Bartholomew (1889–1989), the commissioners prepared three basic maps that showed the location of every building in the city. "One [was] for the control of property uses, another to control the height of buildings, and the third to limit the area of the lot on which buildings could be built." Using these maps Bartholomew and the commissioners studied land-use data and recommended the separation of residential, commercial, and industrial uses, each with its specific regulation for height, use, and area of buildings to be erected.[4]

Controls on use seemed a startling violation of property rights, and Kutz and Brownlow decided to "do everything possible to take the community fully into our confidence and to enlist the help of the citizens generally." The maps were produced by the hundreds, and maps in hand, "General Kutz spent two hours each morning traversing every street in the areas that we were supposed to take up the next day." Before they made their recommendations, the commissioners had walked every street and roadway in the district to determine the appropriate use for every square and neighborhood, addressed citizens' meetings, and met with their staff after 11:00 p.m. In his final report, Bartholomew recommended

"I found a teacher and a mentor, wise, kindly, and sympathetic, in the person of a then major of the Corps of Engineers of the United States Army, a graduate of West Point, a military man with a military mind, who still never permitted for an instant the rigidity of his training to overcome the flexibility of his mind and heart."

"[H]e was somewhat alarmed that I would violate the integrity of the District service by going too far in my partisan activities."

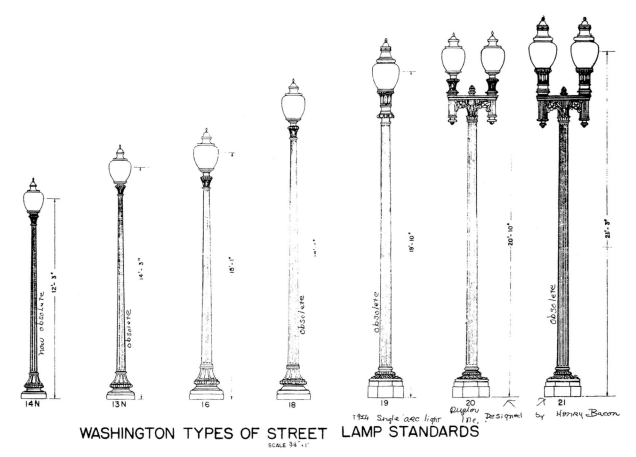

WASHINGTON TYPES OF STREET LAMP STANDARDS
SCALE 3/4"·1'

APPROVED   *Walter Eslem* ELECTRICAL ENGINEER, D.C.   ELECTRICAL DEPARTMENT, D.C.
DATE   *August 8, 1934.*

Sketch of standard street lamp posts for Washington, 1934, compiled by Engineer Commissioner Bell; the tallest and most elaborate was designed by Henry Bacon, architect of the Lincoln Memorial.
Office of the Engineer Commissioner

a commission be created to coordinate zoning with the city's future growth; in 1926 such a commission was established with the Engineer Commissioner at its head.[5]

Under Kutz's chairmanship of the District Zoning Commission, and with advice from the Board of Trade, a city-wide plan took form. Pressure from developers to zone for apartment buildings in the residential area west of Rock Creek Park came to nothing when surveys showed that ample multiple-unit buildings existed elsewhere in the city. When final regulations were adopted on August 30, 1920, Kutz noted that the law marked "a far-reaching step in the advancement of the National Capital...[for]...its symmetrical and beautiful development." Brownlow saw the process as responsive to district citizens who did not choose their local government. "I doubt very much whether any city in the country where the normal electoral processes go on and where the heads of the city government are elected by the people ever undertook such an intensive program for inducing citizen participation or such careful consideration of citizen suggestions."[6]

Although regulating costs of utilities and accomplishing Washington's zoning plan were major achievements during the first quarter of the twentieth century, the District

Commissioners still continued annually to carry out the city's important municipal services. Extending, paving, and naming streets were a highly visible part of their work as widely dispersed subdivisions increased in upper northwest and far northeast. Lighting these streets also was a major undertaking. In 1910 the Commission of Fine Arts approved for city streets an enclosed arc light with a sectional globe on standard ten- to twelve-foot-tall pillars designed by architect Daniel Burnham for Union Station, although only a limited number were erected and only on downtown streets. In 1923 Engineer Commissioner Major Franklin Bell appointed a Committee on Lighting Needs to prepare a comprehensive street lighting plan. They recommended using gas light exclusively throughout the city with standards sixteen to twenty-one feet tall, the tallest having double globes designed by architect Henry Bacon. In 1967 writer John Dos Passos recalled the romantic atmosphere these lights imparted.[7]

> *We walked out southeast toward the Navy Yard. This was still the Washington I remembered: The shadowy streets choked with trees where all the life seemed to be going into vegetation, the street lights shaded and muffled in green leaves,...old women panting in rockers under low-hanging branches, light filtering through the green leaves, the shadows of branches thrown on brick walls....We had come out into the open spaces of trees and grass and shrubbery in front of the Library of Congress before we noticed there was a moon.*[8]

In 1927 now Lieutenant Colonel Bell, who had been appointed Engineer Commissioner in 1923, wrote about his experiences playing such an important role in

(Below left)
Among their many municipal duties, the Engineer Commissioners oversaw paving and maintenance of the district's streets from 1874 until 1967.
Library of Congress, Prints and Photographs Division, LC-USZ62-116217

(Below right)
Cleaning Washington's streets and alleys of refuse and winter snow was supervised by the Engineer Commissioners, the most active of the district's three appointed commissioners who ran Washington's municipal government for nearly a century. In the 1930s trucks spraying water were supplemented by uniformed "white wings" who removed debris daily.
Washington Society of Engineers

Washington's municipal life. He cogently explained the complex governance of the city by many different federal agencies but particularly emphasized the professional and personal difficulties he faced while serving as the Engineer Commissioner. For example, he recounts that he was named in sixty-six lawsuits brought by disgruntled citizens who were unhappy with the decisions made by the commissioners. He became wary of social intercourse with many citizens because some people he met expected preferential treatment. Generally, however, Bell was positive about the experience and urged engineers to elect their colleagues to positions in municipal administration because such jobs fully utilized their training and expertise.[9]

OFFICE OF PUBLIC BUILDINGS AND GROUNDS

While the District Commissioners grappled with a changing city, the Office of Public Buildings and Grounds completed the monumental projects left unfinished at the outbreak of war. In 1913 Congress established a commission to erect a Memorial to Women of the Civil War and appropriated $400,000 for a building to be used as the headquarters of the American Red Cross, provided $300,000 in private funds were raised. The International Red Cross was organized in Geneva, Switzerland, in 1863, as a result of Florence Nightingale's work as a nurse during the Crimean War, but the American Red Cross was not founded until 1881 by Civil War nurse Clara Barton. The Red Cross building, designed by Philadelphia architects Trowbridge & Livingston, was one of three major marble buildings for which Colonel Harts supervised construction; its cornerstone was laid on March 27, 1915, by President Woodrow Wilson who also dedicated it on May 12, 1917, before the "first mobilization of uniformed women war workers ever held in the United States." Between 1927 and 1930 a second memorial building, also designed by Trowbridge & Livingston, but supervised by Lieutenant Colonel U. S. Grant III, was added to the complex. It commemorated the services of American women in World War I. The Red Cross's third office building, designed by Trowbridge & Livingston and supervised by Grant, was built between March 1931 and July 1932.[10]

In 1917 in response to a July 1, 1916, congressional act, Colonel Harts and his successor Clarence S. Ridley compiled a map showing all the buildings in Washington's central area owned, rented, or erected as temporary structures to house World War I workers. Their map particularly noted twenty-nine buildings occupied by different divisions of the War Department. In 1917 the office built three temporary office buildings,

the infamous "temps," on the Mall, followed in 1922–23 by the Navy and Munitions Office, a long range of demountable structures in West Potomac Park that faced Constitution Avenue between 17th and 23rd Streets.[11]

By October 1918 the colonnade of the Lincoln Memorial was completed under the direction of Lieutenant Colonel Ridley. When work began on the Reflecting Pool in November 1919, the presence of the temps forced the elimination of the short north-south arm from the cross-shaped pool planned by the Senate Park Commission in 1902. Constructing the pool's drainage system was the major challenge faced by the Corps' engineers with Ridley in charge at the project's outset. Even with the simpler design without the cross arm, Ridley and his assistant, civil engineer Charles A. Peters, Jr., faced construction problems resembling those that confronted builders of the Lincoln Memorial. An initial plan to build a single concrete conduit to drain into the Tidal Basin 600 feet to the southeast proved impossible because of ground water flooding. (The difference in elevation of the pool's bottom and the river's average high tide was only 3.5 feet.) The engineers then devised an extensive drainage system along the pool's axis with multiple connections to the main conduit. They designed a three-ply surface of reinforced

concrete, membrane, and tile to maximize the pool's mirroring effect and prevent seepage, while remaining flexible enough to adjust to continuous land settlement. A concrete apron and hinged joint connected the pliable bottom of the pool to the rigid coping, which rested on piles driven to bedrock. As the land settled, the pool maintained its fixed relation to the lines of the memorial. Completed in 1923 under Lieutenant Colonel Sherrill, the Reflecting Pool is 2,027 feet long and 160 feet wide; the transverse Rainbow Pool at its east end (also planned by the Senate Park Commission) measures 291 feet long and 160 feet wide. In 1998 the Reflecting Pool's east end was selected as the site of the World War II Memorial, its architect Friedrich St. Florian making the Rainbow Pool the focus of the memorial's commemoration of those lost in that war.[12]

In 1920 Ridley arranged impressive ceremonies to dedicate the Arlington Memorial Amphitheater, which had been built under his supervision. Although first suggested in 1908, the amphitheater's commission was not established by Congress until 1913; the Secretary of War was named its chairman. Ground was broken in 1915 for a one-and-one-half-acre oval amphitheatre to hold ceremonies, such as those held on Memorial Day, that honored all of the nation's war dead. The portico of its reception building provided the backdrop for the Tomb of the Unknown Soldier.

The completion of two other major projects soon added additional memorial sites that commemorated the Civil War. By 1920 sculptor Daniel Chester French finished his statue

"Henry Mervin Shrady has with years of labor and infinite pains here produced one of the great monuments of the world."

of Lincoln for the memorial leaving only the terrace wall, landscaping, and access roads to be completed. On May 30, 1922, Memorial Day, a crowd of tens of thousands and 3,500 invited dignitaries attended the dedication. Robert T. Lincoln, eldest son of President Lincoln, and Secretary of War under Presidents Garfield and Arthur, was introduced by Chief Justice William Howard Taft, the presiding officer. A month earlier, on April 28, Vice President Calvin Coolidge watched the unveiling of the Grant Memorial. Sherrill, who again made all the arrangements for the ceremony and invited its numerous speakers, briefly spoke as the executive officer of the Grant Memorial Commission.[13]

> *Henry Mervin Shrady has with years of labor and infinite pains here produced one of the great monuments of the world. As an adornment to the city of Washington, this memorial ranks with the greatest works of the sculptor's art, and will forever adorn the imposing approach to the Capitol that will result from the completion of the Mall and Union Square in accordance with the plan of George Washington and L'Enfant.*[14]

Posterity has verified Sherrill's assessment. Mindful of the importance of the history of the design and construction of the Lincoln and Grant memorials, Sherrill and his successor

Dedication of the Arlington Memorial Amphitheater, May 15, 1920. Capable of seating five thousand people, the amphitheater was begun in 1915 but delayed by scarcity of materials during World War I and bad winter weather.
Library of Congress, Prints and Photographs Division, LC-H813-A05-022

Ulysses S. Grant III were responsible for the publication of books that were compilations of documents and essays as well as the record of these important ceremonial occasions for each memorial.[15]

ARLINGTON MEMORIAL BRIDGE

Postwar projects were in general more practical, less purely monumental that those of prewar days. One project, however, combined both characteristics—the Memorial Bridge to Arlington Cemetery. Congress long debated whether to construct the bridge, engineers urged it, and the Senate Park Commission made the bridge an essential part of its plan. A new Washington menace—automobile traffic—helped bring the structure at last into being. In November 1921 a spectacular jam occurred as dignitaries and visitors to the dedication of the Tomb of the Unknown Soldier attempted to cross the Potomac River on the highway bridge.

Arriving at the west bank two hours or more late, the crowds found themselves entering the cemetery on a road that led past "a little race track, ...marshes lately used as the city dump, and...the Agriculture Department barns, so designed and constructed as to thrust their ugliness upon one's attention with all the insistence of a spoiled child at table." Dedication of the Lincoln Memorial the following year revealed a great *rond point* situated at the edge of the river with no outlet, while across the Potomac River, Arlington Cemetery with its new amphitheater lay almost inaccessible. Less than two weeks after the dedication of the Lincoln Memorial, Congress voted $25,000 to begin work on the bridge.[16]

In 1916 the Arlington Memorial Bridge Commission, moribund since 1913, was revived with Sherrill named its executive officer. In 1922 both Major Tyler of the Engineer Commissioner's office and now General Beach concurred with Sherrill that the bridge's landfall in Washington should be at New York Avenue near Observatory Hill rather than at the Lincoln Memorial as the Senate Park Commission had planned. They argued that such an alignment would not require a draw (because of its height), would bring users into the heart of the city, and would not interfere with the Lincoln Memorial. The view of the Commission of Fine Arts, led by its secretary Charles Moore, who had been Senator McMillan's secretary, was that a low, arched bridge between Arlington and the Lincoln Memorial would be more in harmony with the Mall's development. Moore released to the public his ten-page report to the Arlington Memorial

Bridge Commission which angered President Warren G. Harding, the bridge commission's chairman. Yet visits to Arlington and the district sites on December 18, 1922, convinced Harding that the Lincoln Memorial landfall was preferable, partly because it was anticipated that the bridge's main users would be tourists traveling between the two sites. The memorial's landfall would also maintain the horizontal vista of the city from Arlington.

In January 1923 Sherrill, who opposed a draw in a low-arched bridge, conducted public hearings about the necessity for a draw. Georgetown business interests convinced him that a draw was vital to local commerce and Sherrill relented. Plans went forward based on a bascule draw in the center arch. Once the large engineering concerns were settled, Sherrill conferred with the Commission of Fine Arts about choosing a suitable architect rather than holding another competition. They chose the New York architectural firm of McKim, Mead & White, a firm whose founding principals, now deceased, were once deeply involved in Washington's revitalization. In January 1926 Sherrill was replaced by Grant, who worked with both John L. Nagle, the bridge commission's own engineer, and the engineers on the architectural firm's staff. The low, Roman aqueduct-inspired bridge designed by William M. Kendall with the McKim, Mead & White office, was based on the bridge depicted on the Senate Park Commission's drawings proposed by its chairman Daniel Burnham in 1901. With broad, graceful arches and pylons at each end topped by symbolic statuary, the bridge was intended to be as unobtrusive as possible, its Roman character a fitting link between the Lincoln Memorial and Arlington House (Robert E. Lee's house at the outbreak of the Civil War) built a century earlier. Memorial Bridge was both a metaphorical and physical link between the North and South, the symbolic linkage between Lincoln and Lee meant to heal the still raw wounds in the aftermath of the war. Moreover, the bridge's superstructure was built using Roman architectural principles: "[T]he visible arches are being built as true granite arches, each stone deep enough to play its part as a voussoir of a real masonry arch and to bear its share of the weight of the bridge deck," Grant reported to President Calvin Coolidge in 1928.[17]

Amid a squabble with Associated General Contractors over the hiring of day labor, work began in 1925 under Sherrill and continued under Grant. Central to the problem of building the bridge was the need to make a practical structure conform to the Senate Park Commission's low-slung, simple design. The bridge had to bear the weight of granite facing and statues, and the bascule draw in the central arch had to be as inconspicuous as possible. Machinery needed to be packed away out of sight beneath the

"[T]he visible arches are being built as true granite arches, each stone deep enough to play its part as a voussoir of a real masonry arch and to bear its share of the weight of the bridge deck."

CONSTRUCTION OF THE ARLINGTON MEMORIAL BRIDGE

First proposed in 1886, the Arlington Memorial Bridge, begun in 1925 and completed in 1932, serves as both the physical bridge and symbolic link between the Lincoln Memorial and the Custis-Lee house, Robert E. Lee's home in Arlington Cemetery. To accommodate the bridge's low Roman aqueduct profile, but allow for a draw span, powerful machinery was concealed in the piers to lift the two particularly broad sections of the draw.

May 1929

n.d.

n.d.

September 1930

n.d.

roadway. The draw itself, though neither the longest nor the widest in the world, had one of the largest areas to be raised; and the concrete deck and ornaments made it one of the heaviest and most costly ever built. While Grant, Nagle, and Strauss Engineering Corporation—designers of the draw span—struggled with these difficulties, the Engineer District diverted the channel of the river beneath the draw, widened approaches, and cut and filled Columbia Island. Completed in 1932, the bridge successfully met both architectural and practical needs while bringing the Senate Park Commission plan a step nearer completion.[18]

BRIDGES, WATER SUPPLY, AND ANACOSTIA RECLAMATION

Corps engineers directed the construction of three additional Washington bridges during the 1920s and 30s: the Francis Scott Key Bridge that linked Georgetown with Rosslyn, Virginia, across the Potomac River; a new Chain Bridge that spanned the wide and rocky Potomac River near Little Falls; and the John Philip Sousa Bridge that carried Pennsylvania Avenue, SE, across the Anacostia River.

The Washington Engineer District built a new, modern bridge across the Potomac near the site of the old, often modified Aqueduct Bridge. The five high reinforced concrete arches (two additional arches were added in 1939) of Key Bridge, designed by Washington architect Nathan C. Wyeth in 1916, paralleled the Aqueduct Bridge that was taken down after the Key Bridge opened in 1923. Wyeth's open spandrel design was constructed entirely in reinforced concrete under the supervision of Colonel Walter L. Fisk and his successor Major Max C. Tyler. The engineers began work in August 1917. Coming out of retirement to head the wartime Engineer District, Fisk encountered the usual problems of the time: Wyeth left the project to take a commission in the Army; labor and materials were hard to come by; and the staff of the District Engineer's office was depleted by military demands. One step the engineers took was to dispense with private contractors and employ day laborers on the project. Their method of pouring the massive amounts of concrete that covered the arches' steel ribs was placing one stationary concrete mixing plant on shore and ferrying containers of concrete to necessary points via a cableway while another mixing plant on a barge was anchored to the river bottom. The bridge was 1,791 feet long and unusually wide for the time, the roadway being fifty feet in width and each of the sidewalks eight feet wide.[19] The completed bridge, equipped for streetcar, automobile, and foot traffic, opened in January 1923. The engineers turned it over to the municipal government for administration, and it was named in honor of former Georgetown resident Francis Scott Key because its land-fall was near his house.[20]

In 1925 the ninety-year-old Aqueduct Bridge was closed to traffic, having been opened as a public thoroughfare in 1868; the Washington and Old Dominion Railway removed its track; the commissioners salvaged railings, floors, and stringers; and the district removed some of the masonry for use in the new Anacostia floodwalls. Four of the salvaged steel trusses went into a bridge over Rock Creek on the Rock Creek and Potomac Parkway, just south of the Connecticut Avenue Bridge, in 1926.

The Engineer Commissioners of the District of Columbia also worked to improve river crossings in the city. They replaced two older bridges on the Potomac and Anacostia rivers. The present Chain Bridge is the eighth on the site, replacing the 1874 bridge erected by the Corps and using its piers. The 1,341-foot-long bridge was designed by Modjeski, Masters & Chase of Harrisburg, Pennsylvania, and built by the Fuller Construction Company of New Jersey in 1938–39. The Sousa Bridge—for which designs were considered in 1936, construction begun in 1938, and completion occurred in 1940—also

The arches of Key Bridge under construction (n.d.). The old Aqueduct Bridge is just north of the arches with Georgetown University visible in the upper right.
Office of History, Corps of Engineers

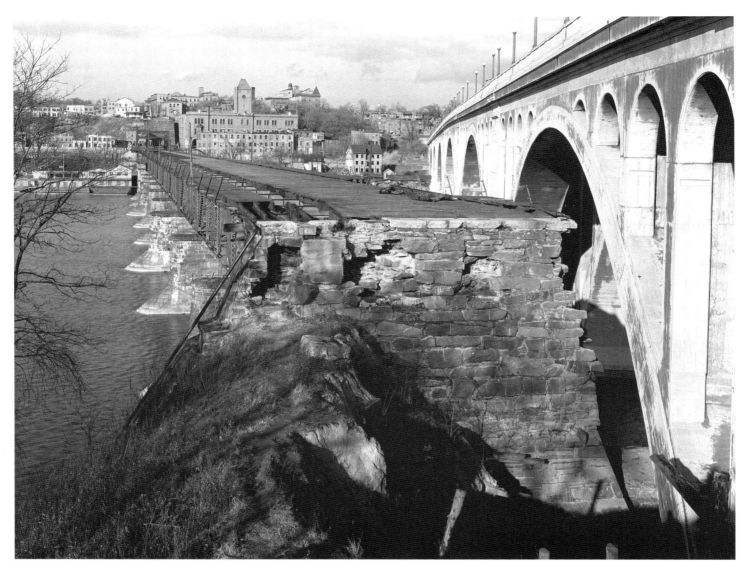

*Aqueduct and Key Bridges
intersecting near the Rossyln
shore, December 1929. The
Aqueduct Bridge was largely
dismantled several years after
Key Bridge was opened for
traffic in 1923.*
Office of History, Corps of Engineers

replaced a nineteenth-century iron bridge erected by the Corps. Engineer Commissioner
Lieutenant Colonel David McCoach, Jr., built the 1,666-foot-long bridge, designed with
nine stone-faced reinforced concrete piers set 154 feet apart carrying low arches rising
thirty feet above high tide. The New York architectural firm of McKim, Mead & White
designed the Sousa Bridge along with the New York engineering firm of Parson, Klapp,
Brinkerhoff and Douglas.[21]

During the previous decade of the 1920s, the Washington Engineer District's aqueduct
division had completed a major expansion of the water supply system. During World War I,
when the city's population had greatly expanded, the system reached its limits. In 1921
Congress approved the most comprehensive expansion of the Washington Aqueduct in its
history, doubling its capacity. The engineers built a new intake structure on the Potomac at
Great Falls and a new ten-foot concrete tunnel under Conduit Road (renamed MacArthur
Boulevard during World War II) and next to Meigs' original conduit. The project proceeded
without mishap except for a washout in 1924 that damaged the old conduit and interrupted

New Washington Aqueduct conduit under construction, May 1923. Steel forms that moved on tracks were used in building the concrete walls of the new conduit.
Washington Aqueduct Division, Baltimore Engineer District

water distribution in the system for two days, almost exhausting the reserve supply in the city's three reservoirs.

To treat the large new intake of raw water, the aqueduct built a major new treatment plant near the old receiving reservoir on the site of the former Dalecarlia farm named for a province in Sweden. The new facilities at Dalecarlia included several basins for chemical treatment and sedimentation, twenty new rapid sand filters, a storage reservoir, and buildings to support these operations. In addition, the aqueduct built a new pumping station with nine new pumps to move water through the distribution system, including several new reservoirs located on high spots in the district. The increased capacity of the aqueduct assured reliable water supply to the city and to a new customer, Arlington County, added in 1927.[22]

In 1916 the Washington Engineer District began work on reclamation of the Anacostia River flats, along the lines originally proposed in the 1902 Senate Park Commission report, and continued for many years, guided by the size of Congressional appropriations. When

Filter plant superstructures under construction, ca. 1926. The 1926 Dalecarlia filter plant, one of the most prominent structures on Conduit Road, was designed in the Colonial Revival style to blend with its residential neighbors and was part of the extensive expansion of Washington Aqueduct facilities during the 1920s.
Washington Aqueduct Division, Baltimore Engineer District

Congress in 1923 asked the engineer board to consider scaling back the project, eliminating reclamation and the development of parkland above Benning Road, the board reported:

> *Already much benefit has resulted from the filling in of the marshes below Benning Road. Malaria, which was formerly a common disease at the navy yard, Government Hospital for the Insane, Washington Barracks, and the District Jail, institutions adjoining these marshes, has now almost disappeared. As the section of Anacostia Park above Benning Road is the only remaining mosquito-breeding marsh in the District of Columbia, the reclamation work should be continued.*[23]

In 1918 Congress made the reclaimed land along the Anacostia River part of the District of Columbia's park system, naming it Anacostia Park. By mid-1920 the project was nearing the halfway mark. Sanitary conditions improved, and deep-draft vessels could use the river as far north as Pennsylvania Avenue. In 1925 part of the reclaimed land was transferred to the Director of Public Buildings and Public Parks for improvement, and another portion set aside as a site for the Agriculture Department's planned U.S. National Arboretum and Botanic Garden.[24]

The Corps of Engineers' dredge Dalecarlia at work on Anacostia River reclamation (n.d.). Like the reclamation of the Potomac flats, the Anacostia work required extensive dredge and fill operations to drain and reclaim its extensive marshland.
Office of History, Corps of Engineers

Anacostia Reclamation Project, July 1929. This aerial photograph shows the work on Section G of the project.
Office of History, Corps of Engineers

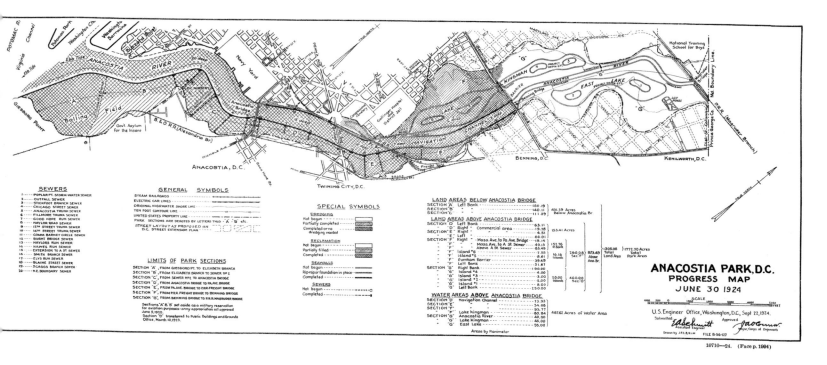

Washington Engineer District map showing the progress of the Corps' dredging and reclamation work and seawall construction on the Anacostia River as of June 30, 1924. The unshaded area on the far right of the map is Section G.

Office of History, Corps of Engineers, ARCE 1924

WASHINGTON PARKS

Land acquisition by the Office of Public Buildings and Grounds for Rock Creek Park continued slowly after Congress appropriated the first funds in 1916, and then released only a limited amount of money each year. A congressional fight in 1925 led to the approval of the first funds for improving the nascent reservation. Grant, who became head of the reorganized Office of Public Buildings and Public Parks in 1926, oversaw much of the final design of the parkway, working with the landscape architectural firm of Olmsted Brothers to modify the general outline developed by Morrow and Markham in 1908, Harts in 1916, and Sherrill's office in 1924. The engineers and civilian landscape architects of his office did all the drafting for the construction: landscape architect James G. Langdon, formerly an employee of Olmsted Brothers who had worked for the Senate Park Commission, drew the 1916 map of the parkway. Aside from some preliminary brush and rubbish clearing, construction began with a bridle path in 1923. Further landscape adjusting and road building occurred in phases all along the path of the road, until by 1933 and the transfer of control over the capital's parks to the National Park Service, only the extensive restoration of the valley between P Street and Pennsylvania Avenue and one major bridge remained to be undertaken.[25]

In 1906 Mary Foote Henderson, wife of Senator John B. Henderson, proposed to Congress that the government build a formal urban park on the hilly twelve-acre site east of 16th Street, NW, on Meridian Hill a mile and a half north of the White House. In 1910 the property was transferred to the Office of Public Buildings and Grounds and a succession of major American landscape architects proposed designs for the site. In 1925 the Office of

Construction of the wall along the Potomac, June 1930. The completed wall and the fill behind it became the foundation for the Rock Creek and Potomac Parkway when it was built later in the 1930s.
Office of History, Corps of Engineers

Public Buildings and Public Parks was organized into divisions with the Design and Construction Division having four sections that included Engineering Design, Landscape Design, and Surveying. Engineer Major M. C. Mehaffey was appointed the division's first chief and construction of Meridian Hill Park was the major landscape project the division undertook before its responsibilities were transferred to the National Park Service in 1933. New York landscape architect Ferruccio Vitale (beginning in 1919) and Washington architect Horace Peaslee (beginning in 1915) were the designers of the park that evolved into a major architectural work in reinforced concrete in imitation of an Italian Renaissance garden. The concrete and mosaic work was executed by Washington's architectural sculptor, John J. Earley, in concrete and overall construction was supervised by Colonel Grant.[26]

OFFICE OF PUBLIC BUILDINGS AND PUBLIC PARKS

Meanwhile, in the heart of the district a new era of major construction opened in 1926 when Congress passed the Public Buildings Act that established the Public Buildings Commission in the Department of the Treasury to develop the Federal Triangle. Under the

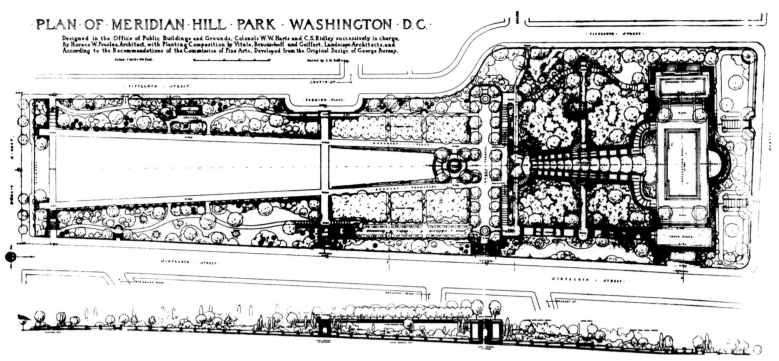

PLAN·OF·MERIDIAN·HILL·PARK·WASHINGTON·D.C.

Designed in the Office of Public Buildings and Grounds, Colonels W.W. Harts and C.S. Ridley successively in charge,
By Horace W. Peaslee, Architect, with Planting Composition by Vitale, Brinckerhoff and Geiffert, Landscape Architects, and
According to the Recommendations of the Commission of Fine Arts, Developed from the Original Design of George Burnap.

(Top)

"The Plan of Meridian Hill Park,
Washington, DC, Designed in the Office of
Public Buildings and Grounds," ca. 1920.
Architect Horace W. Peaslee's and landscape
architect Ferruccio Vitale's plan for the new
park located at 16th and W Streets, NW,
was based on Italian Renaissance gardens
to complement nearby European-inspired
Beaux Arts mansions.
National Archives no. 66-DC-19

(Bottom)

Meridian Hill's upper terrace—as well as
the site's outer retaining walls and other
architectural features—was constructed of
reinforced concrete whose surfaces were
covered with small stones. Because of the
Depression and scarce funding, the park was
not completed until 1936 after it had become
the responsibility of the National Park Service.
*Library of Congress, Prints and Photographs Division,
HABS, DC, WASH, 486-50*

direction of Secretary of Treasury Andrew Mellon and the Supervising Architect of the Treasury, massive government buildings began to rise in the angle between Pennsylvania and Constitution Avenues, on the site suggested by interested Washingtonians in the late 1880s and given official sanction by Bingham in 1899 and the Senate Park Commission in 1902. Grant was the executive and disbursing officer of the Public Buildings Commission, a position that strengthened his role as an influential administrator in the shaping of Washington. Under the general architectural direction of Chicagoan Edward H. Bennett, seven massive and complex Beaux Arts buildings were designed by the country's leading firms. Under Grant's administration, they were all erected in just over a decade—the entire complex larger than the Louvre in Paris or the Vatican in Rome. In 1929 Grant was elected an honorary member of the American Institute of Architects for his outstanding work with the Public Building Commission.[27]

The increased responsibilities of the Office of Public Buildings and Grounds, in both scope and number, led to the Corps' gradual separation from oversight by the War Department in matters relating to public buildings. In many ways it functioned as an independent agency. Though the officer in charge was nominally subject to the Chief of Engineers—and to a supervisory commission in the case of his care of the State, War and Navy Building—the control was largely a formality. As a military aide to the president, the head of buildings and grounds had direct access to the chief executive, and was "effectually subject to the President's direct control." Queried by Congress, the

The future site of the Federal Triangle, seen here in a ca. 1900 photograph, was known as "Murder Bay" when the 1902 Senate Park Commission proposed it for public buildings. All but the Old Post Office (middle left) were replaced by massive executive department buildings for which Col. Grant was the disbursing officer during the 1920s and 1930s. The once commercially important Center Market (upper right) fell victim to the redevelopment.
Library of Congress, Prints and Photographs Division, LC-BH85-34

Secretary of War raised no objection to a proposal to place the office formally under the president alone. On February 26, 1925, the office was reorganized as the Office of Public Buildings and Public Parks, and in 1926 Grant was named its head. He initially oversaw almost 3,428 acres of parkland in 562 reservations, and added almost 100 more reservations before the federal lands were transferred to the National Park Service in 1933.[28]

Grant used his innate judgment about the importance of adequate recreational areas in and near urban areas and hard statistics to foster the increase of recreational areas in Washington's suburbs.

> *The officers in charge of public buildings and grounds, successors to Colonel Bingham, have also naturally followed the plan of 1901 as far as practicable and have given their support to those of its projects which have been adopted. Gratifying as the progress was, it was very inadequate. The method*

Colonel U. S. Grant III
Photograph by Bachrach

It was through the Office of Public Buildings and Public Parks that Grant rose to prominence in Washington. The grandson of the eighteenth president soon established himself as a hard worker, a demanding supervisor, and a press agent's dream. Born in 1881, the son of an Army officer and diplomat, Grant graduated from West Point in 1903, sixth in his class, and four years later married Edith Root, daughter of Elihu Root, who had been Secretary of War, but was Secretary of State in 1907. Stories about him grew into a personal legend, fed by his skill at publicity and a rich supply of quirks and personal oddities. Impatient with fools and visiting firemen, he wore heavy underwear to work in winter so that he could turn off the office heat; unwelcome visitors then fled to warmer regions. In 1928 he got the Washington parks into the newspapers by declaring a "war on neckers." Park users were asked to abide by a pledge that encouraged fire prevention and forbade littering, flower picking, and—the item that caught newsmen's eyes—any "display of amorousness" that might "set a bad example for children" in the puritanical Washington woods. Meantime, black citizens came to know a harsher side of Grant, as he sanctioned a Ku Klux Klan rally on government property, tried to segregate picnic places in Rock Creek Park, and barred blacks from the bathing beach at the Tidal Basin.[29]

of seeking legislation for one project at a time, thereby lining up against it the backers of other projects as well as the enemies of the particular one under consideration, had by 1925, for instance, provided only an addition of 24 per cent to the total park area of 1901, while the population had increased 70 per cent.[30]

Construction of the Post Office Department Building at 13th and D Streets, NW, within the Federal Triangle, 1930s. It was to overlook a landscaped Great Plaza which became a parking lot until replaced by the Reagan Building in the 1990s.
Library of Congress, Prints and Photographs Division, LC-H823-1699

Grant fought effectively for public recreation and an extended park system. "I think," said a civilian planner who worked under him for many years, "he had the highest standard of public service of anybody I've ever known." As head of public buildings and parks, Grant removed as many tempos as he could and cleared and developed the Mall. As a planner he later took a leading role in buying land for Rock Creek and Potomac Parkway and worked with the firm of Olmsted Brothers on the parkway design. When necessary, Grant stood up to his fellow officers. He successfully opposed Washington District Engineer Major Brehon B. Somervell and the Chief of Engineers to preserve a stretch of Potomac shore for parks rather than a power plant. Public tributes to Grant by

BATHING ESTABLISHMENT ON THE TIDAL BASIN
Designed in the Office of Public Buildings and Grounds,
Col. C. S. Ridley in charge, by H. W. Peaslee Architect

'20-'21
Addition
(proposed)   "Raincoat
Check

WOMEN'S
LOCKERS

Life
Guards

High diving
platforms

1919-20
Addition
(authorized)

Overflow
Checking
Space

MEN'S
LOCKERS

Photo by Air Service
War Dept.

MANY ENGINEER PROJECTS
ASSOCIATED WITH WASHINGTON'S
MODERNIZATION OFFERED
ANCILLARY BENEFITS TO RESIDENTS
AND VISITORS ALIKE. A BATHING
BEACH ON THE TIDAL BASIN WAS
FIRST SUGGESTED BY THE
WASHINGTON BEACH ASSOCIATION
IN 1889 AND PROMOTED AS A
MAJOR FEATURE OF THE 1902
SENATE PARK COMMISSION PLAN.
A VARIETY OF FACILITIES WERE
PROVIDED BY THE OFFICE OF
PUBLIC BUILDINGS AND GROUNDS
AND THE DISTRICT COMMISSIONERS
IN SEVERAL LOCATIONS ON THE
RECLAIMED LAND CREATED BY THE
CORPS, WITH THE NORTH SIDE OF
THE INNER BASIN PREFERRED
BECAUSE OF THE WATER'S PURITY.
HOWEVER, ITS DEPTH LED TO MANY
DROWNINGS. IN 1914 COL. HARTS
BEGAN PLANNING FOR A NEW
LOCATION ON THE SOUTHEAST SIDE
OF THE TIDAL BASIN SHADED BY
THE CHERRY TREES PLANTED UNDER
THE DIRECTION OF COL. SPENCER
COSBY, OFFICER IN CHARGE OF
PUBLIC BUILDINGS AND GROUNDS,
IN 1912. FURTHER NORTH, THE
REFLECTING POOL SOON BECAME
A CHOICE LOCATION TO SAIL TOY
BOATS IN THE SUMMER OR,
WEATHER PERMITTING, ICE SKATE
IN THE WINTER—A TRADITION,
SEEN HERE IN THE 1940S, THAT
BEGAN WITH AN EXCEPTIONALLY
COLD JANUARY IN 1925.

those who worked for him attested to not only his integrity, but his personal charm. "He could even handle a commission on which there were both members of Congress and executive officers of the Government, a most difficult job. His many assignments in Washington were in that touchy, nervous area where the Federal and local governments meet, but his diplomacy was adequate."[31]

Grant also carried out a large-scale reconstruction of the White House, which Sherrill had begun. After investigations in April 1923 showed the mansion's roof near collapse, President Warren G. Harding instructed Sherrill to begin repairs during his own absence on an Alaskan trip (from which he did not return alive). After examination showed that "the trusses carrying the roof are no longer acting as trusses, but are now merely a series of beams and struts," Grant warned the new president, Calvin Coolidge, that the whole roof should be replaced at a cost of $500,000. But the Vermonter refused to pay the cost no matter what the danger. "If it is as bad as you say it is,"—an engineer later summed up the president's attitude—"why doesn't it fall down?" Consequently, Grant and the Supervising Architect of the Treasury carried out a less drastic renovation that included rebuilding the roof and third story, fireproofing the interior, and painting. With advice from consulting architects, William Adams Delano and Charles Adams Platt, and experts on American decorative arts, the work was successfully completed in 1927.[32]

Grant also became a key figure in the development of the National Capital Park and Planning Commission (NCPPC). Systematic land acquisition had long been suggested by Harts and other park enthusiasts to ensure the system's growth in the face of rising land prices. Urged on by powerful advocates, including the Chief of Engineers and Washington's city-wide citizens' group, the Committee of 100 headed by district resident Frederic A. Delano, Congress on June 6, 1924, set up a National Capital Park Commission consisting of three officers of the Corps of Engineers, two members of Congress, and two civil servants. Money was to be provided by a yearly appropriation equal to one penny for every inhabitant of the continental United States, and the commission was empowered to acquire land by purchase or condemnation. But first appropriations were less than promised.

Under continued pressure from park advocates, Congress, in April 1926, enlarged the commission by providing for appointment of four leading district citizens, renamed it the National Capital Park and Planning Commission, and gave it authority to plan for the city's growth. The commission was to plan Washington's street system as well, taking over duties that the highway commission had carried out since 1890. Its third responsibility was the

---

"I think he had the highest standard of public service of anybody I've ever known...."

"If it is as bad as you say it is, why doesn't it fall down?"

purchase of land for parks, parkways, and playgrounds. Frederic Delano chaired the commission and Charles Eliot II was the city planner. Grant was secretary and executive officer. His relationship with Presidents Coolidge and Hoover was sufficiently close that Eliot credited him with "managing the White House" in regard to commission projects. Soon the commission took the first steps toward area-wide planning, working with a similar suburban planning commission set up in 1927 by the state of Maryland.[33]

WASHINGTON CHANNEL IMPROVEMENTS

The Depression brought a new Washington District project to improve the Washington Channel. Sheltered by the peninsula of East Potomac Park and flushed by the Tidal Basin, the channel had become an informal recreation spot, with wharves for oyster and melon boats, and landings for river steamers that made trips to Baltimore and Norfolk. But buildings had slipped into decay, and only the federally owned wharves were in good condition. In the 1920s Colonel Bell devised the master plan for the development of the Washington Channel that included commercial and recreational wharfs along the Southwest waterfront and replaced the original Water Street with Maine Avenue. After

Washington Channel Waterfront, Yacht Basin No. 1, July 1939. In the 1930s the Washington Engineer District began a program to improve the Washington Channel waterfront, but sporadic funding during the Depression meant that the district completed only parts of the project by the end of the decade.
Office of History, Corps of Engineers

REBIRTH OF THE MASSACHUSETTS AVENUE BRIDGE

The 1901 viaduct-and-culvert bridge that carried Massachusetts Avenue across Rock Creek was built to serve new suburbs immediately north of the park. In 1925 a roadway was built through the culvert, but frequent floods caused traffic bottlenecks. Construction of the Rock Creek & Potomac Parkway, completed in 1936, required a higher bridge with substantial clearance beneath it. The current Massachusetts Avenue Bridge was designed by Washington's leading modernist architect Louis Justement and engineers Harrington and Cortelyou as a simple, 150-foot-long single reinforced concrete arch faced with stone. During construction, supervised by Captain Herbert C. Whitehurst of the D.C. Highway Division, traffic continued across Massachusetts Avenue on a temporary three-lane bridge as well as on the parkway through the culvert. In April 1941 the south side of the new bridge opened to traffic and in August the old culvert was dynamited to make room for new parkway lanes under the direction of the National Capital Park and Planning Commission.

March 1940

April 1941

July 1941

August 1941

August 1941

(Top)

Dredging and filling for the Mount Vernon Memorial Highway near Gravelly Point and Roaches Run, July 1930. The Corps' first choice for the highway's route was along high ground; creating the roadbed through Potomac River marshes used some of the Corps' most fundamental skills. The Corps' dredge boats Talcott (seen here) and Waletka did much of the work.

Office of History, Corps of Engineers

(Bottom)

This Historic American Engineering Record drawing shows the techniques for constructing the roadway and describes the dredging and filling operations performed by the Washington Engineer District to create land for parts of the road. Similar but more extensive dredging would provide the land for most of National Airport.

Library of Congress, Historic American Engineering Record, National Park Service, Tim Mackey, 1994

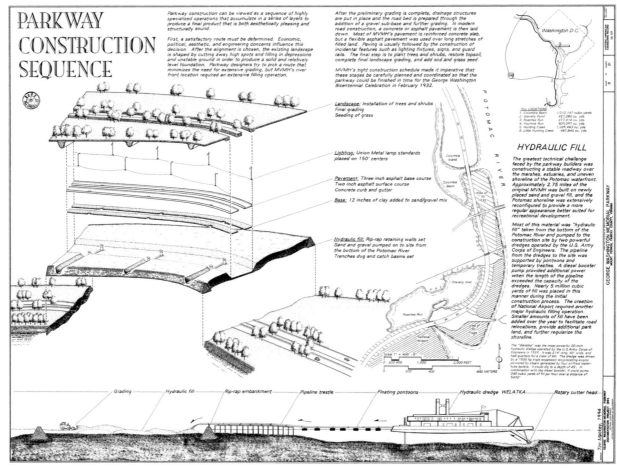

PARKWAY CONSTRUCTION SEQUENCE

Parkway construction can be viewed as a sequence of highly specialized operations that accumulate in a series of layers to produce a final product that is both aesthetically pleasing and structurally sound.

First, a satisfactory route must be determined. Economic, political, aesthetic, and engineering concerns influence this decision. After the alignment is chosen, the existing landscape is shaped by cutting away high spots and filling in depressions and unstable ground in order to produce a solid and relatively level foundation. Parkway designers try to pick a route that minimizes the need for extensive grading, but MVMH's river front location required an extensive filling operation.

After the preliminary grading is complete, drainage structures are put in place and the road bed is prepared through the addition of a gravel sub-base and further grading. In modern road construction, a concrete or asphalt pavement is then laid down. Most of MVMH's pavement is reinforced concrete slab, but a flexible asphalt pavement was used over long stretches of filled land. Paving is usually followed by the construction of incidental features such as lighting fixtures, signs, and guard rails. The final step is to plant trees and shrubs, restore topsoil, complete final landscape grading, and add sod and grass seed.

MVMH's tight construction schedule made it imperative that these stages be carefully planned and coordinated so that the parkway could be finished in time for the George Washington Bicentennial Celebration in February 1932.

Landscape: Installation of trees and shrubs
Final grading
Seeding of grass

Lighting: Union Metal lamp standards placed on 150' centers

Pavement: Three inch asphalt base course
Two inch asphalt surface course
Concrete curb and gutter

Base: 12 inches of clay added to sand/gravel mix

Hydraulic fill: Rip-rap retaining walls set
Sand and gravel pumped on to site from the bottom of the Potomac River
Trenches dug and catch basins set

HYDRAULIC FILL

The greatest technical challenge faced by the parkway builders was constructing a stable roadway over the marshes, estuaries, and uneven shoreline of the Potomac waterfront. Approximately 2.75 miles of the original MVMH was built on newly placed sand and gravel fill, and the Potomac shoreline was extensively reconfigured to provide a more regular appearance better suited for recreational development.

Most of this material was "hydraulic fill" taken from the bottom of the Potomac River and pumped to the construction site by two powerful dredges operated by the U.S. Army Corps of Engineers. The pipeline from the dredges to the site was supported by pontoons and temporary trestles. A diesel booster pump provided additional power when the length of the pipeline exceeded the capacity of the dredges. Nearly 5 million cubic yards of fill was placed in this manner during the initial construction process. The creation of National Airport required another major hydraulic filling operation. Smaller amounts of fill have been added over the year to facilitate road relocations, provide additional park land, and further regularize the shoreline.

Grading — Hydraulic fill — Rip-rap embankment — Pipeline trestle — Floating pontoons — Hydraulic dredge WELATKA — Rotary cutter head

GEORGE WASHINGTON MEMORIAL PARKWAY

long urging by the engineers, Congress authorized an examination and survey of the area. In 1930 the Washington Engineer District proposed a $3.7 million plan to refurbish the waterfront while preserving local landmarks such as the Capital Yacht Club and the fish market. The new wharves and marinas were only partially complete when the outbreak of war ended work.[34]

MOUNT VERNON MEMORIAL HIGHWAY

The Corps contributed to the creation of what one historian called "the first modern motorway built by the federal government," the Mount Vernon Memorial Highway, now a part of the George Washington Memorial Parkway. This scenic road almost fifteen miles in length was constructed between 1929 and 1932 to connect Arlington Memorial Bridge with George Washington's famous estate.[35] Congress ordered the Corps of Engineers to study the possibility of connecting Aqueduct Bridge to Mount Vernon with a formal road in 1889. District Engineer Colonel Peter C. Hains proposed three routes and provided his report with landscape plans and bridge designs.[36] The McMillan Commission in its 1902 park system report endorsed one of Hains's routes.[37] Increased motor tourism in the 1920s and the approach of the 1932 bicentennial of Washington's birth led Congress to authorize the highway's construction in 1928. It was designed by the Bureau of Public Roads to run along the Potomac, passing through and following the river.[38] Sections of the road were built on landfill and two-and-one-half miles of arti-ficial causeway. Numerous bridges were required over creeks that fed into the Potomac. The Corps of Engineers undertook the necessary and extensive hydraulic fill work, first under District Engineer Major Brehon B. Somervell and then under District Engineer Major Joseph D. Arthur.[39]

"[T]he first modern motorway built by the federal government."

WASHINGTON NATIONAL AIRPORT

In 1938 at President Roosevelt's urging, the Civil Aeronautics Authority chose a site for a major new Washington airport. The tiny Washington-Hoover Airport emerged from the combination and expansion in 1930 of Hoover Field (1926) and Washington Airport (1927), built across the road from one another near the Virginia end of the Highway Bridge. Increasing airmail and passenger traffic quickly surpassed its capacity. In 1937 Roosevelt vetoed a bill that would have permitted expansion of Washington-Hoover, believing that a new airport a mile south at Gravelly Point, and only 3.5 miles from downtown Washington, would better serve the capital and national defense needs.

Dredging and filling at the site of National Airport, January 1939. This aerial view looking southeast down the Potomac River shows the outline of the airport beginning to appear. A section of the Mount Vernon Highway that had to be relocated curves though the center of the photograph.
Office of History, Corps of Engineers

The Corps' dredge Talcott *moving dredged material from the Potomac River bottom through pipes to the fill area behind the dike built by the Corps, May 1939. Five hundred of the airport's 729 acres were landfill for which Corps engineers moved twenty million cubic yards of material.*
Office of History, Corps of Engineers

The 1938 passage of the Civil Aeronautics Act, creating the Civil Aeronautics Authority, gave Roosevelt the power to authorize the planning and construction of the new airport.

America's first federally-owned commercial airport resulted from the close cooperation of five federal agencies and was largely funded through New Deal initiatives with 3,500 men from the Works Progress Administration providing much of the labor. The Corps' responsibilities were the survey, design, and preparation of the site that included building a levee around the airport's land reclaimed from the Potomac River. Gravelly Point was a low-lying area on the Potomac's west bank, already being enlarged by Corps of Engineers dredging before the 1938 official approval of the site. It required extensive additional filling before construction could begin. The airport's original 729 acres included 500 that were landfill, brought up from the bottom of the Potomac by Corps of Engineers' dredges. This hydraulic fill construction was a complex problem involving settlement of the river bottom's highly compressible mud, the choice of suitable materials for the runways, and planning for drainage in case of floods. When the airport opened to traffic on June 16, 1941, it was state-of-the-art, with lighted runways to accommodate the heaviest

By March 1940 dredging operations were almost completed under the direction of District Engineer Col. Thomas. The Corps paved the four runways seen in this upriver view, landscaped the site, and built hangars and administration buildings.
Office of History, Corps of Engineers

projected aircraft and the latest flight control and weather forecasting equipment. The airport project also required two miles of the new Mount Vernon Memorial Highway to be realigned.[40]

On September 28, 1940, President Roosevelt laid the cornerstone for the terminal building, designed by Howard L. Cheney of the Treasury Department's Procurement Division in its Office of Public Buildings (the successor to the Supervising Architect of the Treasury Department). Work crews under the superintendence of District Engineer Colonel Robert S. Thomas pumped 20 million cubic yards of fill behind dikes, and graded, landscaped, and paved the field, brought in water and sewage lines, and built hangars and administration buildings.[41]

FORT DRIVE

Fort Drive had been included in the 1902 Senate Park Commission's report as part of Washington's park system, a parkway connecting the Civil War forts encircling the city to serve as a scenic, recreational drive. In 1919 Colonel Ridley submitted a report to Congress calling for Fort Drive and five years later Congress authorized a survey and study. In 1926 under Colonel Grant, a Fort Drive of about 23 miles in extent was one

*The shaded areas on the Engineer Commissioner's 1933
Map of the District's Permanent System of Highways
indicate Fort Drive proposed by the National Capital
Park and Planning Commission, a ring road that
connected the Civil War forts along a scenic parkway.*

of the new National Capital Park and Planning Commission's major proposed projects. During the next two years the Engineer Commissioner approved the plan and in the early 1930s rights of way were acquired and the plan's design was refined. The Depression halted the project because funding was not available. In 1940 engineer Jay Downer proposed changing Fort Drive from a parkway to a freeway, the precursor of Washington's beltway. Although 98.9 percent of the rights of way were in hand by 1953, the freeway was not built because the new chairman of the National Capital Planning Commission had different priorities among many published in the agency's 1953 Comprehensive Plan. Engineer Commissioner Bernard L. Robinson calculated that the freeway was needed because of the volume of traffic at mid-century: 152,000 trips per day were made to the central business district, "while 122,500 trips with other destinations pass through the central area daily." Fort Drive as a "circumferential highway" would route traffic not destined for downtown Washington around the heart of the city.[42]

Wartime Temporary Buildings on the Mall, 1943. From 1922 to 1940 the Corps of Engineers headquarters was located in the Munitions Building, the westernmost section of the World War I "temps" closest to the Lincoln Memorial. These buildings prevented completion of the Reflecting Pool's central cross arm. Temporary office buildings erected during World War II were located on the south side of the Reflecting Pool. The last of the "temps" was removed in 1967.
National Capital Planning Commission

PENTAGON

For many years the U.S. Army had been looking for a location to construct a new central headquarters. It had considered sites around the city—near Walter Reed Hospital and adjacent to the Army War College—before developing a site in Foggy Bottom in 1938. By the middle of 1941 when this 500,000-square-foot building opened, the War Department employed 24,000 people, and they were scattered among seventeen buildings in the district and Virginia. The new headquarters was not even the department's largest building: the 779,000-square-foot Munitions Building, a World War I temporary structure on Constitution Avenue, had that honor. A 25 percent increase in War Department personnel was anticipated by the beginning of 1942, placing an incredible strain on already short supplies of office and storage space available to the department.[43]

In November 1940 the U.S. Army acquired a portion of the Agriculture Department's Government Experimental Farm between Arlington Cemetery and the Potomac, and when Congress appropriated funds for the War Department to construct additional temporary buildings in Washington, Army Chief of Staff General George C. Marshall preferred the more spacious and convenient site at the end of the Memorial Bridge. When planning on the Pentagon began, military construction was under the Quartermaster Corps. On December 1, 1941, President Roosevelt approved an order moving the construction function from the Quartermaster Corps to the Corps of Engineers. Thus, the engineers who began work on the Pentagon were detailed to the Quartermaster Corps until the end of 1941.[44]

The Quartermaster Corps' construction division chief, Brigadier General Brehon B. Somervell, thought a permanent building solution was needed. In the summer of 1941 Somervell, who was an engineer officer, proposed constructing a single permanent building housing forty thousand people to centralize the War Department's operations. Somervell charged Engineer Lieutenant Colonel Hugh J. Casey, chief of the Quartermaster Design Section, and architect George E. Bergstrom, president of the American Institute of Architects and chief consulting architect to the War Department, with designing such a structure. In one hectic weekend, they and their assistants sketched plans for a three-storied, five-sided structure capable of housing forty thousand workers. They sited it on the Arlington Farms land, the bordering roads of which dictated a five-sided design.

The House passed an appropriation to fund the 5.1 million square foot structure one week after Bergstrom and Casey first presented their design. Objections to the building's size, location, and cost delayed Senate approval by a month, but in the end the bill passed with no strings on the structure's site, size, or design.[45]

The Arlington Farms site formed a portion of the original Arlington estate, and it bordered Memorial Drive on the main approach to Arlington Cemetery. Among others, the prominent Frederic A. Delano, chairman of National Capital Park and Planning Commission, and Gilmore D. Clark, chairman of the Fine Arts Commission, objected that the massive new building would dominate the view to and from the cemetery, seriously compromising the dignity of the place. President Roosevelt first approved the site, and then rejected it based in large part on these two men's arguments. Over Somervell's strong objections, he ordered the War Department building built at an alternate site further south, partially on land purchased in July 1941 from the disused Washington-Hoover Airport. Roosevelt also ordered the building be scaled down to accommodate twenty thousand workers.[46]

Redesigned to about four-fifths its original size, the structure's pentagon shape was retained for the new site. John McShain, Doyle & Russell, and Wise Contracting Co., were hired as builders, and extensive work was performed by more than two dozen subcontractors. George Bergstrom served as chief architect until his resignation in April 1942, when his assistant David J. Witmer replaced him. Both were California architects. Witmer served between 1934 and 1938 as chief architectural supervisor for the Federal Housing Administration in southern California. Bergstrom worked in Los Angeles in the 1920s. His firm, Allied Architects, designed the Hollywood Bowl and the Los Angeles County Museum of Science, History, and Art.[47] Their design staff at the Pentagon numbered, at its peak, 110 architects, 54 structural engineers, and 43 mechanical engineers, plus more than one hundred supervisory field architects and inspectors. First under the chief architect, the field workers were later placed under the direction of Arlington District Engineer Major Clarence Renshaw when responsibility for military construction in the War Department passed from the Quartermaster Corps to the Corps of Engineers. Renshaw also directed the contractors, mediating between McShain, the principal contractor, and the architects. General Somervell had final say on all aspects of the project, but gave Colonel Leslie R. Groves (later head of the Manhattan Engineer District) direct oversight.

Groundbreaking was September 11, 1941. The final design placed five concentric rings of offices, broken by light courts, around a central courtyard. Ten crossing wings connected the concentric rings, easing circulation through the building. With five floors, it was built of reinforced concrete mixed on site from sand and gravel dredged out of the Potomac. Its outside perimeter walls were faced in limestone. Efforts to reduce the use of steel in the building led to extensive use of wood, fiber, and concrete in partitions, ducts,

RAPID RISE OF THE PENTAGON

From conception after July 17, 1941, to completion on January 15, 1943, the Pentagon was a remarkable design and construction feat. Built to conserve scarce wartime materials and with little superfluous ornamentation, it was a utilitarian office building bigger than any other in the United States at the time. The period from groundbreaking on September 11, 1941, to the arrival of the first occupants on April 29, 1942, was an incredible seven months. The Pentagon greatly reduced, although did not eliminate, the War and Navy Departments' demand for office space in Washington, although it seemed then far from downtown. It was constructed sturdily enough for records storage after the war in case its services would no longer be required.

September 1941

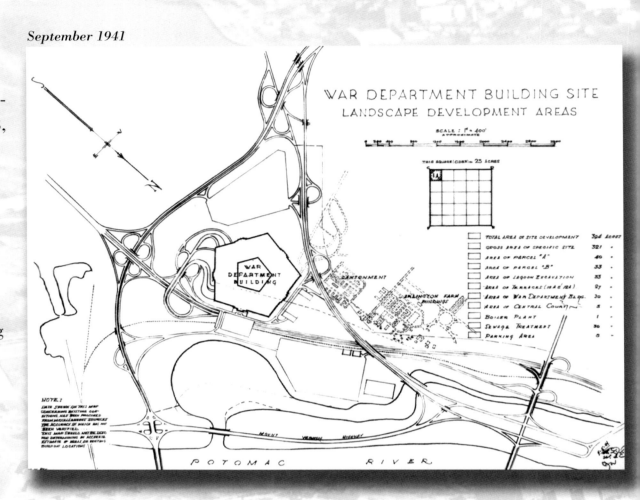

January 1942

July 1942

n.d.

July 1947

and drains, plus the addition of pedestrian ramps between floors to reduce the number of elevators. Provision was made in the Pentagon design for efficient bus, truck, and fire equipment access. Sections of the building were occupied as they were completed, and construction focused on a fifth of the building at a time. The first 300 employees moved in at the end of April 1942, and by the end of May, one million square feet of office space was ready. Twenty-two thousand people worked at the Pentagon by the end of December. Construction finished January 15, 1943, two months after the original completion goal.

The Pentagon construction required architects to lay out more than thirty miles of access roads, greatly accelerating long-term National Capital Park and Planning Commission plans for improving the approaches to Memorial Bridge and the Highway Bridge. They built two giant parking lots, seeded twenty acres of lawn, and landscaped much of the remaining 530 acres that originally surrounded the building. The building required a dedicated heating and cooling plant and a sewage treatment facility that also handled waste from other government buildings in the area.

The creation of the Pentagon, figuring out its many details, and time and material savings ideas, resulted from a dynamic process continuously negotiated between the builders; Renshaw, with the review of his superiors; and the architects. An assessment written in 1942 directly credited now Lieutenant Colonel Renshaw "for the early completion of the building. He alone could represent the War Department, make decisions in the interest of speeding the work and direct the design office, the builder and the inspection force to the end that the work should be accomplished as speedily as possible. The shortness of time from commencement of the building to completion is quite as much due to his driving force and his determination to remove causes of hindrance as [to] the cooperation and efforts of all parties engaged in the work."[48]

But unceasing demands for speed helped create a high on-the-job accident rate, while cost overruns drew criticism from the press and congressional investigators. The sheer size of the Pentagon and the notion that the military was feathering a plush nest for itself at taxpayers' expense drew frequent barbs. Washington wags laughed at the remoteness of the structure, separated by the Potomac from the shopping and dining facilities of downtown.[49]

WORLD WAR II IN WASHINGTON

On December 1, 1941, the engineers took over the construction responsibilities of the Quartermaster Corps, including Bolling Field, now a 600-acre base. Until the end of the war Colonels William J. Barden (who returned to active duty from retirement), Clarence

"The shortness of time from commencement of the building to completion is quite as much due to his driving force and his determination to remove causes of hindrance as [to] the cooperation and efforts of all parties engaged in the work."

Renshaw, and John M. Johnson of the Washington Engineer District directed the building of runways and mess halls, laboratories and boiler plants, a broadcasting studio, electrical and sewage systems, and family housing and recreational facilities. Under district supervision the Public Works Administration built an eight-mile highway, now Suitland Parkway, to connect Bolling to Camp Springs Army Air Field (later Andrews Air Force Base). The district also worked to keep ground transport moving, building between 1942 and 1946 an emergency railroad bridge across the Potomac and four temporary highway bridges—one at 14th Street, two at Roosevelt Island, and one across the Anacostia near the Navy Yard. In 1942 the district also took over construction work at Walter Reed Army Medical Center, where it built laboratories, wards, a gymnasium, and a pool.[50]

In 1944 General Grant proposed a "National Capital Stadium" located on East Capitol Street where it joins the Anacostia River to serve as a "useful memorial" to honor the nation's military heroes as well as to function as an impressive gateway to the city from the

The Washington Engineer District supervised construction of what became known as the Suitland Parkway to allow rapid travel between Bolling Army Airfield and the Camp Springs Army Airfield (later Andrews Air Force Base). The district completed the parkway, seen here in 1949, in late 1944.
Copyright Washington Post; reprinted by permission of the D.C. Public Library

(Top)
Emergency Railroad Bridge, August 1942. The Washington Engineer District built this additional, temporary crossing over the Potomac River from Shepherds Landing, D.C., to Alexandria, Virginia, to transport goods and troops in a national emergency. Authorities worried that the bridge immediately to the north was the only rail crossing of the southern Potomac River.
National Archives no. 77-RH-141B-1

(Bottom)
The Washington Engineer District also built four lighter emergency highway bridges, three across the Potomac River and one spanning the Anacostia River. This one connecting Constitution Avenue near the Lincoln Memorial to Roosevelt Island was photographed in August 1942.
National Archives no. 77-RH-141-B-7

east. Working with city planner John Nolan, Grant proposed a hippodrome-shaped stadium on the north side of East Capitol Street and a monumental parade ground overlooked by a grandstand on axis with the street. As was his practice, Grant invited all concerned citizens to attend a mass meeting about a project that he fostered for a decade. Grant's many civic contributions to Washington included frequent lectures before neighborhood associations and historical organizations. He served as president of the Columbia Historical Society from 1952 to 1968. It was through his efforts from 1954 to 1957 that the Christian Heurich mansion was secured as the society's headquarters.[51]

TRUMAN WHITE HOUSE

During the first three years of his presidency, Harry S Truman and his family were frequently bothered by creaking noises, drafts, cracking plaster, and unusual floor movements in the White House. Studies in 1948 determined that years of use and modification had seriously weakened the White House's structure, making it unsafe for the number of visitors it often contained. Deciding to save what he could, Truman asked Congress for $5.4 million to completely rebuild the White House within its original walls.[52]

In April 1949 Congress created the presidentially appointed Commission on the Renovation of the Executive Mansion. It worked with the Public Buildings Service, the General Services Administration, and architect Lorenzo Winslow. Consulting on the project were architect William Adams Delano and civil engineers Ernest Howard and Emil H. Praeger. In the middle of it all was the commission's executive director, retired engineer officer Major General Glen E. Edgerton, and his assistant, Colonel Douglas H. Gillette of the Corps of Engineers.

The Commissioner of Public Buildings handled the contracting, but the Commission on the Renovation acted as the controlling body guiding the entire project. Throughout, Truman exerted direct influence over the commission and the architects. After the president's household moved across the street to Blair House in 1948, it took a year of planning before demolition began. In 1950 the original interior was dismantled to allow for the excavation of new foundations and sub-basements and the erection of a steel structure and concrete floors. Installing modern utilities and duplicating the interiors took until March 1952. This renovation of the White House was at the vanguard of the new profession of historic preservation and the entire team formulated principles of how to conserve historic properties as they faced the challenges of a major construction project that had to be invisible when completed. The public expected the White House to be aesthetically and

April 1950

May 1950

WHITE HOUSE RENOVATION

President Harry Truman sponsored the most extensive "renovation" of the White House between 1948 and 1952 since its original construction in the 1790s. In reality, only the original exterior walls and some paneling from Theodore Roosevelt's 1902 renovation survived. Yet, conserving both the original plan with its famous East Room, Blue Room, and State Dining Room and the exterior appearance approved by George Washington was critical to the preservation strategy. Truman worked closely with Maj. Gen.(Ret.) Glen Edgerton to retain the White House's national symbolic meaning yet create a functional, up-to-date residence.

July 1950

June 1951

November 1951

symbolically the same but the Executive Branch required a safe home for the president with sufficiently modern service facilities for large-scale entertaining and adequate office space for a large staff. These multiple needs were met by underpinning the original walls and excavating beneath the original footprint as well as along its perimeter to construct multiple basement levels and tunnels connected to the executive office buildings. Steel frames were inserted in original exterior walls while an entirely new steel structural system was built to receive the original interior walls that were saved. Because the underground construction proved to be more time-consuming than anticipated, the interiors had to be hastily built and they were erected with new materials.[53]

During the course of the work, a detailed diary of the renovation was maintained at the direction of General Edgerton. It recorded all daily activities on site from October 28, 1949, to March 27, 1952, including this entry for March 3, 1952: "Capital Parks grading and tearing down shacks. Plasterer patching in misc. locations. make inspection of cabinets in pantries and kitchen and tell Jamestown man what to do in way of corrections. Meeting in General Edgerton's office. Matter of ice cream maker comes up and Mr. Crim says it must be installed. Matter of oiling soapstone in fireplaces discussed." Truly, the daily duties of Corps engineers were a constant round of trivial details and momentous decisions.[54]

"Meeting in General Edgerton's office. Matter of ice cream maker comes up and Mr. Crim says it must be installed."

The Truman renovation preserved the original exterior stone walls designed by Hoban, but tons of wood, brick, and plaster became landfill at Fort Myer, Virginia. Although the architects made detailed plans to reuse original woodwork and ornamental plaster, little was reused because of damage, time pressures, and cost cutting. The State Dining Room dating from Theodore Roosevelt's 1902 White House renovation, its oak paneling painted light green, was the only room substantially reinstalled with pre-renovation materials.

After the excitement of building structures associated with the great era of monumental Washington was over about 1920, Corps members spent much of the first half of the twentieth century devising and implementing modern civic infrastructures as important as the engineering and architectural ones that occupied their predecessors. They brought to this essentially political and bureaucratic work the same creative energies that others expended on building bridges and raising complex and impressive monuments. Moreover, the commitment of many Corps members went far beyond completing their assigned jobs expeditiously but extended to their life as Washington citizens. Kutz, who graduated second in West Point's 1893 class, served his third term as Engineer Commissioner from 1941 to 1945 as a retired general called back to public service. Grant was away from

Washington from 1933, the year the responsibilities of the Office of Public Buildings and Grounds were transferred to the National Park Service, until 1942. When he returned, Grant took over the chairmanship of the National Capital Park and Planning Commission and expanded his civic service to membership on several public and private commissions for the preservation of Washington's and the nation's historic heritage. He was one of the first ten trustees of the National Trust for Historic Preservation, created by Congress in 1949, for example. The allegiance of such men to their profession was matched by their commitment to the nation's capital.[55]

THE CONNECTICUT AVENUE BRIDGE (1897—1907) SPANNING THE ROCK CREEK VALLEY WAS DESIGNED BY GEORGE S. MORISON AND EDWARD P. CASEY UNDER THE SUPERVISION OF ENGINEER WALTER J. DOUGLAS OF THE BRIDGE DIVISION IN THE OFFICE OF THE DISTRICT COMMISSIONERS. EACH OF ITS SEVEN ARCHES IS BUILT OF PRE-CAST AND POURED CONCRETE, ONE OF THE EARLIEST AND LARGEST CONCRETE BRIDGES IN THE WORLD THAT DOES NOT DEPEND ON METAL REINFORCEMENT; RATHER, THE SPANDRELS OF EACH ARCH ARE COMPOSED OF A SERIES OF ARCHES. ORIGINALLY CALLED THE MILLION DOLLAR BRIDGE (ACTUAL ESTIMATED COST $846,331), IT WAS RENAMED THE WILLIAM H. TAFT MEMORIAL BRIDGE IN 1931. THE 1891 STEEL TRUSS CALVERT STREET BRIDGE THAT CROSSES THE NORTH LANDFALL OF THE TAFT BRIDGE WAS REPLACED IN 1935 BY ONE DESIGNED BY PAUL CRET, RENAMED THE DUKE ELLINGTON MEMORIAL BRIDGE IN 1974.

THE FOOT OF 11TH STREET, SE, HAS BEEN THE LANDFALL OF SEVERAL ANACOSTIA RIVER BRIDGES BUILT TO SERVE THE NAVY YARD. ENGINEER DOUGLAS REPLACED AN 1875 IRON BRIDGE WITH THE STEEL ARCH 11TH STREET BRIDGE (1905–07) THAT INCORPORATED A COUNTERWEIGHTED DOUBLE BASCULE SPAN AND CARRIED DOUBLE STREETCAR TRACKS AS WELL AS ITS ROADWAY AND SIDEWALKS. BY 1970 TWIN PARALLEL STEEL GIRDER BRIDGES SPANNING THE ANACOSTIA WERE LINKED MORE TO THE AREA'S REGIONAL HIGHWAY SYSTEM THAN TO WASHINGTON'S STREETS.

National Archives no. 66-DC-1
Office of History, Corps of Engineers

Engineers Modjeski and Masters and consulting architect Paul Cret won the limited design competition for the present South Capitol Street Bridge in 1942, but World War II delayed its construction until 1949. The river's angle and the position of the Anacostia shoreline required that the bridge deviate from the true north-south axis of South Capitol Street. Because it separated two industrial parts of the city, the bridge needed a 386-foot-long swing span to allow a forty-five-foot vertical clearance for large ships to pass upriver. In 1965 the South Capitol Street Bridge was dedicated to Frederick Douglass, whose Cedar Hill home is located near the bridge's Anacostia landfall.

6 | *Metropolis 1950–2004*

INTRODUCTION

The Corps of Engineers, through its key position on the District of Columbia Board of Commissioners until 1971, confronted the same issues faced by other cities nationwide in the middle of the twentieth century: the emergence of "inner cities," racial tensions, uncontrolled suburban growth, increased traffic congestion, and pollution of both air and water. The commissioners, however, also worked under the close scrutiny of a population that fervently desired a new form of government that allowed for full enfranchisement of Washington's citizens. Unlike the governments of other cities, that of the district was constrained by federal authority. Congress retained line-by-line control over the city budget—a budget whose federal contribution continued to dwindle.

In the decade ending in 1960 the percentage of Washington metropolitan area inhabitants living in the district dwindled from 53 percent to 37 percent, turning Washington into an inner city surrounded by burgeoning suburbs. As middle-class white households moved to the suburbs, the African-American population remained in the city, augmented by migrations from the rural south. By the late 1960s the percentage of African-American students in the city's public school system exceeded 90 percent. By the 1980s Washington was again vital, thriving, and diverse with many widespread revitalized centers because of the collaboration of federal and district agencies and the commitment of residents.[1]

One day in 1960 Engineer Commissioner Brigadier General Frederick J. Clarke and his wife were speaking with Elizabeth Kutz, widow of Charles W. Kutz who served three terms as the Engineer Commissioner, his last term ending in 1945. She asked Clarke, "Tell me, dear, are the Eisenhowers treating you properly?" Clarke replied that he supposed so. He and his wife had been invited to the White House "for one of those big mass affairs," and had shaken hands with the president. Elizabeth Kutz remembered a different Washington. She said, "You know, when Papa [General Kutz] and I were there, we went to the White House at least every two weeks for lunch with the President. We were the city fathers. And we were always being asked to the White House for things, to represent the city." By the time of Clarke's tenure as commissioner, he and his fellow commissioners never had an audience with the president on the city's problems.[2] President John F. Kennedy did, however, appoint a Special Assistant for District Affairs who served as an intermediary between the White House and the District Building.[3]

Although numerous congressionally mandated planning and executive agencies or commissions also played roles in running the city, D.C. commissioners continued to serve on these bodies as their predecessors had done for the better coordination of all aspects of the city's affairs. For example, Clarke served on, and sometimes chaired, at least eighteen such agencies during his term as Engineer Commissioner. They included the National Capital Planning Commission, the Council of Governments, the Public Utilities Commission, and commissions on zoning, mass transit, regional sanitation, and traffic safety.[4]

When he assumed his post in 1967, Engineer Commissioner Brigadier General Robert E. Mathe knew he would be the last engineer officer to have a direct hand in the District of Columbia government.[5] Public sentiment in the city had long favored a new form of government. In August 1967 President Johnson's Reorganization Order No. 3 took effect, replacing the three-person Board of Commissioners with a presidentially-appointed chief executive, deputy, and a nine-person appointed council. Mathe and one of the civilian commissioners agreed to stay in their posts long enough to assist in the transition to a new government. The terms of the reorganization provided for the Corps to assign up to three engineer officers to assist the new city government, but General Clarke—then Deputy Chief of Engineers—and the new mayor's staff agreed not to assign any officers, opting instead for a clean break with the past.[6]

"You know, when Papa [General Kutz] and I were there, we went to the White House at least every two weeks for lunch with the President. We were the city fathers."

Washington's city planners blamed alley dwellings and "slums" for crime and disease and launched large-scale efforts using the District of Columbia's Redevelopment Land Agency to turn huge tracts of the district from "blighted areas" into "healthy communities."
Library of Congress, Prints and Photographs Division. LC-USF34-T01-246-D

URBAN REDEVELOPMENT

The Engineer Commissioners, as they always had, dealt primarily with public works, although they voted on all aspects of city government. They received no policy direction from their superiors in the Corps, and they freely exercised their own judgment on all issues—save one—that arose in the governance of the city. The Chief of Engineers did instruct the engineer officers serving in the city government to remain silent about proposals for government reorganization. In the 1960s a government official described city government this way: "It's divided into sixths—four-sixths for the engineer commissioner and one-sixth for each of the others. He makes the big decisions—on urban renewal, streets, freeways, and so on. He can do anything he wants."[7]

Urban renewal was one of the most pressing issues facing Washington at mid-century. Brigadier General U. S. Grant III, serving as chairman of the National Capital Park and Planning Commission, wrote in 1952, "It is generally recognized that the blighted and slum areas [of Washington], now so expensive to the city as the breeders of disease and crime, can be redeemed only by complete and well planned redevelopment into balanced and healthy communities." Congress established the District of Columbia Redevelopment Land Agency (RLA) in 1945 to facilitate the "redevelopment of slums and blighted areas in the city of Washington." The RLA was run by a five-member board, with two presidentially-appointed members and three chosen by the district

"It's divided into sixths— four-sixths for the engineer commissioner and one-sixth for each of the others. He makes the big decisions."

commissioners. After receiving funding to begin operations in 1950 from the Housing and Home Finance Agency, the RLA worked with the Board of Commissioners and the National Capital Park and Planning Commission (on which the Engineer Commissioner also sat) to plan the redevelopment of three areas in the city.[8]

Large areas of Washington's Southwest quadrant received immediate attention because it was perceived that while the residential and commercial blocks of older buildings were decaying, they housed a close-knit community. A study commissioned by the RLA and the NCPPC found buildings in Southwest in poor repair, frequently lacking central heating and indoor plumbing. Many residents lived in tiny alley dwellings, which planners regarded as particularly unhealthy physically as well as socially. In reality, the majority of Southwest's residents were poor or working class African Americans and the crime rate was high. The housing stock was similar to that of Capitol Hill; its historic buildings began to be renovated little more than a decade after most of Southwest was leveled.

Two plans for the redevelopment of Southwest were considered. The first, proposed by city planner Elbert Peets, called for rehabilitation of buildings and some new construction, with little long-term displacement of current residents and businesses. The second, by two of Washington's leading modernist architects Chloethiel Woodard Smith and Louis Justement, called for demolishing the old neighborhood completely in favor of creating

a modernist Utopia following the most avant-garde socially responsible architectural ideas and ideals. Rebuilding in a variety of architectural typologies from high-rise apartment buildings to row houses, all in extensive landscape settings would, they argued, provide better conditions for some of the former residents, but primarily would attract higher-income professionals back from the suburbs. In the end, the RLA, with the approval of the District of Columbia Commissioners and the newly-reorganized National Capital Planning Commission, favored a plan based on the Smith-Justement model. Decried by many for decades as socially irresponsible because the neighborhood's cohesion was broken and historically important buildings were lost, Southwest's extensive Modernist landscape was again appreciated at the beginning of the twenty-first century as its open spaces were threatened by new buildings.[9]

Between 1954 and 1958 the RLA acquired and demolished most of the buildings in Southwest—churches, homes, and businesses—and dispersed more than twenty thousand residents to other parts of the city. The RLA then leased the land to private

The Redevelopment Land Agency favored the Smith-Justement proposal to completely demolish Southwest and start over. By October 1959 most of Southwest's buildings had been razed, making room for a new freeway (shown under construction) and the first of the high-rise and garden apartment complexes.

developers who, with federal subsidies, rebuilt the area over the next decade with high-rise apartment buildings, townhouses, office buildings, churches, and a shopping center. The federal government used RLA land adjacent to the Mall for office buildings of its own.[10] The Southwest redevelopment had considerable racial overtones. The old Southwest was a majority African-American neighborhood, and, forced to move, its relocated residents frequently encountered difficulty finding non-discriminatory and affordable housing elsewhere in the city, or they moved into public housing. When new housing was ready in the new Southwest, its high rents effectively excluded many of the former, low-income inhabitants. Disturbed by the injustice and extensive physical and community destruction that came with the Southwest redevelopment, citizens in other parts of the city organized. In such neighborhoods as Shaw and Adams-Morgan, they were effective in influencing further RLA planning to avoid the clean-slate approach adopted in Southwest. In retrospect, relocation subsidies provided some former Southwest residents with the means to educate themselves and their children, thus breaking the poverty cycle.[11]

The elegant 1965 Tiber Island complex, designed by the Washington architectural firm of Keyes, Lethbridge & Condon, exemplified Modernism's urban renewal ideal of multiple middle-class housing types arranged amidst extensive public parks. It consisted of low-rise townhouses and four high-rise apartment buildings surrounding a central plaza.
Office of History, Corps of Engineers, Layton Personal Papers

HIGHWAY PLANNING

Intimately related to urban redevelopment was highway planning. In 1946 Engineer Commissioner Brigadier General Gordon R. Young released for public comment a six-year plan for the Capital. In it he warned of the dangers that population dispersion posed for the central city, promoting the idea of beltline and lateral freeways to keep the spreading suburbs in close contact with the traditional downtown. In the 1950 study *Washington Present and Future*, the National Capital Park and Planning Commission posited that traffic congestion could be moderated by locating places of employment away from the central city, but only if freeways existed to serve as a circulatory system for the whole metropolis. The commission proposed connecting the district and its suburbs with radial freeways and easing movement around and into the city with a system of three circumferential freeways, two in the district and one around it.[12]

The design for the Inner Loop Freeway was announced in 1955. Almost eighteen miles in length with an estimated cost of $273 million, its construction threatened sixty-five thousand buildings, a quarter of the city's total. Plans for the Southeast-Southwest Freeway, a portion of the full Inner Loop, proceeded quickly, as the Southwest's redevelopment had already freed up most of the required land. Southwest had long been physically isolated from the rest of the city—in the nineteenth century by the Washington City Canal and in the twentieth by the Pennsylvania Railroad's tracks. When the freeway set up a new barrier, the RLA welcomed it as a natural buffer between the federal offices to its north and the new residential communities on its south. But this attitude was rejected in neighborhoods that felt threatened. During the early 1960s citizens in the Southeast sector objected to demolition of houses in impoverished areas. The racial situation worked further to discredit the freeway program. "White men's roads through black men's homes" became a rallying cry for freeway opponents.[13]

Protests from one citizens' group after another forced the commissioners to abandon plans for any freeways to the north. The Southeast freeway, which was intended to loop past the new stadium at the east end of Capitol Hill and continue around the center part of the city, remained truncated in midair. The inner loop controversy also marked one of the rare occasions when the two civilian commissioners voted counter to the Engineer Commissioner—General Clarke favored completing the freeway system—on a public works issue.[14]

Activists in near Northwest and Northeast in 1968 protested the destruction of their neighborhoods that would be required to extend the Inner Loop Freeway (I-95) through the heart of the city. Protestors and neighborhood opposition played a large part in the eventual abandonment of the plans for the Inner Loop Freeway.
National Capital Planning Commission

"White men's roads through black men's homes…"

The construction of Rochambeau Bridge, the first of three mid-twentieth century 14th Street bridges, was well under way by July 1949. The Highway Bridge, heir to Long Bridge, at left, would give way in 1962 and 1971 to two new lower-level spans connecting Southwest D.C. with Arlington, Virginia.
Washingtoniana Division, D.C. Public Library

"On the contrary, he proved to be the right man at the right time for a monumental undertaking....There have been no scandals in the construction of the nation's largest public works project."

Although the last Engineer Commissioners generally favored highway construction, they also embraced the new emphasis on improved public transportation including a subway system. In 1966 the commissioners became members of the new congressionally established Washington Metropolitan Area Transit Authority (Metro) that hired a retired engineer officer, Major General Jackson Graham, to be the first general manager of Metro. Graham brought in other retired engineers, including Brigadier General Roy T. Dodge, to help run the massive project. Hired in 1967, Graham saw construction begin in 1969 and he resigned in 1976 just a few months before the first Metro trains began regular service. In spite of the problems and criticism he encountered, according to *The Washington Post*, Graham "owes no apology for his service to this community. On the contrary, he proved to

By August 1965 the Roosevelt Bridge spanned the Potomac River and reached Theodore Roosevelt Island but was not yet connected to the Virginia shore. The Roosevelt Memorial Association bought Analostan Island in 1931 and gave it to the government the following year as a nature sanctuary when it was renamed.
Washingtoniana Division, D.C. Public Library

be the right man at the right time for a monumental undertaking." Two years later Dodge announced his retirement as the design and construction chief of Metro. *The Washington Post* commented that he had "forged a remarkable reputation for integrity.... There have been no scandals in the construction of the nation's largest public works project."[15]

Bridge construction went more smoothly in postwar Washington than highway construction, although bridge designs came under the jurisdiction of the Commission of Fine Arts and National Capital Planning Commission. Congress approved two new four-lane bridges from Southwest Washington across East Potomac Park with the Virginia landfall north of National Airport to replace the Highway Bridge in 1947. The first, Rochambeau Bridge (now Arland D. Williams, Jr., Bridge), opened in 1950, the work supervised by Engineer Commissioner General Young. The second, George Mason Bridge, opened in 1962. A third bridge was authorized in 1966 while there was still an engineer commissioner but not completed until 1971; collectively the three bridges that divide East Potomac Park comprise the present Fourteenth Street Bridge. The Theodore Roosevelt Bridge, also partially supported by a landmass in the Potomac River—Theodore Roosevelt Island—was built by the District of Columbia Highway Department. Both the Commission of Fine Arts and the National Capital Planning Commission—as well as numerous citizens' groups—opposed the Roosevelt bridge both because of its industrial appearance and because it intruded on the nature sanctuary and memorial dedicated to the conservation-minded president.[16]

Senator Robert C. Byrd (left) of West Virginia and Brig. Gen. Frederick J. Clarke at the construction site of the Theodore Roosevelt Bridge, 1961. Clarke, who went on to become the Chief of Engineers (1969–73), was the Engineer Commissioner from 1960 to 1963, with only two successors.
©1961, Washington Post. Photo by David Chevalier. Reprinted with permission.

MAINTAINING AND EXPANDING GOVERNMENT FACILITIES

The U.S. Soldiers' Home (renamed the Soldiers' and Airmen's home in 1972) required renovation and expansion in the late 1940s and early 1950s to meet the coming influx of veterans from both world wars. In 1947 Chief of Engineers Lieutenant General Raymond A. Wheeler, president of the Soldiers' Home Board of Commissioners, oversaw the preparation of a master plan by Washington architects Porter & Lockie for expansion from 1,500 occupants to 3,500, and began work on air conditioning and fire protection of existing buildings. The plan featured a new 850-bed residence hall and a 200-bed hospital, plus needed modernization of the heating and electrical systems.[17]

The hospital plan had been expanded to 500 beds by 1949, and the design of the modern limestone buildings had been approved by the Commission of Fine Arts. A waiting list of 400 veterans precluded the option of tearing down the oldest buildings from the 1870s, generally viewed as "firetraps."[18] In 1950 the Soldiers' Home ceded 148 of its 500 acres to the General Services Administration in exchange for funding for an approximately $14 million expansion program. The home retained the historic Anderson Cottage (1843), where Abraham Lincoln wrote the Emancipation Proclamation while the cottage was still the country home of Washington banker George W. Riggs. The new residence hall, completed in 1953, was named for General Winfield Scott, who played the leading role in establishing the home in the mid-nineteenth century. In response to a declining population, between 1988 and 1990, the Corps renovated the Scott Building's interiors, which included creating private rooms and revamping the cafeteria. Between 1990 and 1992 Baltimore District Project Engineer David Hand oversaw the largest building to be erected at the home in four decades, the $29 million LaGarde Building, a 200-bed home health care facility that incorporated a "town center," an internal group of services as diverse as barber and beauty shops and a post office. Designed by the Detroit architects Smith, Hinchman and Grylls Associates, the LaGarde building brought modern concepts of assisted health care to the home's diverse group of retired service personnel.[19]

The Cold War years brought the Washington Engineer District a project designed to withstand nuclear attack, the Armed Forces Institute of Pathology at Walter Reed Army Medical Center. Completed in 1954, the $6 million windowless building of reinforced concrete rose eight stories, including three underground. The blast-resistant twelve- to sixteen-inch walls, of which the thickest faced downtown Washington, provided protection to an emergency power plant, laboratories, records and specimens, and medical education facilities and was the first deliberately planned atomic-bomb-resistant building in Washington.[20]

The Corps oversaw restoration of Arlington Cemetery's amphitheater in 1957 to accommodate increasingly larger numbers of visitors who came to view the ceremonies held at the Tomb of the Unknown Soldier. Two lateral cracks in the forty-eight-ton marble tomb progressed to the stage that repairs were carried out between 1987 and 1989 by Oehrlein and Associates, a difficult job that combined historic preservation and artistic conservation because of the tomb's delicate sculpture and famous inscription: "Here rests in honored glory an American Soldier known only to God." In 1996 large parts of the amphitheater's deteriorating marble were replaced or cleaned, a new sound system was installed, and the lighting was improved.

The creation of the John F. Kennedy gravesite on the central axis between Arlington House and Memorial Bridge led Corps planners by the mid 1960s to consider new projects relating to education, crowd control, and expanded facilities. The cemetery's 1977 master plan,

The Corps of Engineers' involvement with Arlington National Cemetery also included renovation work on the Tomb of the Unknown Soldier, 1974–75.
Office of History, Corps of Engineers

The new visitors' center at Arlington National Cemetery, built under the supervision of the Baltimore Engineer District and dedicated in 1988, won the Department of Defense's Excellence in Design Award.
Office of History, Corps of Engineers

developed in conjunction with the NCPPC, focused on public and private transportation to and within the cemetery for thousands of daily visitors. Their plan included a new permanent visitors' center, featuring an exhibit on the history of the site. Designed by David Volkert and Associates, the new center was dedicated in December 1988. Expanded parking, including an underground structure and tour bus facilities, was built adjacent to the visitors' center. Annexation of adjacent Army-owned land for 9,500 gravesites and columbaria for interment of cremated remains ensured adequate burial sites for America's future heroes. In a departure from its usual engineering studies, the Baltimore District conducted a sociological study on the columbarium concept and determined that the public would accept it. In March 1997 ground was broken for the sixth of nine columbaria to contain sixty thousand niches.[21]

During the 1990s the Corps was involved in renovation projects for two complex Washington buildings whose diverse functions were intended to continue while construction was underway. In 1992 the General Accounting Office (GAO) asked the Corps to evaluate the possibility of modernizing its massive 1951 headquarters building. The Corps began its planning based on the GAO's stacking plan that identified the movement and interactions of its employees laterally and vertically between seven floors. In 2000 Corps of Engineers' headquarters moved from the leased space at the Pulaski Building on the corner of Massachusetts Avenue and North Capitol Streets, NW, to part of the newly-renovated Government Accounting Office building.

On November 23, 1963, while the nation was still in shock over the assassination of President John F. Kennedy the day before, the Corps of Engineers was surveying Arlington National Cemetery in order to recommend a location for a gravesite. The next day, then Chief of Engineers Lt. Gen. Walter K. Wilson, Jr., learned of Mrs. Kennedy's desire for an eternal flame at the burial site and was tasked to provide it. He assigned the mission to Maj. Gen. William F. Cassidy, commandant of the Engineer School. Over the next thirty hours the engineers worked to produce a functioning flame in time for the burial the next morning, November 25. Starting from scratch, they built the device out of welded metal strips, a "luau lamp," and several small propane tanks. Once the flame was in place, Wilson tested it only once. When Mrs. Kennedy lit the flame during the burial ceremony, it ignited, and remained lit. The Corps' makeshift creation remained in place for more than a year. In 1967 President Kennedy was quietly reinterred in the current permanent gravesite.

In the mid-1990s Corps engineers began working on the team to renovate the John F. Kennedy Center for the Performing Arts. Although the Kennedy Center was only twenty-five years old, its more than 2,800 annual performances and related activities led to a proposed fifteen-year comprehensive plan to improve its safety, security, and accessibility; renovate its four theaters and halls; and extend and landscape its site. The Corps' major work was to renovate the Concert Hall, which required rebuilding the stage area, updating its acoustical environment, and refurbishing its interiors.[22]

On September 27, 1991, President George H.W. Bush dedicated Marshall Hall, the new $27 million academic operations center at the National Defense University, at Fort Lesley J. McNair, the nation's oldest operating Army post. Designed by the Minneapolis architects and engineers Ellerbe-Becket, the award-winning three-story concrete and brick structure consciously paid homage to the Army War College's historic Colonial Revival and Beaux Arts buildings initiated by President Theodore Roosevelt and overseen by his Secretary of War, Elihu Root. The Corps' construction oversight team consisting of project engineer Robert Wilson, Major Dale Schweinsberg, and Joe Reynolds were particularly proud of their joint achievement, which Reynolds referred to as "the Taj Mahal of military construction." The operation center's avant-garde design "is one of the most

"[T]he Taj Mahal of military construction..."

"[O]ne of the most striking pieces of architecture I've ever seen on any military post."

Marshall Hall, on the grounds of Fort Lesley J. McNair in Southwest Washington, was designed by the architect-engineer firm of Ellerbe-Becket; its construction was supervised by the Baltimore Engineer District. President George H. W. Bush attended its dedication ceremony in September 1991. Marshall Hall won the Military Programs Merit Award in the 1992 Chief of Engineers Design and Environmental Awards Program for its success in "resolv[ing] the demands of a large and complex function on an historic installation, while reinforcing the original 1903 master plan and respecting the character of the existing architecture."
Office of History, Corps of Engineers

striking pieces of architecture I've ever seen on any military post," commented former Corps officer John Bandera. Renovations of existing academic buildings in the National Defense University complex were also undertaken during the 1990s, most notably Theodore Roosevelt Hall, a National Historic Landmark designed by McKim, Mead & White and built between 1903 and 1907. The Corps' oversight of its $7 million renovation by Ellerbe-Becket was praised by the District of Columbia Preservation Office as a model of cooperation between review agencies, the Military District of Washington, and the architects and consultants.[23]

WASHINGTON AQUEDUCT

Water projects formed much of the Washington Engineer District's peacetime post-World War II work. Along with improvement and expansion of the Aqueduct, the engineers devoted considerable effort to studying and planning the development of the Potomac River water supply. Population growth and an expanded service area created greater demands on the Washington Aqueduct. Congress authorized the Aqueduct to supply water to Arlington County, Virginia, in 1926, and to Falls Church, Virginia, in 1947. World War I, the Depression, World War II, peacetime prosperity, and the Cold War all increased the population of the national capital region. In 1930 the Washington metropolitan area held six hundred seventy thousand people; by 1960 more than two million; by 1970 almost three million. Consequently, the Washington area demanded 103 million gallons of water per day in 1940, and 126 million gallons in 1950. Demand steadily climbed until the metropolitan area average topped 400 million gallons a day in the mid-1970s.[24]

To address the pressure on the Aqueduct, Congress, for the fourth time in thirty-five years, requested that the Corps of Engineers study the future of the district water supply in 1940 and 1941. The resulting report, submitted to Congress in February 1946, outlined a broad program for expanding and improving the collection, purification, pumping, storage, and distribution facilities of the water system to meet projected population needs for the next half century.[25]

The Washington Aqueduct Division began the next year to improve its reservoirs, filters, mains, and pumping stations, while the District of Columbia upgraded some of the pipelines and pumping stations in its water distribution system. Significant among these improvements was the completion in 1959 of a 450 million-gallon-per-day raw water pumping station at Little Falls. Complete with a new diversion dam at the falls and a tunnel to the receiving reservoir at Dalecarlia, this project represented a major addition to the 200 million gallons of capacity available at the Great Falls intake works. Equally important, it provided a backup conduit in the event of repairs or damage to the two existing conduits.[26]

Washington's waste water treatment plant at Blue Plains, which in 1950 allowed 80 percent of the pollutant load to enter the Potomac, was expanded from a capacity of 130 to 240 million gallons a day during the next decade. In 1960 Engineer Commissioner Brigadier General Alvin C. Welling reported in a newspaper editorial that neighboring jurisdictions had constructed sewers and mains to carry their wastewater to the expanded Blue Plains facility, resulting in an almost two-thirds reduction of organic pollution loads discharged into the river.[27]

Also of note, Washington became one of the first cities in the nation to fluoridate its water supply, beginning in June 1951. Engineer Commissioner Brigadier General Bernard L. Robinson decided in favor of fluoridation based on the Surgeon General's endorsement of its safety.[28]

Between 1960 and 1964 the Corps built new filter and chemical buildings at the Dalecarlia Reservoir that increased its filtration and treatment capacity. From 1967 to 1970 the engineers constructed a single unobtrusive replacement intake structure for both conduits at Great Falls. Aqueduct personnel could monitor the new intake structure from the control room at the Dalecarlia Pumping Station and thus reduce 24-hour surveillance.[29]

The Aqueduct Division, responding to concerns in the late 1960s that drought conditions might result in insufficient water flowing to the Great Falls and Little Falls intakes, designed the Emergency Estuary Pumping Station on the Potomac just above Chain Bridge. As the station was located within the C&O Canal National Park, public and National Park Service pressure led the engineers to create a low-lying design surrounded by local stone that blended into the landscape. The station was completed 1979 and never used. It was abandoned in 1985 when other water supply solutions made it unnecessary.

Broad environmental concerns in the 1990s led to the Corps' participation in a task force of federal agencies that undertook a feasibility study of creating a fishway at Little Falls to repopulate the Potomac River with many species of fish. This project was part of the Washington Aqueduct's wider efforts to clean up hazardous wastes and debris in the river and along its shoreline. The Aqueduct's recently completed, underway, or proposed projects totaling $75 million in 2000 focused on updating physical plants, improving water quality, and following EPA guidelines to reduce the quantity of disinfection by-products.[30]

Beginning in 1982 the construction of new rapid sand filters at the McMillan reservoir, just east of Howard University, obviated the need for the slow sand filters built in 1905. The sand storage "silos" (extreme lower left) remained standing in 2004 as remnants of the earlier technology.
Washington Aqueduct Division, Baltimore Engineer District

In 1991 the 1913 fountain dedicated to Senator James McMillan (who had proposed the reservoir) was returned to the McMillan Reservoir grounds near its original hilltop setting, which had been obliterated during the site's expansion and the fountain's removal in 1941. Improvements to the filtration plant at the reservoir, first suggested in 1946, began in 1982. The deteriorating slow sand filters from 1905 were abandoned upon completion three years later of a new filter and chemical building containing twelve new rapid-sand filters. During the 1990s water quality concerns continued to plague the Aqueduct and its reservoirs. The Environmental Protection Agency (EPA) called for an independent study in 1993 after bacterial contamination was found during routine testing of the district government's water distribution system. Two years later Virginia activists urged lawmakers to turn control of the entire system over to the Fairfax County Water Authority, a suggestion that was seconded by Assistant Secretary of the Army John Zirschky in 1996. Some officials suggested that a new federal agency run the Aqueduct. In 2001 Virginia Senators John Warner and George Allen urged congressional hearings on the discharge of sediment into the Potomac River from the Dalecarlia Reservoir, wishing to prohibit it during the spawning season. In December 2002 the EPA was pushing to reduce the concentration of sediment unleashed into the river by 90 percent. Although the Aqueduct experienced continuing pressure to improve its services, it remained in 2004 a part of the Baltimore District of the Corps of Engineers.[31]

POTOMAC AND ANACOSTIA RIVER BASIN PLANNING AND MAINTENANCE

The Aqueduct report of 1946 did not address the development of future water resources on the Potomac. The Corps began studying this thorny topic—which involved questions of water supply and quality, flood control, pollution control, and recreation—at the request of Congress in 1956, releasing its report in February 1963. During this long preparation time, the Baltimore Engineer District in 1961 assumed the duties of the Washington District, which was abolished, including its responsibility for studying the Potomac. An adequate supply of water to the Washington vicinity and clean water were the two main issues faced by the Corps' engineers. Although the Potomac's average flow was in the billions of gallons, it could and did fall during summer months to less than half a billion gallons a day. (On September 10, 1966, the flow fell to a record low of 388 million gallons.) In 1957 the U.S. Public Health Service declared the river unsafe for swimming. Consequently, the engineers' report made certain recommendations concerning land management and conservation, and it suggested wastewater treatment goals that extended to the year 2010. At its core was a proposed massive system of impoundments throughout the Potomac River basin, including sixteen major reservoirs and 418 smaller headwater reservoirs, estimated to cost $500 million.[32]

The storage capacity gained by this system would have assured an adequate supply of water even in times of severe drought. Furthermore, it was designed to provide a sufficient flow of water beyond the Washington Aqueduct's intakes in order to flush pollutants downstream and into the Chesapeake Bay. The report sought immediate authorization to build eight of the major proposed projects. As early as 1957, when aspects of its general approach became known, the Corps' proposal was widely criticized. Residents of four states and the District of Columbia objected to the condemnation of large amounts of upriver real estate to serve the needs of downriver Washington and to the flooding of sizable areas of the basin. Responses to the plan also noted that it did not seek to prevent "present or future pollution from being dumped into the waterways of the Potomac...on the thesis that this is unpreventable and will become progressively worse."[33]

The Seneca Project, a dam and reservoir slated for the main stem of the Potomac, was one of the most controversial parts of the proposal. Had the largest of the potential impoundments been built, its creation would have displaced about 460 families and flooded out twenty-nine miles of the C & O canal—16 percent of the canal's length—including the Monocacy Aqueduct. In his 1965 State of the Union address, President Lyndon Johnson declared: "We hope to make the Potomac a model of beauty here in the Capital." To this end, he sent the Corps' report to the Secretary of the Interior for review. A specially created Federal Interdepartmental Task Force on the Potomac worked with Chief of Engineers Lieutenant General William F. Cassidy to scale back the Corps' plan for the Potomac to six major reservoirs. None of these were funded and the Corps built only one major impoundment as part of this long effort. The Bloomington Lake Project, authorized by the Flood Control Act of 1962, went into service in 1981. Severe flooding in 1985 cost twenty lives and $300 million in damages in Virginia and West Virginia, but the Bloomington Dam "absorbed

"We hope to make the Potomac a model of beauty here in the Capital."

Construction of the concrete abutments for the tainter gates at the spillway of the Bloomington Dam on the Maryland-West Virginia border, (n.d.). The resulting reservoir was later renamed William Jennings Randolph Lake.
Baltimore Engineer District

After delays caused by the Depression and World War II, in 1948 the Corps resumed work on improvements to the Washington Channel, including construction of Pier No. 4, seen here in May 1950, before turning over responsibility for the channel to the district government in 1951.

Office of History, Corps of Engineers

the flood and protected the residents along the North Branch. Bloomington was the right dam at the right place. It prevented approximately $113 million in flood damages."[34]

One outgrowth of the contested planning for Potomac water development was a provision in the 1974 Water Resources Development Act. Congress mandated the construction of what became the Experimental Estuary Water Treatment Plant, the result of the Corps' study into the feasibility of treating water from the Potomac estuary in cooperation with the Environmental Protection Agency. Constructed at Blue Plains by the Corps' Aqueduct Division in 1980, the $10 million facility tested a variety of chemical and mechanical processes. The 1983 final report from the studies conducted at the plant concluded that the estuary water could be made potable, but at an unreasonable cost. But pollution was reduced at Blue Plains by the construction of eight new settling tanks in the 1980s that employed nitrification to process waste water, making Blue Plains one of the nation's few state-of-the-art facilities and the largest such plant in the world. The EPA's resident engineer Arthur H. Smit was able to say in 1988: "The Potomac River is much cleaner now than it was 10 to 15 years ago because of this plant."[35]

In 1942 the Corps used mechanical cutters on boats, developed and constructed by the Washington Engineer District, to attempt to rid the Potomac and its tributaries of their infestation of water chestnuts.
National Archives no. 77-RH-141A-3

Despite valid pollution concerns and the Corps' mitigation efforts, the Potomac is certainly not a lifeless river. Water chestnut (*trapa natans*) spread wildly on a forty-eight-mile stretch of the Potomac after first being detected in 1919, interfering with commercial navigation and recreational boating. The year 1939 marked the Corps' first effort to remove aquatic weeds from the Potomac with mechanical cutters. Annual cuttings continued through 1977, when the vegetation subsided. It was at that time that the National Park Service mistakenly introduced *hydrilla verticillata* into the Reflecting Pool as part of an experiment to reduce green algae. Hydrilla's escape and spread first came to public notice in 1982, after it had already choked waterways in California and Florida. Naturalists, however, viewed the return of vegetation to the Potomac as an "indicator of the health" of the river.[36]

The Corps of Engineers' river crew based at a small boat dock under the 11th Street Bridge on the Anacostia River normally spent its days clearing debris and other navigation hazards from the area's rivers. Their routine changed on January 13, 1982, when Air Florida Flight 90 crashed after takeoff from National Airport, struck the 14th Street Bridge, and plunged into the Potomac. Although the frozen river prevented the Corps' boats from immediately reaching the scene to aid in rescue operations, once the ice had been broken the crew spent thirteen days retrieving wreckage and bodies from the river. The crash killed seventy-four airline passengers and crew and four motorists on the bridge.

In 1982 hydrilla covered ten acres of the Potomac but within four years had expanded to a three- to four-thousand-acre range, which it maintained through 1989. In 1984 Maryland and Virginia asked the Corps to study the infestation and recommend a solution. The Baltimore District focused its investigation on the herbicide Diquat and mechanical harvesting, both of which had effectively controlled hydrilla on other waters. They eliminated Diquat because both states objected on environmental grounds, and because the herbicide was no more cost effective than the mechanical alternative. In early 1986 the Baltimore District decided mechanical harvesting was preferable to keep channels to marinas open. Boating interests urged complete elimination of hydrilla, but limited control made the most economic and environmental sense.[37]

Congressional approval for resumption of reclamation and development work on key parts of the Anacostia River's 158-square-mile basin came in 1955, when Congress authorized a Corps study. The unfinished work on 900 acres of water and land included dredging Kingman Lake and East Lake, dredging the river channel to Bladensburg, building seawalls, filling in low-lying areas with dredged material, and installing tidal gates. The Washington Engineer District noted that additional silting and deterioration of partially completed work would add to the original cost. Flood control work on the Anacostia, including channel improvements, levees, conduits, pumping stations, and a boat basin, was completed in 1959 and turned over to the Washington Suburban Sanitary Commission for operation. The engineer district retained responsibility for maintenance dredging. Years of piecemeal and sporadic improvement efforts did little to counteract the lower Anacostia's severe pollution.[38]

The Baltimore District of the Corps released its *Anacostia River Basin Reconnaissance Study* at the end of 1990, a study that was stimulated in part by citizen activism. It set forth a basin-wide plan to restore 600 acres of fish and wildlife habitat lost in previous Corps flood control works. The plan included wetland restoration, planting of trees and shrubs, removal of barriers to seasonal fish movements, and channel modifications to create riffles and pools for fish. The reconnaissance study concluded that the federal government had an interest in pursuing a detailed feasibility study leading to a federal project costing an estimated $46 million.[39]

Restoring the Anacostia got underway in 1991, an effort requiring multiple local government agencies, and for the Corps, environmental engineering, a relatively new area of expertise. The Corps and Coast Guard used skimming techniques and vacuum suction to clean up a mile-long oil spill near the Navy Yard in 1992 that ran from shore

Chapter 6

to shore. This accident hampered work on restoring the Kenilworth marsh, a key component in restoring the lower Anacostia's viability as a river. Corps engineers built up the marsh using material dredged from the main channel, which was contained by straw bales. The $2 million project restored thirty-two acres of wetlands destined to become a natural habitat for waterfowl and a feeding ground for fish. Stream-bank planting of trees and protection by placing riprap along muddy banks of the Anacostia and its tributaries followed in the mid 1990s. In 1996 President Bill Clinton designated the Anacostia one of the ten ecosystems nationwide to receive priority attention; in 1995 the National Capital Planning Commission's Legacy Plan earmarked both sides of the Anacostia's shores from its mouth to the National Arboretum as one of Washington's major future recreation areas. In the twenty-first century the Corps had joined local governments and private organizations in rallying citizen commitment to restoring the Anacostia as

In the 1990s, in part stimulated by citizen activism, the Corps began restoring wetlands and wildlife habitats on Kingman Lake in the Anacostia River that were lost due to earlier twentieth-century reclamation efforts by the Corps.
Baltimore Engineer District

The 4th Battalion of the 20th Engineers (Forestry) posed for the camera in December 1917 at Camp American University. Beginning in 1917 the Army used land near the post as a weapons range, a training ground for defense against toxic gas attacks, and a testing area for its own military gases. The land is now part of the upscale residential neighborhood of Spring Valley in northwest Washington.
Office of History, Corps of Engineers

the key to the revitalization of its adjacent neighborhoods. By 2002 the Corps had thirteen environmental restoration projects along the Anacostia River's watershed. A major strategy was to repopulate the wetlands with native plants. During the summer of 2002 the Corps collaborated with the National Park Service on Lake Kingman, which abuts the east end of Capitol Hill.[40]

MUNITIONS CLEANUP AT SPRING VALLEY AND CAMP SIMMS

In the last decades of the twentieth century several problems with government and city sites, as well as structures particularly associated with the military, involved the Corps and its Baltimore District once again in a diverse mixture of building projects. In 1993 the routine laying of sewer pipes uncovered buried chemical munitions containers dating from World War I in Northwest Washington's Spring Valley neighborhood located between the American University campus and the Dalecarlia Reservoir. Between 1917 and 1920 the American University Experiment Station, a chemical warfare research center and experiment station located at American University, used 661 acres of the sparsely settled neighborhood for testing ranges. The soldiers dug trenches modeled from those on the Western Front—where allied forces from 1915 on were subject to attacks by toxic chlorine (and later thirty other types of gas)—to replicate chemical weapons attacks and test protective clothing and equipment. More importantly, the Army began developing many kinds of noxious gases on the site and carried out many experiments, including chemical munitions explosions, in conditions now known to be unsafe. Such work was halted on

December 31, 1918, but significant amounts of high explosives and containers of chemicals were left behind and buried.[41]

In 1993 Operation Safe Removal, the collaboration of the District's Office of Emergency Preparedness, the Army's Service Response Force, the EPA, and the Corps, began investigating the initial area. Test trenches and electromagnetic surveys on 492 properties revealed two possible burial pits. During the ensuing years, evidence of contamination over a broader area has surfaced raising particular concerns about high illness and death rates among the neighborhood's population and arsenic that had leached into the soil at a day care center. These serious concerns led to 1,602 properties being slated for soil sample or subsurface investigation by 2003. The area's difficult rolling landscape, coupled with the amount of land covered by structures, contributed to the complex problem facing the Corps, which took the lead in the investigations. During the early 2000s removal of actual artifacts was accompanied by soil removal and replacement. In 2003–04 a local newspaper, the *Northwest Current,* coordinated a survey of the health of Spring Valley's residents, reporting its findings in a twelve-page supplement to the November 10, 2004 issue. The *Current* compiled a map of Spring Valley that outlined the Army's 1918 central testing area within the entire original defense site boundary. The survey identified lots where the Corps found high concentrations of arsenic and households "where significant diseases were reported to the *Current* in a yearlong health survey."[42]

In 1994 while the Metro was doing preliminary work on its Green Line subway in Southeast, six mortar rounds were discovered on what had been part of Camp Simms, a 169-acre fort used by the District of Columbia National Guard for a small arms target range. Between 1995 and 1997 the Corps detonated or safely removed forty-seven ordnance items from the site before testing the soil and ground water for lead and other heavy metals. During 2000 and 2002 the Corps' ordnance specialists investigated another site slated for commercial and residential development that also had been part of Camp Simms and removed various magnetic and construction elements although no hazardous materials were found.[43]

DISTRICT OF COLUMBIA PUBLIC SCHOOLS

In April 1998 the Corps offered its services to the District of Columbia government to renovate and modernize 147 public schools. Structural repairs as extensive as new roofs (33 in 1998), removal of asbestos, and extensive window replacement were begun immediately with $76 million of the school system's funds. Removal of approximately 200 underground storage tanks was a preliminary step to replacing antiquated heating systems with natural gas furnaces and air conditioning systems. Much of the major work had to be carried out while the schools were not in session and beginning in 1998 the Corps repeatedly met their goal of opening the schools on time each September. Federal standards of construction and procurement resulted in dramatically improved facilities throughout the city. By the fall of 2000 some improvements had been carried out in every school. Once the safety and security of the 68,000 students attending the existing schools was accomplished, the Corps began oversight of the design and construction of eight new schools, with construction of Key Elementary School beginning in 2000 and completed in 2002. In November 2001 the Corps broke ground for Miner Elementary

Chief of Engineers Lt. Gen. Joe N. Ballard and the District of Columbia Superintendent of Schools, Dr. Arlene Ackerman, discussed the Corps' role in the rehabilitation of Washington's schools, October 1998.
Office of History, Corps of Engineers

Following completion of a new building for Barnard Elementary School on 4th Street, NW, between Crittenden and Decatur Streets, the 1926 structure was demolished to make room for playgrounds.
Baltimore Engineer District

The Corps has made extensive repairs and built additions to the Thomson Elementary School in downtown Washington at 12th and L Streets, NW, which was scheduled to reopen for the 2005–06 school year.
Photograph by Darren Santos

School designed by Grimm and Parker, Architects, of Alexandria, Virginia. By 2003 the Corps managed more than $300 million in the projected $1 billion capital improvements related to the district's schools. The D.C. Board of Education hoped to renovate or replace all the city's schools by 2015.[44]

KOREAN WAR MEMORIAL

The Korean War Veterans Memorial was authorized in October 1986 to honor those Americans who had joined the armed forces and civilian personnel from twenty-two countries that served under the United Nations' mandate from 1950 to 1953. In 1989 four faculty members at Pennsylvania State University won the design competition that featured thirty-eight realistic statues of marching soldiers; veterans in interviews repeatedly had recalled memories of walking all over South Korea. "The number 38 was selected because it was the basic battle unit of the war, about the size of a single platoon. The war lasted 38 months. It took 38 years for our country to commemorate the war from its beginning in 1950 to the memorial's conception. The 38th parallel now divides the two Koreas, who signed an armistice there July 27, 1953, at the village of Panmunjom." The memorial was located on a seven and one-half-acre site at the west end of the Mall on the south side of the Reflecting Pool, opposite the Vietnam Veterans Memorial. Moreover, the architects of record of both memorials, Washington's Cooper Lecky Architects, modified the winning design of the Korean War Memorial by adopting a polished black granite wall as one of its major elements, the idea borrowed from the Vietnam Veterans Memorial.[45]

Working for the American Battle Monuments Commission, the Baltimore Engineer District managed construction of the Korean War Memorial, consisting of the 164-foot

The Corps of Engineers managed the construction of the Korean War Veterans Memorial for the American Battle Monuments Commission. By April 1995 most of Frank Gaylord's stainless steel statues were in place and the memorial was dedicated only three months later.
Office of History, Corps of Engineers

Beginning in December 1941 the Corps assumed responsibility for construction at the Walter Reed Army Medical Center in northwest Washington. In August 1994 Daria Hasselman, Project Engineer, and Debbi LoCicero, of the Medical Facilities Office of the Baltimore Engineer District, visited the site of a clinic under construction.
Office of History, Corps of Engineers

mural wall etched with nearly 2,400 digitized photographs of actual participants in the war's broad-ranging efforts, nineteen stainless steel statues (the number reduced during the review process by federal planning agencies) by Frank Gaylord, walkways with curbs inscribed with the names of the participating countries, and a memorial pool of remembrance. Construction for the $16.5 million memorial began in 1993, its dedication taking place on July 27, 1995, the forty-second anniversary of the armistice. Two years later the pool had to be rebuilt and part of a memorial grove of trees replanted, the work done under the Corps' aegis and completed in 1999; the National Park Service claimed poor original construction by the Corps' contractors and the Corps claimed poor maintenance by the Park Service.[46]

THE PENTAGON

In 1989 the Baltimore District began an anticipated ten-year, $600 million project to renovate the Pentagon and the following year Anthony Leketa was named as the program manager. In August 1991 Leketa described his team's task as creating a modern work environment by replacing the entire heating and refrigerating plant as well as all mechanical and electrical systems; consolidating all the building's light industrial functions; replacing all windows for better environmental control; and renovating the entire interior by opening up and connecting offices for ease of communication. This massive undertaking would be done in stages, with each of the five sides vacated and the work completed before moving on to an adjacent side, a logistical problem for a building occupied by 25,000 members and employees of the five armed services. By 1991 the price tag for the Pentagon's rehabilitation had escalated to $1.4 billion and would continue to grow as was often the case with large and complex renovation projects. Even after work moved inside in 1995, the daily operations of the Pentagon's workforce continued uninterrupted.

In the summer of 2000 the Defense Department transferred management of the Pentagon renovation project to the Washington Headquarters Services (WHS), a Defense Department agency responsible for operating the building among other things. By that time, the Baltimore District had constructed a new Heating and Refrigeration Plant south of the building, begun an extensive renovation of the basement, started two new pedestrian bridges to improve access to the building and a Remote Delivery Facility where trucks would unload and their cargo allowing them to be processed away from the main building, and made substantial progress on renovation of the first of five segments or "wedges." In the process of the renovation, the Corps recommended increased protection against blast for not only the exterior windows but for the walls as well. This increased blast resistance proved its worth on September 11, 2001, when terrorists crashed American Airlines Flight 77 into the Pentagon near the intersection of renovated and old segments of the building. The WHS director of the renovation commented that without the increased blast resistance, "this could have been much, much worse."[47]

In November 2001 the Corps was charged with selecting the site and conducting the design competition for the Pentagon Memorial to commemorate those who lost their lives when terrorists attacked the building. From the outset, the families of the 184 victims (fifty-nine of whom were in the plane) played a key role on a team that included several federal agencies in choosing both the site and the design. Carol Anderson-Austra acted as the Corps project manager. The Corps established eleven criteria to evaluate ten sites in close proximity to the Pentagon with family acceptability, nearness to the impact area, and public accessibility leading the list. In April 2002 the team's choice of a 1.93-acre site 165 feet west of the Pentagon's west face under the plane's flight path was approved. The open, two-stage design competition was conducted between May 2002 and March 2003, six finalists chosen from 1,126 entries. The winning design by New York architects Julie Beckman and Keith Kaseman, announced on March 3, 2003, called for 184 cantilevered benches lit internally and arranged in a landscaped park, each personalized according to the age of the victim and whether they were on the plane or in the Pentagon itself.[48]

Immediately following the terrorist attacks on September 11, 2001, the Corps of Engineers responded by deploying personnel to New York City and to the Pentagon to perform rescue operations, debris removal, structural integrity analyses, and structural stabilization. The Engineer Company of the Military District of Washington, a unit based at Fort Belvoir, Virginia, and specially trained in search and rescue missions, arrived at the Pentagon within hours of the attack and later displayed the Corps flag at the site. In the months to follow the Corps would also select the site for a Pentagon Memorial and coordinate its design competition.
Corps of Engineers

"[T]his could have been much, much worse."

"...*outstanding teamwork in the areas of communication, customer care, flexibility, innovation, and responsiveness.*"

The successful completion of the competition ended the Corps' involvement but during the two-year process the Baltimore District's Pentagon Memorial team won two awards. The first was the *2002 Baltimore District Team Honors Award* for "outstanding teamwork in the areas of communication, customer care, flexibility, innovation, and responsiveness," the second the *2003 U.S. Army Corps of Engineers Project Delivery Team Honor Award* for "an extraordinary job well done" on a project that was "unique in the emotion, teamwork, commitment, and coordination required." The Corps' continuing contributions to Washington's development builds on nearly two centuries of an honorable commitment to public service.[49]

SUMMATION

It is more than two centuries since Army Engineer Peter Charles L'Enfant designed the federal city, yet Corps of Engineers officers continue to contribute their expertise to the betterment of Washington. The length of their commitment is matched by the diversity of the Corps' involvement. Design and construction of Washington's fortifications and bridges and management of its rivers' navigation repeated the Corps' traditional roles being carried on simultaneously in other parts of the country. Washington's unique position as the federal capital involved the Corps in two major aspects of the city's development for a century beginning in the 1860s: construction oversight of the nation's most important monuments, memorials, and public buildings as Officers in Charge of the Office of Public Buildings and Grounds and management of its municipal affairs as Engineer Commissioners. This crucial century saw Washington evolve from a loose conglomeration of widely dispersed neighborhoods to a coherent national capital, center of international power, and genuine community; the Corps of Engineers played no little role in this transformation.

Appendix

Engineer Commissioners of the District of Columbia

Name	Years	Name	Years	Name	Years
William J. Twining	1878–82	Jay J. Morrow	1907–08	David McCoach, Jr.	1938–41
Garret J. Lydecker	1882–86	William V. Judson	1909–13	Charles W. Kutz	1941–45
William Ludlow	1886–88	Chester Harding	1913–14	Gordon R. Young	1945–51
Charles W. Raymond	1888–90	Charles W. Kutz	1914–18	Bernard L. Robinson	1951–52
Henry M. Robert	1890–91	John G.D. Knight	1917–18	Louis W. Prentiss	1953–54
William T. Rossell	1892–93	Charles W. Kutz	1918–21	Thomas A. Lane	1955–58
Charles F. Powell	1893–97	Charles Keller	1921–23	Alvin C. Welling	1958–60
William M. Black	1898–1901	J. Franklin Bell	1923–27	Frederick J. Clarke	1960–63
Lansing H. Beach	1898–1901	William B. Ladue	1927–30	Charles M. Duke	1963–67
John Biddle	1901–07	John C. Gotwals	1930–33	Robert E. Mathe	1967
		Daniel I. Sultan	1934–37		

Officers in Charge of the Washington Aqueduct

Name	Years	Name	Years	Name	Years
Montgomery C. Meigs	1852–62	Thomas Lincoln Casey	1878–82	Charles E.L.B. Davis	1895
Henry W. Benham	1860	Garret J. Lydecker	1882–89	David D. Gaillard	1895–98
James St. C. Morton	1860–61	John M. Wilson	1889	Charles J. Allen	1896
Nathaniel Michler	1867–70	George H. Elliot	1889–95	Edward Burr	1898
George H. Elliot	1870–71	John G.D. Knight	1895	Theodore A. Bingham	1898
Orville E. Babcock	1871–77			Alexander M. Miller	1898–1904

District Engineers, Washington District

Name	Years	Name	Years	Name	Years
Sylvanus T. Abert (Civil Engineer)	1875–82	William C. Langfitt	1910–14	Robert G. Guyer	1935
		Henry C. Newcomer	1914–15	Walter D. Luplow	1937–38
Peter C. Hains	1882–91	Charles W. Kutz	1915	Robert S. Thomas	1938–40
Lewis C. Overman	1891	Harry F. Hodges	1915	William J. Barden	1940–42
Thomas Turtle	1891–92	Clement A.F. Flafler	1915–17	Donald A. Phelan	1942
Charles E.L.B. Davis	1892–96	Walter L. Fisk	1917–19	Clarence Renshaw	1942–44
Charles J. Allen	1896–1904	Max C. Tyler	1919–23	John M. Johnson	1944–45
Alexander M. Miller	1904	J.A. O'Connor	1923–26	Donald G. White	1945–48
William P. Wooten	1904	Brehon B. Somervell	1926–30	John W. Califf (Acting)	1948
Smith S. Leach	1904–05	Joseph D. Arthur, Jr.	1930–34	Henry C. Wolfe	1948–50
Richard L. Hoxie	1905	Leland H. Hewitt	1934	Harry R. Davis (Acting)	1950
Spencer Cosby	1905–08	John C.H. Lee	1934	Alan J. McCutchen	1950–53
Elliott J. Dent	1908	Frank O. Bowman	1934	Ray Adams	1953–56
Jay J. Morrow	1908–10	Robert W. Crawford	1934–35	George B. Sumner	1956–60
Warren T. Hannum	1910	William J. Matteson	1935–37	J.U. Allen	1960–61

Officers in Charge of Public Buildings and Grounds (after 1925 the Office of Public Buildings and Public Parks of the National Capital)

Name	Years	Name	Years	Name	Years
Nathaniel Michler	1867–71	Oswald H. Ernst	1889–93	Spencer Cosby	1909–13
Orville E. Babcock	1871–77	John M. Wilson	1893–97	William W. Harts	1913–17
Thomas Lincoln Casey	1877–81	Theodore A. Bingham	1897–1903	Clarence S. Ridley	1917–21
Almon F. Rockwell (Quartermaster Corps)	1881–85	Thomas W. Symons	1903–04	Clarence O. Sherrill	1921–26
		Charles S. Bromwell	1904–09	Ulysses S. Grant, III	1926–33
John M. Wilson	1885–89			James A. Woodruff	1933

Notes

Chapter 1: The Grand Design, 1790–1800

1 "Essay on the City of Washington," *Washington Gazette*, November 19, 1796. Pamela Scott, "L'Enfant's Washington Described: The City in the Public Press, 1791–1795," *Washington History*, vol. 3, no. 1 (Spring/Summer 1991), pp. 96–111.

2 J. J. Jusserand, *With Americans of Past and Present Days* (New York: Charles Scribner's Sons, 1916). Elizabeth S. Kite, *L'Enfant and Washington, 1791–1792* (Baltimore: Johns Hopkins University Press, 1929). H. Paul Caemmerer, *The Life of Pierre Charles L'Enfant* (Washington: National Republic Publishing Co., 1950). Joseph R. Riling, *Baron von Steuben and his Regulations* (Philadelphia: Ray Riling Arms Book Co., 1966). Daniel D. Reiff, *Washington Architecture, 1791–1861* (Washington: Commission of Fine Arts, 1971).

3 Letter, P. Ch. L'Enfant to the President of Congress [Richard Henry Lee], December 15, 1784, National Archives and Records Administration (hereafter NARA), Record Group 360 (hereafter RG), Papers of the Continental Congress. John C. Fitzpatrick, ed., *Journals of the Continental Congress, 1774–1789* (Washington: GPO, 1933), vol. 28, pp. 16–7.

4 Paul K. Walker, *Engineers of Independence: A Documentary History of the Army Engineers in the American Revolution, 1775–1783* (Washington: GPO, 1981), p. 358.

5 Fitzpatrick, *Journals of the Continental Congress*, vol. 28, pp. 16, 37, footnote 2.

6 P. Ch. L'Enfant, [Memorial to Congress], January 30, 1824. NARA, RG 233, Record of the House of Representatives. Letter, L'Enfant to the Marquis de Lafayette, November 2, 1785. Henry Knox Papers, Massachusetts Historical Society. For a general discussion of the alternate site for the federal city, see Kenneth R. Bowling, *The Creation of Washington, D.C.: The Idea and Location of the American Capital* (Fairfax, Virginia: George Mason University Press, 1991).

7 Letter, L'Enfant to Washington, September 11, 1789, Library of Congress (hereafter LOC), Manuscript Division, George Washington Papers, series 7, reel 120.

8 Edgar Erskine Hume, "The Diplomas of the Society of Cincinnati," *Americana*, vol. 29, no. 1 (January 1935), pp. 5–45.

9 Whitfield J. Bell, Jr., "The Federal Processions of 1788," *New York Historical Society Quarterly*, vol. 46 (1962), pp. 29–38.

10 Louis Torres, "Federal Hall Revisited," *Journal of the Society of Architectural Historians* (hereafter *JSAH*), vol. 29, no. 4 (December 1970), pp. 327–28.

11 Letter, Jefferson to Johnson, January 29, 1891, NARA, Papers of the Continental Congress. Letter, Washington and Jefferson to Deakins and Stoddert, March 2, 1791, LOC, Manuscript Division, District of Columbia Letters and Papers.

[12] Letter, Jefferson to L'Enfant, March 2, 1791, Digges-L'Enfant-Morgan Papers, LOC.

[13] Silvio A. Bedini, "Andrew Ellicott," John A. Garraty and Mark C. Carnes, eds., *American National Biography* (hereafter *ANB*) (New York: Oxford University Press), vol. 7 (1999), pp. 414–5. See also: Catharine VanCortlandt Mathews, *Andrew Ellicott, His Life and Letters* (New York: Grafton Press, 1908).

[14] Report from P. Ch. L'Enfant to Washington, n.d., LOC, Manuscript Division, Papers of Pierre Charles L'Enfant, Covering sheet in clerk's hand: No. 1. (P B & G 1791), L'Enfant, Peter Charles, Major, "Reporting to President Washington the suitability of the location of the City for the Capital of a mighty Empire, the sites of houses of Congress & Presidents Palace.—The above was personally handed to the Executive on his arrival at Georgetown at that time. 5-a."

[15] Donald Jackson and Dorothy Twohig, eds., *The Diaries of George Washington* (Charlottesville: University Press of Virginia, 1979), vol. 6, p. 103.

[16] John C. Fitzpatrick, *The Writings of George Washington* (Washington: GPO, 1931), vol. 31, pp. 256–7.

[17] Letter, L'Enfant to Hamilton, April 8, 1891, LOC, Manuscript Division, Alexander Hamilton Papers. Letter, Washington to L'Enfant, April 4, 1791, LOC, Manuscript Division, Digges-L'Enfant-Morgan Papers.

[18] Letter, L'Enfant to Jefferson, April 4, 1791, Jefferson Papers, LOC.

[19] Letter, Jefferson to L'Enfant, April 10, 1791, Digges-L'Enfant-Morgan Papers, LOC.

[20] *Ibid.*

[21] Letter, L'Enfant to Washington, June 22, 1791, L'Enfant Papers, LOC. A copy of this report, with some omissions, in Isaac Roberdeau's hand, is in the Digges-L'Enfant-Morgan Papers, LOC. Washington's diary entry, June 29, 1791, Jackson and Twohig, *Washington Diaries*, vol. 6, p. 165.

[22] *Ibid.*

[23] "L'Enfant's Reports to President Washington, March 26, June 22, and August 19, 1791," *Records of the Columbia Historical Society* (hereafter *RCHS*), vol. 2 (1899), pp. 38–48. Letter, Tobias Lear to L'Enfant, August 27, 1791, Digges-L'Enfant-Morgan Papers, LOC. Letter, Jefferson to the Commissioners of the District of Columbia, August 28, 1791, in Charles T. Cullen, et al., ed., *The Papers of Thomas Jefferson* (Princeton: Princeton University Press, 1986), vol. 22, pp. 88–9.

[24] NARA, RG 42, Records of the Office of Public Buildings and Public Parks of the National Capital, Entry 21, Proceedings, September 24, 1791 and October 6, 1791. Cullen, *Jefferson Papers* (1990), vol. 23, p. 237. William Seale, *The President's House: A History* (Washington: White House Historical Association, 1986), p. 18.

[25] Letter, Commissioners to Jefferson, April 11, 1792. Cullen, *Jefferson Papers*, vol. 23, pp. 396–7.

[26] Quoted in [H. W. Crew], *Centennial History of the City of Washington, D.C.* (Dayton, Ohio: United Brethren Publishing House, 1892), p. 184.

[27] Letter, Washington to the Commissioners, December 18, 1791, Fitzpatrick, *Washington's Writings*, vol. 21, p. 446.

[28] Pamela Scott, "Stephen Hallet's Designs for the United States Capitol," *Winterthur Portfolio*, vol. 27, no. 2–3 (1992), pp. 145–70. Bob Arnebeck, *Through a Fiery Trial: Building Washington 1790–1800* (Lanham, Maryland: Madison Books, 1991), p. 314.

[29] *Georgetown Weekly Ledger*, July 2, 1791. *Centinel of Liberty*, September 9, 1800.

[30] L'Enfant's "Observations…" were published on the front page of *Dunlap's American Daily Advertiser*, December 26, 1791. See Scott, "L'Enfant's Washington…," pp. 102–3. In his June 22, 1791, report to Washington, L'Enfant claimed that he first chose the locations for squares, then overlaid the grid, inserting the diagonal avenues later.

[31] Letter, Commissioners to L'Enfant, September 9, 1791, Saul K. Padover, ed., *Jefferson and the National Capital* (Washington: GPO, 1946), pp. 74–5. Letter, Ellicott to L'Enfant, September 12, 1791, Kite, *L'Enfant and Washington*, pp. 73–4.

[32] Pamela Scott, "'This Vast Empire': The Iconography of the Mall, 1791–1848," in Richard Longstreth, ed., *The Mall in Washington, 1791–1991* (Washington: National Gallery of Art, 1991), pp. 41–5.

[33] Cullen, *Jefferson Papers*, vol. 23, pp. 141, 150–9, 161.

[34] Russell I. Fries, "European vs. American Engineering: Pierre Charles L'Enfant and the Water Power System of Paterson, N.J.," *Northeast Historical Archaeology*, vol. 4, nos. 1 and 2 (Spring 1975), pp. 68–96. John W. Jackson, *Fort Mifflin, Valiant Defender of the Delaware* (Philadelphia: Old Fort Mifflin Historical Society, 1986). William Dunlap, *A History of the Rise and Progress of the Arts of Design in the United States* (Boston: C. E. Goodspeed & Co., 1918 reprint of 1834 edition), vol. 2, p. 12.

CHAPTER 2: THE ANTEBELLUM CITY, 1850–65

[1] Pamela Scott, "Moving to the Seat of Government," *Washington History*, vol. 12, no. 1 (Spring/Summer 2000), pp. 70–3. "Extract from an Address [reprint of Oliver Wolcott's 1802 report to Congress on the expense of moving the government to Washington]," *RCHS*, vol. 9 (1906), pp. 219–41. Elaine Everly and Howard H. Wehmann, "The War Office Fire of 1800," *Prologue*, vol. 31–1 (Spring 1999), pp. 22–35.

[2] Scott, "Moving," p. 72.

[3] *Ibid.*, p. 71.

[4] Edward C. Boynton, *History of West Point and the United States Military Academy* (New York: D. Van Nostrand, 1863), p. 176.

5   Gary D. Ryan, "War Department Topographical Bureau, 1831–1863: An Administrative History," Ph.D. diss., American University, 1968, p. 103. The technical system of educating West Point engineers on the French system was established early in its history. Peter Michael Molloy, "Technical Education and the Young Republic: West Point as America's Ecole Polytechnique, 1802–1833," Ph.D. diss., Brown University, 1975. Theodore Crackel, *West Point: A Bicentennial History* (Lawrence, Kansas: University Press of Kansas, 2002), pp. 39, 50–62.

6   Crackel, *West Point*, pp. 194–5.

7   *Ibid.*, p. 194. John C. Fredriksen, "Jonathan Williams," *ANB*, vol. 23, pp. 483–5.

8   John K. Mahon, "George Bomford," *ANB*, vol. 3, pp. 151–3.

9   Letter, Knox to John Vermonnet, May 12, 1794, *American State Papers*, vol. 16, p. 93.

10 Anthony S. Pitch, *The Burning of Washington: The British Invasion of 1814* (Annapolis, Maryland: Naval Institute Press, 1998), p. 153.

11 Quoted in Amy Cheny Clinton, "Historic Fort Washington," *Maryland Historical Magazine*, vol. 32 (September 1931), p. 237.

12 Pitch, *Burning*, p. 154.

13 Pitch, *Burning*, pp. 156–7. James Dudley Morgan, "Historic Fort Washington on the Potomac," *RCHS*, vol. 7 (1904), p. 15. David L. Salay, "'Very picturesque, but regarded as nearly useless': Fort Washington, Maryland, 1816–1872," *Maryland Historical Magazine*, vol. 81 (1986), p. 67. Two maps show the relationships between Fort Warburton and Fort Washington. NARA, RG 79, NCP 117.8-3 and NCP 117.8-4.

14 Jeffrey A. Cohen and Charles E. Brownell, *The Architectural Drawings of Benjamin Henry Latrobe* (New Haven: Yale University Press, 1994), vol. 2, pp. 587–9.

15 *Ibid.*

16 Russell F. Weigley, *History of the United States Army* (New York: The MacMillan Company, 1967), pp. 134–5. Joseph G. Swift, *The Memoirs of Gen. Joseph Gardner Swift* (Privately printed, 1890), pp. 168, 173. Michael A. Burke, "Joseph Gardner Swift," *ANB*, vol. 21, pp. 208–9. Frank N. Schubert, ed., *The Nation Builders: A Sesquicentennial History of the Corps of Topographical Engineers* (Fort Belvoir, Virginia: Office of History, U.S. Army Corps of Engineers, 1988), pp. 4–6.

17 Roberdeau Buchanan, *Genealogy of the Roberdeau Family* (Washington: Joseph L. Pearson, 1876), p. 117. Richard Rathbun, "The Columbian Institute for the Promotion of Arts and Sciences," *United States National Museum and Bulletin* (Washington: GPO, 1917), vol. 101, p. 9. William Dzombak, "Roberdeau's Treatise on Canals," *American Canals*, no. 76 (February 1991), pp. 8–9. Pamela Scott, "Isaac Roberdeau," *ANB*, vol. 20, pp. 590–2. *The History of the U.S. Army Corps of Engineers* (Alexandria, Virginia: Office of History, Headquarters, U.S. Army Corps of Engineers, 1998), p. 142.

18 *The Metropolitan and Georgetown Commercial Gazette*, October 19, 1824. Buchanan, *Genealogy*, pp. 115, 120.

19 Henry Ways, *The Washington Aqueduct, 1852–1992* (Washington: U.S. Army Corps of Engineers, n.d.), 1–2. *To Improve Pennsylvania Avenue in Washington City*, 22nd Cong., 1st sess., H. Rpt. 291 (1832) reprints and repeats the recommendations of 21st Cong., 1st sess., H. Rpt. 184 (1830); 22nd Cong., 2nd sess., H. Doc. 11 (1832).

20 *Report on the Potomac Bridge*, 22nd Cong., 2nd sess., H. Doc. 22 (1832).

21 *Contract for Construction of Bridge Over Potomac River*, 23rd Cong., 1st sess., H. Rpt. 264 (1834); 24th Cong., 1st sess., H. Doc. 53 (1836).

22 *Report from the Secretary of War on the Employment of the Topographical Engineers*, 24th Cong., 1st sess., S. Doc. 419 (1836), p. 9.

23 *Potomac Aqueduct*, 25th Cong., 2nd sess., H. Doc. 459 (1838) [reprinting 24th Cong., 1st sess., H. Doc. 261 (1836)], pp. 19, 24. Walter S. Sanderlin, *The Great National Project: A History of the Chesapeake and Ohio Canal* (Baltimore: Johns Hopkins University Press, 1946), pp. 59–60. Constance McLaughlin Green, *Washington: Village and Capital, 1800–1878* (Princeton: Princeton University Press, 1962), pp. 114–6. Letter, Abert to Turnbull, August 29, 1832, NARA, RG 77, Records of the Topographical Bureau, Letters Sent. Donald Beekman Myer, *Bridges and the City of Washington* (Washington: Commission of Fine Arts, 1974), p. 11. Sackett L. Duryee, *The Corps of Engineers in the Nation's Capital, 1852–1952* (Washington: U.S. Army Engineer District, 1952), p. 53.

24 NARA, RG 77, Monthly Returns of the Corps of Topographical Engineers, March 1842–December 1843; June–July 1843; April 1845–August 1846; March–October 1847; August 1848–July 1849. 25th Cong., 2nd sess., S. Doc. 346 (1838). 26th Cong., 2nd sess., S. Doc. 51 (1841). NARA, RG 77, Register of Letters Received by the Topographical Bureau, 1849; Report, Mills to Secretary of War, December 20, 1841, and Letter, Strickland to Abert, December 6, 1843, in Letters Received by the Topographical Bureau. Schubert, *Nation Builders*, pp. 20–1.

25 Pamela Scott, ed., *The Papers of Robert Mills, 1781–1855* (Wilmington, Delaware: Scholarly Resources, Inc., 1990), pp. 98, 122.

26 Ryan, "War Department Topographical Bureau," pp. 73–110. Schubert, *Nation Builders*.

27 B. Brown Goode, "The Genesis of the National Museum," *Annual Report of the Smithsonian Institution* (Washington: Smithsonian Institution, 1891), pp. 273–335.

28 Kenneth Hafertepe, *America's Castle: The Evolution of the Smithsonian Building and Its Institution, 1840–1878* (Washington: Smithsonian Press, 1984), p. 27.

[29] *Ibid.*, pp. 71, 106. Sara E. Wermiel, *Army Engineers' Contributions to the Development of Iron Construction in the Nineteenth Century* (Kansas City, Missouri: Public Works Historical Society, 2002), pp. 31–3.

[30] [Crew], *Centennial History*, p. 650.

[31] *Ibid.*, p. 124.

[32] *Ibid.*, pp. 126, 135–7. Alexander continued to experiment with wrought iron and in 1855, when the government's great construction program of courthouses and custom houses was just getting underway, his knowledge was crucial. "Letter to the Secretary of the Treasury," 33rd Cong., 2d Sess., S. Exdoc. 54 (1855).

[33] James B. Richardson, *A Compilation of the Messages and Papers of the Presidents, 1789–1908* (Washington: GPO, Bureau of National Literature and Art, 1908), vol. 6, p. 2628. *Statutes* vol. 9, p. 523. 32nd Cong., 2nd sess., H. Doc. 33 (1853).

[34] NARA, RG 77, Letters Sent. Totten to W. W. Corcoran, August 12, 1852; H. H. Steward, August 14, 1852; Totten to Fillmore, September 1852; Totten to Smith, September 15, 1852. On background and selection of Meigs, see Russell F. Weigley, *Quartermaster General of the Union Army: A Biography of M. C. Meigs* (New York: Columbia University Press, 1959), pp. 13–30, 49, 52, 59; Ways, *Aqueduct*, pp. 3–7, and David W. Miller, *Second Only to Grant: Quartermaster General Montgomery C. Meigs* (Shippenburg, Pennsylvania: White Mane Books, 2000), pp. 18–24.

[35] Meigs' report was published as 32nd Cong., 2nd sess., S. Exdoc. 48 (1853); quote from Weigley, *Quartermaster General*, p. 61. Warren T. Hannum, "Water Supply of the District of Columbia," *Professional Memoirs, Corps of Engineers, U.S. Army*, vol. 4 (1912), p. 226. Edwin A. Schmitt and Philip O. Macqueen, "Washington Aqueduct," *The Military Engineer*, vol. 61 (1949), p. 205.

[36] Quote from letter, Meigs to Davis, April 18, 1853, NARA, RG 77. See also: letter, Meigs to Davis, February 22, 1855. Weigley, *Quartermaster General*, p. 62.

[37] Ways, *Aqueduct*, p. 11.

[38] William T. S. Curtis, "Cabin John Bridge," *RCHS*, vol. 2 (1899), pp. 295–6; Harold K. Skramsted, "The Engineer as Architect in Washington: The Contribution of Montgomery Meigs," *RCHS*, vols. 69–70 (1969–70), p. 268; Philip O. Macqueen, "Cabin John Bridge," *The Military Engineer*, vol. 24 (1932), pp. 566–8 and "Rock Creek Bridge," *The Military Engineer*, vol. 28 (1936), pp. 111–3.

[39] Harry C. Ways, "Montgomery C. Meigs and the Washington Aqueduct," in William C. Dickinson, et al., *Montgomery C. Meigs and the Building of the Nation's Capital* (Athens: Ohio University Press, 2001), p. 27. *Annual Report of the Secretary of War, 1857*, 35th Cong., 1st sess., S. Exdoc. 11 (1857), pt. III, p. 26.

[40] 35th Cong., 1st sess., S. Exdoc. 34 (1858), p. 5.

[41] James M. Goode, "Architecture and Politics: Thomas Ustick Walter and the Enlargement of the United States Capitol, 1850–1865," Ph.D. diss., The George Washington University, 1995. William C. Allen, *History of the United States Capitol* (Washington: GPO, 2001), pp. 140–4.

[42] *Estimates and Plans for Alteration of Capitol*, 28th Cong., 1st sess., H. Doc. 51 (1843–44). Pamela Scott, "Robert Mills and the United States Capitol," AIA symposium *American Architectural Practice: The Formative Years* (1989), pp. 16–7.

[43] Allen, *History of the Capitol*, pp. 203–4. Susan Brizzolara Wojcik, "Thomas U. Walter and Iron in the United States Capitol: An Alliance of Architecture, Engineering, and Industry," Ph.D. diss., University of Delaware, 1998, pp. 258–65.

[44] *Daily Union*, April 5, 1854; see also April 8, 11, and 15. *Washington Sentinel*, April 8 and 9, 1854; see also, April 5, 25, and 28.

[45] Dean A. Herrin, "The Eclectic Engineer: Montgomery C. Meigs and His Engineering Projects," in Dickinson, et al., *Meigs*, pp. 3–20.

[46] Allen, *History of the Capitol*, pp. 218, 303–4. In April, 1860, Captain William B. Franklin, Meigs's replacement, responding to a Senate resolution to move its chamber to an outside wall, noted that such a move would require major demolition and rebuilding of half the north wing's interiors at a cost of about $365,000 and two years of work. The alterations were not undertaken.

[47] *Ibid.*, p. 218.

[48] *Ibid.*, pp. 245–6. Charles E. Fairman, *Art and Artists of the Capitol of the United States of America* (Washington: GPO, 1927), p. 143.

[49] Wendy Wolff, *Capitol Builder: The Shorthand Journals of Montgomery C. Meigs, 1853–1859, 1861* (Washington: GPO, 2001), *passim*.

[50] Allen, *History of the Capitol*, pp. 221–3.

[51] *Ibid.*, p. 224.

[52] Wolff, *Capitol Builder*, p. 178.

[53] *Ibid.*, p. 183. August Schoenborn was Walter's chief draftsman employed by him at the Capitol beginning in 1851.

[54] Allen, *History of the Capitol*, pp. 229–36.

[55] Pamela Scott, *Temple of Liberty: Building the Capitol for a New Nation* (New York: Oxford University Press, 1995) p. 100. Allen, *History of the Capitol*, pp. 253–5. Wolff, *Capitol Builder*, p. 358.

[56] Allen, *History of the Capitol*, pp. 234–42.

[57] *Ibid.*, pp. 247, 250. Barbara Wolanin, *Contantino Brumidi, Artist of the Capitol* (Washington: GPO, 1998).

[58] [Crew], *Centennial History*, p. 667.

[59] Allen, *History of the Capitol*, pp. 268–9.

[60] *Ibid.*, p. 270.

[61] Wolff, *Capitol Builder*, p. 653.

62 *Ibid.*, pp. xxvii, 300.

63 History of the Civil War defenses summarized from Benjamin Franklin Cooling III and Walton H. Owen II, *Mr. Lincoln's Forts: A Guide to the Civil War Defenses of Washington* (Shippensburg, Pennsylvania: White Mane Publishing Co., Inc., 1988).

64 J. G. Barnard, quoted in Cooling and Owen, *Mr. Lincoln's Forts*, p. 28.

65 *Ibid.*

66 *Ibid.*, p. 26.

CHAPTER 3: THE VICTORIAN CITY, 1865–90

1 William Stull Holt, *The Office of the Chief of Engineers of the Army: Its Non-Military History* (Washington: Brookings Institute, 1923), pp. 50–5. Between 1871 and 1874, Washington was governed by a territorial governor and Board of Public Works charged with repairing damage done to the city during the Civil War and instituting modern public works.

2 Monthly Returns of the Corps of Engineers, May 1867, NARA, RG 77.

3 William Tindall, *Standard History of the City of Washington from a Study of the Original Sources*, (Knoxville, Tennessee: H. W. Crew and Co., 1914), p. 472. *Statutes*, vol. 14, p. 466. The Aqueduct had been controlled by the Secretary of the Interior since mid-1862 (*Statutes*, vol. 12, p. 620).

4 John Reps, *Washington on View* (Chapel Hill: University of North Carolina Press, 1991), p. 151.

5 U.S. Congress, House. Report of the Secretary of War (hereafter Rpt. Sec. War). *Report of Brevet Brigadier General N. Michler*, 40th Cong., 2nd sess., H. Exdoc. 1 (1867), p. 522.

6 *Ibid.* p. 531. William Seale, *The White House: The History of an American Idea* (Washington: American Institute of Architects Press, 1992), pp. 116–21.

7 Letter, R. D. Mussey to Thaddeus Stevens, June 12, 1866, NARA, RG 233, Records of the House of Representatives, H.R. 39A–F2.4.

8 "Communication of N. Michler, Major of Engineers," 39th Cong., 2d Sess., Sen. Misc. Doc. 21 (February 13, 1867), p. 1.

9 *Ibid.*, p. 2.

10 *New York Times*, July 19, 1881.

11 "Communication…Michler," *op. cit.*, p. 3.

12 *Ibid.*, pp. 4–5.

13 *Survey of the Potomac River*, 40th Cong., 2nd sess., H. Exdoc. 292 (1868).

14 U.S. Congress, House. Rpt. Sec. War. Report of the Chief of Engineers (hereafter cited as Rpt. Ch. Eng.), 42nd Cong., 2nd sess., H. Exdoc. 1 (1871), p. 969.

15 U.S. Congress, House. Rpt. Ch. Eng., 58th Cong., 3rd sess., H. Doc. 2 (1904), p. 3917, and Rpt. Ch. Eng., 56th Cong., 1st sess., H. Doc. 2 (1899), p. 3822.

16 *Statutes*, vol. 30, p. 570.

17 Rpt. Ch. Eng., 1904, pp. 3912–8.

18 Rpt. Ch. Eng., 1871, p. 976.

19 U.S. Congress, House. Rpt. Sec. War. *Improvement and Care of Public Buildings and Grounds in the District of Columbia*, 56th Cong., 1st sess., H. Exdoc. 2 (1899), p. 3823.

20 U.S. Congress. House. Rpt. Ch. Eng., 59th Cong., 1st sess., H. Doc 2 (1905), pp. 2653–4.

21 Rpt. Ch. Eng., 1871, p. 969.

22 U.S. Congress, House. Rpt. Ch. Eng., 44th Cong., 2nd sess., H. Exdoc. 1 (1876), pp. 683–4, and 45th Cong., 2nd sess., H. Exdoc. 1 (1877), p. 1065.

23 Rpt. Ch. Eng., 1877, p. 1065.

24 U.S. Congress, House. *Report of the Board of Public Works of the District of Columbia from its Organization until November 1, 1872*, 42nd Cong., 3rd sess., H. Exdoc. 1 (1872), pt. VI, p. 6.

25 The activities of the Office of Public Buildings and Grounds are detailed in the Annual Reports of the Chief of Engineers from 1871 until the office ceased to exist in 1925, except for 1868–70, when Michler made no reports. Mary Clemmer Ames, *Ten Years in Washington* (Hartford: A.D. Worthington & Co., 1874), p. 73.

26 Mary-Jane M. Dowd, comp., *Records of the Office of Public Buildings and Public Parks of the National Capital* (Washington: NARA, 1992), pp. 58–9. James M. Goode, *The Outdoor Sculpture of Washington, D.C.* (Washington: Smithsonian Institution Press, 1974), p. 281.

27 "Interview with Professor Baird," *Forest and Stream*, vol. 10 (1878), p. 214. U.S. Congress, House. Rpt. Ch. Eng., "Annual Report of Colonel O. E. Babcock," 43d Cong., 2d Sess., H. Exdoc. 1 (1874), pp. 385–6.

28 George Alfred Townsend, *New Washington, or the Renovated City* (Washington: Chronicle Publishing Company, 1874), pp. 17–8.

29 Rpt. Sec. War, 1872, p. 1017.

30 Rpt. Ch. Eng., 1904, p. 3939.

31 Alan Lessoff, *The Nation and Its City: Politics, "Corruption," and Progress in Washington, D.C., 1861–1902* (Baltimore: Johns Hopkins University Press, 1994), p. 56. No record of their meetings (if any) has been found.

32 *Ibid.*, p. 63.

33 Brooks D. Simpson, "Orville Elias Babcock," *ANB*, vol.1 (1998), pp. 813.

34 Ben Perley Poore, *Perley's Reminiscences of Sixty Years in the National Metropolis* (Philadelphia: Hubbard Brothers, 1886), vol. 2, pp. 313–4.

35 Quoted in "Babcock," *ANB*, p. 813.

36 Pamela Scott, "Robert Mills and American Monuments," in John Bryan, ed. *Robert Mills, Architect* (Washington: AIA Press, 1991), pp. 143–72.

37 Letter, J. C. Ives to Thomas Carbery, August 10, 1859, RG 42, Papers of the Washington National Monument Society (hereafter WNMS), Secretary's Correspondence, Box 10. Mills described both the foundations and the preparations for laying them in a report published in the *National Intelligencer* on September 15, 1848, just as they were nearly level with the ground. The only known Mills drawing showing the foundations (in plan and section) survives in Thomas Lincoln Casey's papers at the Society for the Preservation of New England Antiquities.

38 Louis Torres, *"To the immortal name and memory of George Washington": The United States Army Corps of Engineers and the Construction of the Washington Monument* (Washington: Office of the Chief of Engineers, n.d.), p. 33.

39 Frederick L. Harvey, *History of the Washington National Monument and Washington National Monument Society* (Washington: GPO, 1903), p. 80.

40 Quoted in Torres, *"immortal name,"* p. 34.

41 Letter, J. G. Barnard, Z. B. Tower, and H. G. Wright to A. A. Humphreys, August 7, 1874, RG 42, Papers WNMS, Secretary's Correspondence, Box 10.

42 Henry R. Searle, *Washington Monument Monograph* (Washington: Gibson Brothers Printers, [1877]) p. 8. Several designs and their sources are published in Bates Lowry, *The Architecture of Washington, D.C.* (Washington: The Dunlap Society, 1976), Chapter V, microfiche 2.

43 Torres, *"immortal name,"* pp. 34–7. Samuel Willard Crompton, "Joseph Christmas Ives," *ANB*, vol. 21, pp. 722–3.

44 Torres, *"immortal name,"* pp. 47–8.

45 *Ibid.*, p. 54.

46 *Ibid.*, pp. 55–7, 59–80.

47 George J. Binczewski, "The Point of the Monument: A History of the Aluminum Cap of the Washington Monument," *Journal of the Minerals, Metals and Materials Society*, vol. 47, no. 11 (1995), pp. 20–5.

48 See Pamela Scott, "Montgomery C. Meigs and Victorian Architectural Traditions," in Dickinson, et al., *Meigs*, pp. 73–9.

49 NARA, RG 233, Records of the House of Representatives, HR39A–F2.16, Committee on Appropriations, Department of War. Scott, *Meigs*, p. 79.

50 Quoted in Jennifer Laurie Ossman, "Reconstructing a National Image: The State, War and Navy Building and the Politics of Federal Design, 1866–90," Ph.D. diss., University of Virginia, 1996, p. 48.

51 The Executive Office of the President, *The Old Executive Office Building: A Victorian Masterpiece* (Washington: GPO, 1984), pp. [17–8] (unpaginated).

52 Ossman, "Reconstructing," pp. 180–5. U.S. Congress, House. *State, War and Navy Building: Letter from the Secretary of War*, 50th Cong., 1st sess., H. Exdoc. 337 (1888), p. 3. Donald Lehman, *Executive Office Building* (Washington: General Services Administration, 1964), p. 47.

53 "A Notable Career: The Retirement of General Casey by Operation of Law," *Washington Star*, May 4, 1895. *State, War and Navy*, pp. 4–5.

54 Lehman, *Executive*, pp. 47–8.

55 Elsa M. Santoyo, ed., *Creating an American Masterpiece* (Washington: American Institute of Architects Press, 1988), p. 69.

56 Ossman, "Reconstructing," *State, War and Navy*, pp. 200–1.

57 Executive Office, *Old Executive…*, footnote. 47.

58 *Report of the U.S. National Museum…for the year ending June 30, 1903* (Washington: GPO, 1905), p. 240.

59 H. Rpt. 244, 45th Cong., 1st sess. (1878), quoted in *Report of the U.S. National Museum*, p. 243.

60 *Report of the U.S. National Museum*, p. 244.

61 *Ibid.*, p. 247.

62 "Fire-Proof Building for the Army Medical Department," 47th Cong., 2d sess., H. Rpt. 1995 (1883).

63 Robert S. Henry, *The Armed Forces Institute of Pathology: Its First Century, 1862–1962* (Washington: Department of the Army, 1964), pp. 73–83. Tanya Beauchamp, "Adolph Cluss and the Building of the U.S. National Museum: An Architecture of Perfect Adaptability," M.A. thesis, University of Virginia, 1972, pp. 56–60.

64 Linda Brody Lyons, *A Handbook to the Pension Building: Home of the National Building Museum* (Washington: National Building Museum, 1993).

65 "Fireproof Buildings," unidentified newspaper clipping dated February 4, 1882, and signed M. C. Meigs, Montgomery C. Meigs Papers, Manuscript Division, LOC.

66 Joyce L. McDaniel, "Caspar Buberl: The Pension Building Civil War Frieze and Other Washington, D.C., Sculpture," *RCHS*, vol. 50 (1980), p. 335.

67 Linda B. Lyons, "The Pension Building: Function and Form," in Dickinson, et al., *Meigs*, p. 106.

68 Beth Sullebarger, *Historic Structures Report, U.S. Pension Building* (Washington: Privately printed, 1984), pp. 3.2.1 to 3.3.19.

69 *Ibid.*, p. 3.3.10.

70 Robert Dale Owen, *Hints on Public Architecture* (New York: Da Capo Press, 1979 reprint of 1849 edition), p. 98. *American Architect and Building News*, vol. 12 (November 18, 1882), p. 1106.

71 Frances Mary Brousseau, "The Library of Congress, 1873–1897: The Building, Its Architects, and the Politics of Nineteenth-Century Architectural Practice," Ph.D. diss., University of Delaware, 1998. John Y. Cole, "Struggle for a Structure: Ainsworth Rand Spofford and a New Building for the Library of Congress," in John Y. Cole and Henry Hope Reed, *The Library of Congress: The Art and Architecture of the Thomas Jefferson Building* (New York: W. W. Norton & Company, 1997), pp. 31–63.

72 Cole, "Struggle," p. 50–51. *Washington Evening Star*, September 24, 1889. Green's Diary is in the Manuscript Division, LOC.

73 Brousseau, "Library," p. 392.

74 Charles H. Baumann, *The Influence of Angus Snead Macdonald and the Snead Bookstack on Library Architecture* (Methchen, New Jersey: Scarecrow Press, 1972), pp. 65–75.

75 Cole, "Struggle," p. 51.

76 [John L. Smithmeyer,] *History of the Construction of the Library of Congress, Washington, D.C.* (Washington: Beresford, printer, 1906), p. 65.

77 U.S. Congress, House. *Report of Thomas Lincoln Casey, Brigadier General United States Army, in Charge of Construction of New Library of Congress*, 54th Cong., 1st sess., S. Doc. 5 (1895) and *Building for the Library of Congress*, 54th Cong., 2nd sess., H. Doc. 20 (1896).

78 Thomas P. Somma, "The Sculptural Program for the Library of Congress," in Cole and Reed, *Library of Congress*, p. 320.

79 Charles Moore, *The Life and Times of Charles Follen McKim* (Boston: Houghton Mifflin Company, 1929), pp. 70–1.

80 Richard Murray, "Painted Words: Murals in the Library of Congress," in Cole and Reed, *Library of Congress*, pp. 200, 308, footnote 10.

81 Quoted in Cole, "Struggle," p. 51.

82 Murray, "Painted Words," p. 199. Somma, "Sculptural Program," p. 230.

83 Cole, "Struggle," pp. 51, 56–7. Smithmeyer, *History*, p. 20.

84 Brousseau, "Library," p. 413.

85 Smithmeyer, *History*, p. 60.

86 *Communication from the Chief of Engineers, U.S. Army, Transmitting a Report on the Construction of the Building for the Library of Congress*, 51st Cong., 1st sess., S. Misc. Doc. 8, December 4, 1889, pp. 1–2.

87 Brousseau, "Library," pp. 430, 435–7. Cole, "Struggle," pp. 51, 306. Green's defense of his and Casey's work appears in U.S. Congress, Joint Committee on the Library, "Condition of the Library of Congress," March 3, 1897, 54th Cong., 2d sess., S. Rpt. 1573 (1897), p. 5. "Protest Against Placing Name of General Casey's Son on Table of Library Building," 54th Cong., 2d sess., S. Doc. 88 (1897).

88 Green's two-volume diary is among his papers in the Manuscript Division, LOC. Bernard R. Green, "The Building for the Library of Congress," *Smithsonian Institution Annual Report, 1897*, p. 627.

89 James E. Miller, Jr., *Walt Whitman* (Boston: Houghton Mifflin, 1959), p. 82.

90 Tindall, *Standard History*, pp. 254–5. Green, *Washington, Village and Capital*, p. 302. Franklin T. Howe, "The Board of Public Works," *RCHS*, vol. 3 (1900), pp. 257–78. William M. Maury, *Alexander "Boss" Shepherd and the Board of Public Works*, GW Washington Studies, no 3 (Washington: George Washington University, 1975).

91 *Evening Star Index*, Washingtoniana Division, Martin Luther King, Jr. Library.

92 C. H. Forbes-Lindsay, *Washington: The City and the Seat of Government* (Philadelphia: John C. Winston Co., 1908), pp. 224–5.

93 Phillip Ogilvie, "Chronology of Events in the History of the District of Columbia," 1988 typescript, Historical Society of Washington, D.C. William Tindall, *Origin and Government of the District of Columbia* (Washington: GPO, 1908), pp. 116–7.

94 Tindall, *Standard History*, pp. 249–50. Green, *Washington, Village and Capital*, pp. 357–8. *Statutes*, vol. 16, p. 419. Rpt. Sec. War, 1867, pp. 523–30.

95 Tindall, *Standard History*, p. 269. Green, *Washington, Village and Capital*, p. 360.

96 Tindall, *Origin and Government*, p. 116.

97 "The New Washington," *Century Magazine* (March 1884), reprinted in Terry Oppel and Tony Meisel, *Washington, D.C.: A Turn-of-the-Century Treasury* (Secaucus, New Jersey: Castle, 1987), pp. 117–36.

98 Report of Lt. F.V. Greene on the work of filling up the old canal in Washington City, 47th Cong., 1st sess., S. Misc. Doc. 28 (1882), p. 1.

99 Constance McLaughlin Green, *Washington: Capital City, 1879–1950* (Princeton: Princeton University Press, 1963), p. 36.

100 Quoted in Roland M. Brennan, "Brigadier General Richard L. Hoxie, United States Army, 1861–1930," *RCHS*, vols. 57–59 (1961), p. 91.

101 Rufus Rockwell Wilson, *Washington: The Capital City and Its Part in the History of the Nation* (Philadelphia: J.P. Lippincott Company, 1902), vol. 2, pp. 379–80.

102 Brennan, "Hoxie," pp. 87–95.

103 Alison K. Hoagland, "Nineteenth-Century Building Regulations in Washington, D.C.," *RCHS*, vol. 52 (1989), pp. 57–77. In 1860, New York enacted America's first building regulations (based on those of London instituted in 1855), but it was the destruction by fire of all or large sections of several American cities that led to their issuance beginning in the early 1870s.

104 *Ibid.*

105 Ed Hatcher, "Washington's Nineteenth-Century Citizens' Associations and the Senate Park Commission Plan," *Washington History*, vol. 14, no. 2 (Fall/Winter 2002), pp. 70–95.

106 Michael R. Harrison, "The Evil of the Misfit Subdivisions: Creating the Permanent System of Highways of the District of Columbia," *Washington History*, vol. 14, no. 1 (Spring/Summer 2002), pp. 26–55; Annual Report of the Board of Commissioners of the District of Columbia for 1879, p. 386–7; 1880, p. 218; 1881, p. 226.

107 *Statutes at Large* 25 (1888), p. 451, Annual Report of the Board of Commissioners of the District of Columbia for 1888, pp. 257–8.

108 *Statutes at Large* 27 (1893), pp. 532–7. Senate Report 207, "Highways in the District of Columbia," 52nd Cong., 1st Sess. (February 10, 1892).

109 *Statutes at Large* 30 (1898), pp. 519–20.

110 U.S. Congress, House. *Improvement and Care of Public Buildings and Grounds in the District of Columbia*, 45th Cong., 2nd sess., H. Exdoc. 1 (1877), p. 1070.

111 U.S. Congress, House. Rpt. Ch. Eng., *Annual Report of Colonel O. E. Babcock, Corps of Engineers*, 43rd Cong., 2nd sess., H. Exdoc. 1 (1874), p. 392. Myer, *Bridges*, pp. 3–5. U.S. Congress, House. Rpt. Sec. War. *Rpt Ch. Eng.* 43rd Cong., 1st sess., H. Exdoc. 1 (1873), p. 1159.

112 *Annual Report*, 1874, p. 394.

113 Myer, *Bridges*, p. 45. U.S. Congress, House. Rpt. Ch. Eng., *Annual Report of O. E. Babcock, Corps of Engineers*, 44th Cong., 1st sess., H. Exdoc. 1 (1875) pp. 806–7. U.S. Congress, House. Rpt. Ch. Eng., *Annual Report of O. E. Babcock, Corps of Engineers*, 44th Cong., 2nd sess., H. Exdoc. 1 (1876) p. 687. "Letter of the Secretary of War Relative to the Report and Survey of the Commissioner of Public Buildings and Grounds on a New Navy Yard Bridge across the Anacostia River," 41st Cong., 1st sess., S. Exdoc. 10 (1869).

114 J. G. Barnard, *A Report on the Defenses of Washington, to the Chief of Engineers, U.S. Army*, professional paper 20, Corps of Engineers, Washington (1871), quoted in Cooling, *Mr. Lincoln's Forts*, p. 27; Myer, *Bridges*, p. 12. *Statutes*, vol. 21, p. 329; Duryee, *Corps of Engineers*, p. 54–5; U.S. Congress, House. Rpt. Ch. Eng., *The Aqueduct Bridge*, 49th Cong., 2nd sess., H. Exdoc., 128 (1887), pp. 3, 6; Joanna Schneider Zangrando, "Monumental Bridge Design in Washington, D.C., as a Reflection of American Culture, 1886–1932," Ph.D. diss., The George Washington University, 1974.

115 Myer, *Bridges*, p. 47; U.S. Congress, House. Rpt. Ch. Eng., *Bridge across the Eastern Branch of the Potomac River at the Foot of Pennsylvania Avenue East*, 50th Cong., 2nd sess., H. R. 1807 (1888). U.S. Congress, Senate. *Letter from the Acting Secretary of War transmitting...a report...concerning the bridge over the Eastern Branch...*, 51st Cong., 1st sess., S. Exdoc. 218 (1890).

116 Barnard, *Report on the Defenses of Washington, op. cit.*

117 Myer, *Bridges*, pp. 50–1; U.S. Congress, House. *Survey for Bridge across Anacostia River*, 54th Cong., 1st sess., H. Doc. 163 (1896), p. 8.

118 *Ibid.*

119 Peter C. Hains, "Reclamation of the Potomac Flats at Washington, D.C.," *Transactions of the American Society of Civil Engineers*, vol. 36 (January 1894), p. 57.

120 U. S. Congress, House. Rpt. Ch. Eng. *River Channel Improvements*, 40th Cong., 3rd sess., H. Exdoc. 1 (1868), pp. 889–90.

121 U.S. Congress, Senate. Rpt. Ch. Eng., *Report of the Board on the Improvements of the Harbors of Washington and Georgetown*, 42nd Cong., 3rd sess., S. Misc. Doc. 15 (1872), p. 2.

122 U.S. Congress, Senate. Rpt. Sec. War, *Letter of the Secretary of War relative to the improvement of the sanitary condition of Washington, and for deepening the channel of the Potomac River*, 45th Cong., 3rd sess., S. Exdoc. 32 (1879). Lt. Col. Thomas L. Casey also wrote a Potomac Flats report in 1878, see, 45th Cong., 3rd sess., H. Exdoc. 70 (1878).

123 U.S. Congress, Senate. *Letter...Transmitting a Report of S. T. Abert, Relative to the Survey of the Potomac River in the Vicinity of Washington*, 47th Cong., 1st sess., S. Exdoc. 126 (1882).

124 *Testimony before the Select Committee...on the Condition of the Potomac River Front of Washington*, 47th Cong., 1st sess., S. Misc. Doc. 133 (1882).

125 *Statutes*, vol. 22, p. 198.

126 "Memoir of Peter Conover Hains," *Transactions of the American Society of Civil Engineers*, vol. 85 (1822), pp. 1682–3.

127 Hains, "Reclamation," pp. 55–80.

128 U.S. Congress, House. Rpt. Sec. War, *National Road From the Aqueduct Bridge to Mount Vernon, Va.*, 51st Cong., 1st Sess., H. Exdoc. 106 (1890), p. 3.

129 The technical system of educating West Point engineers had been established early in the century. Molloy, "Technical Education."

CHAPTER 4: THE PROGRESSIVE CITY, 1890–1915

1 "Commission to Consider Certain Improvements in the District of Columbia," 56th Cong., 2d Sess., S. Rpt. 1919 (Jan. 18, 1901), p. 1.

2 John W. Reps, *Monumental Washington* (Princeton: Princeton University Press, 1967), pp. 96–140.

3 "The New Executive Mansion," *Washington Evening Star,* January 10, 1891. Seale, *White House,* pp. 154–9.

4 *Architecture and Building,* vol. 13, no. 23 (Dec. 6, 1890), p. 317.

5 "The White House Too Small," *New York Times,* July 11, 1893. "Journal of Joseph Dentz, Georgetown cabinet maker," Curator's Office, The White House. George Kennan, "The White House: The Plans for Its Reconstruction," *The Outlook,* February 1, 1902, p. 321.

6 William V. Cox, *Celebration of the One Hundredth Anniversary of the Establishment of the Seat of Government in the District of Columbia* (Washington: GPO, 1901), pp. 61–4.

7 "The A.I.A. and the White House," *New York Times,* December 18, 1900.

8 Seale, *White House,* pp. 160–1. William Seale, *President's House,* pp. 637–8.

9 Esther Singleton, *The Story of the White House* (New York: The McClure Company, 1907), vol. 2, p. 287.

10 "Transforming the White House into a Magnificent Dwelling," *The Architect and Builders Journal,* vol. 3 (June 1902), p. 17.

11 Biographical files, Office of History, Headquarters, U.S. Army Corps of Engineers, Alexandria, Virginia. "Col. Bingham Leaves," *Washington Post,* February 12, 1903, and "Col. Bingham Badly Hurt," *Washington Post,* March 20, 1904.

12 Autograph, undated note, McKim to Root, Elihu Root Papers, LOC. Letter, Moore to McKim, January 31, 1907, McKim, Mead & White Papers, NYHS. Dozens of newspapers mentioning Bingham are found among his papers in the Manuscript Division, Library of Congress.

13 Annual Report of the Chief of Engineers (hereafter ARCE), 1895, p. 4136. *Biographical Register of the Officers and Graduates of the U.S. Military Academy at West Point, New York,* Supplement, vol. 7, 1920–30. *Seventy Second Annual Report of the Association of Graduates of the United States Military Academy at West Point, New York,* June 10, 1941, pp. 198–203. "The Printing Office Site," *Washington Evening Star,* September 26, 1890.

14 "The Government Printing Office," *Washington Evening Star,* February 26, 1891. "Erection of New Building for GPO," ARCE, 1901, pp. 3801–22.

15 Annual Reports of the War Department, ARCE, part 5, GPO, 1901, Appendix HHH, "Erection of New Building for Government Printing Office," p. 3803.

16 Annual Reports of the War Department, ARCE, part 5, GPO, 1901, pp. 3802–11 and 1904, pp. 3819–60. *Washington Post,* January 1, 1902.

17 William R. Roberts, "Reform and Revitalization, 1890–1903," in Kenneth J. Hagen and William R. Roberts, eds., *Against All Enemies: Interpretations of American Military History from Colonial Times to the Present* (New York: Greenwood Press, 1986). Benjamin Franklin Cooling, "To Preserve the Peace," *Washington History,* vol. 1, no. 1 (Spring 1989), pp. 71–86. Leland M. Roth, *McKim, Mead & White Architects* (New York: Harper & Row, 1983), pp. 280–2. Letters, McKim to Root, July 21, 1902, and September 19, 1902, McKim Papers, LOC.

18 ARCE, 1904, IV, pp. 3866–70. ARCE, 1906, II, pp. 2259–68. *Seventy-Second...Graduates...West Point, op. cit.* Andrea Kim Foster, "The Conflict Between the Engineers and Architects over Control of Washington Barracks, 1902," paper dated July 2, 1986, American Studies Department, George Washington University. NARA, RG 42, Entry 193, "Copies of Correspondence Relating to the Design of the Army War College, June–July 1902."

19 Dana G. Dalrymple, "Agriculture, Architects, and the Mall, 1901–1905: Implementing the Park Commission's Vision," in *The Senate Park Commission Plan, 1901–1902* (Washington: Commission of Fine Arts, forthcoming). David J. Murphy, "Architects, Engineers, and the New Agriculture Department Buildings: A Reinterpretation of the Fight Over Implementing the McMillan Plan," unpublished paper delivered at the annual meeting of the Society for American City and Regional Planning, Richmond, Virginia, November 1991.

20 *Seventy-Second Report...West Point,* p. 314.

21 Cynthia R. Field and Jeffrey T. Tilman, "Creating a Model for the National Mall: The Design of the National Museum of Natural History," *JSAH,* vol. 63, no. 1 (March 2004), pp. 52–73.

22 Letter by Charles F. McKim to Bernard R. Green, April 18, 1904, p. 7, McKim, Mead & White Papers, Library of Congress.

23 *Ibid.,* pp. 7–8.

24 Glenn Brown, ed., "Proceedings of the Thirty-Sixth Annual Convention of the American Institute of Architects," *Journal of Proceedings AIA* (Washington: Gibson Bros., 1903), pp. 8–9. [John S. Sewell], "The Relation of the Architect and Engineer to the Design and Erection of Government Buildings," in Brown, *Proceedings, op. cit.,* p. 80. Antoinette J. Lee, *Architects to the Nation: The Rise and Decline of the Supervising Architect's Office* (New York: Oxford University Press, 2000), pp. 163–88.

25 Roth, *McKim,* pp. 363–8. Brown, *Proceedings,* pp. 7–8. Letter, McKim to Green, April 18, 1904, and Letter, Green to McKim, April 23, 1904, McKim, Mead & White Papers, NYHS.

26 "Programme of Competition for the Grant Statue or Memorial, Washington, D.C.," pamphlet dated April 10, 1901, copy in the McKim, Mead & White Papers, NYHS. Pamela Scott, "'A City as a Work of Art': The Emergence of the Senate Park Commission's Monumental Core," in *Senate Park Commission Plan*.

27 Scott, "City as a Work of Art."

28 Clarence O. Sherrill, *The Grant Memorial in Washington*, ed. James William Bryan (Washington: GPO, 1924). Kathryn Allamong Jacob, *Testament to Union: Civil War Monuments in Washington, D.C.* (Baltimore: Johns Hopkins University Press, 1998). NARA, RG 42, Records of the Grant Memorial Commission, 1901–28.

29 Dennis Robert Montagna, "Henry Merwin Shrady's Ulysses S. Grant Memorial in Washington, D.C.: A Study in Iconography, Content, and Patronage," Ph.D. diss., University of Delaware, 1987, pp. 12, 24–5, 38, 46–7.

30 *Ibid.*, pp. 48–59.

31 Christopher A. Thomas, "The Lincoln Memorial and Its Architect, Henry Bacon (1866–1924)," Ph.D. diss., Yale University, 1990, pp. 327–419. Edward F. Conklin, *The Lincoln Memorial in Washington* (Washington: GPO, 1927), pp. 16–7.

32 Sue A. Kohler, *The Commission of Fine Arts: A Brief History, 1910–1995* (Washington: Commission of Fine Arts, c. 1996), pp. 1–6.

33 Thomas, "Lincoln Memorial," pp. 444–72.

34 Thomas, "Lincoln Memorial," pp. 445–528. Concklin, *Lincoln Memorial, op. cit.*, pp. 15–21.

35 Thomas, "Lincoln Memorial," pp. 528–41.

36 Thomas, "Lincoln Memorial," p. 538. Statement of Maj. W. V. Judson, Engineer Commissioner of the District of Columbia," *Hearings Before the Committee on the Library*, H.R. 13045, March 5–6, 1912. (Washington: GPO, 1912), pp. 60–4. "Memoir of William Voorhees Judson, M. Am. Soc. C. E.," *Transactions of the American Society of Civil Engineers*, vol. 88 (1925), pp. 1405–8.

37 Thomas, "Lincoln Memorial," pp. 541–77.

38 "Lincoln Memorial Award in Dispute," *Washington Herald*, October 18, 1913. "Lincoln Memorial Delay Held Likely," *Washington Evening Star*, December 4, 1913, and "The Lincoln Memorial Contract," *Washington Evening Star*, December 5, 1913. Letter, Henry Bacon to William W. Harts, January 27, 1914. NARA, RG 42, Records of the Office of Public Buildings and Public Parks of the National Capital (hereafter RG 42).

39 Thomas, "Lincoln Memorial," pp. 579–82. Douglas L. Weart, "The Foundations of the Lincoln Memorial," in Concklin, *Lincoln Memorial*, pp. 55–61. Col. W. W. Harts, "Cylinder-Pier Foundations for Lincoln Memorial, Washington, D.C.," *Engineering News*, vol. 71 (May 7, 1914), p. 1019. Christopher A. Thomas, "The Marble of the Lincoln Memorial: Whitest, Prettiest, and…Best," *Washington History*, vol. 2 (Fall/Winter 1993–94), pp. 43–63. Christopher A. Thomas, *The Lincoln Memorial and*

American Life (Princeton: Princeton University Press, 2002), p. 115.

40 Michael Richman, *Daniel Chester French, An American Sculptor* (Washington: National Trust for Historic Preservation, 1976), p. 180.

41 *William Wright Harts, His Story*, written in Rome 1934 (Privately published, c. 2001), p. 47.

42 *Ibid., passim.*

43 "Petition for Public Park," July 10, 1866. NARA, RG 233, Records of the House of Representatives (hereafter RG 233) HR 39A–H20.2. Quote from Michler report, reprinted in William V. Cox, "Notes on the Establishment of a National Park in the District of Columbia…" Senate Committee on the District of Columbia Park Improvement Papers No. 7, 1901, p. 16. ARCE, 1867, p. 567.

44 S. Rpt. 549 quoted in Cox, "Notes," pp. 22–3. William Bushong, *Historic Resources Study of Rock Creek Park, District of Columbia* (Denver: National Park Service Denver Service Center, 1990), pp. 65–6, 68–9. *Report of the Secretary, Board of Control of Rock Creek Park, District of Columbia, Operations from the Establishment of the Park September 27th, 1890, to May 1, 1907*, p. 5.

45 Bushong, *Rock Creek*, pp. 69–70; Cornelius W. Heine, "The Contributions of Charles Carroll Glover and Other Citizens to the Development of the National Capital," *RCHS*, vols. 53–56 (1953–56), pp. 232–8. *Washington Evening Star*, December 29, 1888.

46 Bushong, *Rock Creek*, p. 71. William Cox writes, "for when it was proposed to attach the Rock Creek Park bill as an amendment [to the zoo bill,] the Zoological Park, with a smaller appropriation, was accepted as a compromise and became law." Cox, "Notes," p. 4.

47 Public Law No. 297, *Statutes at Large* 1889–91, vol. 26, pp. 492–5.

48 Bushong, *Rock Creek*, pp. 73–4. The records of the Rock Creek Park Commission and the Board of Control of Rock Creek Park are in NARA, RG 42.

49 Bushong, *Rock Creek*, pp. 1, 77–8. Today Rock Creek Park comprises 1,754.62 acres.

50 *Ibid.*, pp. 96, 104. Bushong notes that the creation of Rock Creek Park's central road system "required considerable grading and innovative construction and represents the most conspicuous contribution of the Army Corps of Engineers to the park's designed character," p. 103. Berry Mackintosh, *Rock Creek Park: An Administrative History* (Washington: National Park Service History Division, 1985), p. 19.

51 *Washington Evening Star*, September 1, 1900, quoted in Cox, "Notes," *op. cit.*, p. 15.

52 Bushong, *Rock Creek, op. cit.*, p. 97.

53 *Ibid.*, pp. 97-8; Timothy Davis, "Beyond the Mall: The Senate Park Commission's Plan for Washington's Park System," in *Senate Park Commission. Annual Report of the Commissioners of the District of Columbia*, 1917, vol. 2, p. 181.

54 "Rock Creek Park, a report by Olmsted Brothers, December 1918," quoted in Bushong, *Rock Creek*, p. 99. ARCE, 1918, p. 1937 and ARCE, 1919, p. 2044. *Statutes*, vol. 40, p. 650 made Rock Creek Park a part of the D.C. park system as defined in legislation of July 1, 1898. *Annual Report of the Commissioners of the District of Columbia*, 1918, vol. 2, p. 17.

55 Rossell quoted in Timothy Davis, "Rock Creek and Potomac Parkway, Washington, DC: The Evolution of a Contested Urban Landscape," *Studies in the History of Gardens and Designed Landscapes*, vol. 19, no. 2 (April–June 1999), p. 152. Rossell's report is 52nd Cong., 2nd sess., S. Misc. Doc. 21 (1893). F. L. Olmsted, Jr., "Report of interview on Rock Creek Parkway with Capt. Beach, Engineer Commissioner," September 25, 1901, Job 2820, Olmsted Associates Papers, Manuscript Division, Library of Congress.

56 Davis, "Rock Creek," pp. 154-5. Reps, *Monumental Washington*, pp. 78-80.

57 Reps, *Monumental Washington*, pp. 74-8. Jon A. Peterson, "The Hidden Origins of the McMillan Plan for Washington, D.C., 1900-1902," in *Historical Perspectives on Urban Design: Washington, D.C. 1890-1910*, edited by Antoinette J. Lee, Conference Proceedings, October 7, 1983, Center for Washington Area Studies, Occasional Paper No. 1, pp. 4-6.

58 ARCE, 1883, p. 2080 and ARCE, 1887, p. 2536; Ways, *Aqueduct*, pp. 71, 76; Frederick Gutheim, *Worthy of the Nation: The History of Planning for the National Capital* (Washington: Smithsonian Institution Press, 1977), p. 91. In March 1895 additional funds were appropriated to raise the overall height of the dam two and a half feet, work that occupied the engineers until November 1896.

59 Aqueduct extension authorized by act of July 15, 1882, *Statutes* vol. 22, p. 168.

60 ARCE, 1883, pp. 2081-2.

61 Ways, *Aqueduct*, pp. 81-4.

62 Lydecker was subjected to a court-martial that fined him and sent him to a posting far from Washington. The two civil engineers who conducted the investigation were Henry Flad of St. Louis and Frederick Graff of Philadelphia. *Washington Aqueduct Tunnel*, 50th Cong., 2nd sess., S. Rpt. 2686 (1889), pp. 2, 12, 73.

63 *Ibid.*, p. 77. 49th Cong., 2nd, sess., H. Exdoc. 1 (1886), pp. 2021-43.

64 *Washington Evening Star*, November 9, 1894 and January 10, 1896.

65 Ways, *Aqueduct*, p. 76.

66 *Ibid.*, pp. 92-3, 95, 97.

67 Quote from *Statutes*, vol. 29, p. 624; Glover's involvement described in Heine, "The Contributions of Charles Carroll Glover and Other Citizens," pp. 240-2.

68 ARCE, 1896, part II, p. 1023; ARCE, 1899, part II, p. 1415.

69 ARCE, 1904, p. 3940. Quote from Report, Bingham to Chief of Engineers, July 19, 1899, Reports of the Office of Buildings and Grounds, p. 384. NARA, RG 42; ARCE, 1901, part V, p. 3718 ff; ARCE, 1902, part IV, p. 2739; ARCE, 1903, p. 2552-5; ARCE, 1915, part I, pp. 1669-70.

70 ARCE, 1905, p. 2621. Quote from ARCE, 1917, p. 1891. ARCE, 1908, p. 2399. Quote from ARCE, 1914, p. 3355. See ARCE, 1917, p. 1891 for legislative history of the park. ARCE, 1913, p. 3225. ARCE, 1917, p. 1892.

71 "Col. Cosby, 94, Dies; Placed Cherry Trees," *Washington Star*, March 27, 1962. "Do You Know? The Corps' Connection to the Washington, D.C., Tidal Basin and its Beloved Cherry Trees?" U.S. Army Corps of Engineers, Office of History, Vignette No. 48. www.hq.usace.army.mil/history.

72 ARCE, 1892, part II, pp. 1064-9. Hains's report also was printed as 52nd Cong., 1st sess., H. Exdoc. 30 (1891). Duryee, *Corps of Engineers*, p. 77. *Survey of the Anacostia River*, 55th Cong., 3rd sess., H. Doc. 87 (1898), pp. 4, 6.

73 *Ibid.*, p. 7; ARCE, 1892, pp. 1080-3. *Survey of the Anacostia River*, p. 9. *Anacostia River Flats*, 59th Cong., 1st sess., H. Doc. 194 (1905). *Improvement of the Anacostia Flats*, 59th Cong., 1st sess., H. Doc. 903 (1909).

74 *Anacostia River and Flats, D.C.*, 64th Cong., 1st sess., H. Doc. 1357 (1916), pp. 2, 5. National Building Museum, "D.C. Builds. The Anacostia Waterfront," exhibition text, 2004.

75 Myer, *Bridges*, p. 29, and ARCE, 1870, p. 519, and ARCE, 1871, p. 974.

76 Barnard, *Report on the Defenses of Washington*, quoted in Cooling, *Mr. Lincoln's Forts*, p. 26. ARCE, 1871, p. 974. Myer, *Bridges*, p. 31. *Statutes*, vol. 31, p. 772-3.

77 "Principal Local Events During 1904," *RCHS*, vol. 8 (1904), p. 203. *Bridge Across the Potomac River*, H. Doc. 138, 57th Cong., 1st sess. (1901). Myer, *Bridges*, p. 32; "Principal Local Events in the Year 1906," *RCHS*, vol. 10 (1906), p. 255.

78 *Report of the Arlington Memorial Bridge Commission* (Washington: GPO, 1924), pp. 21-8.

79 Myer, *Bridges*, pp. 65-9.

80 *Title of the United States to Lands in the District of Columbia*, H. Doc. 1055, 64th Cong., 1st sess. (1916); *Map of the Public Lands under Federal Jurisdiction in the District of Columbia* (Washington: War Department, Corps of Engineers, 1915).

81 *Public Buildings in the District of Columbia*, 65th Cong., 2nd sess., S. Rpt. 155 (1917), pp. 146-7.

82 Harts, *His Story*, pp. 43, 46, 49.

CHAPTER 5: THE EXPANDING CITY, 1915–50

1. Louis Brownlow, *A Passion for Anonymity: The Autobiography of Louis Brownlow* (Chicago: University of Chicago Press, 1958), pp. 4–5, 22–3.

2. Green, *Washington, Capitol City*, pp. 237, 246–249. ARCE, 1918, part III, p. 3782. ARCE, 1919, part I, p. 2041. *Annual Report of the Commissioners of the District of Columbia*, 65th Cong., 3d sess., H. Doc. 1431 (1918), Part II, pp. 6, 21–2.

3. Brownlow, *Autobiography*, pp. 4–5. Gutheim, *Worthy of the Nation*, pp. 160–1. "General Kutz, Ex-Engineer Commissioner, Dies," *Washington Evening Star*, January 25, 1951.

4. Quoted in Brownlow, *Autobiography*, p. 97. See also, Gutheim, *Worthy of the Nation*, p. 160–1, and Eldridge Lovelace, *Harland Bartholomew: His Contributions to American Urban Planning* (Urbana, Illinois: University of Illinois, 1993).

5. Brownlow, *Autobiography*, p. 97.

6. *Annual Report of the Commissioners of the District of Columbia, 1921* (Washington: 1921), p. 10. Brownlow, *Autobiography*, p. 98.

7. Lt. Col. J. Franklin Bell, "Street Lighting Versus Street Trees," *American City* (October 1928), p. 122–3. Sarah Pressey Noreen, *Public Street Illumination in Washington, D.C.: An Illustrated History*, GW Washington Studies, no. 2 (Washington: George Washington University, May 1975.)

8. John Dos Passos, "Washington Evening," in Bill Adler, ed., *Washington: A Reader* (New York: Meredith Press, 1967), pp. 174, 178.

9. J. Franklin Bell, "City Engineering in Washington," *The Military Engineer*, vol. 19, no. 107 (September–October 1927), pp. 359–62.

10. ARCE, 1914, part 3, pp. 3372–3. "Wilson to Lay Stone," *Washington Post*, March 27, 1915, and "Wilson to Review Women Marchers at Dedication of Red Cross Building," May 5, 1917. Quote from "Red Cross Home Dedication May 12," *Washington Post*, April 16, 1917. Dowd, *Office of Public Buildings*, pp. 95–6. http://www.redcross.org/museum/history/square.asp.

11. Colonel W. W. Harts and Colonel C. S. Ridley, "Washington. The Mall and Vicinity. Buildings and Occupancy by Various Government Activities," 1917, NARA, Cartographic Division, RG 42 (oversize).

12. Conklin, *Lincoln Memorial*, p. 64. Charles A. Peters, Jr., "The Lincoln Memorial Reflecting Pool," *The Military Engineer*, vol. 15 (1923), pp. 209–13. ARCE, 1918, part III, p. 3801. ARCE, 1920, part I, p. 2028.

13. Conklin, *Lincoln Memorial*, pp. 73–91. Dowd, *Office of Public Buildings*, op. cit., pp. 83–4. C. O. Sherrill, "The Arlington Memorial Amphitheater," *The Military Engineer*, vol. 17, no. 92 (April 1925), pp. 152–3.

14. Bryan, *Grant Memorial*, p. 58.

15. Sherrill, *Grant Memorial*, and Conklin, *Lincoln Memorial*.

16. Quote from Fine Arts Commission Report, in Green, *Washington, Capitol City*, p. 282. *Statutes*, vol. 43, p. 983.

17. Myer, Bridges, pp. 17–25. *Report of the Arlington Memorial Bridge Commission*. Zangrando, "Monumental Bridge Design," *op. cit.*, chapters 8 and 9, quote p. 407.

18. *Constructor*, vol. 7 (June 1925), p. 20; (December 1925), pp. 27–8, 47, 49. John L. Nagle, "The Arlington Memorial Bridge," *The Military Engineer*, vol. 20 (1928), pp. 154–60. George A. Follett, "The Constriction of a Cofferdam," *The Military Engineer*, vol. 20 (1928), pp. 29–31. The Corps often hired contractors but sometimes acted as contractors, hiring day laborers directly.

19. H. Paul Caemmerer, "The Corps of Engineers and the Capital City," *The Military Engineer*, vol. 45, no. 305 (May–June 1953), p. 209. Myer, *Bridges*, p. 13.

20. Myer, *Bridges*, p. 13; *Statutes at Large*, vol. 43, p. 1338.

21. Caemmerer, *Corps…*, p. 208. Myers, *Bridges*, p. 47.

22. ARCE, 1918, part I, pp. 1912–3; ARCE, 1925, part I, pp. 1913–7. Zack Spratt, "Rock Creek's Bridges," *RCHS*, vols. 53–56 (1953–56), pp. 101–5, 123. Ways, *Aqueduct*, pp. 101–5.

23. *Anacostia River and Flats*, 68th Cong., 1st sess., S. Doc. 37 (1924), p. 2.

24. ARCE, 1918, part I, p. 512; ARCE, 1923, part I, pp. 1990–3; ARCE, 1919, part II, p. 2390; ARCE, 1920, part I, pp. 2005–6; ARCE, 1925, part I, pp. 1907–8; ARCE, 1924, part I, p. 1994.

25. Davis, "Rock Creek," pp. 167, 178. The development of large public parks within Washington's outlying suburbs were a major concern of the reorganized agency in 1926. Parks adjacent to public schools are one result.

26. J. C. Pearson and J. J. Earley, "Successful Building in Stucco," *American Architect*, vol. 117, no. 2309 (March 24, 1920), pp. 386–92. Sue A. Kohler and Jeffrey R. Carson, *Sixteenth Street Architecture* (Washington: Commission of Fine Arts, 1978), vol. 1, pp. 323–35. HABS No. DC-532, "Meridian Hill Park," 1985. Dowd, *Office of Public Buildings*, pp. 79–80.

27. "An Architect's Views," *Washington Evening Star*, April 17, 1886. 69th Cong., 2nd sess., S. Doc. 240 (1926), p. 6. Sally Kress Tompkins, *A Quest for Grandeur: Charles Moore and the Federal Triangle* (Washington: Smithsonian Institution Press, 1993).

28. Quote from *To Consolidate the Office of Public Buildings and Grounds and the Office of the Superintendent of State, War, and Navy Department Buildings*, H. Rpt. 1363, 68th Cong., 2nd sess. (1925), p. 2; *Statutes at Large*, vol. 43, p. 983; Executive Order 6166, June 10, 1933, in *Executive Orders: President Hoover and President Roosevelt* (Washington, 1933), not paginated. Elizabeth Barthold, "The Predicament of the 'Parklets': Understanding Washington's Smaller Parks," *Washington History*, vol. 5, no. 1 (Spring/Summer 1993), pp. 28–39.

29. Charles W. Eliot II, "U. S. Grant, 3rd: A Word of Personal Reminiscence," *RCHS*, vols. 66–68 (1966–68), p. 364; *Annual*

Report of the Director of Public Buildings and Public Parks, 1926 (Washington, 1926), pp. 6–7; *Washington Post,* August 10, 1928; *Washington Star,* August 10, 1928; *Washington Evening News,* August 10, 1928; Green, *Washington: Capital City,* pp. 328–9, 383.

30 U. S. Grant, III, "The L'Enfant Plan and Its Evolution," *RCHS,* vols. 32–33 (1932), p. 16.

31 Interview with John Nolan, Jr., Washington, D.C., February 1, 1974. U. S. Grant III, "The National Capital: Reminiscences of Sixty-Five Years," *RCHS,* vols. 57–59 (1957–59), pp. 10–1; Letter, Grant to Harlan Bartholomew, October 21, 1953, U. S. Grant III Collection, Historical Society of Washington, D.C.; Eliot, "U. S. Grant, 3rd," p. 364. Albert W. Atwood, "General Grant, The Man," *RCHS,* vols. 66–68 (1966–68), p. 360.

32 See letters of W.C. Lyon to Superintendent Architect of the Treasury, April 23, 1923; George B. Christian, Jr. to Sherrill, June 18, 1923; Delano to Grant, October 24, 1927, and Grant to Delano, November 4, 1927. Report, Charles A. Peters, Jr. to Grant, August 12, 1925. Specifications, November 19, 1926, pp. 6–7, RG 42, Office of Public Buildings and Grounds, NARA, White House Correspondence. For Coolidge paraphrase, see D.H. Gillette, "Reconstruction of the White House," *The Military Engineer,* vol. 45 (January-February 1953), p. 8. Seale, *President's House,* vol. 2, p. 864.

33 *Statutes at Large,* vol. 43, p. 463; Eliot quote from Gutheim, *Worthy of the Nation,* p. 187; Green, *Washington: Capital City,* pp. 284–7; U. S. Grant III, "Planning the National Capital: Objectives and Problems of Attainment," *Transactions of the American Society of Civil Engineers,* vol. 117 (1952), p. 122. *Work of the National Capital Park and Planning Commission* (Washington: GPO, 1928).

34 *Potomac River, North Side of Washington Channel, D.C.,* 71st Cong., 2nd sess., H. Doc. 127 (1929); ARCE, 1930, part I. pp. 497, 530; ARCE, 1935, part I, pp. 361–2; ARCE, 1940, part I, pp. 474–8; *Statutes,* vol. 44, p. 1031. J. E. Wood, "Improvement of Washington Channel," in vol. 15, no. 83 (September–October 1923), pp. 435–7. Caemmerer, "Corps of Engineers," pp. 208–9.

35 Timothy Davis, "George Washington Memorial Parkway," pamphlet in the National Park Service series "Highways in Harmony," n.d., n.p.

36 *National Road from the Aqueduct Bridge to Mount Vernon, Va.,* 51st Cong., 1st sess., S. Exdoc. 106 (1889).

37 Charles Moore, ed., *The Improvement of the Park System of the District of Columbia,* 57th Cong., 1st sess., S. Rpt. 106 (1902), pp. 121–2.

38 Davis, "Memorial Parkway" pamphlet. Duryee, *Corps in Washington,* pp. 93–5.

39 Duryee, *Corps in Washington,* pp. 93–5. R. E. Royall, "The Mount Vernon Memorial Highway," *The Military Engineer,* vol. 24, no. 135 (May–June 1932), pp. 238–42.

40 R. C. Tripp, "Washington National Airport," *The Military Engineer,* vol. 31, no. 179 (September–October 1939), pp. 319–25. Nancy N. Knickerbocker, "Aircraft Noise and Property Values," Ph.D. diss., 1991, University of Maryland, pp. 51–2.

41 Duryee, *Corps in Washington,* pp. 94–5, 119–20; Howard Lovewell Cheney, "Inspection of the Washington National Airport," *The Military Engineer,* vol. 33, no. 190 (July–August 1941), pp. 283–6. Howard Lovewell Cheney, "Washington National Airport," *Architectural Record,* vol. 90, no. 4 (October 1941), pp. 49–57. James M. Goode, "Flying High: The Origin and Design of Washington National Airport," *Washington History,* vol. 1, no. 2 (Fall 1989), pp. 4–25.

42 *Work of the National Capitol Park,* pp. 23–9. "The Story of the Fort Memorial Freeway, 1894–1953," Geography & Map Division, LC, G3852 .F56G45 1953 .R6. Gutheim, *Worthy of the Nation,* pp. 242–3.

43 Pentagon history largely summarized from Alfred Goldberg, *The Pentagon: The First Fifty Years* (Washington: Department of Defense, 1992). See also: Lenore Fine and Jesse A. Remington, *The Corps of Engineers: Construction in the United States* (Washington: Office of the Chief of Military History, U.S. Army, 1972), pp. 434–7.

44 Goldberg, *Pentagon,* p. 14.

45 *Ibid.,* pp. 24–5.

46 *Ibid.,* pp. 14, 24–8.

47 Diane Tepfer, Washingtoniana II, Documentation on Washington Architectural Drawings, LOC Prints and Photographs Division.

48 "Planning the Pentagon Building" quoted in Goldberg, *Pentagon,* p. 86. Carl M. Brauer, *The Man Who Built Washington: A Life of John McShain* (Wilmington, Delaware: Hagley Museum and Library, 1996) pp. 80–8.

49 Fine and Remington, *The Corps,* pp. 438, 514–5; *Life* (December 21, 1942), pp. 83–4.

50 *Ibid.,* pp. 471–6; Duryee, *Corps in Washington,* 109, 119–20.

51 "City Unites in Drive for Memorial Stadium," *Washington Post,* November 12, 1944. "General Grant and the Christian Heurich Memorial Mansion," *RCHS,* vols. 66–68 (1966–68), pp. 365–8.

52 *Report of the Commission on the Renovation of the Executive Mansion* (Washington: GPO, 1952); William P. O'Brien, "Reality and Illusion: The White House and Harry S. Truman," *White House History,* vol. 5 (Spring 1999), pp. 4–12.

53 Gillette, "Reconstruction," pp. 8–13.

54 *Diary of Progress on the Renovation and Remodeling of the Executive Mansion for General Glen E. Edgerton, Executive Director of the Commission* (Alexandria, Virginia: Office of History, Headquarters, U.S. Army Corps of Engineers), p. 144.

55 Milton Rubincam, "Major General U. S. Grant, 3rd, 1881–1968," *RCHS,* vols. 66–68 (1966–68), pp. 369–408.

CHAPTER 6: METROPOLIS, 1945–2004

1 Green, *Washington: Capital City*, p. 505. "Interview with Brig. Gen. Robert E. Mathe, USA (Ret.)" (hereafterr Mathe Interview), by Albert E. Cowdrey, February 12, 1974, Oral History Files, Office of History, U.S. Corps of Engineers, Washington, D.C., pp. 21–4.

2 *Ibid.*

3 Green, *Washington: Capital City*, p. 435. *Engineer Memoirs: Lieutenant General Frederick J. Clarke* (hereafter *Clarke Memoirs*) (Washington: Office of the Chief of Engineers, 1979), pp. 275–8, 285–6. Hereafter, *Clarke Memoirs*.

4 *Clarke Memoirs*, pp. 80, 143, 254. In 1952, Congress established the National Capital Planning Commission as successor to the National Capital Park and Planning Commission. The same year, the National Capital Regional Planning Council was established. That body was turned over in 1966 to the Metropolitan Council of Governments, which had been established in 1957.

5 Mathe interview, p. 6.

6 Philip W. Ogilvie, "Chronology of some events in the history of the District of Columbia," D.C. Office of Public Records, 1989. *Clarke Memoirs*, p. 279.

7 Telephone interview with Robert E. Mathe, Washington, D.C., May 30, 1991. Mathe interview, p. 3. Steven J. Diner and Anita Henderson, *A History of the District of Columbia, Unit II: The Center of a Metropolis, Washington since 1954* (Washington: Associates for Renewal in Education, Inc., 1980), p. 34.

8 Ulysses S. Grant, III, "Planning the Nation's Capital," *RCHS*, vol. 50 (1980), p. 56. "D.C. Redevelopment Land Agency Annual Report," 1951, p. 1.

9 Detailed demographic data and an assessment of two proposed redevelopment plans appeared in Harland Bartholonew & Associates, *Redevelopment Plans for the Southwest Survey Area in the District of Columbia*, May 1952. Howard Gillette, Jr., *Between Justice and Beauty: Race, Planning, and the Failure of Urban Policy in Washington, D.C.* (Baltimore: Johns Hopkins University Press, 1995), p. 156; D.C. Redevelopment Land Agency Annual Report 1958, p. 4.

10 The progress of the redevelopment is readily seen in the annual reports of the D.C. Redevelopment Land Agency between 1951 and 1971.

11 Gillette, *Between Justice*, pp. 163–4, 173–6.

12 Brig. Gen. Gordon R. Young, *A Preliminary Six-year Plan for Postwar Washington* (Washington, 1946). *Washington Present and Future: A General Summary of the Comprehensive Plan for the National Capital and its Environs* (Washington: National Capital Park and Planning Commission, 1950).

13 De Leuw, Cather & Company, *Report on Inner Loop Freeway System, District of Columbia* (Chicago: De Leuw, Cather & Company, 1955), pp. 1–3; Gillette, *Between Justice*, p. 165. Quote from Keith Melder, *City of Magnificent Intentions: A History of Washington, District of Columbia* (Washington: Intac, Inc., 1997), p. 530. Bob Levey and Jane Freundel Levey, "Lost Highways: The Plan to Pave Washington and the People Who Stopped It," *Washington Post Magazine*, November 26, 2000.

14 *Clarke Memoirs*, pp. 145–6, 255–6.

15 "Jackson Graham's Resignation," *Washington Post*, December 13, 1975. "Jackson Graham, General Manager, Washington Metropolitan Area Transit Authority," Biographical Files, Office of History. Douglas B. Feaver, "Building Supervisor for Metro Reveals Plans to Retire May 1," *Washington Post*, February 3, 1978.

16 Myer, *Bridges*, pp. 16, 32–3.

17 "Soldiers' Home Plans $10,000,000 Building Program in 2 Years," *Washington Star*, October 5, 1947. "Soldiers' Home Plans 10-Million Apartments for 900," *Washington Post*, October 5, 1947.

18 William P. Moseley, "Soldiers' Home Still Presses Building Plans," *Washington Times Herald*, December 7, 1949.

19 Wes Barthelmes, "Soldiers' Home Now Boasts 2 New Buildings," *Washington Post*, December 7, 1953. Fran Feldman, "Gabel Builds over and in the Water and Sometimes on Dry Land," *Constellation*, vol. 14, no. 8 (August 1988), pp. 4–5. Fran Feldman, "Veterans Enjoy Modern Living in Renovated Soldiers' and Airmen's Home," *Constellation*, vol. 16, no. 5 (June 1990), pp. 4–5. "Secretary of Army Dedicates $29 Million Health Care Residence," *Constellation*, vol. 18, no. 6 (June 1992), p. 4.

20 Duryee, *Corps in Washington*, pp.117–8.

21 "Arlington Amphitheater Renovation Completed," *Washington Star*, September 6, 1957. "District Repairs Tomb of Unknown Soldier," *Constellation*, vol. 15, no. 11 (November 1989), p. 3. Debi Horne, "Memorial Amphitheater Gets Facelift," *Constellation*, vol. 22, no. 8 (August 1996), p. 11. "Visitors Center Dedicated at Arlington," *Constellation*, vol. 15, no. 1 (January 1989), p. 2. "Arlington Visitors Center Wins Award," *Constellation*, vol. 17, nos. 5–6 (May–June 1991), p. 3. Interview with Joseph G. Kemper and Donald Lynne, Baltimore, Maryland, May 16, 1991. Jim Maxwell, "Sixth Columbarium Construction under Way," *Constellation*, vol. 23, no. 8 (August 1997), pp. 10–1.

22 "Tackling the GAO," *Constellation*, vol. 20, no. 11 (November 1994), pp. 4–5. Bernard Tate, "Headquarters Moves to New Home," *Engineer Update* (September 2000), accessed on 8/11/2005 at www.hq.usace.army.mil/cepa/pubs/sep00/story4.htm. Denise Tann, "A New Face for the Kennedy Center," *Constellation*, vol. 23, no. 1 (January 1997), pp. 4–5.

23 Robert Cook, "President Attends NDU Dedication," *Constellation*, vol. 17, no. 9 (September 1991), pp. 1, 4–5. "Support to Fort McNair," *Constellation*, vol. 24, no. 10 (October 1997), pp. 8–9. Ted Henry, "Preparing for the Military's Future within the Walls of History," *Constellation*, vol. 25, no. 8 (August 1999), p. 3. "National War College Completes Historic Renovation, 4/18/2000," www.ellerbebecket.com.

24 Ways, *Aqueduct*, pp. 129–30. Interstate Commission on the Potomac River Basin, *Healing a River: The Potomac, 1940–1990*, p. 11. *Water for the Future of the Nation's Capital Area* (Washington: National Academy Press, 1980), pp. 1, 3.

25 *Adequate Future Water Supply for District of Columbia*, 79th Cong., 2nd sess., H. Doc. 480 (1946), pp. 1–13.

26 *Adequate Future Water Supply*, p. 8. Pages 2–3 of the same document summarize the previous Potomac River study reports. "Little Falls Water Shaft Nearly Done," *Washington Post*, August 27, 1957; Ways, *Aqueduct*, p. 120. Robert Cook, "WAD Quenches D.C.'s Thirst," *Constellation* (January 1991), pp. 4–5.

27 *Healing a River*, pp. 6, 9. Alvin C. Welling, "Pollution in the Potomac River," *Medical Annals of the District of Columbia* (May 1960) pp. 289–90.

28 Bernard L. Robinson interview, November 8, 1978, Oral History files, Office of History, U.S. Army Corps of Engineers, Washington, D.C., pp. 6–7.

29 ARCE, 1964, vol. 2, p. 306. Ways, *Aqueduct*, p. 122.

30 *Ibid.*, pp. 138–9. Patty Gamby and Erika Hieber, "Little Falls Fish Passage Project," *Constellation* (April 1996), p. 5. "Washington Aqueduct's Environmental Mission," *Constellation* (April 1996), p. 9. Mary Beth Thompson, "Capital Projects Move Forward at WA," *Constellation*, vol. 26, no. 7 (July 2000), pp. 1–2.

31 Harry Ways, "Fountain Returns Home to WAD," *Constellation*, vol. 17, no. 2 (February 1991), p. 1. Thomas P. Somma, "The McMillan Memorial Fountain: A Short History of a Lost Monument," *Washington History*, vol. 14, no. 2 (Fall/Winter 2002), pp. 96–107. Joseph L. Arnold, *The Baltimore Engineers and the Chesapeake Bay, 1961–1987* (Baltimore: U.S Army Corps of Engineers, 1988), p. 124. "EPA Wants Independent Study of D.C. Water Purification," *Washington Post*, October 5, 1993. "Fairfax Seeks Control of Reservoirs," *Washington Post*, December 7, 1995. "Clean Water for the District," *Washington Post*, March 3, 1996. "New Agency May Run Aqueduct," *Washington Post*, August 21, 1997. "Hearings Urged on Discharge from Dalecarlia Plant," *Washington Post*, August 24, 2001. "EPA Is Proposing Tougher Rules for Water Plant in D.C.," *Washington Post*, December 18, 2002.

32 Charles D. Pierce, "D.C. to Get Bill for Dam Share," *Washington Star*, April 26, 1961. Ways, *Aqueduct*, p. 134. *Healing a River*, pp. 6, 10. U.S. Army Engineer District, Baltimore, *Potomac River Basin Report*, February 1963, part I, syllabus. "Why Washington Has Enough Water," *Potomac Basin Reporter*, vol. 43, no. 9 (October 1987), pp. 1–3. Arnold, *Baltimore Engineers and the Chesapeake Bay*, pp. 67–76.

33 *Public Hearing on the Potomac River Basin Report*, Board of Engineers for Rivers and Harbors, Corps of Engineers, U.S. Army, Sept. 4, 1963. Coordinating Committee on the Potomac River Valley, *Potomac Prospect: A study and report with recommendations for action concerning…the Potomac River Basin*, 1961, p. 65.

34 Potomac River Basin Report, part II, p. 100. *Annual Message to the Congress*, January 4, 1965. The Secretary of the Interior's report was titled *The Nation's River*, and it was submitted to the President on Oct. 1, 1968. *Potomac River Basin Report*, 1970, is the revised report sent to Congress. Ways, *Aqueduct*, p. 133. Quote from Fran Feldman, "Corps Studies Potomac Flood Control," *Constellation*, vol. 13, no. 3 (March 1987), p. 1.

35 *Ibid.*, pp. 139–40. Katharine L. Vaughn, "Smit Swears He Can't Smell It Any More," *Constellation*, vol. 14, no. 9 (September 1988), pp. 4–5. "Happy Anniversary, Blue Plains," *Potomac Basin Reporter*, vol. 44, no. 10 (November–December 1988), pp. 1–3.

36 Duryee, *Corps of Engineers*, pp. 105–8. ARCE on Civil Works Activities, 1977, vol. 2, pp. 4–11. Rupert Welch, "Green Monster Vine Spreading in Potomac," *Washington Times*, June 6, 1984. Paul Hodge, "Hydrilla in Potomac Found Well-Rooted," *Washington Post*, September 11, 1984.

37 Arnold, *Baltimore Engineers and the Chesapeake Bay*, pp. 75–6. Charlie Walker, "District Recommends Mechanical Harvester to Control Hydrilla," *Constellation* (January 1986.) "Potomac Mowing Underway," *Potomac Basin Reporter*, vol. 42, no. 8 (August–September 1986), pp. 1–3. Harold K. Clingerman, "Hydrilla Control Program Begins," *Constellation*, vol. 13, no. 7 (July 1987), pp. 3–4. "Hydrilla Falls, Rises," *Potomac Basin Reporter*, vol. 47, no. 7 (July 1991), p. 1

39 ARCE, 1956, vol. 2, pp. 315–9. John W. Stepp, "Reclamation Plan Revived for Anacostia Swamps," *Washington Star*, September 11, 1955. ARCE, 1964, vol. 2, p. 270.

39 "A River Unfulfilled," *Potomac Basin Reporter*, vol. 43, no. 3 (March 1987), pp. 1–4.

40 Robert Cook, "Anacostia River Cleanup Gets Corps Help," *Constellation*, vol. 17, no. 11 (November–December 1991), pp. 3, 7. "Anacostia Oil Spill Gets Help from Baltimore District," *Constellation*, vol. 18, no. 3 (May 1992), pp. 6–7. "Kenilworth Key to Future Success," *Constellation*, vol. 19, no. 2 (February 1993), p. 4. "District Celebrates Rebirth of Kenilworth Marsh," *Constellation*, vol. 19, no. 10 (October 1993), pp. 6–7. "New Project Promotes Team Baltimore Concept," *Constellation*, vol. 22, no. 2 (February 1996), p. 11. James Johnson, "Anacostia River Gets Priority Attention," *Constellation*, vol. 22 special edition (April 1996), p. 14. Doug Garman, "Kingman Lake Focus of Earth Day Celebration," *Constellation*, vol. 26, no. 5 (May 2000), p. 1. Mary Beth Thompson, "Corps Helps Polluted Anacostia Watershed Recover," *Constellation*, vol. 28, no. 8 (August 2002), pp. 1–6. National Building Museum, "D.C. Builds. The Anacostia Waterfront," exhibition text, 2004.

41 Martin K. Gordon, Barry R. Sude, and Ruth Ann Overbeck, "Chemical Testing in the Great War: The American University Experiment Station," *Washington History*, vol. 6, no. 1 (Spring/Summer 1994), pp. 28–45. Harold Clingerman, "Excavations Begin in Spring Valley Area," *Constellation*, vol. 19, no. 11 (November 1993), p. 1.

42 U.S. Army Corps of Engineers, Baltimore District, "Spring Valley, Washington, D.C. Project Overview," 2003, www.nab.usace.army.mil. "District Meets Spring Valley Challenge," *Constellation*, vol. 19, no. 2 (February 1993), pp. 6–7. "District Makes Home in Spring Valley," *Constellation*, vol. 19, no. 3 (March 1993), pp. 1, 6–7. "Spring Valley Is at It Again," *Constellation*, vol. 20, no. 4 (April 1994), p. 7. "Spring Valley Bunker Work Completed," *Constellation*, vol. 20, no. 2 (February 1995), p. 14. "Spring Valley Investigation of WWI Munitions Complete," *Constellation*, vol. 21, no. 7 (July 1995), p. 3. "Excavation for WWI Remnants Complete at Spring Valley," *Constellation*, vol. 26, no. 5 (May 2000), p. 3. "Excavation by Military Forces Some AU Closings," *Washington Post*, January 8, 2001. "Arsenic Illnesses Worry D.C.," *Washington Post*, January 27, 2001. "More Arsenic Tests to Come," *Washington Post*, February 1, 2001. "Some D.C. Sites Need More Arsenic Tests," *Washington Post*, August 22, 2001. *The Northwest Current*, vol. 37, no. 45 (November 10, 2004), pp. B6–7.

43 U.S. Army Corps of Engineers, Baltimore District, "Camp Simms, Former Defense Site, Washington, D.C.," 2003, www.nab.usace.army.mil. "Munition Discovery Leads to On-Site Detonation," *Constellation* (April 1995), p. 3. "Discovered Munitions Change Project Work Plans," *Constellation* (December 1995), p. 4. "Digging Begins Again at Camp Simms Project," *Constellation* (July 1996).

44 U.S. Army Corps of Engineers, Baltimore District, "District of Columbia Public Schools Capital Improvements Program Project Brief," 2003, www.nab.usace.army.mil. Ted Henry, "Improvements Continue in the Nation's Capital," *Constellation*, vol. 25, no. 6 (June 1999), p. 4. Doug Garman, "D.C. Schools Open on Time," *Constellation*, vol. 26, no. 10 (October 2000), pp. 1, 3. Mary Beth Thompson, "Corps People: Improving Schools for the Children," *Constellation*, vol. 27, no. 5 (May 2001), pp. 6–7. "Corps Struggles With Role in D.C. Schools," *Washington Post*, July 2, 2000. "Despite Sinking Enrollment, Proposal Calls for Rebuilding," *Washington Post*, December 7, 2000. "District and D.C. Schools Break Ground for New Elementary School," *Constellation*, vol. 28, no. 1 (January 2002), p. 10. Doug Garman, "Work Progresses on New D.C. Elementary Schools," *Constellation*, vol. 28, no. 5 (May 2002), p. 4.

45 "Architects to Oversee 2nd Memorial," *Washington Times*, May 4, 1990. "Architects Sue Over Redesign of Memorial," *Washington Post*, December 19, 1990. "The Korean Controversy," *Washington Post*, February 2, 1991. Quote from Robert Cook, "District to Build Memorial," *Constellation*, vol. 16, no. 11 (November 1990), p. 6.

46 Robert Martin, ed., *Korean War Veterans Memorial: A Tribute to Those Who Served* (Paducah, Kentucky: Turner Publishing, 1995). "Statues Arrive for Korean War Memorial," *Constellation* (May 1995), p. 3. Derek Walker, "District Leads Project of Completion," *Constellation* (August 1995), pp. 1, 8–9. "A Shadow Has Fallen on Korean Memorial," *Washington Post*, May 10, 1997. "Corps to Receive Funds to Finish Korean War Memorial Modification," *Constellation* (December 1998), p. 3

47 "District Will Renovate Pentagon," *Constellation*, vol. 15, no. 5 (May 1989), p. 1. "Pentagon Renovation Office Approved," *Constellation*, vol. 15, no. 8/9 (August/September 1989). Fran Feldman, "Leketa Heads Pentagon Renovation," *Constellation*, vol. 16, no. 4 (May 1990), pp. 4–5. "Pentagon Office Is Gearing Up," *Constellation*, vol. 17, no. 8 (August 1991), pp. 1, 4–5. Robert Cook, "Pentagon's Heating/Refrigeration Plant Begins to Take Shape," *Constellation*, vol. 20, no. 3 (March 1994), pp. 6–7. "Moving Indoors at the Pentagon," *Constellation*, vol. 21, no. 1 (January 1995), pp. 4–5. "Many Jobs at PenRen, Much Experience," *Constellation*, vol. 22, no. 8 (August 1996), p. 10. "Pentagon Renovation Projects Move to Construction," *Constellation*, vol. 23, no. 8 (August 1997), pp. 1, 8–9. Tom Fontana, "Pentagon Renovation Moves Ahead," *Engineer Update* (October 1997); Tom Fontana, "Pentagon Renovation," *Engineer Update* (February 2000); and Bernard Tate, "Corps Designed Pentagon Protection, Managing Memorial Contest," *Engineer Update* (September 2003), all accessed on 8/10/2005 at www.hq.usace.army.mil/cepa/pubs/oldpubs.htm.

48 U.S. Army Corps of Engineers, Baltimore District, "The Pentagon Memorial Project," 2004, http://pentagonmemorial.nab.usace.army.mil/, includes "Pentagon Memorial Site Evaluation Summary," March 2, 2002, and three issues of the *Pentagon Memorial News*, "Competition Entries Stream in at Deadline" (September 2002), "Competition Jury Selects Six Finalists" (November 2002), "Memorial Design Chosen: Light Benches" (March 2003). "Six Wide-Open Visions Vie for a Pentagon Memorial," *Washington Post*, October 18, 2002.

49 "The Pentagon Memorial Project Overview," homepage, http://pentagonmemorial.nab.usace.army.mil/.

Bibliography

SECONDARY SOURCES

Adler, Bill, ed., *Washington: A Reader* (New York: Meredith Press, 1967).

Allen, William C., *A History of the United States Capitol* (Washington: GPO, 2001).

American National Biography (New York: Oxford University Press, 1999).

Arnebeck, Bob, *Through a Fiery Trial: Building Washington 1790–1800* (Lanham, Maryland: Madison Books, 1991).

Arnold, James R., "The United States Army Corps of Engineers and the Lincoln Memorial," n.d., unpublished paper, Humphreys Engineer Center.

Arnold, Joseph L., *The Baltimore Engineers and the Chesapeake Bay, 1961–1987* (Baltimore: U.S. Army Corps of Engineers, 1988).

Atwood, Albert W., "General Grant: The Man," *Records of the Columbia Historical Society*, vols. 66–68 (1966–68), pp. 358–62.

Barthold, Elizabeth, "The Predicament of the 'Parklets': Understanding Washington's Smaller Parks," *Washington History*, vol. 5, no. 1 (Spring/Summer 1993), pp. 28–45.

Baumann, Charles H., *The Influence of Angus Snead Macdonald and the Snead Bookstack on Library Architecture* (Metuchen, New Jersey: Scarecrow Press, 1972).

Beauchamp, Tanya, "Adolph Cluss and the Building of the U.S. National Museum: An Architecture of Perfect Adaptability," M.A. thesis, University of Virginia, 1972.

Bell, Lt. Col. J. Franklin, "City Engineering in Washington," *The Military Engineer*, vol. 19, no. 107 (September–October 1927), pp. 359–62.

_____, "Street Lighting Versus Street Trees," *American City* (October 1928), pp. 122–3.

Binczewshi, George J., "The Point of the Monument: A History of the Aluminum Cap at the Washington Monument," *Journal of the Minerals, Metals and Materials Society*, vol. 47 (1995), pp. 20–5.

Bowling, Kenneth R., *The Creation of Washington, D.C.: The Idea and Location of the American Capital* (Fairfax, Virginia: George Mason University Press, 1991).

Boynton, Edward C., *History of West Point and the United States Military Academy* (New York: D. Van Nostrand, 1863).

Brauer, Carl M., *The Man Who Built Washington: A Life of John McShain* (Wilmington, Delaware: Hagley Museum and Library, 1996).

Brennan, Roland M., "Brigadier General Richard L. Hoxie, United States Army, 1861–1930," *Records of the Columbia Historical Society*, vols. 57–59 (1961), pp. 87–95.

Brousseau, Frances, "The Library of Congress," Ph.D. diss., University of Delaware, 1998.

Brown, Glenn, ed., "Proceedings of the Thirty-Sixth Annual Convention of the American Institute of Architects," *Journal of the Proceedings of the AIA* (Washington: Gibson Bros., 1903).

Brownlow, Louis, *A Passion for Anonymity: The Autobiography of Louis Brownlow* (Chicago: University of Chicago Press, 1958).

Bryan, James William, ed., *The Grant Memorial in Washington* (Washington: GPO, 1924).

Buchanan, Roberdeau, *Genealogy of the Roberdeau Family* (Washington: Jospeh L. Pearson, 1876).

Bushong, William B., "Glenn Brown, the American Institute of Architects, and the Development of the Civic Core of Washington, D.C.," Ph.D. diss., The George Washington University, 1988.

_____, *Historic Resources Study of Rock Creek Park, District of Columbia* (Denver: National Park Service Denver Service Center, 1990).

Caemmerer, H. Paul, "The Corps of Engineers and the Capital City," *The Military Engineer*, vol. 45, no. 305 (May–June 1953), p. 209.

_____, *The Life of Pierre Charles L'Enfant* (Washington: National Republic Publishing Co., 1950).

Centennial History of the City of Washington (Dayton, Ohio: United Brethren Publishing House, 1892).

Cheney, Howard Lovewell, "Washington National Airport," *Architectural Record*, vol. 90, no. 4 (October 1941), pp. 49–57.

Clinton, Amy Cheny "Historic Fort Washington," *Maryland Historical Magazine*, vol. 32 (September 1931), p. 237.

Cohen, Jeffrey A. and Charles E. Brownell, *The Architectural Drawings of Benjamin Henry Latrobe* (New Haven: Yale University Press, 1994).

Cole, John Y. and Henry Hope Reed, eds., *The Library of Congress: The Art and Architecture of the Thomas Jefferson Building* (New York: W. W. Norton & Company, 1997).

Colket, Meredith B., Jr., "General Grant and the Christian Heurich Memorial Mansion," *Records of the Columbia Historical Society*, vols. 66–68 (1966–68), pp. 365–8.

Conklin, Edward F., *The Lincoln Memorial, Washington* (Washington: GPO, 1927).

Cooling, Benjamin Franklin III and Walton H. Owen, *Mr. Lincoln's Forts: A Guide to the Civil War Defenses of Washington* (Shippensburg, Pennsylvania: White Mane Publishing Co., 1988).

_____, "To Preserve the Peace," *Washington History*, vol. 1, no. 1 (Spring 1989), pp. 71–86.

Coordinating Committee on the Potomac River Valley, *Potomac Prospect: A Study and Report with Recommendations for Action Concerning the Potomac River Basin*, 1961.

Cowdrey, Albert E., *A City for the Nation* (Washington: GPO, 1978).

Cox, William V., *Celebration of the One-Hundredth Anniversary of the Establishment of the Seat of Government in the District of Columbia* (Washington: GPO, 1901).

Cullen, Charles T. et al., eds., *The Papers of Thomas Jefferson* (Princeton: Princeton University Press, 1986).

Cullum, George W., *Biographical Register of Officers and Graduates of the U.S. Military Academy* (Boston: Houghton Mifflin & Co.).

"Current News and Comment, The Lincoln Memorial Site," *American Architect*, vol. 100, no. 1866 (September 27, 1911), p. 5.

Curtis, William T. S., "Cabin John Bridge," *Records of the Columbia Historical Society*, vol. 2 (1899), pp. 293–307.

Davis, Timothy, "George Washington Memorial Parkway," pamphlet (Washington: National Park Service, n.d.).

_____, "Rock Creek and Potomac Parkway, Washington D.C.: The Evolution of a Contested Urban Landscape," *Studies in the History of Gardens & Designed Landscapes*, vol. 19, no. 2 (April–June 1999), pp. 123–237.

DeLeuw, Cather & Company, *Report on Inner Loop Freeway System, District of Columbia* (Chicago: Privately printed, 1955).

[Diaz, Jean R.], "Do You Know the Corps' Connection to the Washington, D.C., Tidal Basin and its Beloved Cherry Trees?" U.S. Army Corps of Engineers, Office of History, Vignette No. 48. www.hq.usace.army.mil/history.

Dickinson, William C. et al., eds., *Montgomery C. Meigs and the Building of the Nation's Capital* (Athens, Ohio: Ohio University Press, 2001).

Diner, Steven J. and Anita Henderson. *A History of the District of Columbia, Unit II: The Center of a Metropolis, Washington Since 1954* (Washington: Associates for Renewal in Education, Inc., 1980).

District of Columbia Redevelopment Land Agency Annual Report, Washington, 1951.

Dowd, Mary Jane, *Records of the Public Buildings and Public Parks of the National Capital* (Washington: National Archives, 1992).

Dunlap, William, *A History of the Rise and Progress of the Arts of Design in the United States* (Boston: C. E. Goodspeed & Co., 1918).

Duryee, Sackett L., *The Corps of Engineers in the Nation's Capital, 1852–1952* (1952).

Dzombak, William, "Roberdeau's Treatise on Canals," *American Canals*, vol. 76 (February 1991), pp. 8–9.

Eliot, Charles W., II, "U.S. Grant, 3rd: A Word of Personal Reminiscence," *Records of the Columbia Historical Society*, vols. 66–68 (1966–68), pp. 363–4.

Everly, Elaine and Howard H. Wehmann, "The War Office Fire of 1800," *Prologue*, vol. 31, no. 1 (Spring 1999), pp. 22–35.

Executive Office of the President, *The Old Executive Office Building: A Victorian Masterpiece* (Washington: GPO, 1984).

Fairman, Charles E., *Art and Artists of the Capitol of the United States of America* (Washington: GPO, 1927).

Field, Cynthia R. and Jeffrey T. Tilman, "Creating a Model for the National Mall: The Design of the National Museum of Natural History," *Journal of the Society of Architectural Historians*, vol. 63, no. 1 (March 2004), pp. 52–73.

Fine, Lenore and Jesse A. Remington, *The Corps of Engineers: Construction in the United States* (Washington: GPO, 1972).

Fitzpatrick, John C., ed., *Journal of the Continental Congress, 1774–1789* (Washington: GPO, 1933).

_____, *The Writings of George Washington* (Washington: GPO, 1931).

Follett, George A., "The Construction of a Cofferdam," *The Military Engineer*, vol. 10 (1928), pp. 29–31.

Forbes–Lindsay, C. H., *Washington: The City and the Seat of Government* (Philadelphia: John C. Winston Co., 1908).

Foster, Andrea Kim, "The Conflict Between the Engineers and Architects Over Control of the Washington Barracks, 1902," class paper dated 1986, American Studies Department, The George Washington University.

Fries, Russell I., "European vs. American Engineering: Pierre Charles L'Enfant and the Water Power System of Paterson, N.J.," *Northeast Historical Archaeology*, vol. 4, nos. 1–2 (Spring 1975), pp. 68–96.

"General Grant and the Christian Heurich Memorial Mansion," *Records of the Columbia Historical Society*, vols. 66–68 (1966–68), pp. 365–8.

Gillette, D. H., "Reconstruction of the White House," *The Military Engineer*, vol. 45 (1953), p. 8.

Gillette, Howard, Jr., *Between Justice and Beauty: Race, Planning, and the Failure of Urban Policy in Washington, D.C.* (Baltimore: Johns Hopkins University Press, 1995).

_____, *Washington: The City and the Seat of Government* (Baltimore: Johns Hopkins University Press, 1995).

Goldberg, Alfred, *The Pentagon: The First Fifty Years* (Washington: Department of Defense, 1992).

Goode, B. Brown, "The Genesis of the National Museum," *Annual Report of the Smithsonian Institution* (Washington: Smithsonian Institution, 1891), pp. 273–335.

Goode, James M., "Architecture, Politics, and Conflict: Thomas Ustick Walter and the Enlargement of the United States Capitol, 1850–1865," Ph.D. diss., The George Washington University, 1995.

_____, *The Outdoor Sculpture of Washington, D.C.* (Washington: Smithsonian Institution Press, 1974).

_____ "Flying High: The Origin and Design of Washington National Airport," *Washington History*, vols. 1–2 (Fall 1989), pp. 4–25.

Gordon, Martin K., Barry R. Sude, and Ruth Ann Overbeck, "Chemical Testing in the Great War, The American University Experiment Station," *Washington History*, vol. 6, no. 1 (Spring/Summer 1994), pp. 28–45.

Grant, U. S., III, "Planning the National Capital: Objectives and Problems of Attainment," *Transactions, American Society of Civil Engineers*, vol. 117 (1952), p. 122.

_____, "The L'Enfant Plan and Its Evolution," *Records of the Columbia Historical Society*, vols. 33–34 (1932), pp. 1–23.

_____, "The National Capital: Reminiscences of Sixty-Five Years," *Records of the Columbia Historical Society*, vols. 57–59 (1957–59), pp. 1–15.

Green, Bernard R., "The Building of the Library of Congress," *Smithsonian Institution Annual Report* (Washington: Smithsonian Institution, 1897).

Green, Constance McLaughlin, *Washington: Capital City, 1879–1950* (Princeton: Princeton University Press, 1963).

_____, *Washington: Village and Capital, 1800–1878* (Princeton: Princeton University Press, 1962).

Gutheim, Frederick, *Worthy of the Nation: The History of Planning for the National Capital* (Washington: Smithsonian Institution Press, 1977).

Hafertepe, Kenneth, *America's Castle: The Evolution of the Smithsonian Building and Its Institution* (Washington: Smithsonian Institution Press, 1984).

Hagen, Kenneth J. and William R. Roberts, eds., *Against All Enemies: Interpretations of American Military History from Colonial Times to the Present* (New York: Greenwood Press, 1986).

Hains, Peter C., "Reclamation of the Potomac Flats at Washington, D.C.," *Transactions of the American Society of Civil Engineers*, vol. 36 (January 1894), pp. 55–80.

Hannum, Warren T., "Water Supply of the District of Columbia," *Professional Memoirs, Corps of Engineers, U.S. Army*, vol. 4 (1912), p. 226.

Harland Bartholomew & Associates, *Redevelopment Plans for the Southwest Survey Area in the District of Columbia*, May 1952.

Harrison, Michael R., "The Evil of the Misfit Subdivisions: Creating the Permanent System of Highways of the District of Columbia," *Washington History*, vol. 14, no. 1 (Spring/Summer 2002), pp. 26–55.

Harts, Col. William W., "Cylinder-Pier Foundations for Lincoln Memorial, Washington, D.C.," *Engineering News*, vol. 71 (May 7, 1914), p. 1019.

_____*William Wright Harts, His Story* (Privately printed, c. 2001).

Harvey, Frederick L., *History of the Washington National Monument and the Washington National Monument Society* (Washington: GPO, 1903).

Hatcher, Ed, "Washington's Nineteenth-Century Citizens' Associations and the Senate Park Commission Plan," *Washington History*, vol. 14, no. 2 (Fall/Winter 2002), pp. 70–95.

Heine, Cornelius W., "The Contributions of Charles Carroll Glover and other Citizens to the Development of the National Capital," *Records of the Columbia Historical Society*, vols. 53–55 (1959), pp. 229–48.

Henry, Robert S., *The Armed Forces Institute of Pathology: Its First Century, 1862–1962* (Washington: Department of the Army, 1964).

Hoagland, Alison K., "Nineteenth-Century Building Regulations in Washington, D.C.," *Records of the Columbia Historical Society*, vol. 52 (1989), pp. 57–77.

Holt, William Stull, *The Office of the Chief of Engineers of the Army: Its Non-Military History* (Washington: Brookings Institute, 1923).

Howe, Franklin T., "The Board of Public Works," *Records of the Columbia Historical Society*, vol. 3 (1900), pp. 257–78.

Hume, Edgar Erskine, "The Diplomas of the Society of Cincinnati," *Americana*, vol. 29, no. 1 (January 1935), pp. 5–45.

Interstate Commission on the Potomac River Basin, *Healing a River: The Potomac, 1940–1990* (Washington: GPO, 1991).

"Interview with Professor Baird," *Forest and Stream,* vol. 10 (1878), p. 214.

Jackson, Donald and Dorothy Twohig, eds., *The Diaries of George Washington* (Charlottesville: University Press of Virginia, 1979).

Jackson, John W., *Fort Mifflin, Valiant Defender of the Delaware* (Philadelphia: Old Fort Mifflin Historical Society, 1986).

Jacob, Kathryn Allamong, *Testament to Union: Civil War Monuments in Washington, D.C.* (Washington: Smithsonian Institution Press, 1998).

Jusserand, J. J., *With Americans of Past and Present Days* (New York: Charles Scribner's Sons, 1916).

Kennan, George, "The White House: The Plans for Its Reconstruction," *The Outlook* (February 1, 1902), p. 321.

Kite, Elisabeth S., *L'Enfant and Washington, 1791–1792* (Baltimore: Johns Hopkins University Press, 1929).

Knickerbocker, Nancy N., "Aircraft Noise and Property Values," Ph.D. diss., University of Maryland, 1991.

Kohler, Sue A., *The Commission of Fine Arts: A Brief History, 1910–1995* (Washington: Commission of Fine Arts, [1996]).

_____ and Jeffrey Carson, *Sixteenth Street Architecture,* vol. 1 (Washington: Commission of Fine Arts, 1878).

_____ and Pamela Scott, eds., *The Senate Park Commission Plan of 1901 for Washington, D.C.: A Collaboration of Art and Politics* (Washington: Commission of Fine Arts, 2005).

[Kousoulis, Mary], "D.C. Builds: The Anacostia Waterfront," National Building Museum, 2004.

Lee, Antoinette J., *Architects to the Nation: The Rise and Decline of the Supervising Architect's Office* (New York: Oxford University Press, 2000).

_____, ed., *Historical Perspectives on Urban Design: Washington, D.C., 1890–1910,* Conference Proceedings, October 7, 1983. Center for Washington Area Studies Occasional Papers No. 1.

Lehman, Donald, *Executive Office Building* (Washington: General Services Administration, 1964).

"L'Enfant's Reports to President Washington, March 26, June 22 and August 19, 1791," *Records of the Columbia Historical Society,* vol. 2 (1899), pp. 38–48.

Lessof, Allan, *The Nation and Its City: Politics, "Corruption," and Progress in Washington, D.C., 1861–1902* (Baltimore: Johns Hopkins University Press, 1994).

Longstreth, Richard, ed., *The Mall in Washington, 1791–1991* (Washington: National Gallery of Art, 1991).

Lovelace, Eldridge, *Harland Bartholomew: His Contributions to American Urban Planning* (Urbana, Illinois: University of Illinois, 1993).

Lowry, Bates, ed., *The Architecture of Washington, D.C.* (Washington: The Dunlap Society, 1976).

Lyons, Linda Brody, *A Handbook to the Pension Building: Home of the National Building Museum* (Washington: National Building Museum, 1993).

Mackintosh, Barry, *Rock Creek Park: An Administrative History* (Washington: National Park Service History Division, 1985).

Macqueen, Philip O., "Cabin John Bridge," *The Military Engineer,* vol. 24 (1932), pp. 566–8.

_____, "Rock Creek Bridge," *The Military Engineer,* vol. 28 (1936), pp. 111–3.

Martin, Robert, ed., *Korean War Veterans Memorial: A Tribute to Those Who Served* (Paducah, Kentucky: Turner Publishing, 1995).

Mathews, Catharine VanCortlant, *Andrew Ellicott, His Life and Letters* (New York: Grafton Press, 1908).

Maury, William M., *Alexander "Boss" Shepherd and the Board of Public Works,* GW Washington Studies, no. 3 (Washington: George Washington University, 1975).

McDaniel, Joyce L., "Caspar Buberl: The Pension Building Civil War Frieze and Other Washington, D.C., Sculpture," *Records of the Columbia Historical Society,* vol. 50 (1980), pp. 309–44.

Melder, Keith, *City of Magnificent Intentions: A History of Washington, District of Columbia* (Washington: Imac, Inc., 1997).

"Memoir of Peter Conover Hains," *Transactions of the American Society of Civil Engineers,* vol. 85 (1922), pp. 1682–3.

"Memoir of William Voorhees Judson, M. Am. Soc. C.E.," *Transactions of the American Society of Civil Engineers,* vol. 88 (1925), pp. 1405–8.

Miller, David W., *Second Only to Grant: Quartermaster General Montgomery C. Meigs* (Shippensburg, Pennsylvania: White Mane Publishing Co., 2000).

Miller, James E., Jr., *Walt Whitman* (Boston: Houghton Mifflin, 1959).

Molloy, Peter Michael, "Technical Education and the Young Republic: West Point as America's Ecole Polytechnique, 1802–1833," Ph.D. diss., Brown University, 1975.

Montagna, Dennis, "Henry Mervin Shrady's Grant Memorial in Washington, D.C.: A Study in Iconography, Content, and Patronage," Ph.D. diss., University of Delaware, 1987.

Moore, Charles, ed., *The Improvement of the Park System of the District of Columbia* (Washington: GPO, 1902).

_____, *The Life and Times of Charles Follen McKim* (Boston: Houghton Mifflin Company, 1929).

Morgan, James Dudley, "Historic Fort Washington on the Potomac," *Records of the Columbia Historical Society,* vol. 7 (1904), p. 15.

Murphy, David J., "Architects, Engineers, and the New Agriculture Department Building: A Reinterpretation of the Fight Over Implementing the McMillan Plan," unpublished paper delivered at the annual meeting of the Society for American City and Regional Planning, Richmond, Virginia, November 1991.

Myer, Donald Beekman, *Bridges and the City of Washington* (Washington: Commission of Fine Arts, 1974).

Nagle, John L., "The Arlington Memorial Bridge," *The Military Engineer*, vol. 20 (1928), pp. 154–60.

"National War College Completes Historic Renovation, 4/18/2000," www.ellerbebecket.com.

Noreen, Sarah Pressey, *Public Street Illumination in Washington, D.C.: An Illustrated History*, GW Washington Studies, no. 2, (Washington: George Washington University, May 1975).

O'Brien William P., "Reality and Illusion: The White House and Harry S. Truman," *White House History*, vol. 5 (Spring 1999), pp. 4–12.

Ogilvie, Philip W., "Chronology of Events in the History of the District of Columbia," typescript, D.C. Office of Public Records, 1989.

Oppel, Terry, and Tony Meisel, *Washington, D.C.: A Turn-of-the-Century Treasury* (Secaucus, New Jersey: Castle Publishing Co., 1987).

Orlin, Glenn S., "The Evolution of the American Urban Parkway," Ph.D. diss., The George Washington University, 1992.

Ossman, Jennifer L., "Reconstructing a National Image: The State, War and Navy Building and the Politics of Federal Design, 1866–90," Ph.D. diss., University of Virginia, 1996.

Owen, Robert Dale, *Hints on Public Architecture* (New York: Da Capo Press, 1979 reprint of 1849).

Padover, Saul K., *Jefferson and the National Capital* (Washington: GPO, 1946).

Pearson, J. C. and J. J. Earley, "Successful Building in Stucco," *American Architect*, vol. 117, no. 2309 (March 24, 1920), pp. 386–92.

Peters, Charles A., Jr., "The Lincoln Memorial Reflecting Pool," *The Military Engineer*, vol. 15 (1923), pp. 209–13.

Peterson, Jon A., "The Hidden Origins of the McMillan Plan for Washington, D.C., 1900–1902," *Historical Perspectives on Urban Design: Washington, D.C., 1890–1910*, edited by Antoinette J. Lee, Conference Proceedings, October 7, 1983, Center for Washington Area Studies, Occasional Papers No. 1.

Pitch, Anthony S., *The Burning of Washington: The British Invasion of 1814* (Annapolis, Maryland: Naval Institute Press, 1998).

Poore, Ben Perley, *Perley's Reminiscences of Sixty Years in the National Metropolis* (Philadelphia: Hubbard Brothers, 1886).

"Principal Local Events During 1904," *Records of the Columbia Historical Society*, vol. 8 (1904), p. 203.

"Principal Local Events During 1906," *Records of the Columbia Historical Society*, vol. 10 (1906), p. 255.

Rathbun, Richard, "The Columbian Institute for the Promotion of Arts and Sciences," *United States National Museum and Bulletin* 101 (Washington: GPO, 1917).

Reiff, Daniel D., *Washington Architecture, 1791–1861* (Washington: Commission of Fine Arts, 1971).

Report of the Arlington Memorial Bridge Commission (Washington: GPO, 1924).

Report of the Commission on the Renovation of the Executive Mansion (Washington: GPO, 1952).

Report of the U.S. National Museum (Washington: GPO, 1905).

Reps, John, *Monumental Washington* (Princeton: Princeton University Press, 1967).

_____, *Washington on View* (Chapel Hill: University of North Carolina Press, 1991).

Richardson, James B., *A Compilation of the Messages and Papers of the Presidents, 1789–1908* (Tennessee: Bureau of National Literature and Art, 1908).

Richman, Michael, *Daniel Chester French, An American Sculptor* (Washington: National Trust for Historic Preservation, 1976).

Riling, Joseph R., *Baron von Steuben and His Regulations* (Philadelphia: Ray Riling Arms Book Co., 1966).

Roth, Leland M., *McKim, Mead & White Architects* (New York: Harper & Row, 1983).

Royall, R. E., "The Mount Vernon Memorial Highway," *The Military Engineer*, vol. 24, no. 135 (May–June 1932), pp. 238–42.

Rubincam, Milton, "Major General U.S. Grant, 3rd, 1881–1968," *Records of the Columbia Historical Society*, vols. 66–68 (1966–68), pp. 369–408.

Ryan, Gary D., "War Department Topographical Bureau, 1831–1863: An Administrative History," Ph.D. diss., American University, 1968.

Salay, David L., "'Very picturesque, but regarded as nearly useless': Fort Washington, Maryland, 1816–1872," *Maryland Historical Magazine*, vol. 81 (1986), p. 67–.

Sanderlin, Walter S., *The Great National Project: A History of the Chesapeake and Ohio Canal* (Baltimore: Johns Hopkins University Press, 1946).

Santoyo, Elsa M., ed., *Creating an American Masterpiece* (Washington: American Institute of Architects Press, 1988).

Schmitt, Edwin A. and Philip O. Macqueen, "Washington Aqueduct," *The Military Engineer*, vol. 61 (1949), p. 205.

Schubert, Frank N., ed., *The Nation Builders: A Sesquicentennial History of the Corps of Engineers, 1838–1863* (Fort Belvoir, Virginia: U.S. Army Corps of Engineers, 1988).

Scott, Pamela, "L'Enfant's Washington Described," *Washington History*, vol. 3, no. 1 (Spring/Summer 1991), pp. 96–111.

_____, "Moving to the Seat of Government," *Washington History*, vol. 12, no. 1 (Spring/Summer 2000), pp. 70–3.

_____, "Stephen Hallet's Designs for the United States Capitol," *Winterthur Portfolio*, vol. 27, nos. 2–3 (1992), pp. 145–70.

_____, *Temple of Liberty: Building the Capitol for a New Nation* (New York: Oxford University Press, 1995).

_____, ed., *The Papers of Robert Mills* (Wilmington, Delaware: Scholarly Resources, Inc., 1990).

Seale, William, *The President's House: A History* (Washington: White House Historical Association, 1986).

_____, *The White House: The History of an American Idea* (Washington: American Institute of Architects Press, 1992).

Searle, Henry R., "Washington Monument Monograph," (Washington: Gibson Brothers Printers, [1877]).

Sherrill, C. O., "The Arlington Memorial Amphitheater," *The Military Engineer*, vol. 17, no. 92 (April 1925), pp. 152–3.

Singleton, Esther, *The Story of the White House* (New York: The McClure Company, 1907).

Skramsted, Harold K., "The Engineer as Architect in Washington. The Contribution of Montgomery Meigs," *Records of the Columbia Historical Society*, vols. 69–70 (1969–70), pp. 266–84.

[Smithmeyer, John L.], *History of the Construction of the Library of Congress* (Washington: Beresford, printer, 1906).

Somma, Thomas P., "The McMillan Memorial Fountain: A Short History of a Lost Monument," *Washington History*, vol. 14, no. 2 (Fall/Winter 2002), pp. 96–107.

Spratt, Zack, "Rock Creek's Bridges," *Records of the Columbia Historical Society*, vols. 53–56 (1953–56), pp. 101–34.

Steinberg, Michael S., "The United States Army Corps of Engineers in the Federal City" (manuscript, n.d.).

Sullebarger, Beth, *Historic Structures Report, U.S. Pension Building* (Washington: Privately printed, 1984).

Swift, Joseph G., *The Memoirs of Gen. Joseph Gardner Swift* (Privately printed, 1890).

Thomas, Christopher A., "The Lincoln Memorial and Its Architect, Henry Bacon," Ph.D. diss., Yale University, 1990.

_____, "The Marble of the Lincoln Memorial: 'Whitest, Prettiest, and …Best,'" *Washington History*, vol. 2, no. 2 (Fall/Winter 1993–94), pp. 43–63.

Thompson, Gilbert, *The Engineer Battalion in the Civil War*, Occasional Papers, No. 44, Engineer School, United States Army (Washington: The Engineer School, 1910).

Tindall, William, *Origin and Government of the District of Columbia* (Washington: GPO, 1908).

_____, *Standard History of the City of Washington from a Study of the Original Sources* (Knoxville, Tennessee: H. W. Crew and Co., 1914).

Tompkins, Sally Kress, *A Quest for Grandeur: Charles Moore and the Federal Triangle* (Washington: Smithsonian Institution Press, 1993).

Torres, Louis, "Federal Hall Revisited," *Journal of the Society of Architectural Historians*, vol. 29, no. 4 (December 1970), pp. 327–28.

_____. *"To the immortal name and memory of George Washington," The United States Army Corps of Engineers and the Construction of the Washington Monument* (Washington: Office of the Chief of Engineers, 1984).

Townsend, George Alfred, *New Washington, or the Renovated City* (Washington: Chronicle Publishing Company, 1874).

"Transforming the White House into a Magnificent Dwelling," *The Architect and Builders Journal*, vol. 3 (June 1902), p. 17.

U.S. Army Corps of Engineers, Baltimore District, "Camp Simms, Former Defense Site, Washington, D.C.," 2003, www.nab.usace.army.mil.

_____, "District of Columbia Public Schools Capital Improvements Program Project Brief," 2003, www.nab.usace.army.mil.

_____, "The Pentagon Memorial Project," 2004, http://pentagonmemorial.nab.usace.army.mil.

_____, "Spring Valley, Washington, D.C. Project Overview," 2003, www.nab.usace.army.mil

Vermeil, Sara E., *Army Engineer's Contributions to the Development of Iron Construction in the Nineteenth Century* (Kansas City, Missouri: Public Works Historical Society, 2002).

Walker, Paul K., *Engineers of Independence: A Documentary History of the Army Engineers in the American Revolution, 1775–1783* (Washington: GPO, 1981).

Washington Present and Future: A General Summary of the Comprehensive Plan for the National Capital and its Environs (Washington: National Capital Park and Planning Commission, 1950).

Water for the Future of the Nation's Capital Area (Washington: National Academy Press, 1980).

Ways, Harry C., *The Washington Aqueduct, 1852–1992* (Washington: U.S. Army Corps of Engineers, c. 1993).

Weigley, Russell F., *Quartermaster General of the Union Army: A Biography of M. C. Meigs* (New York: Columbia University Press, 1959).

_____, *History of the United States Army* (New York: The MacMillan Company, 1967).

Welling, Alvin C., "Pollution in the Potomac River," *Medical Annals of the District of Columbia* (May 1960), pp. 289–90.

Wilson, Rufus Rockwell, *Washington: The Capital City and Its Park in the History of the Nation* (Philadelphia: J.P. Lippincott Company, 1902).

Wojcik, Susan Brizzolara, "Thomas U. Walter and Iron in the United States Capitol: An Alliance of Architecture, Engineering, and Industry," Ph.D. diss., University of Delaware, 1998.

Wolanin, Barbara, *Constantino Brumidi, Artist of the Capitol* (Washington: GPO, 1998).

Wolff, Wendy, ed., *Capitol Builder: The Shorthand Journals of Montgomery C. Meigs, 1853–1859* (Washington: GPO, 2001).

Wood, J. E., "Improvement of Washington Channel," *The Military Engineer*, vol. 15, no. 83 (September–October 1923), pp. 435–7.

Work of the National Capital Planning Commission (Washington: GPO, 1928).

Young, Brig. Gen. Gordon R., *A Preliminary Six-year Plan for Postwar Washington* (Washington, 1946).

Zangrando, Joanna Schneider, "Monumental Bridge Design in Washington, D.C., as a Reflection of American Culture, 1886–1932," Ph.D. diss., The George Washington University, 1974.

NEWSPAPERS

Centinel of Liberty, 1800

Constellation, 1988–2002

Engineer Update, 1997–2003

Georgetown Weekly Ledger, 1791

Metropolitan and Georgetown Commercial Gazette, 1824

National Intelligencer, 1814

New York Times, 1881–1900

Northwest Current, 2004

Potomac Basin Reporter, 1986–88

Washington Evening News, 1928

Washington Evening Star, 1886–1962

Washington Gazette, 1796

Washington Herald, 1913

Washington Post, 1928–2004

Washington Times, 1984–90

Washington Times Herald, 1949

PRIMARY SOURCES

LIBRARY OF CONGRESS

Digges-L'Enfant-Morgan Papers

District of Columbia Letters and Papers

Bernard R. Green Papers

Alexander Hamilton Papers

Thomas Jefferson Papers

Pierre Charles L'Enfant Papers

McKim, Mead & White Papers

Montgomery C. Meigs Papers

Olmsted Associates Papers

Elihu Root Papers

George Washington Papers

HISTORICAL SOCIETY OF WASHINGTON, D.C.

Philip W. Ogilvie Collection

U.S. Grant III Collection

OFFICE OF HISTORY, U.S. ARMY CORPS OF ENGINEERS

Glen E. Edgerton, "Diary of Progress on the Renovation and Remodeling of the Executive Mansion," 1948–52

Brigadier General Robert E. Mathe Papers

Engineer Memoirs: Lieutenant General Frederick J. Clarke

Bernard L. Robinson Papers

Biographical Files

MARTIN LUTHER KING MEMORIAL LIBRARY

Evening Star Collection

MASSACHUSETTS HISTORICAL SOCIETY

Henry Knox Papers

NATIONAL ARCHIVES AND RECORDS ADMINISTRATION

R.G. 42, Records of the Office of Public Buildings and Grounds

R.G. 77, Records of the Chief of Engineers

R.G. 233, Records of the House of Representatives

R.G. 360, Papers of the Continental Congress

NEW YORK HISTORICAL SOCIETY

McKim, Mead & White Papers

SOCIETY FOR THE PRESERVATION OF NEW ENGLAND ANTIQUITIES

Thomas Lincoln Casey Papers

THE WHITE HOUSE

Journal of Joseph Dentz

GOVERNMENT PRINTED DOCUMENTS

Annual Reports of the Chief of Engineers (ARCE), 1867–1984

Annual Reports of the Commissioners of the District of Columbia, 1879–1921

Annual Reports of the Commission of Fine Arts, 1913–44

House and Senate Reports, 1830–1925

U.S. Statutes at Large

NOTES ON ILLUSTRATIONS

The largest source of images for this book is the Research Collections maintained by the Office of History, Headquarters, U.S. Army Corps of Engineers. The Office of History has accumulated its large image collection over many years and it continues to grow. In addition to the visual materials maintained by the U.S. Army and the Corps of Engineers, the collection includes materials culled from other repositories and sources. Where information on the originating source was available, credit in this publication is given to that organization or individual. Where no information was available, or where the originating source was another element of the U.S. Army, credit is given to the Office of History, Corps of Engineers. In addition, illustrations were gleaned from the *Annual Reports of the Chief of Engineers* and other reports, as well as the Office of History's Personal Papers collections that have been donated by individuals. Images from the Baltimore Engineer District—both the headquarters office and the Washington Aqueduct Division—are credited to those organizations.

Substantial research also was conducted in other archives and repositories. The Library of Congress has a vast collection of Washington-related photographs, maps, and drawings and its holdings were tapped considerably. Many images were located at the National Archives and Records Administration in College Park, Maryland. The Washingtoniana Division at the Martin Luther King branch of the D.C. Public Library was an invaluable source of photographs. Other important repositories consulted included the Smithsonian Institution Archives, the Curator's Office of the Architect of the Capitol, and the Historical Society of Washington, D.C. Images were acquired from the library and the museum of the U.S. Military Academy at West Point, as well as: AP/Wide World Photos; Avery Architectural and Fine Arts Library of Columbia University; the Historical Society of Pennsylvania; the Image Archives of the Historical Map and Chart Collection of the National Oceanic & Atmospheric Administration; the National Park Service, including its Historic American Buildings Survey/Historic American Engineering Record; the New York Historical Society; the New York Public Library, The Society of the Cincinnati; *The Washington Post*; and Picture History, an internet-based photograph supplier. Local photographer Darren Santos captured current images of D.C. public schools. Greg Knott of McFarland Photography, Inc., photographed the highway map on the inside cover flap. Jean Diaz and Douglas J. Wilson scanned the original 59-inch by 28-inch map that is the basis for the cover of the book. Using skill, ingenuity, and patience, Ms. Diaz produced a clear and accurate copy of this striking map. The author, Pamela Scott, generously offered several images, maps, and illustrations from her personal collection; these images are credited to their original sources.

All efforts were made to properly credit the images and, where necessary, to obtain permission to publish them. Permissions granted are greatly appreciated.

Image captions are based primarily on information from the text, or from sources cited in the text, and from the information supplied with the original visual material. Additional sources of information for the captions include:

Annual Reports of the Chief of Engineers (ARCE)

Brewster, Casondra, "'Extractors' Put Training to Test. Special Unit Vital in 'Operation Noble Eagle' at Pentagon Site." *MDW News Service*, http://www.mdw.army.mil/news/Extractors_put_training_to_test.html.

Data pages of the Historic American Buildings Survey (HABS) and Historic American Engineering Record (HAER) of the National Park Service, http://www.loc.gov/rr/print/catalog.html.

D.C. Highway Department Map of Truxton Circle, 1946, http://www.truxtoncircle.org/doclib/DChighwaydept1946.doc.

Engineer Memoirs: Lieutenant General Walter K. Wilson, Jr., Office of History, Corps of Engineers, May 1984, http://www.usace.army.mil/inet/usace-docs/eng-pamphlets/ep870-1-8/toc.htm.

Government of the District of Columbia, Department of Transportation, "Thomas Circle Restoration Project," http://www.ddot.dc.gov/ddot/lib/ddot/information/pdf/Thomas_Circle.pdf.

James, Clayton, "Corps of Engineers' Watermen Keep Channels Clear." *Pentagram*, July 25, 1997, http://www.dcmilitary.com/army/pentagram/archives/july25/pt_d725.html.

Myer, Donald Beekman, *Bridges and the City of Washington* (Washington: GPO, 1974).

National Transportation Safety Board website, http://www.ntsb.gov/publictn/1982/AAR8208.htm.

Newell, Frederick Haynes, ed., *Planning and Building the City of Washington* (Washington: Ransdell, Inc., 1932).

Office of History, Corps of Engineers, Biographical Files.

The Washington Post, 1900, 1921, 1947.

Ways, Harry C., *The Washington Aqueduct, 1852–1992* (Baltimore: U.S. Army Engineer District, Baltimore, n.d.).

Direct quotations used in the image captions are extracted from the text except as noted here:

Page 142, Government Printing Office. *ARCE*, 1901

Page 162, Willow Tree Park. *ARCE*, 1919

Page 163, Dupont Circle. *ARCE*, 1916

Page 169, Truxton Circle. D.C. Highway Department Map of Truxton Circle, 1946, http://www.truxtoncircle.org/doclib/DChighwaydept1946.doc

Page 183, Calvert Street Bridge. Paul Cret, architect, to Commission of Fine Arts, November 13, 1935, as quoted in Historic American Engineering Record, Calvert Street Bridge (Duke Ellington Bridge), HAER no. DC-23 (HAER, DC, WASH, 578-), by Amy Ross, Summer 1992

Page 255, Marshall Hall. Headquarters, U.S. Army Corps of Engineers, slide show presentation on the 1992 Chief of Engineers Design and Environmental Awards Program, Office of History, Corps of Engineers, unprocessed Baltimore District PAO images

Index

Page references in *italic* refer to photos and illustrations.